I DID NOT COMMIT ADULTERY

Marital Conflict and the Law in Ontario in the 1870s

PATRONS OF THE SOCIETY

Professor Constance Backhouse

Chernos, Flaherty, Svonkin, LLP

Gowling WLG

Hull & Hull LLP

Mr. Wayne Kerr

The Law Foundation of Ontario

McCarthy Tetrault

Osler, Hoskin & Harcourt LLP

Pape Chaudhury

Paliare Roland Rosenberg Rothstein LLP

The Hon. Robert Sharpe

Torys LLP

WeirFoulds LLP

The Osgoode Society is supported by a grant from The Law Foundation of Ontario

The Law Foundation of Ontario
Building a better foundation for justice in Ontario

The Society also thanks The Law Society of Ontario for its continuing support.

JIM PHILLIPS

I Did Not Commit Adultery

Marital Conflict and the Law in Ontario in the 1870s

Published for the Osgoode Society for Canadian
Legal History by University of Toronto Press
Toronto Buffalo London

Toronto Buffalo London
utppublishing.com
Printed and bound by CPI Group (UK) Ltd, Croydon, CR0 4YY

ISBN 978-1-4875-1744-1 (cloth)
ISBN 978-1-4875-1746-5 (EPUB)
ISBN 978-1-4875-1745-8 (PDF)

Library and Archives Canada Cataloguing in Publication

Title: I did not commit adultery : marital conflict and the law in Ontario in the 1870s / Jim Phillips.
Names: Phillips, Jim, 1954– author
Series: Osgoode Society for Canadian Legal History series.
Description: Series statement: Osgoode Society for Canadian Legal History series | Includes bibliographical references and index.
Identifiers: Canadiana (print) 20250217104 | Canadiana (ebook) 20250217112 | ISBN 9781487517441 (cloth) | ISBN 9781487517465 (EPUB) | ISBN 9781487517458 (PDF)
Subjects: LCSH: Married women – Legal status, laws, etc. – Ontario – History – 19th century. | LCSH: Divorce – Law and legislation – Ontario – History – 19th century. | LCSH: Marital conflict – Ontario – History – 19th century.
Classification: LCC KEO207.W6 P45 2025 | LCC KF521 .P45 2025 kfmod | DDC 346.71301/66 – dc23

Cover design: Will Brown
Cover images: Albert Ellery Berg, *The Universal Self-Instructor* (New York: Thomas Kelly, Publisher, 1883) 275; (bottom) Unknown Artist. *Ottawa. The Opening of Parliament. Arrival of His Excellency at the Grand Entrance.* Canadian Illustrated News (1879).

We wish to acknowledge the land on which the University of Toronto Press operates. This land is the traditional territory of the Wendat, the Anishnaabeg, the Haudenosaunee, the Métis, and the Mississaugas of the Credit First Nation.

University of Toronto Press acknowledges the financial support of the Government of Canada, the Canada Council for the Arts, and the Ontario Arts Council, an agency of the Government of Ontario, for its publishing activities.

Canada Council for the Arts | Conseil des Arts du Canada

ONTARIO ARTS COUNCIL
CONSEIL DES ARTS DE L'ONTARIO
an Ontario government agency
un organisme du gouvernement de l'Ontario

Funded by the Government of Canada | Financé par le gouvernement du Canada

Canada

Contents

Illustrations

Foreword

I Did Not Commit Adultery: Marital Conflict and the Law in Ontario in the 1870s chronicles the breakdown of the marriage of Whitby residents Robert and Eliza Campbell in 1873, which precipitated a six-year battle in the Ontario courts and the Parliament of Canada. Eliza's alleged adultery led to a series of suits and counter-suits between the spouses that produced somewhat contradictory results and could not provide Robert with the relief he really wanted: an end to the marriage. He thus petitioned Parliament for an Act of Divorce, the only way to get a divorce in Ontario before 1930. In 1876 he failed to persuade the Senate divorce committee that Eliza had committed adultery, the sole ground for a divorce at that time, but Eliza succeeded in having an Act of Separation passed in her favour. This highly unusual measure raised important constitutional questions as well as revealed a range of attitudes of legislators about the nature of marriage and the family. *I Did Not Commit Adultery* by Professor Jim Phillips, Editor-in-Chief of the Osgoode Society for Canadian Legal History, provides a detailed study of the law governing marriage and divorce in the later nineteenth century, revealing the ways in which it was particularly disadvantageous for married women. Along the way Professor Phillips also examines the operations of the civil courts, the forensic skills of leading members of the Ontario legal profession, constitutional law, and parliamentary divorce – the last a topic never before examined in detail by Canadian historians.

The purpose of the Osgoode Society for Canadian Legal History is to encourage research and writing in the history of Canadian law. The Society, which was incorporated in 1979 and is registered as a charity, was founded at the initiative of the Honourable R. Roy McMurtry and officials of the Law Society of Upper Canada. The Society seeks to stimulate the study of legal history in Canada by supporting researchers, collecting oral histories, and publishing volumes that contribute to legal-historical scholarship in Canada. This year's books bring the total published since 1981 to 129, in all fields of legal history – the courts, the judiciary, and the legal profession, as well as the history of crime and punishment, women and the law, law and economy, the legal treatment of Indigenous peoples and racial and ethnic minorities, and famous cases and significant trials in all areas of the law.

Paul Schabas
President

Philip Girard
Associate Editor

Acknowledgments

Completing a book always requires assistance from others, and one of the pleasures of completion is the opportunity to thank a variety of people and organizations. I begin with the Osgoode Society for Canadian Legal History, which, I like to say, is the most successful legal historical organization in the common law world. The Society allows me to keep one foot rooted in each of two great professions, the legal and the historical. This is the ninth book I have written or edited that has been published with the Society, starting in 1990, a relationship which has sustained me throughout my legal academic career.

All of those nine books have been published by the University of Toronto Press, and I am equally grateful to that venerable publisher. Special mention should go to Len Husband, Canadian history editor, with whom I have worked as author and as editor-in-chief of the Osgoode Society for nearly three decades. I also thank Leah Connor, managing editor, who saw the book through the production process, and Michael Waldin, copy editor who improved the book in numerous ways.

Over the last three years I have given talks on this book to a variety of audiences, and many people who attended those events made useful suggestions. I thank participants at the Australia-New Zealand Legal History conference, the Whitby Historical Society and the Whitby Public Library Lecture Series, the Osgoode Society Legal History Workshop, and the Legal History Series at Western University.

Four people were indispensable in finding sources: Sarah Ferencz, archivist at the Whitby Public Library; Sufei Xu at the Bora Laskin Library of the University of Toronto Law School (now retired); and Briana De Valk, graduate student in history at the University of Nebraska. Most of all I thank Sooin Kim, reference librarian at the Bora Laskin Library of the University of Toronto Law School, unfailingly efficient and professional and over many years a delightful friend.

I have been fortunate enough to have been helped by a number of research assistants, including Anna Jarvis, history graduate student at York University, and four students at the University of Toronto law school. Nina Patti, Natan Snowbell, Hannah West, and, especially, Zoe Brown, all made my life much easier and ensured that the book would come out when it did. Zoe's intelligence and diligence must be singled out, qualities matched only by her sheer enthusiasm for the project. Alyssa Mintzberg of Toronto prepared some of the illustrations.

A number of friends were kind enough to read all or part of this book, and all of them made it better. I thank Phil Augustine, Rosemary Gartner, Philip Girard, Preston Lim, Ian Radforth, and Bob Sharpe. I am also grateful to Bettina Bradbury of Wellington, New Zealand, who read the manuscript as one of the anonymous reviewers for the Osgoode Society and the University of Toronto Press. Her generous assessment came with useful suggestions for improvement and some references to additional sources. She later kindly agreed to my knowing it was her, and I take pleasure in thanking her here.

Special thanks are due to two people. I took classes in property law and legal history with Philip Girard in the 1980s at Dalhousie Law School, and that collaboration produced our first edited collection of legal history essays. Forty years later we are still collaborating, and the best of friends in all matters personal and professional.

Above all I thank my kind and beautiful wife, Christine Davidson. She has brought me much joy since we met in 2007, and among many other things has always supported my work. As this book was in production she suffered a potentially life-altering medical set-back, an event which, to be honest, has taken some of the gloss off the pride and pleasure that all academics feel in publishing books. I would gladly sacrifice this book for a full recovery for her. I can only dedicate it to her, as I now dedicate my life to improving hers.

Abbreviations and Short Forms

Reported Cases

Six reported cases are used in this book. Since all of them have the name Campbell in the style of cause, and three of them are *Campbell v. Campbell*, I have not referred to them in the notes by the names of the parties but by their subject matter.

Alimony Case Report	*Campbell v. Campbell*, [1875] Ontario Judgments [OJ] No. 202, 22 Grant's Chancery Reports 322.
Defamation Case Report	*Campbell v. Campbell*, [1875] Ontario Judgments [OJ] No. 136, 25 *Upper Canada Common Pleas Reports* 368
Dower Case Report No 1	*Re Campbell*, [1877] OJ No. 24, 25 Grant's Chancery Reports 187
Dower Case Report No 2	*Re Campbell*, [1878] OJ No. 187, 25 Grant's Chancery Reports 480
Interim Alimony Case Report	*Campbell v. Campbell*, [1873] OJ No. 306, 6 Practice Reports 128 (Chancery Chambers)
Legal Fees Case Report	*McDougall v. Campbell*, [1877] OJ No. 100, 41 Upper Canada Reports 332 (Queen's Bench).

Law Reports

AC	Appeal Cases
NBR	New Brunswick Reports
NSR	Nova Scotia Reports
OJ	Ontario Judgments
SCJ	Supreme Court Judgments

Parliamentary Records

Commons Debates	Debates of the House of Commons
Commons Journals	Journals of the House of Commons
Commons Rules	*Rules, Orders and Forms of Proceedings in the House of Commons of Canada* (Ottawa: Hunter Rose & Co, 1868)
Minutes of Evidence	*Report of the Select Committee of the Senate on the Bill Intituled An Act for the Relief of Robert Campbell Together with the Minutes of Evidence, 31 March 1876, in Senate Journals*, 1876, Appendix 1.
Senate Debates	Debates of the Senate
Senate Journals	Journals of the Senate
Senate Rules	*Rules, Orders and Form of Proceedings of the Senate of Canada* (Ottawa: McLean, Rogers & Co, 1876)

Other Abbreviations

AO	Archives of Ontario
BNA Act	*British North America Act*, 1867, UK Statutes 1867, c 3
DCB online	Dictionary of Canadian Biography online – www.biographia.ca
LAC	Library and Archives Canada
LSO/PMD	Law Society of Ontario Archives, Past Member Database
RSO	*Revised Statutes of Ontario*
SC	*Statutes of Canada* – Annual
SO	*Statutes of Ontario* – Annual
Whitby Archives	Whitby Public Library, Digitized Photograph collection with accompanying biographical sketches – www.whitbylibrary.ca/digital-content

Principal Members of the Campbell and Byrne Families

The Campbell Family

Robert Campbell Sr.	Whitby merchant; husband of Eliza Byrne
James Campbell	Brother and business partner of Robert Campbell Sr.
Jane Anderson, née Campbell	Sister of Robert and James Campbell; wife of John Anderson
Eliza Campbell, née Byrne	Wife of Robert Campbell Senior
John Anderson	Whitby butcher. Husband of Jane Campbell and brother-in-law to James and Robert Campbell
Rebecca Campbell, née Tweedie	Wife of James Campbell
James Bremner Campbell	Son of Robert and Eliza Campbell
Robert Campbell Jr.	Son of Robert and Eliza Campbell
Edith Holmes Campbell	Daughter of Robert and Eliza Campbell
Francis William Campbell	Son of Robert and Eliza Campbell

The Byrne Family

Rev. James Thomas Byrne	Congregationalist minister. Father of Eliza Campbell (née Byrne), Bethiah Ham (née Byrne), James Byrne, and Annie Byrne
Henrietta Byrne	Wife of Rev. James Byrne
Bethiah Ham, née Byrne	Daughter of Rev. James and Henrietta Byrne, widow of Norman Ham, later married Thomas Johnston of Toronto

James Byrne	Son of Rev. James and Henrietta Byrne. Whitby druggist
Mary Byrne, née Lewis	Wife of James Byrne
Eliza Campbell, née Byrne	Daughter of Rev. James Thomas Byrne; wife of Robert Campbell Sr.
Annie Byrne	Daughter of Rev. James and Henrietta Byrne, unmarried
Henrietta Ham (Hettie)	Daughter of Bethiah Ham
Norman and George Ham	Sons of Bethiah Ham

Timeline of the Three Court Cases, 1873–1875

1873

September, early, various dates – All three lawsuits involving the Campbells are started, although they were tried at different times.

October 15 and 16 – The case of *Robert Campbell v. George Gordon* for criminal conversation is tried in Toronto.

November 21 – Argument is heard in George Gordon's application for a new trial. Judgment not given until September 1875.

1874

March 26 and 27 – The case of *Eliza Campbell v. James Campbell* for defamation is tried in Toronto.

April 23–26 – *Viva voce* evidence in the alimony case taken in Whitby.

May 21 – James Cambell wins a rule *nisi* for a new trial in the defamation case.

1875

May 14 – Legal argument in Toronto in the alimony case of *Eliza Campbell v. Robert Campbell.*

May 21 – Legal argument in Toronto in James Campbell's application for a new trial in the defamation case.

September 15 – Blake issues his judgment in the alimony case.

September 17 – Court rules against George Gordon's application for a new trial in the crim. con. case.

December 22 – New trial granted to James Campbell in the defamation case.

I DID NOT COMMIT ADULTERY

Marital Conflict and the Law in Ontario in the 1870s

1
Introduction

A Unique "Divorce" Act

In 1879 the Parliament of Canada passed a private Act of separation for Elizabeth (Eliza) Maria Campbell from her husband Robert.[1] It was the only Act among the 266 passed between 1868 and 1914 that was the result of a marital breakdown but not for a divorce *a vinculo matrimonii*, (divorce from the bonds of matrimony), which dissolved the marriage and allowed the parties to marry again. Rather it was for what was called by some a separation, and by others a divorce *a mensa et thoro* (separation from bed and board), which did not dissolve the marriage but did regularize the couple living apart. Largely because it was a unique statute, the leading contemporary Canadian expert on Canadian divorce called the Campbell Act "one of the most peculiar in the history of divorce in Canada."[2] As will be discussed at length in this book, the question of whether the Act was a "divorce" under section 91 (26) of the *BNA Act*, which gave Parliament jurisdiction over "marriage and divorce," was a hotly debated one.[3] Eliza's 1879 Act was the only one of the 266 that began, in 1876, as a bill to grant her husband Robert a divorce *a vinculo* from her and was transformed along the way into an Act to grant her a separation from him.* The Campbell matrimonial dispute was a part of parliamentary proceedings each year between 1876 and 1879, taking up over 100 pages of the Senate and Commons Hansards. It also involved 22 days of hearings before a Senate divorce committee in 1876 and 1877, and a further three days before a differently constituted committee in 1879. Before 1876 the breakdown of the

* Henceforth I will refer to the principal protagonists in this story as Robert and Eliza, to avoid endless repetition of the Campbell name.

Campbell marriage generated three civil suits in the Ontario courts, discussed below in chapters 5 through 7, cases which involved some of the leading lights of the Ontario bar of the 1870s.

Within the confines of Parliament, the Campbell divorce case produced passionate and at times vituperative debate, accusations of conspiracies, and denunciations of MPs and senators as either hoodwinked by a beguiling and shameless harlot or as heartless accomplices to a husband's cruelty. The case was extensively reported on, not just in the local newspapers in the Campbells' hometown of Whitby, but in Toronto, various other newspapers in Ontario, and other parts of Canada, and even internationally, with the same themes dominant. It consumed Whitby throughout. Local residents, inhabitants of Toronto, Montreal, and elsewhere, and senators and MPs all had opinions about the case that reflected both their attitudes to marriage and their views of the behaviour of the individuals concerned. Both Eliza and Robert were judged against the prevailing Victorian gendered views of how respectable husbands and wives should comport themselves.

In Parliament the Campbell case also raised a number of legal and constitutional questions. The most important of these was the meaning of section 91 (26) of the *BNA Act*. Did the word "divorce" in that section include both kinds of "divorce" mentioned above, or only divorce *a vinculo matrimonii*? A related question was whether Parliament was precluded from passing a statute for a separation from bed and board because in doing so it legislated in respect of custody and support (alimony), both subjects which normally came under the provincial property and civil rights power, section 92 (13) of the *BNA Act*. A third major point of contention was that the Ontario Court of Chancery had previously decided that Eliza Campbell had been guilty of adultery and denied her alimony on that ground. The Campbell Act stated that she had not committed adultery and awarded her support. Thus for some Parliament passed legislation that was effectively a successful appeal judgment from the Ontario Court of Chancery.

A Case Study in Socio-Legal History

This book is a case study of one parliamentary divorce, a topic that has been almost entirely neglected by Canadian social and legal historians.[4] The Campbell case itself is not mentioned in the lengthy and otherwise comprehensive *Dictionary of Canadian Biography* entry for one of the principals, Eliza's lawyer William McDougall.[5] This book has its genesis in research I did for the second volume of *A History of Law in Canada*, dealing with the 50 years after Confederation and published in 2022. One chapter of that book examines "Women and the Law," a topic that includes marital breakdown and divorce. Although I was able to say a good deal about judicial divorce in the provinces in which it was available by using the work of other historians, I found that practically nothing had been written about parliamentary divorce. Yet a petition to Parliament for a private Act of divorce was the only way that most Canadians could get a divorce in the period I was writing about. Judicial divorce was only available in British Columbia, Nova Scotia, and New Brunswick. Residents of Ontario, Quebec, Prince Edward Island, the Prairie provinces, and the Territories had to go to Parliament for a divorce. The research for my section on parliamentary divorce included reading all the divorce Acts passed by Parliament between 1867 and 1914, and, for the reasons noted above, the Campbell measure stood out as unique among those Acts. Further investigation into the case made me quickly realize that it would make a fascinating case study of the law and its operation.

Although this book is a legal history of the events following the breakdown of the Campbell marriage, the social and legal aspects of this story were inextricably linked. As one recent case study argues, there is much to be learned from "infus[ing] accounts of doctrine and procedure with the earthy details of everyday life.... [S]ocial histories of superficially unremarkable cases [are] particularly well-suited to excavating the multiple meanings of law."[6] In other words, the content and operation of the law can never be properly understood without placing it in its personal, social, and ideological context, and the Campbell case serves as a vivid illustration of that fact. This book is, therefore, both a legal history and one that throws light on the lives of ordinary people, not just judges, lawyers, and parliamentarians. Although the Campbells were not ordinary people in the sense of being lower class agricultural or industrial workers, the fact that they were relatively well-off, middle-class people still distinguished them from the MPs, senators, superior court judges, and elite lawyers who were frequently embroiled in political and legal controversies.

This book is of the genre that has been variously called legal history "case studies," "micro-history," or "legal archaeology." I will use the last named term here because the metaphor of archaeology most effectively captures the process of excavating the dominant legal principles involved, the social and political ideologies that shaped those legal principles, and the lives and circumstances of the people affected by the law.[7] This genre of historical writing is usually seen as originating with social historian Natalie Zemon Davis's *The Return of Martin Guerre* and the work of legal scholar Brian Simpson, who coined the term "legal archaeology" and penned a number of such studies.[8]

In recent decades legal archaeology has become a prominent form of scholarship about the history of the law. I have made my own contributions to it in very different areas of law, including an essay that deals with the Campbell case.[9] Legal archaeological work is of two kinds. Sometimes historians take a well-known case that is still cited for standing for a principle of law, and investigate the background to the case, often background that does not appear in the limited accounts provided in the law reports. The identities and motivations of the litigants are scrutinised, the broader social, economic, and political context is explicated, and much emphasis is placed on the ways in which the litigation unfolded and was resolved. The result is that sometimes the authority of the leading case is undermined. Lawyers and judges feature prominently in such work, but as products of their time and place in the same way that the legal principles themselves are contextualized historically.[10]

Another form of legal archaeology takes as its starting point a legal dispute that did not result in a jurisprudentially significant court decision. Generally this work, like studies of leading cases, highlights how the law was used in a particular dispute, using a similar methodology to studies of leading cases. The background to the dispute, the motives and actions of litigants, and the roles of lawyers, judges, and jurors are all placed under scrutiny. Also, as with studies of jurisprudential landmarks, the law and the legal system are treated as socially embedded phenomena and are always central to the story. But the purpose of this work is not to show how a leading case was shaped, but to explicate how case law, statutes, or constitutional provisions operated in a particular dispute. Invariably the result of the legal dispute was determined as much by socio-political attitudes as it was by legal principle.

Legal history case studies are always also contributions to other genres of history – gender history, race relations history, religious, family and class histories, and others. While the operation of the criminal law is the most common legal setting for this work, other areas of law, especially what we would now call family law and labour law, have also been central to many case studies.[11] Such studies often reveal the workings of what might be termed "non-state law," popular but unofficial attitudes and beliefs that at times decided the outcome in contradiction to how state law should have operated. Notable examples include Carolyn Strange's study of the treatment of two women charged with murder in turn-of-the-century Toronto who were acquitted despite having no "legal" defence. Their cases were turned into trials of the behaviour of the men they had killed.[12] To similar effect, a young man who gunned down a radical Christian preacher in early twentieth-century Seattle was acquitted because he was able to persuade the jury that he had followed the "unwritten law," a popular notion that a man had the right to take the life of another who had sexually dishonoured a family member.[13] While many historical case studies are not about the law, legal archaeology is used because records generated by legal proceedings are often the principal, sometimes the sole, source providing insight into the lives of the featured individuals. In this regard legal archaeology is particularly valuable for telling us about the lives and experience with the law of society's dispossessed, particularly among racial and ethnic minorities.[14]

As one of Canada's leading historians has recently noted, legal archaeology has its critics.[15] It has in particular been argued that the emphasis it places on the single case, or group of cases, obscures the large and important questions that legal history should address. It does not in itself tell us enough about the dominant ideologies, the deep-rooted belief systems that shaped the development of the law. In my view this critique misses the point, because legal archaeology does not pretend to answer these kinds of questions in a comprehensive way. Rather it supplements the work of the "generalists," sometimes supporting, sometimes modifying, but always adding colour and richness to the work of others. As American legal historian Richard Danzig succinctly put it half a century ago, "cases are of different vintages; they arise in different settings."[16] Legal archaeology is one way of examining not just the content and operation of legal doctrine and procedure in the abstract, but also the links between law and other broad historical processes in context. This book, for example, has much to tell us about the inequality between men and women within the marriage bond and the consequent limitations on the agency of married women in Ontario in the 1870s. Yet at the same time it shows that the gender inequality of the time could, in the appropriate case, work both ways, on occasion giving a "win" to a woman who had "bucked the system."

Another flaw with legal archaeology identified by some critics is related to what I have said but distinct from it. We should not care about the particular, they say, because it is too much so; it tells us only about one area of law in one place at one time. In emphasizing local contexts and the contingency of the outcomes of legal disputes, it substantially reduces the usefulness of the case study for understanding the past. I would not deny that there is often an emphasis on the particular but would disagree that looking at particular cases and other legal disputes is therefore an unrevealing enterprise. The opposite is true. Examining contingency and particularity is examining how the law operated then and operates now. Of course there is much in law that appears stable and timeless, but this is an illusion. As the aforementioned Richard Danzig long ago argued persuasively, examining one case in its historical context provides an "experiential supplement to the reader's steady diet of logic."

This book is thus firmly in the vein of case studies that examine the operation of the law as it affected relatively ordinary people at a particular place and time. As noted above, the breakdown of the Campbell marriage produced a number of lawsuits in the Ontario courts, three of which pitted the Campbells against each other, either directly or indirectly. They produced contrasting results, largely the result of the law of evidence in force at the time and the differing attitudes of judges and juries. When the venue for the dispute moved from courts to Parliament, Eliza ultimately triumphed, persuading enough senators and MPs to pass the unique separation Act with which this chapter began. Yet according to prevailing legal doctrines that Act should probably not have been passed. To understand why it was we must analyse not just the law but, as importantly, the attitudes to marital relations that underpinned that law. Eliza was able to invoke the chivalrous sympathies of enough elite men to persuade them that she deserved to be given "justice," whether or not the formal law supported that conclusion. Central to the debates over the bill was the law of marital relations in the 1870s, but not just the law. The social attitudes on which the law was based mattered just as much.

A Man's World: Gender and the Law in the 1870s

In multiple ways women occupied an inferior position to men in mid- to late nineteenth-century Canada.[17] They could not vote or hold provincial or federal elected office, nor join the professions of medicine or law. When they were employed outside the home, which was only in certain occupations, they earned less than men. When they turned to the law and the legal system to assert their rights to bodily autonomy and integrity they received minimal protection in practice, even if the formal law guaranteed it.[18] Canada was truly a patriarchy – a social, economic, and political system run by and for men. One practical result of this can be seen in this book. Although Eliza Campbell is the central figure, involved in different ways in many lawsuits and the subject of extensive debate in the Parliament of Canada over three years, she rarely spoke for herself. She did so only as a witness, in court and in the Senate divorce committee. The lawyers who presented the witnesses and made arguments to the juries, judges, and senators, those jurors, judges, and senators, the legislators (MPs and again senators) were all men. Even the journalists who reported on her case were men. Eliza Campbell is not recorded as having made a single speech, penned a single newspaper article or letter to the editor. Men often commented on her actions, her character, her demeanour, and of course her clothes and physical appearance, but they showed little or no interest in her thoughts about the world or the dilemmas she faced. It was a man's world.

Patriarchy also aptly describes the legal system, the rules and procedures governing relations between men and women and between women and all societal institutions. This was as true for the institution of marriage as for any other, indeed more so, for marriage very substantially subordinated wives to husbands, in what we call private law as well as public law. It is telling that while Canadians in this period often referred to "the sacred character of the matrimonial tie," and the family as "the source and life of Christian civilization," marriage was, in the words of Canada's leading historian of women and law, "pure patriarchy."[19] Although the common law afforded single women the same rights to hold property, to contract with others, to sue and be sued for injuries in court, referring formally to them as *femes soles*, everything changed when a woman married. Marriage made a woman a *feme covert*, made husband and wife, in the words of William Blackstone, the foremost eighteenth-century English writer on the common law, "one person in law" with "the very being or legal existence of the woman … suspended."[20] She was "not in legal contemplation a person" when she married.[21] Hence authors of law books in the nineteenth century did not speak, as we now do, of something called "family law." They referred to the law of "husband and wife" or, more broadly, the law of "domestic relations," the latter encompassing the husband's authority over domestic servants as well as his wife and children.[22] Numerous studies have documented the reality of these abstract legal principles in the nineteenth-century Canadian law of married women's property,[23] child custody,[24] women's reproduction,[25] and the civil action that could be taken by a father against the seducer of his daughter.[26] In this period the dominance of men was reinforced, not mitigated, by the doctrine of separate spheres, "the idea that the natural inclinations of and abilities of women fitted them for a submissive role within the private world of the household, while men took on public duties."[27]

The dominant concept which underlay the law of husband and wife was coverture, or the unity of legal personality. The common law of husband and wife was "strongly oriented to preserving the power of men" as "husbands and heads of households," as patriarchal potentates.[28] Coverture was "grounded … on the overwhelming concentration of power in the hands of the husband."[29] The marriage bond was seen as the cornerstone of social stability, and the authority of the husband was integral to that bond.[30] Courts in the United Kingdom and North America rarely interfered with contractual or testamentary freedom in the second half of the nineteenth century. But they refused to enforce contracts or to uphold dispositions of property that encouraged separation or divorce, on the ground that they were contrary to public policy.[31]

In concrete terms coverture gave the husband near absolute authority over the children while the parties lived together. It also meant that a married woman was unable to contract, to make a will, operate a business, sue and be sued in the common law courts, or choose where the couple should live. The husband's right to select the couple's domicile was absolute. A married woman's rights to hold property, including property she owned before her marriage, were also very heavily circumscribed. Her personal property became her husband's absolutely, with the exception of her "paraphernalia" – clothing and jewellery appropriate to her social status. Her real property remained hers, in that she retained title, but her husband had the sole right to administer it without her consent and to receive any income generated. The Court of Chancery developed doctrines to enable women to overcome some of these disadvantages, but Chancery was effectively available only to the better off and did nothing for working class women. Some of these legal disabilities related to property were statutorily reformed in the second half of the nineteenth century, to different degrees in different jurisdictions at different times. The changes to the law of Ontario are discussed briefly in chapter 6 of this book. For current purposes suffice it to say that in the 1870s the process of reform had still only partially given a married woman the same status as a *feme sole*.

The common law was not just a one-way street. In return for being the dominant partner within the union of legal personality the husband was liable for his wife's pre-marital debts and for any torts she committed while married to him. He also had a legal duty to support his wife and children, to provide shelter, food, and clothing. As one legal treatise of the period put it, "[t]he husband is bound to furnish his wife with a suitable home" and "to provide according to his means and condition of life for her maintenance and support." He was also to "love, cherish, and support, ... to defend her from personal insult and wrong, ... to be kind to her..., and generally to conduct himself not according to the strict letter of the matrimonial contract, but in its spirit."[32] A deserted wife not supported by her husband could go to the Court of Chancery for alimony, about which I will have more to say in chapter 7, which deals with Eliza's unsuccessful application for it to the Ontario

Court of Chancery. Husbands and wives also had concomitant duties of living together and of obedience and fidelity in matters sexual and non-sexual. Eliza's alleged offence of a sexual liaison with someone not her husband was as great an affront to the required standards of appropriate wifely behaviour as could be imagined.[33]

If a wife survived her husband her independent legal status was revived, but there was no obligation on the husband to provide for his wife in his will. The common law gave a widow only an indirect form of "widow's pension" in the form of a dower right. She was entitled to the use for life, or to receive the income from, one-third of the realty that he had owned at any point in the marriage and in which the wife had not "barred" her dower, that is, relinquished her right to it. As we will see in chapter 13, Robert tried unsuccessfully to do this without Eliza's consent after he had separated from her.

A husband or a wife who no longer wished to be in the marriage had limited legal recourse. The parties could agree to separate, and make an agreement to that effect, but the Ontario courts did not have the power to order a separation although they would enforce a privately negotiated agreement. Judicial divorce, going to court to end the marriage, was available only in some provinces. In others, including Ontario, spouses were required to petition the Parliament of Canada. Even though it was available in a very limited way, divorce was seen as carrying a stigma, as shameful, a belief most strongly expressed in Article 185 of the Civil Code of Lower Canada, which declared marriage to be dissolvable only by death. Among Protestants, the Anglican church retained its pre-Reformation "Catholic" doctrine that a marriage could only be dissolved by the death of one of the spouses and thus did not permit the remarriage in church of divorced persons. Other protestant denominations were accepting of divorce in exceptional cases, but it was always frowned upon, seen as an occasional necessary evil. Even in the United States, which had much more liberal divorce laws than Canada and the United Kingdom, it was disapproved of by many. As the legal text writer James Schouler put it in 1870, divorces should only be granted when "the grossly immoral conduct" of one spouse "brings unmerited shame upon the other" and thereby "inflicts a wound upon the community."[34]

One result of divorce being so difficult to get was that many unhappy couples simply agreed on "self-divorce," living separately either by agreement or by the insistence of one party in leaving the other and moving elsewhere. This was an immeasurable phenomenon precisely because it took place outside the legal system and generally involved people from the less affluent social classes. Self-divorce was not a choice made by the Campbells, middle-class people and leading citizens of the town of Whitby, Ontario. Eliza said that Robert had deserted her, but that he should support her if she was to accept that. Robert said that he had grounds for a legal divorce, one which relieved him of any obligation to support her. In the event Robert tried but failed to get a parliamentary divorce, and Eliza succeeded in getting a parliamentary separation, the "unique divorce Act" referred to in the first sentence of this chapter.

The Argument and Organization of This Book

The central argument in this book brings together what I have said about legal history case studies and the law of marital relations. The Campbell case was one that very much involved the law, which defined the parties' rights and obligations. But it did not determine the final result of the parliamentary divorce controversy. Rather, that result was shaped by parliamentarians' views of Robert's conduct as a husband. Although the opponents of Eliza's separation bill were probably "right" that the 1879 Act should not have been passed because it was unconstitutional, it did succeed. It succeeded because enough elite men were persuaded that Eliza had been wronged by her husband, who had not lived up to his side of the bargain as laid down by the law of husband and wife. He had demonstrated unmanly, disrespectful behaviour not consonant with his station in life as a respectable middle-class leader of his community. When those same elite men were confronted with the fact that the law as it stood could not provide a remedy for Eliza, they effectively ignored the law. They resolved that it was their manly duty to defend and protect her, to provide a remedy no matter what the law said. Thus a married woman, while she was far from equal in the eyes of the law, could in the appropriate circumstances prevail in a legal dispute with her husband. Voting for Eliza's bill was an act of what, in a different context, has been termed "chivalric justice."[35]

I tell this story in two parts. The first part, chapters 2 through 7, provides the background to the parliamentary divorce controversy that began in 1876. Chapter 2 describes the Campbell and Byrne (Eliza's maiden name) families, their hometown of Whitby, Ontario, and the Campbell marriage down to August 1873. Chapters 3 and 4 cover the period from Robert's return to Whitby in August 1873 from a business trip to the United Kingdom, when he became convinced that his wife had been unfaithful, to his forcible removal of Eliza from the family home a month or so later. Chapters 2, 3, and 4 are set in Whitby, Ontario, and largely based on records created after the events they describe, the testimony given in the three court cases litigated in 1873 and 1874, and the evidence given before the Senate divorce committee in 1876. What was said before the Senate divorce committee was transcribed verbatim and printed as an appendix to the Senate *Journal* for 1876.

Chapters 5 through 7 cover the period from October 1873 until the end of 1875, and deal with the three major lawsuits involving, directly or indirectly, Eliza on one side and Robert on the other. These chapters are set mostly in Toronto, because two of the three lawsuits were heard entirely in the provincial capital as was the third case, in part. In the first Robert Campbell sued George Gordon for criminal conversation, an action that could be taken by a man against another man who had allegedly had sex with his wife. The suit was heard in the Court of Common Pleas before a presiding judge and a jury. The second case, also heard in Common Pleas with a jury, involved Eliza suing Robert's brother James Campbell for defamation, the specific defamatory statement being that he had said that his sister-in-law had had sex with Gordon. The third case, a suit by Eliza against Robert in the Court of Chancery for alimony, is set in Toronto and Whitby because the evidence was taken in the latter on circuit with legal argument being made and judgment given later in the provincial capital.

The records of the three lawsuits are not as complete as the Senate *Journals*. The testimony given in the first two was not transcribed, although the bench books in which the judges took notes have survived. The testimony given in the third, conducted in the Court of Chancery, was transcribed and read over afterwards to the witnesses for them to sign. We also know more about this Chancery case than about the other two because it was a reported case, a case in which the judge, Vice-Chancellor Samuel Hume Blake, wrote a judgment that was published in one of the law reports series produced for the legal profession. His judgment included long extracts from the evidence given and transcribed for the witnesses to sign.[36] The principal source used for the first two lawsuits are the extensive reports, but by no means complete, published in newspapers, the Toronto *Globe* and the *Mail*, and the *Whitby Chronicle* and the *Whitby Gazette*. These newspaper reports are not as reliable or as full as the accounts produced by the shorthand note-takers in Chancery and the Senate. They were produced from reporters' notes, which did not include everything said, nor were they likely to have got everything right. Moreover, the newspaper reports rarely give a "blow by blow" account of questions and answers. They do sometimes summarize the lawyers' question(s) at the start of a report of a witness' appearance, but the witnesses' answers are invariably reproduced in the form of one continuous narrative, moving from one subject to another and giving no sense of the cut and thrust of initial and follow-up questions. On some occasions the reporter said nothing about the questions, simply noting that the lawyer cross-examined the witness and then summarizing what the witness said. One therefore has to work out the questions from the answers.

Despite these shortcomings of the historical record, enough can be discerned from the accounts we do have of what was said in testimony and therefore of what happened before any of the cases got to court. The lawsuits and the Senate divorce committee hearings were all about different legal questions – what lawyers call the causes of action – but common to them was one factual question: Had Eliza been unfaithful to her husband? Had she had sexual intercourse with a man other than her husband in the parlour of the marital home on one evening in August 1873 while Robert was out of town? What did, or did not, take place that evening was argued about later, with Eliza vehemently denying the accusation of adultery, and in turn accusing Robert and his brother James of fabricating evidence in order to free the former from his duties as a husband, including supporting his wife financially.

For the second half of the book, chapters 8 through 14, the locale shifts to Ottawa. These chapters examine how the Campbell matrimonial dispute was handled in Parliament, from 1876 to 1879. Chapters 8 to 11 cover Robert's unsuccessful application for a parliamentary divorce in 1876. The only ground for a parliamentary divorce was adultery, and the evidence Robert presented did not convince a majority of the Senate divorce committee that Eliza had committed adultery. He could have tried the next year, with more persuasive evidence, and/or evidence that would persuade a differently constituted committee. But as detailed in chapter 12, in 1877 Eliza's lawyer was able to persuade the Senate to pass a bill giving her a divorce *a mensa et thoro* instead. That bill did not pass the Commons, but two years later, in 1879, a similar bill passed both Houses of Parliament (chapter 14). The last legal act in this drama came in May 1879 when Governor-General the Marquis of Lorne gave Eliza's Act royal assent. The sources for all the chapters on the parliamentary proceedings are principally the *Journals* and *Debates* of the House of Commons and the Senate.

Chapter 15, the final substantive chapter, traces the fate of Eliza and Robert and their families from 1879. Robert may have lost twice in Parliament, but that had little effect on his fortunes or future life. He prospered, obtained an American divorce, was married twice more, moved to the United States, and died there in 1915 at the age of 82. Eliza never remarried, and moved to Toronto, where she died five years before Robert, in 1910, 67 years old and living in genteel poverty. Chapter 16 concludes, with some observations on the social and legal meanings of the story told in this book.

2
The Town of Whitby, the Campbell and Byrne Families, and the Campbell Marriage to August 1873

The Town of Whitby

Robert Campbell and Eliza Byrne were both residents of Whitby, Ontario, when they met and married in the early 1860s. The Township of Whitby, called Norwich before 1801, had been first settled by Europeans in the 1780s and 1790s, loyalists and others who had moved north after the revolutionary war.[1] They settled on land surrendered, according to English law and policy – but not by the light of the Indigenous Mississauga of Scugog Island people – by the still controversial Gunshot Treaty of 1787–1788, signed at what is now Carrying Place.[2] The growth of the European population was slow because much of the land was taken up by speculators. In 1804 the European population was only just over 100, and the number increased slowly until the War of 1812. After the war more settlers came, not from the republic to the south but from Britain. They were not impoverished immigrants, but people able to buy land from existing grantees who were given incentives to sell. In 1820 the population of European origin had increased five-fold to just over 500, consisting mainly of farmers in scattered settlements. Over the next two decades the Township grew to over 5,000 and by mid-century Whitby was a town of nearly 7,000, mostly immigrants from the British Isles and their descendants.

Whitby grew and prospered because of a thriving agricultural export trade. Its natural harbour became a busy port, receiving lumber and wheat that was harvested inland and brought to the shores of Lake Ontario via a plank road that ran from Port Perry in the north to Whitby. There, merchants from nearby Toronto (York until 1834) and the more distant Montreal would buy these goods and raw materials and export them to the United States.

In the 1850s Whitby was the third largest point of origin in Canada West for exports to the US, after Toronto and Kingston.[#] The lake-based trade also created a ship-building industry and a variety of other businesses in the town. By 1861 the town had grown to over 7,000 people supporting two tanneries, one flour mill, one foundry, one planing mill, one match factory, one brewery, 12 carriage and implement shops, a number of boot and shoe and blacksmiths shops, 22 stores, and 12 taverns.[3] The completion of the Grand Trunk railway between Montreal and Toronto in 1856 made getting the region's exports to market quicker and cheaper, but it also precipitated the slow decline of trade by water. Nonetheless, Whitby remained important in the county as the outlet for agricultural produce, especially so after 1872 and the opening of the Port Whitby and Port Perry Railway. It was also the administrative centre, the county town of the County of Ontario, created in 1852 when what became Ontario county was separated from York county. As a result the county court house, jail, and registry office, and the armoury of the county militia regiment were all located in Whitby. The process of building them was completed in 1854, and Whitby was proclaimed the county town. It was incorporated the same year and thereby separated from Whitby Township.[4]

In the 1870s the town had two weekly newspapers, only one of which, the *Whitby Chronicle*, which supported John A. Macdonald's Conservative party, has a more or less complete run extant. Much less is known about the *Whitby Gazette*, because very few issues from this period have survived. The editor and publisher in this period was William H. Higgins, an Irish Catholic, born in 1830, who emigrated to the Province of Canada in his early 20s.[5] He worked for some years as a parliamentary reporter in Quebec City. In the mid-1850s he decided to acquire his own newspaper and the then mayor of Whitby, James Wallace, loaned him enough money to buy the *Chronicle*. Through his Irish Catholic connections Higgins was friendly with some well-known figures in Canada West, most notably Thomas D'Arcy McGee, one of the fathers of Confederation and briefly a minister in John A. Macdonald's first cabinet until he was assassinated by a radical Fenian in 1868. Higgins regularly published the "Tim O'Day Letters" in the *Chronicle*, a humour column written in an Irish dialect. They were commentaries on life and events in Whitby and the politics of the day. He has also been called the town's first historian for his articles in an historical atlas of the 1870s, which were later republished as a book.[6] None of Higgins's articles were about the Campbell affair. He left Whitby

– As is well known, the area that became the province of Ontario was called Upper Canada from 1791 to 1841, and Canada West from 1842 to 1867. In this book I use all three names, depending on the time period being discussed.

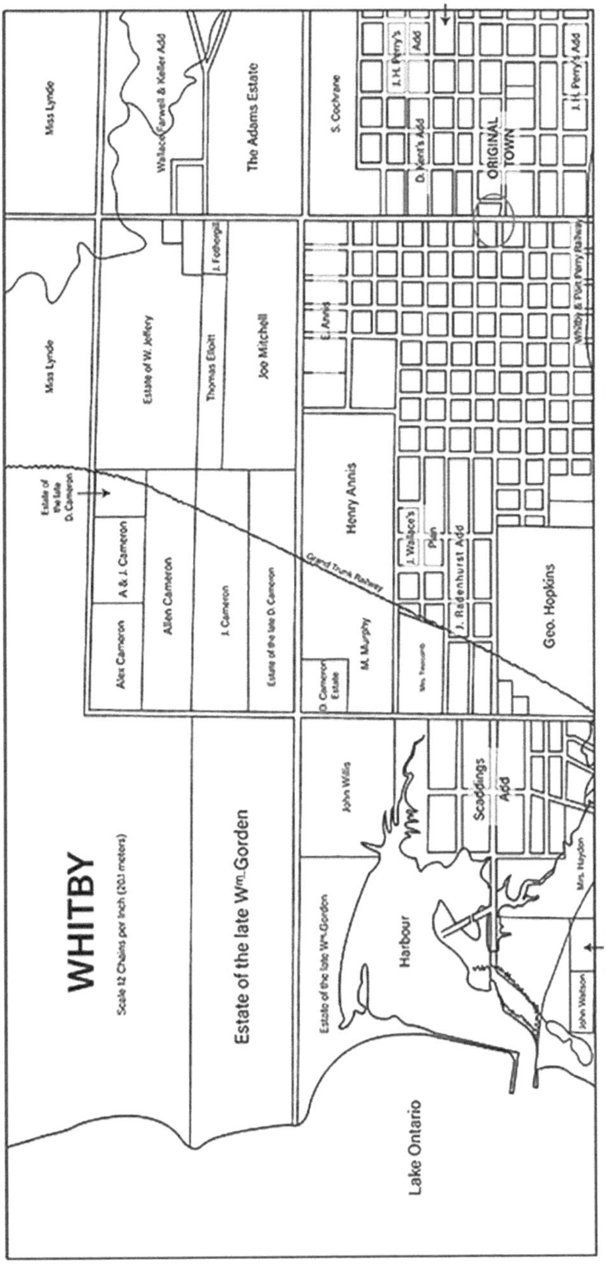

Figure 2.1. Whitby Street Plan in the 1870s (Campbell's store circled)

Source: Drawn by Alyssa Mintzberg, from *Illustrated Historical Atlas of Ontario County, Ontario* (Toronto: J.H. Beers, 1877).

in 1883, discouraged by the town's stagnation as the railway put the port out of business. He moved to Toronto and died there in 1904.

The 1850s and 1860s were the apogee of Whitby's growth. Thereafter it entered a slow decline; its population shrank by some 500 people to around 6,600 by 1871, and Oshawa became the county's major centre for manufacturing and other industries. By the 1880s the railway had almost entirely replaced the harbour as the principal means of commercial transport. Nonetheless Whitby was still a significant market town in the 1860s and 1870s, as attested to by the fact that in 1870 it hosted the Queen's Plate, the province's premier horse race, which was run in various towns before it got a permanent home in Toronto in 1883. It was also a venue visited by travelling fairs and other exhibitions, and the location chosen for the Ontario Ladies College, a private boarding school for girls that opened in 1872. Rather less a matter for civic pride, it had its own brothel as well, run by the "notorious Mrs. Glass."[7]

The Byrne Family

The Byrne family were immigrants to Upper Canada from the British Isles, arriving in New York in 1838 and settling initially in L'Orignal, Ontario.[8] The Reverend James Thomas Byrne was a 28-year-old Congregationalist minister. Congregationalists were part of the Calvinist tradition within low Protestantism, different from other Calvinist sects like Presbyterians because individual churches were autonomous and self-governing, not controlled by elders. They originated in sixteenth-century England, where they were called separatists or independents to distinguish them from Presbyterians. Colonial branches of Congregationalists were often founded by men sent to the colonies by the London Missionary Society (LMS), which is how Rev. Byrne came to Upper Canada.[9] His wife Henrietta, 32 years old when the family emigrated to North America, was a few years older than her husband. From L'Orignal the Byrnes moved to Ottawa, then to Brockville, and then, sometime before the 1851 census was taken, to Whitby, where Rev. Byrne was the minister of the Congregationalist Church, a wooden building on the west side of Byron Street. Like many Christian ministers he left his mark on the historical record through his work as a vocal supporter of the anti-slavery movement in Canada West.[10]

The Byrnes brought with them to North America four children born in the UK: Henrietta, born in 1832; Bethiah, 1834; James, about 1835 or '36, and Samuel, around 1836. Henrietta and Samuel are not important players in this book.[11] Bethiah and James, conversely, were major figures in the events of the early to mid-1870s. Bethiah, named for an unusually virtuous daughter of a Pharoah who converted to Judaism,[12] married a Whitby lawyer,

Norman George Ham, in 1851, and had three children with him – a daughter, Henrietta, invariably called Hettie, and sons Norman and George Philip Ham, respectively born in 1855, 1858, and 1859. Norman Ham Senior died in 1864, and for the next decade Bethiah stayed in Whitby, a widow raising three teenaged children. Norman Ham worked for the Campbell brothers, discussed in the next section, as an office odd-job man.[13]

James Byrne initially worked as a clerk in Prescott, having elected to stay in eastern Canada West when the rest of his family moved to Brockville and Whitby. By 1860 he lived in Hamilton, where on 24 September of that year he married 16-year old Sarah Lewis, whose mother ran a patent medicine business in that city. Sarah Lewis died at 18 in 1861, and three years later James Byrne was married by his father to another much younger wife, the daughter of a Hamilton physician, 18-year-old Mary Mason, also in Hamilton.[14] James and Mary had five children. By 1864 they had moved to Whitby and James had established a business as a druggist, advertising his "long experience … as a Dispensing Chemist."[15] He played an important role in this story as a financial and emotional supporter of Eliza when marital problems transformed her life.

The Byrnes had three other children after they moved to North America. Alex Francis, born in 1840; Eliza Marie, the central character in this book, born in 1844; and Ann Sophia, born in 1846 or 1847. Alex Francis lived at home with his parents until 1862, when he married a local girl, 18-year-old Georgina Godsman. At some point, probably before 1871 because they are never listed in any federal census, Alex and Georgina relocated to Owatonna City in Minnesota.[16] Ann Sophia, known as Annie, was still single in the early 1870s when the Campbell marriage broke down, and indeed never married. She lived with her parents until Rev. Byrne died in 1874, and then with her mother. Eliza Marie Byrne was married to Robert Campbell by her father, in the Byrne home, on 6 April 1863, at the respective ages of 19 and 29.[17]

The Campbell Family

The Campbell family were Scottish immigrants to Canada West in 1849, buying land in the Saugeen region of Bruce County, on the Lake Huron shore.[18] Robert's parents, James and Janet Findlay Campbell, came from northeast Scotland in 1849. They were originally from Elgin, but moved first to Forres and then to Inverness, and both were 49 when they emigrated. They brought with them to Canada six children: Ann (24 in 1849), Catherine (22), Elizabeth (20), Jane (18), Robert (16), and James (12). A seventh child, also named James, had died in infancy in Scotland. James Campbell Senior and Janet Campbell were, like most people from that region, Presbyterians, adherents of the Free Church

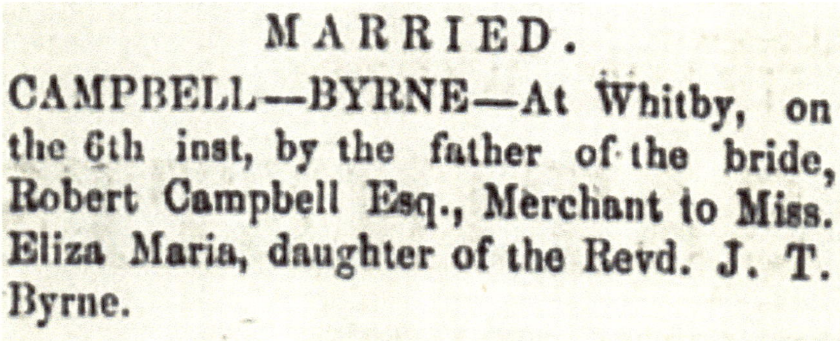

MARRIED.

CAMPBELL—BYRNE—At Whitby, on the 6th inst, by the father of the bride, Robert Campbell Esq., Merchant to Miss. Eliza Maria, daughter of the Revd. J. T. Byrne.

Figure 2.2. The marriage notice of Robert Campbell and Eliza Byrne
Source: Whitby Chronicle, 9 April 1863

of Scotland, established in 1843 when a large number of congregations broke away from the established Church of Scotland in what became known as the Great Disruption because they objected to state interference with the independence of the church.[19]

The Campbell family all lived on a farm in the Saugeen district of Bruce County, near Southampton, for a few years. Janet Findlay Campbell did not long survive after emigration, dying in Southampton in 1852. Catherine and Ann Campbell stayed in that area and both married men named Ross. Catherine's husband was Duncan Ross, the first name of Ann's husband is not known. James Campbell Senior lived another 30 or so years, dying in Walkerton, Bruce County, in 1883, aged 80. At some point in the early 1850s, presumably after the death of their mother, the four younger Campbell children all left for other places in southern Ontario. Robert had completed high school in Inverness and started work in a law office expecting to qualify to practise, but his apprenticeship was cut short by his parents' decision to emigrate. Having spent his formative years in Scotland it was always "home." He visited Scotland almost annually once he was successful in business, and he had lived in Scotland long enough to likely speak with that accent in the subsequent decades. He certainly acquired Scottish idioms, which he continued to use in his new home.[20] Although he was listed in the 1851 census as a labourer and still on the Bruce county farm, he did have an education and that year left the farm to work in a retail store in St Catharine's for a short time and then in a similar establishment in Whitby. Having learned something of the trade, he started his own wholesale and retail dry goods and grocery business in Whitby in 1851, the same year he left the farm.[21]

Elizabeth, Jane, and James Campbell all moved to Whitby as well, though it is not known whether they went with Robert or joined him in

Figure 2.3. Robert Campbell

Source: Whitby Archives Photograph 31-009-319

later years. On 1 November 1860, Jane Campbell married John Anderson, a farmer until 1870 when he became a butcher.[22] John Anderson features prominently in this book. Elizabeth was a life-long spinster who lived with Robert after his marriage to Eliza broke down, and on her own in Whitby and Toronto after Robert had left Canada. She then moved to Missouri to live with Robert and died there in 1907.[23]

James Campbell followed Robert into the retail trade. In 1862 the brothers entered into a formal business partnership, R. & J. Campbell. The *Whitby Chronicle* welcomed the news, noting that "young blood" would bring "additional energy and vigour" into the business, while also pointing out that Robert's business had always been "well conducted."[24]

Figure 2.4. James Campbell, 1881

Source: Whitby Archives Photograph 31-002-051

Operating from a number of different locations in Whitby's business district R. & J. Campbell quickly became one of the leading dry goods and grocery businesses in the town, and they diversified into a wide variety of merchandise – men's and women's clothing of all kinds and made of a great variety of materials, as well as haberdashery, shoes, bedding, curtains, and seeds. They bought their principal building, at 119–121 Brock Street, known as the "Glasgow Warehouse," in the early 1860s and expanded it over the years by adding two storeys, rebuilding their premises after a fire in 1877. Some of their clothing stock was imported from the United Kingdom, and both Campbells travelled

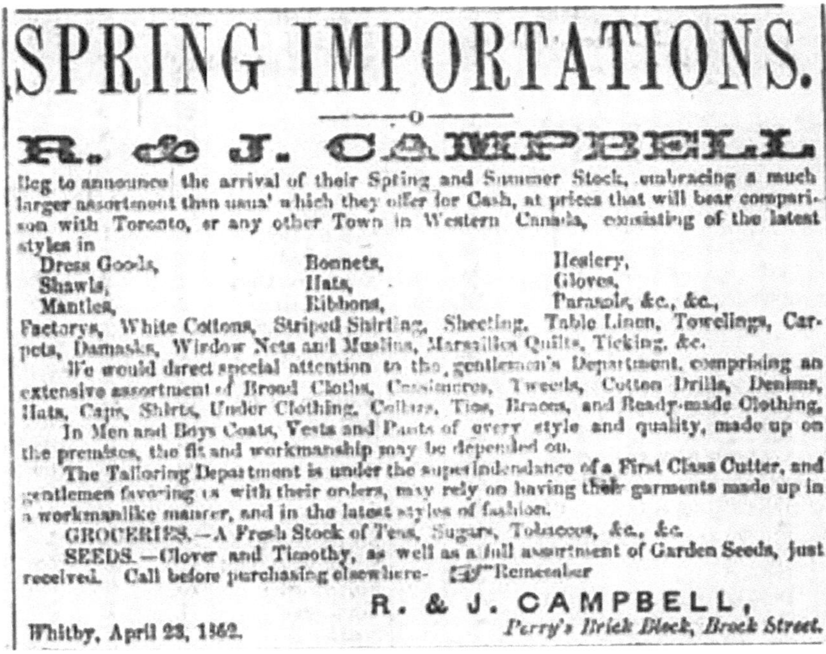

SPRING IMPORTATIONS.

R. & J. CAMPBELL

Beg to announce the arrival of their Spring and Summer Stock, embracing a much larger assortment than usual which they offer for Cash, at prices that will bear comparison with Toronto, or any other Town in Western Canada, consisting of the latest styles in

Dress Goods,	Bonnets,	Hosiery,
Shawls,	Hats,	Gloves,
Mantles,	Ribbons,	Parasols, &c., &c.,

Factorys, White Cottons, Striped Shirting, Sheeting, Table Linen, Towelings, Carpets, Damasks, Window Nets and Muslins, Marseilles Quilts, Ticking, &c.

We would direct special attention to the gentleman's Department, comprising an extensive assortment of Broad Cloths, Cassimeres, Tweeds, Cotton Drills, Denims, Hats, Caps, Shirts, Under Clothing, Collars, Ties, Braces, and Ready-made Clothing.

In Men and Boys Coats, Vests and Pants of every style and quality, made up on the premises, the fit and workmanship may be depended on.

The Tailoring Department is under the superintendance of a First Class Cutter, and gentlemen favoring us with their orders, may rely on having their garments made up in a workmanlike manner, and in the latest styles of fashion.

GROCERIES.—A Fresh Stock of Teas, Sugars, Tobaccos, &c., &c.

SEEDS.—Clover and Timothy, as well as a full assortment of Garden Seeds, just received. Call before purchasing elsewhere- ☞Remember

R. & J. CAMPBELL,

Perry's Brick Block, Brock Street.

Whitby, April 23, 1862.

Figure 2.5. Advertisement for R & J Campbell

Source: *Whitby Chronicle*, 22 May 1862

there on business and visited with their extended family frequently in the 1860s and early 1870s. In 1873, for example, a propitious year in our story, a large advertisement in the *Whitby Chronicle* announced that their fall and winter stock had just arrived from the UK and was available from the Glasgow Warehouse at the best prices.[25] The Campbells' store was a landmark, other advertisements not infrequently telling customers that their place of business was at "premises opposite R. & J. Campbell's store," or "next door to the store of R. & J. Campbell, Brock Street."[26] The Campbell brothers were very much leading citizens of the town, James also serving on the township and county councils a number of times in the 1860s and 1870s and as deputy reeve in 1873. Robert did not run for local office, but he too was a prominent member of the community, being elected a vice-president of the Whitby branch of the St Andrew's Society, the leading organization promoting Scottish culture in nineteenth-century Ontario.[27]

Despite the depression, which started in 1873 and lasted some five years, the Campbells' fortunes did not fall precipitously, likely attributable to their diversification. Indeed in the 1870s they were consistently said to be wealthy. In 1874 Robert told the Ontario Court of Common Pleas that he was a businessman who owned his house and other real estate in Whitby, but was not, as some claimed, worth $75,000. In 1876, when the Campbell brothers were becoming widely known, albeit, as we will see not for good reasons, the *Hamilton Weekly Times* said that he and James had, for "a considerable number of years," run "the largest and most lucrative business ... in Whitby." Robert himself was rumoured to be worth $100,000. Whatever the actual amount, in 1875 he was said by Samuel Hume Blake, vice-chancellor of the Ontario Court of Chancery, about whom more in chapter 7, to have amassed "what, in this country, is looked upon as a considerable fortune."[28]

Both brothers married women from Whitby. In October 1864 James Campbell married Rebecca Tweedie at Broadfield, the Tweedie family home. Rebecca was the daughter of deceased "pioneer farmer" and prominent citizen James Tweedie, who had emigrated from Scotland about 1829. They had six children, all boys, born between 1865 and 1875, three of whom became lawyers. Two became physicians, and one a veterinarian.[29] As noted above, in 1863 Robert Campbell married the central character in this book, Eliza Maria Byrne.

The Campbell Marriage to June 1873

On the surface Robert and Eliza's marriage seemed like a perfect match. Eliza was by all accounts very attractive,* a good musician and singer who liked to dance, the life and soul of church socials and house parties. Yeoman Gibson, a local grocer and later mayor of Whitby who lived near the Campbells, would often pause on his evening walk to listen to her when she sang in the house. Wellington Adams, a young dentist who set up his practice in Whitby in the fall of 1871, told the Senate divorce committee of going to a number of parties at the Campbell home with other young people.[30] Robert must have believed he had made a catch. Eliza likely felt that she, too, had done well. She had married a mature man who was rising in the world, and who was somewhat captivated by her even if he did not share her tastes and accomplishments. By 1873 the Campbells had three children: two boys, James Bremner Campbell and Robert Campbell Junior, born in 1864 and 1865 respectively, and a daughter, Edith Holmes Campbell, born in 1867. In early 1873 Eliza became pregnant

* I was not able to find a photograph of Eliza, but she was referred to often as very attractive.

with what would become their fourth child, Francis William Campbell, born on 12 December 1873.[31]

The Campbell family lived in a spacious, although by no means palatial, two-storey house set well back from the street. Half a dozen steps led up to a wide porch and the front door, and at the end of the hallway were the stairs to the second floor. Off the hallway to the right were, in turn, the dining room, a breakfast room, and the kitchen. To the left were the parlour and a spare bedroom. The pantry and back kitchen completed the first-floor layout. Upstairs were four rooms – the master bedroom, the children's bedroom, the one servant's bedroom, and a lumber room.[32] Their servant for all of 1872 and much of 1873 was Martha Newsom, a local girl. Martha left the Campbells' service on 15 August 1873, for an extended visit to her sister in the village of Taunton, just north of what is now Oshawa. She was replaced by her sister Jane, who until then was the servant to James Byrne. Jane had also preceded Martha as the Campbells' live-in servant, from mid-1870 through all of 1871. The Newsoms were not a well-regarded family. Hardware merchant George Gross said the father was not a "person of credit and character"; indeed, he was "about the biggest loafer in the place." Jane had had a child out of wedlock in 1868, which would not have been approved of, but that did not prevent the Campbells employing her.[33]

All accounts state that there was no overt evidence of difficulties with their marriage during its first decade. Martha Newson, for example, told the Court of Common Pleas in 1873 that they lived "on good terms" until August 1873.[34] Yet they were not a well-suited couple. In court testimony and before the Senate divorce committee James Campbell said that Eliza had told him that Robert had married her for her beauty and she had married him for his money. Having heard testimony from them and others in the alimony case, discussed in chapter 7, Vice-Chancellor Samuel Hume Blake provided a succinct account of their different personalities and the effect their differences had on the relationship. He described Eliza's fondness for music and the social life of the town, and contrasted this with Robert, a man "of good business habits" who "took but little, if any, interest in that which pleased his wife." When Eliza threw parties for the young men and women of the town Robert often stayed late in the office and worked. The marriage, said Blake, "was not ... a well assorted one" for "neither party sought to accommodate" their differences. Robert was absorbed by his business, "and he gave himself up to that to the exclusion, ... to some extent, of the attention which his wife might have reasonably asked of him." As he increasingly did so, "she looked for and obtained, in the society of others, the enjoyment and admiration which she vainly sought at the hands of her husband. Gradually that which amounted almost to estrangement grew up between them."[35]

Blake's suggestion that Robert paid little attention to his wife and children was reflected in some of the testimony given in the various lawsuits. In the defamation trial in March 1874 he testified that he married Eliza in 1862 or 1863 and that their daughter had been born "about six years ago"; in both cases he could not remember which year, and he was similarly unable to remember whether his youngest son had been born in 1873 or 1874 when he testified before the Senate divorce committee in 1876. Also at the defamation trial he admitted that he "paid no particular attention" to what Eliza read or to her apparent ambition to write for publication.[36]

Robert's relative inattention to his wife and children was also a contrast to the closeness between him and his brother James. Their fraternal loyalty was a source of friction in the Campbell marriage, because James Campbell and Eliza did not care for each other. James dropped by the Campbell home almost every evening when Robert was in town, chatted for 15 or 20 minutes, and then attended to a horse he stabled on some waste ground next to the house. But when Robert was away he limited himself to caring for the horse. He did not visit Eliza – he had "business to attend to."[37] Indeed there were occasional spats between him and Eliza. She and James, Eliza said, "were never on friendly terms," never "on intimate terms." Eliza's father, Rev. Byrne, also knew of the coldness between them. The relations between Eliza and James Campbell were symptomatic of those between the Campbell and Byrne families generally; they were "only on speaking terms."[38] The lack of familiarity extended to John Anderson, Robert's brother-in-law. He visited from time to time, but he was not invited to the house parties that Eliza threw at the Campbell home. The problems between Eliza and James Campbell seem to have been deeper than those between any other members of the two families, and animosity might describe their feelings towards each other. James thought Eliza frivolous, and, as we shall see in later chapters, Eliza was adamant that James had it in for her as a result.

Samuel Hume Blake's assessment of Eliza's response to Robert's indifference, that she looked for "enjoyment" in "the admiration of others," led to the occasional confrontation. In 1871 Robert took Eliza with him on his annual business trip to the United Kingdom, and on the voyage back to Canada she became too familiar for Robert's liking with a young man called Millard Pugsden. She walked around the deck with him every day for many hours, Robert only seeing her at mealtimes. Robert complained that she seemed to think more of Pugsden than of him, and after they had landed he upbraided her for her conduct, and said that had they been travelling on a Canadian ship, where presumably other passengers would have known him or known of him, "he would have felt himself disgraced."[39] Despite this one incident, Robert consistently stated that as far as he knew the marriage was otherwise cloudless until early 1873, although that perhaps had much to do with the fact that he simply did not notice her dissatisfaction.

In January 1873 Robert was disabused of his complacency, as Eliza began to openly express her feelings, in words and actions. Robert perceived that she "was very much dissatisfied with the house, and her lot, and her children." She went out a good deal and "neglected the house." She took up with "frivolous people."[40] On one occasion she apparently said that she wished the children were dead, and that if they did die she would leave him. On another occasion she asked what Robert would be prepared to give to have her leave him. She could not have been very happy with his reply. He would give her nothing, and if she wanted to leave him, she should do it honourably, and not disgrace him. The coldness which had descended on their marriage did not prevent Eliza becoming pregnant in April, which Robert may have known before he went away on his annual trip to the UK on 26 June. On previous occasions arrangements had been made for someone else to live in the house while he was away, but not this time. There had been talk of Eliza's niece Hettie Ham staying there, but she did not.

Eliza Campbell's Social Summer of 1873

Before and after Robert's departure Eliza developed friendships with two different young men, one of whom, 32-year-old George Brand Gordon, she had known since childhood. The other, Godfrey Parks, was a recent arrival in Whitby from the United Kingdom, turning up in the town in the fall of 1872. Why he ended up in Whitby is not known, but it was not unusual for young Englishmen to emigrate to Canada to seek a better life in the new and expanding Dominion. He first met Eliza at her father's house where he and other young people had been invited for an evening. According to Eliza they met "frequently" while he was in Whitby.[41] Some of these meetings were in the Campbell house, with others present, on social occasions. Parks decided to try and stay in the town, and for that purpose answered an advertisement placed by the Campbell brothers for a post as bookkeeper. Eliza took an interest in the application and asked Robert about it. The Campbell firm did not hire him, and he left Whitby in mid-February 1873 and took a job in Concord, some 50 kilometres to the east and north of Toronto, in what is now Vaughan. He and Eliza did not forget each other. The nature and precise extent of their relationship is unknown, but it did involve a clandestine correspondence, which began shortly after Parks left Whitby and continued thereafter, and which included words of endearment and statements about how enjoyable it would be to meet. Our knowledge of their relationship derives principally from a letter that Parks sent to Eliza and another letter written by her to him, but probably not sent, which was found in August 1873 in one of the drawers of her secretaire.

The letter written by Parks to Eliza was dated 14 August 1873, and sent from Concord. It was addressed to Eliza "care of" the Campbell firm, and read:[42]

> Concord, August 14th, 1873
>
> Dear Marie – I wrote to you from here three or four weeks since, but have never had an answer. I was thinking of coming about the first or second week in next month, should I be in time to escape the G-d-n" I asked in my last for some envelopes, will you write by return and send me a few; I have been very busy all day and have hardly a minute to spare, and have to walk to the post with this as I cannot allow anyone to see the address. Be sure and write by return. In haste Believe me to remain, My Dear Marie, Yours in sincerity
>
> G. H.
>
> I think if you have written to me, your letter must have gone to the States as there is a place of the same name there. Please address to me at Concord Post Office, County of Vaughan, Ontario
>
> Tell me where you think the suspicion is?

This letter obviously raised suspicions in Robert. It appeared to be one link in a chain of correspondence, and to intimate that Parks was considering visiting Eliza in Whitby in early September if the "G-d-n," "guardian," the word that Parks and Eliza used to refer to Robert, was not yet returned from the United Kingdom. It asked Eliza about "the suspicion," presumably Robert's suspicion of Eliza, and the reference to "envelopes" was to envelopes that Eliza had addressed to herself and sent to Parks so that when he wrote to her people in her household would not see a letter to her with strange handwriting on the envelope. For all that it seemed to be from Parks, it was written in a disguised hand – what was referred to as a "backhand," with letters sloping backwards.[43]

The other letter, the draft or copy of one from Eliza to Parks, was, from internal evidence, written before Robert went to the UK in June 1873 and while Parks was probably briefly in Toronto before he moved to Concord. It read:[44]

> I have been very remiss in not answering yours ere this, but I have been out so often in the evenings that really I've not had time. *I hope it has not seriously affected you though. "Incognito"* came safely and was delivered into my own hands at the office. I thank you for your interesting letter. I have just come in from a "ramble" with two or three *other girls*. I think if you ever *honour* this fair town with your presence again, you might find someone to take a ramble with you as of *yore;* a great deal may have been thought, but I have never had a word hinted to me of the past. How happy I should have been to have complied with your request, in coming to give you a drive, and then having you drive me home again. That dream is too sweet to indulge in. I haven't the slightest idea when I shall come to Toronto. The "Guardian" was up for two days last week, but I suppose you had not the extreme felicity of *beholding* him. I am not certain if the *Guardian* will take that journey you spoke of or not, but if it is taken it will be sometime in June or the beginning of July. I am glad you enjoy attending Holy Trinity. You say it is what you like, a little "High." I would much prefer attending something a shade or two lower in the same denomination; there are too many Ritualistic performances there to suit my liberal views. I should go with you there if I came up. You suggest the probability of someone giving me a walk after service. I assure you, on my honour, nothing of the kind has occurred. I do not so easily forget those I *like* as to run with another the moment they are out of sight. You seem to have had some trouble in your mind as to whether you should write.
>
> BOOK-KEEPER

These letters provide clear, albeit limited, evidence that Eliza had formed a close friendship with Parks while he was in Whitby. The undated letter, even if it was never sent, shows that she corresponded with Parks after he had left Whitby. It was an affectionate, dreamy letter involving thoughts of the good time they could have if they did meet again. She used a pseudonym which referenced Parks's profession. Yet there is nothing in the undated letter that refers to any physical love. The only really "racy" thing alluded to is that the daughter of a Congregationalist minister would agree to attend a high Anglican service with Parks. It is consistent with Eliza's sense of dissatisfaction with her dull life and her dour and business-obsessed husband, and also with her romantic nature and a willingness to break the bounds of conventional behaviour.

In fact, in telling Parks that she did not "run with another" when one friend was "out of sight" Eliza was not truthful. Through 1873 she also spent an increasing amount of time with George Gordon, a single man who lived with and assisted his father, William M. Gordon, on the family farm, Bayside, about one and a half kilometres outside of Whitby. He was a tall man and solidly built, about 5 foot 11 and 200 pounds, and an officer in the county militia, the 34th Battalion, which had been formed in 1866 in anticipation of expected Fenian raids launched from the United States. The Gordons had emigrated to Whitby from Scotland in 1837, and Eliza had known George Gordon since they were children. Indeed the Gordon, Byrne, and Campbell families were all well acquainted. George Gordon visited Eliza's parents and her brother James at their homes, and Robert, who knew the Gordon family from the time of his first settling in Whitby, was sufficiently close to them that he signed the $500 bond that George Gordon's older brother, James Keith Gordon, had to provide when he joined the Law Society of Upper Canada as an articling student. James articled in a law office in Toronto from 1859, and was called to the bar in 1864. He practised law in Whitby for the next 35 years before retiring in 1899, one of only five lawyers with offices in Whitby in 1873, although lawyers based elsewhere also advertised their services in the *Chronicle*.[45] As we will see, he was one of the lawyers involved in the various lawsuits involving Robert and Eliza. George Gordon was also well acquainted with John Anderson, Robert's brother-in-law, the one-time farmer who had known Gordon since about 1850 when they were both teens.

Gordon attended evening parties put on by Eliza, where James and Henrietta Byrne were also among those present, and occasionally called at the house on his own. On one occasion, in April 1873, he called in the evening when the Campbell family were at tea. Eliza showed him into the parlour and was still there with him when Robert, as was his wont, left after tea to work in his store. They were still there when Robert returned at 8 p.m., although he did not join them. Gordon finally left after 10, by which time Robert had let his anger stew. He told Eliza that "it was very imprudent and wrong for her to entertain young men in the way she had been doing," and although Robert thought his words were spoken in "half joke and whole earnest," his evident anger made her cry.[46] She asked Robert to forgive her and to sleep with her that night, but he refused.

Despite this incident and his knowledge that matters generally were not good between him and Eliza, Robert was confident that nothing

Figure 2.6. George Gordon and family. James K. Gordon is in the back row, second from left, and George Gordon is on his left.

Source: https://www.familysearch.org/tree/person/about/9NP7-P3P

beyond "imprudent" behaviour had occurred before he left for the United Kingdom towards the end of June 1873, even though he suspected Gordon of having too much interest in his wife. Whether he was right regarding Parks depends on one's definition of "imprudent," but it is reasonable to speculate that if he had known of the correspondence he would have called it more than that. He would have called Eliza's friendship with Gordon something stronger had he known how much it appeared to some in Whitby to advance while he was away. As Robert Harrison, Robert's counsel, put in an opening address to the Court of Common Pleas in October 1873, Gordon went from being an "occasional visitor" before June to being a "constant" one thereafter.'[47] That was the gravamen of the evidence that the Campbell family's live in servant Martha Newsom, gave in all the later court cases and before the Senate divorce committee. She said that Gordon had started visiting on his own in late June, shortly after Robert left, and often stayed very late, until after she went to bed. He came about once a week, usually on a Saturday night. Only once did he come with another person, a John Mitchell. Newsom could not say what Eliza and Gordon talked about, nor did she ever see or hear anything untoward. But she could say that Gordon visited alone, that he and Eliza sat in the parlour together as late as midnight and, indeed, sometimes much later than that. On one occasion she heard Eliza go to bed "shortly before daylight."[48] She provided four specific dates in August – the 2nd and the 9th, which were Saturdays, the 13th, a Wednesday, and Friday the 15th.

There was more. Eliza would "dress herself more carefully" on the evenings Gordon visited, and on more than one occasion she had found Eliza's shoes in the parlour when she went there in the morning. The implication was that Eliza had removed them before going to bed so that Newsom would not hear her doing so at a late hour. In addition, on three occasions Newsom had found the curtains pinned together with a footstool placed on the curtains where they met the floor. Thus Eliza took extra precautions against anybody outside being able to see what went on. Newsom also found used glasses in the parlour. All in all Martha Newsom thought Gordon's frequent visits "strange," and "not proper."[49] She also thought it odd that Eliza would occasionally talk to her about Gordon, asking her if she did not think he was a fine-looking man. Newsom also claimed to have noticed a marked change in Eliza's general demeanour and routines after Robert had left. She had never been an early riser, sleeping usually until 8. But the mornings after Gordon's visits she stayed in bed until 10 or 11. More generally, she was not as fastidious about looking after the house and children that summer; she left things to Newsom. All of this related only to the period before 15 August because, as noted above, Martha Newsom's sister Jane replaced her as the family servant on that date, which was also one of the evenings that Gordon visited. Martha had been out all day at a picnic in Oshawa with Jane and came back to the house with her. She wanted to say goodbye to Eliza but heard Gordon's voice in the parlour and did not go in.

The most potentially damning piece of evidence that Martha Newsom gave related to a spare bedroom on the ground floor and to one snippet of conversation she did hear. She thought that the bed was "unnecessarily mussed up at times" after Gordon's visits. However, she could not say whether it had been "used." Nor did she ever say that she had seen any intimate behaviour or heard any suggestive words pass between Eliza and Gordon.[50] The one possible exception to this was that she had heard Gordon ask Eliza if she was sincere. But she did not hear the answer.

Eliza did not dispute that Gordon had visited her in the evening while Robert was away, but she said it was only five or six times. She denied all the other things said by Martha Newsom and insisted that the visits were nothing more than childhood friends getting together to talk and listen to her play the piano and sing. Both she and Gordon later stated that he did not stay that late when he visited, invariably leaving before midnight.

Although there is no direct evidence for it, and although she denied telling anybody but her sister Jane under cross-examination in the criminal conversation (crim. con.) trial and at the senate divorce committee hearing, it is reasonable to think that Martha Newsom talked about Gordon's visits to other domestic servants, who might have then mentioned them to their employers. In any event when Robert returned to Whitby on 18 August 1873, stories were circulating about the unseemly behaviour of Eliza with Gordon. Three people who testified in later court cases and may well have talked about what they claimed to have seen while Robert was absent were George Cameron, Charles Scott, and William Henry Fagan. Cameron, a shoemaker and the son of Whitby's chief constable, claimed that he saw the two walking together one evening, with Gordon's arm around her shoulder. Scott also said that he had seen the two walking together, although he had never seen Gordon pay more attention to Eliza "than to any other lady," suggesting that Gordon was perhaps something of a "ladies' man." Fagan, a moulder in the local foundry who had lived in Whitby for just two years, claimed that he saw Gordon one evening in August walking from the Campbell house front door towards the gate, with his arm around a woman's neck in "a kind of loving attitude," and he also claimed that he had heard Gordon say to the woman, whom he did not know, "You must not say anything of this to Robert."[51] Another person who knew about Gordon's visits to the Campbell house was James Campbell's wife Rebecca, who heard it from a friend, Mrs. Mary Jameson, the wife of Robert Jameson, a local wine and spirits merchant and grocer.[52] It was also later claimed that the rumours reached Bethiah Ham, Eliza's older sister, and that she wrote to Eliza to "[warn] her of the consequences of her conduct, if she were not more discreet."[53] Bethiah, however, denied doing so. One person who does not seem to have talked about Gordon or known of his visits was James Campbell, which is perhaps surprising because while Robert was away he went frequently to the field next to the Campbell family home to take care of his horse which was stabled there.

Robert had a good summer trip to the UK, buying a lot of stock for the business at good prices, which he arranged to ship to Whitby for the fall season.[54] When he got home he discovered the letter of 18 August from Parks and heard some, if not all, of these stories. The next chapter discusses his subsequent actions.

3
Robert Campbell's Separation from Eliza, August 1873

Robert Campbell's Decision to Separate

Robert got back to Whitby from his UK trip at midnight on Monday, 18 August 1873. He and Eliza had sex that night, as many couples would do after a long absence. Eliza had not known in advance that he was about to return home; he telegraphed James Campbell from Quebec City, not his wife. The following day when he went down to his store he got his first intimation that Eliza might have behaved inappropriately over the preceding weeks. He discovered the letter of 14th August written to her by Parks. It was lying on his desk. It was the usual practice that mail for the Campbell family was delivered to the office, but it was then taken to the house. On this occasion James Campbell had apparently forgotten to send it up the previous day when it arrived and had instead placed it on Robert's desk. A letter addressed to Eliza being left on Robert's desk was unusual, and it would later be alleged that it was not genuine or that it was and had been read first by James who left it for Robert to find. Robert opened and read it. He mulled the matter over for an hour or two, and then spoke to James about it, telling him that he was shocked but not surprised. Robert instantly jumped to the conclusion that Eliza had behaved improperly with Parks, but the one thing he did not do was ask her for an explanation of the letter. He gave it to James and told him to go to Toronto and have it copied, which James did on Wednesday, 20 August. James was also to engage someone to go to Concord, if possible to secure any letters he found in Parks's residence written by Eliza and mail the original of the letter of 14 August to Eliza. The letter was duly copied and posted from Concord, but no letters from Eliza were found there. When the letter arrived for a second time in Whitby it was given by James Campbell to Norman Ham to be delivered to Eliza. This subterfuge with the letters was done to keep from Eliza the knowledge that Robert had seen the letter while also having it arrive and be given to Eliza unopened.

Whatever the reason, Robert's suspicions of his wife's improper conduct were firmly focused on Parks. In the few hours after he had found the letter Robert decided that Eliza had had some sort of dalliance with Parks, but did not ask her about it. Instead he was "quite friendly" with her while he set about gathering evidence to confirm his suspicions.[1]

In the evening after he had opened the letter Robert went home, taking with him a bunch of keys from his hardware store. On the following day, with Eliza absent from the house, he used one of the keys to open a secretaire in which she kept personal items and found other papers in her handwriting, three of which confirmed his suspicions. One was the undated letter, possibly a draft, discussed in the previous chapter. Another was a short passage written in pencil, which read like part of a draft of another letter, as it was written in the first person and apparently addressed to someone else. The style was excessively florid. It read:[2]

> Come when thou wilt I've a welcome for thee (song), – If you should ever come over there, would you come to see us? I should be most happy to see you, so understand that if you please your reception would be princely; do you understand? Do not keep me in such fearful suspense, but send me a line expressive of your feelings. I hope you will not forget our last fond meeting so reft with bliss. Oh, that it could be renewed; what rapture fills my mind to think no pleasure on earth so exquisite. Think me not flighty; it is only the outpouring of a deep passionate love which I bear for you, a love which so few comparatively feel for one another – Adieu cherished one.*

It is not difficult to conceive that reading such prose would not only confirm Robert's suspicions but send him into a near apoplectic rage. His wife had composed a letter to another man promising him a "princely" reception, and asking him to express his feelings towards her. Worse, Eliza referred to a previous meeting she had had as leaving her "reft with bliss," and talked of the "deep passionate love" she bore for him.

The third piece of writing found in the secretaire was a single page that also might have been a letter, this time one written to Eliza. Its content must have been equally alarming to Robert, because it seemed to refer to an encounter she and someone else had had in which the other person had been compelled to "yield," presumably to his physical desire for her. Yet it also seemed that the unknown male author was rebutting any

* Emphasis added. I discuss below why some passages are emphasized.

possibility of he and Eliza ever marrying, as if she had suggested it. But that, of course, did not make sense, unless he and Eliza had discussed their decamping together. The "letter," if that was what it was, read:[3]

> Here I am vacillating between two opinions, whether shall I stay here or stray afar off – Duty says stay. You were so enchantingly persuasive that I could not help but yield – I might say I was prompted by an irresistible impulse to come to you. My world is in a corner of my brain and when I have finished my day's work, I wander in dream through the enchanted city. I believe there are certain men who can be happy when they have learned where their ideal lies. We never can be perfectly happy, although a great deal of our happiness consists in being contented. We must be sorrowful sometimes in order to compare the difference of happiness or misery. I have no wish to marry, and it is not likely that I shall ever sacrifice my independence to any woman. So much the worse for you! You will never know what love is, for we love only virtuous women, my dear, and never loved except by them. Now, the virtuous women demand marriage, and it is their due. Every reasonable man in marrying should choose a woman who, he thinks, is worthy of his confidence, and "who will prove to him a companion; not a slave, but a helpmeet."*

As it turned out these pieces of paper in Eliza's handwriting were not what Robert thought they were. He thought they were letters from Parks or drafts of letters from Eliza. But they were not. Each piece of paper contained a melange of passages taken from published books or song lyrics, with other phrases, sentences, and paragraphs that were either Eliza's own jottings or were also from publications that I have not been able to identify. Three of the sentences from the last passage, underlined, were copied from the 1866 novel *Monsieur Sylvestre*, by George Sand, the pen name of Amantine Lucile Aurore Dupin de Francueil, the leading French novelist of the period. A North American edition of the novel, one of 70 written by Sand, was published in 1870 by Roberts Brothers of Boston.[4]

Other phrases from what were often later referred to as Eliza's "jottings" can be located in a variety of other published work. A phrase from the first quoted passage, "no pleasure on earth so exquisite," was from an early nineteenth-century religious tract.[5]

The opening sentence of the same passage, "Come when thou wilt I've a welcome for thee," was from a songbook.[6] The word "helpmeet"

* Emphasis added.

in the phrase in the second "jotting," "not a slave, but a helpmeet," originates from Genesis 2:18 and the creation of Eve: "And the Lord God said, it is not good that the man should be alone; I will make him an help meet for him."

Robert knew none of this as he read the papers he found in Eliza's secretaire. Had he known that Eliza was in the habit of copying things written by George Sand he would have probably been shocked. Sand was a very controversial figure. Briefly married to one François Casimir Dudevant, she separated from her husband after five years and two children and had open affairs with many men, including Frédéric Chopin, and at least one woman, the actress Marie Dorval. She championed the rights of women, castigated marriage, sometimes dressed in male attire, smoked openly in public at a time when that was not accepted, and advocated sexual freedom. She was also a political radical, member of the provisional government formed after the 1848 revolution.[7] But that could hardly have bothered Robert because he did not know the origins of any of the sentences and phrases in Eliza's writings. He could have discovered where those sentences and phrases, and likely others, had come from had he asked Eliza for an explanation, but he did not. The papers he found in the secretaire simply reinforced his conclusion reached the day before when he read the Parks letter. Eliza "was not a proper guardian for my children." It was an expression he used often in the subsequent court cases and before the Senate divorce committee. He did not talk of her as an unsuitable mother, or as an unfaithful wife, but as "not a proper guardian," as if the children were wholly his and Eliza was simply a person with the legal responsibility of caring for them. As she was not a suitable guardian, he decided there and then, in his own words, to "part with his wife."[8]

Ironically given that Eliza's correspondence with him had been what aroused Robert's suspicions in the first place, Godfrey Parks played no further part in this story. Whether he thought it best to get out of Ontario before he became embroiled in a matrimonial dispute, or whether he sought opportunity and adventure, he went to the Northwest Territories. He joined the newly formed North-West Mounted Police as a constable and was among the detachment of some 300 men who made the "Great March West" from Fort Dufferin (Emerson, Manitoba) to southern Alberta in the summer and fall of 1874 to assert Canadian authority in the area. The Great March West was a fiasco, planned and executed by men in equal parts ignorant of the country they were travelling through and incompetent. Many men suffered from the privations of the march, but only one died. Parks contracted typhoid and succumbed to it on 26 October 1874, a week or so after the force reached

Fort MacLeod in what is now Alberta. His fate was known in Whitby by the time Robert applied to Parliament for a divorce in 1876.[9]

Robert's next move was to show Eliza's writings to her family members – her brother James Byrne and her parents. The Byrne family urged him to talk to Eliza to get an explanation, but he did not. Robert told Rev. Byrne "that there was no necessity for me to see her, as a separation must take place." Robert's certainty was derived not just from the writings he had found but also from conversations he and James Campbell had with others about George Gordon's visits to the Campbell home, including Mary Jameson, Martha Newsom, and one Walter Coulthard, who ran a local parcel delivery business.[10] They told Robert that Gordon "had been going to his house at night and leaving at all hours of the morning." With the information provided by these local residents, but again without talking to Eliza other than to tell her that he considered Gordon "a man with whom he did not wish to be acquainted," Robert decided by the Thursday, having been back in Whitby two full days, to get the children out of the way before he confronted Eliza. He did not want them to witness "the trouble."[11]

He chose to take them to Southampton on Friday, 22 August, ostensibly to visit his father and his two sisters. He also told Eliza that he was going because he was not feeling well, and the lakeside air would do him good. He told James Campbell a different story He was going to take the children to Southampton and leave them there. Before going he also asked James Campbell to "watch the house" every night while he was away. He then changed his mind about leaving immediately because his youngest child, his daughter Edith, did not have enough clean clothes for a sojourn away from home, and he put his departure off until the Monday. Robert spent the weekend in the house, although he is unlikely to have conversed much, if at all, with Eliza. He certainly said nothing about his suspicions or plans to her. On the Saturday Eliza and a number of her friends, but not Robert, attended a church soirée. Robert spent the evening with James, watching to see who accompanied Eliza home, but nothing untoward transpired. Robert was nonetheless so "prostrated with feeling" that he went to James's house and lay down for a time. On Sunday he told John Anderson what he knew, which was that he suspected Eliza and Parks – he did not mention Gordon. Anderson asked Robert "if it was necessary to watch the house," and Robert said, "You may do so." Robert did not go to church with Eliza even though, unsuspecting of where his mind was, she asked him to. Gordon did go to church and spoke to Eliza there.[12]

Robert left on Monday morning, 25 August, kissing Eliza goodbye. She had no idea of it, but it was goodbye in more than one sense. Robert told the Senate divorce committee in 1876 that that was the day he separated from Eliza. Eliza accompanied her family part of the way as far as Toronto, and after she had left the train and returned to Whitby Robert asked each of the children separately who was in the habit of visiting their mother, "and they all said George Gordon."[13]

Robert's Suspicions Apparently Confirmed: The Night of 26–27 August 1873

James Campbell dutifully watched the house on the night of Monday, 25 August, concealed in the bushes, but saw and heard nothing. Eliza was at home, entertaining a lady friend. He was back again the next evening, Tuesday, 26 August, with his brother-in-law John Anderson, and this time he had a lot to report. He telegraphed Robert on Wednesday morning, giving no details but telling him to come home immediately. Robert got back on either Thursday, 28 August or Friday, 29 August (the accounts are inconsistent), and James had much to tell. Campbell and Anderson alleged that in the late evening of the 26 of August into the early morning the 27th, Eliza and Gordon had had sexual intercourse. Eliza and George Gordon consistently denied that. Campbell and Anderson repeated their stories in the three court cases litigated in 1873 and 1874 and before the Senate divorce committee in 1876. The newspaper reports drew a veil over the explicit and salacious details, but rather less reticent were the written judgment of Vice-Chancellor Samuel Hume Blake in the alimony case and the Senate divorce committee report. What follows therefore relies on Blake's judgment and the divorce committee proceedings more than the newspaper reports of the trials.

Some facts were never in dispute. Gordon walked Eliza home to the Campbell house at about 9 p.m., from the Byrne family home. Eliza had been visiting her mother and met Gordon there. Gordon had walked Eliza's sister Annie and her niece Hettie Ham back to the Byrne residence after they had been visiting at the Gordon farm. Gordon then offered to walk Eliza home. James Campbell had been at the house earlier in the evening, at about 7, to tend to his horse. He did not stay long but must have remained in the vicinity because he saw Gordon and Eliza come back together. He went to the parlour window, which he called the west window (see figure 3.1 on the next page), that was a few feet above the ground, as was the whole of the first floor. He half stood, half crouched there, his head at the level of the sill, and satisfied himself that Eliza and Gordon were in the parlour. He then walked the three blocks to Anderson's house to ask him to come along and "be prepared

GROUND AND CHAMBER FLOORS OF THE RESIDENCE OF ROBERT CAMPBELL, MERCHANT, WHITBY, ONTARIO

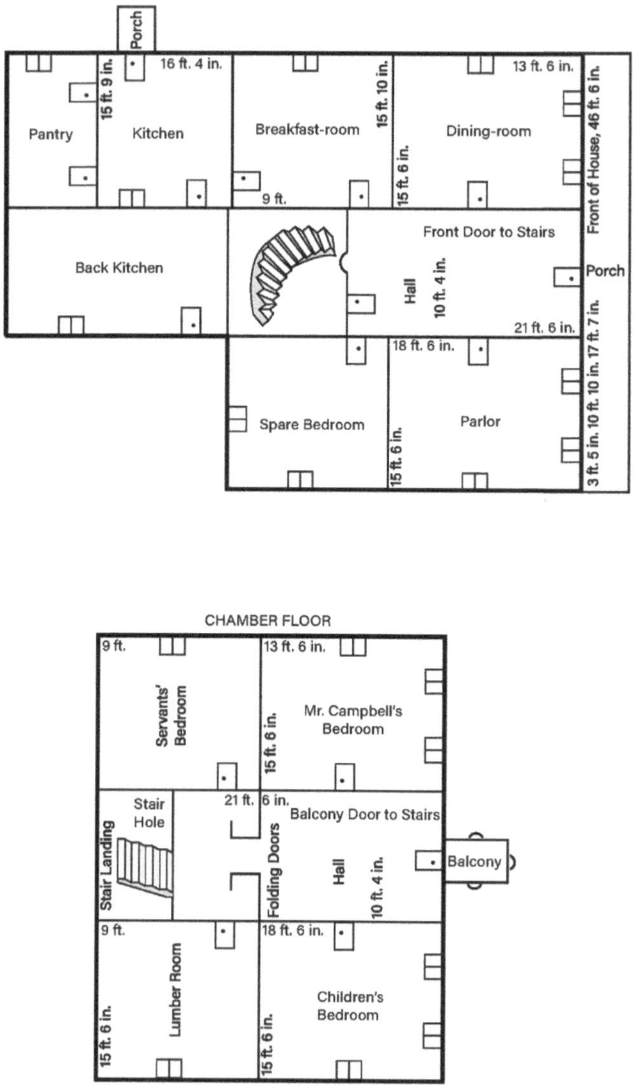

Figure 3.1. Floor plan of the Campbell family home

Source: Drawn by Alyssa Mintzberg, from Minutes of Evidence taken before the Senate Divorce Committee, Senate Journals 1876, Appendix A, 33

to act as a witness in case there was any criminal intercourse" between Eliza and Gordon.[14] He had earlier that day told Anderson that Gordon was the "suspect," which was the first Anderson had heard of Gordon as Eliza's alleged paramour.

The two returned to the house. As they entered the front gate they removed their shoes and hats, the former to avoid making noise the latter because they were white Panama hats which would be visible in the dark. They threw the hats over a wall. They both went to the west window, from which a light in the parlour could be seen, and listened for about half an hour, crouching there in stockinged feet. Campbell then moved to the veranda and stayed there listening at the front door and window, what they called the southwest window, for some hours, because, he later claimed, he could hear better from there. Both men were trying to see the couple inside and/or hear what was said by them. Campbell left the veranda twice during the evening, as described below. Anderson stayed at the west window the whole time. Sometime between 11 p.m. and 12 a.m., Jane Newsom, who had been in the back kitchen entertaining her young man, David Smith, for about an hour and a half, went up to bed carrying a lamp. Campbell came off the veranda long enough to satisfy himself that the lamp light was showing in her bedroom. He then returned to the veranda and resumed his listening vigil.

At this point we leave the region of uncontested and uncontroversial facts and enter that of strongly disputed accounts. I will provide first the account of Campbell and Anderson, and then the version told by Eliza and Gordon. Campbell and Anderson saw nothing of what was happening in the parlour, for the curtains remained closed and the blinds fixed throughout the evening. Nor did they suggest that Gordon and Eliza left the parlour and went upstairs. But they did say that they had heard a lot of what was said in the parlour. Until midnight they could hear only the sound of voices, but not the words or phrases used because Eliza and Gordon were "very guarded" in their conversation and noise from the street interfered. They were adamant about what they did not hear – no music playing and no singing in the parlour. Jane Newsom said the same thing when she later testified in the various lawsuits. After Newsom had gone to bed, Campbell claimed that he had been able to hear "every word distinctly" of the conversation, and other sounds.[15] At around midnight they heard words that made them think something was about to happen. Eliza said to Gordon "Robert might suspect," and Gordon asked her if she and Robert had had sex since he had returned. Eliza said "Only the first night" and Gordon responded "All right then, Robert cannot suspect."[16] This worried James Campbell enough that he decided to fetch a stout stick from the woodpile to break the window so that he could catch them in the act. He got the stick, but Anderson dissuaded him from using it. They resumed listening and heard an earful.

Chancellor Blake's reported judgment in the alimony case included a written statement by Anderson, which read: "Heard G. Gordon remark, you are getting stout. She answered, young men should not take notice of these things; he replied, I always do. Heard Mrs. C. tell G. Gordon that she was going to California, but would not go unless he would go with her. Heard G. Gordon ask, 'What is this?' 'That is my navel.'" The implication of this last question and answer must, of course, have been that Gordon was touching Eliza's at least partly unclothed body, and in his fumbling around with the underclothing of a five-months pregnant woman he had mistaken her navel for her vagina. The next part of Anderson's statement left no doubt about the purport of the alleged conversation:

> Heard Mrs. C. tell Gordon that he might put it in halfway. He asked why? She said, it hurt her. G. Gordon asked Mrs. C. to put her arms around him and let him stretch her out. Heard no objections, a short interval without conversation, and then laughter. Heard Mrs. C. crying. G. Gordon asked, what is the matter, what are you crying for? You hurt me, and then immediate laughter. On three different occasions heard Gordon say he would go away; and he got up to leave, but she called him back. Heard Mrs. C. ask him to kiss her.

The final part of Anderson's statement was somewhat contradictory to the above: "This was after ½ past one on Wednesday morning. Heard Gordon frequently after this time ask her to let him do it, but she said no, no; he asked why? She replied, I don't want to. Heard Gordon call Mrs. C. his dear love."[17]

A very similar account of what the listeners allegedly heard was given by James Campbell in his *viva voce* evidence at the alimony trial, and reproduced by Chancellor Blake:

> I heard him call her "his dear love"; they were then, I suppose, on the sofa.... I heard Gordon say that the floor was as good as a bed. I could hear rustling on the floor. I heard Gordon tell her that if he gave her all that it would hurt her. He said he would only put it in half way. In a minute or so, or less, she was crying or wheezing, and in a minute or two after she was laughing. I heard her asking him which way he preferred it. I am quite satisfied they had criminal connection once. There was other

> improper and indecent conversation between them. I heard Gordon asking her what that was, and she said it was her navel. I heard her, while on the sofa, I think, say would he come half way if she came the other half, and Gordon said, "Yes."[18]

Before the Senate divorce committee James Campbell and John Anderson also reported very similar exchanges, some of which were also testified to in the other court cases. They are not presented here as one continuous and coherent conversation, but as snippets, and they appeared in evidence in the same way, in a different order depending on the source. In the Senate, James Campbell testified to hearing these items of conversation:

> ELIZA: Which way do you like it best, George? Sideways, topways or bottomways? Oh, bottomways is the best, Gordon replied.... Why are you so crazy tonight, George?... And George replied that he was crazy for it.
>
> ELIZA: "What pleasure is it living here this way, having no pleasure in life only by taking a walk down town".... [A] man made a woman unhappy, and if she was single she would never marry. Her views were 'liberal,' and "she did not like to be tied to one man." She wanted to go to California; she would do that "if ever there was trouble or difficulty" between her and Robert. "Robert Campbell married me for my beauty, and I married him for his money."
>
> Eliza asked Gordon: "If he had a wife, and she entertained a young man as she had done that night, what would he think of her?" "They all do it," or "all married women do it" was the reply.
>
> GORDON: "[t]hose are nice breasts you've got Eliza."
>
> ELIZA: "Will you come half way if I go the other?" Gordon: "Yes, I will."
>
> ELIZA: Well, do you come then George." Gordon: "No, you proposed, do you come first and I will follow."
>
> GORDON: "The floor is as good as a bed."
>
> ELIZA: "If you give me all that it will hurt me." Gordon: "I will only put it in halfway."[19]

The listeners also reported hearing various noises, including the unlikely sound of the "smacking of lips." James Campbell said he heard "rustling on the floor and the springs of the sofa and the castors ... as it was being shoved along the floor. I heard both springs and castors all at the same time." The listeners had different evidence on one point. Anderson thought that intercourse had taken place twice, the first time while Campbell was away fetching the stick. "They had got through," he told Campbell on his return from the woodpile.[20] Campbell could only testify to them doing it once, after he had come back, on the floor by the sofa, which had been pushed back a little to make room.

As noted above, although essentially the same evidence was presented in all three court cases and before the Senate divorce committee, the newspapers that reported what was said in *viva voce* evidence were reticent to repeat what Campbell and Anderson said about sexually explicit matters. In its report of what Anderson said in the criminal conversation case in 1873, for example, discussed in chapter 5, the *Globe* merely said "[t]he witness here testified to hearing conversation which showed the guilt of the parties." When the same evidence was given at the defamation trial in 1874, dealt with in chapter 6, the *Globe* said that the conversations between Gordon and Eliza that the witnesses recounted were "unfit for publication." The *Whitby Gazette* was a little more forthcoming but still left the details to its readers' imagination. Its report of the crim. con. case had James Campbell saying that he heard Eliza ask Gordon to move close to her on the sofa, and that he "heard springs of sofa, and imagined they were having connection." The *Whitby Chronicle* was even less forthcoming, finding asterisks preferable to words in reporting James Campbell's evidence: "During the carrying on heard Mrs. Campbell ask which way (the vile language said to be used is of the most filthy and disgusting character, and unfit for publication ***)." The *Globe's* report of the defamation trial was equally unilluminating. Campbell "detail[ed] at length the criminal conduct alleged to have been witnessed by him, and also the disgusting language which he said he had heard."[21]

Anderson and Campbell both said in all fora that Gordon did not leave until about 3 a.m. In the crim. con. trial Campbell added that he was tired and cold by then, "standing with my bare head and stocking feet from 9 to 3, my limbs were getting sore and cold."[22] As a result he knelt down for a rest, and fortuitously in that position he was able to see through a corner of the blind that Gordon got up to go two or three times saying he had to go because he had a hard day's work on the farm ahead. But Eliza called him back each time, asking him to kiss her.

I turn to Eliza's and Gordon's very different accounts of the evening. The newspapers were not reticent about reporting this testimony because it told a very different, and innocent, story. Both denied that they had had sex, or done anything remotely improper, and claimed that the conversations the listeners reported were either fabricated or involved misunderstandings of the words used. Certainly no profane language was used by Eliza as Campbell and Anderson claimed. They described an evening of general conversation about Eliza's walk that day, seeing her niece, and Gordon's anticipated hard day of work on the farm the next day. When they were not talking she played the piano and sang for him, and read to him, and at different points they played drafts (checkers) and looked at images in a stereoscope.[23] The songs they claimed were sung and the books from which the readings were taken can all be located. This does not mean, of course, that there was singing and reading rather than sexual activity; all it means is that when Eliza and Gordon gave sworn evidence in court some time later they had plausible stories not just about the fact that there was singing and reading but also about which songs were sung and which books read from. The principal songs that they consistently claimed were sung were "The Pirates' Serenade," a love song about a young man going to sea, "Kathleen Aroon," a sentimental ballad, and "You'll Not Forget Kathleen," which was probably "I'll Take You Home Again Kathleen," which starts with the line "You'll Soon Forget Kathleen." All three songs were widely available in published American song book collections.[24] Gordon joined in occasionally on choruses, but it was agreed by both of them that his voice could not match Eliza's.

The two literary works that Eliza and Gordon claimed that Eliza read from were *The Language of Flowers* and Samuel Butler's *Hudibras*. The *Language of Flowers* was very probably a long poem of that name by Catharine Waterman Esling, first published in 1839 and continuously in print over the ensuing decades. Esling wrote poems and hymns, and *The Language of Flowers* was a well-known text in the floriography movement, which was popular in the Victorian period in both the United Kingdom and North America. Floriography was a form of communication in which flowers stood for certain sentiments or attributes. How they were arranged, and who they were sent to, were a form of coded message, and Eliza's interest in the movement comports with her sentimental character.[25] *Hudibras* was also a revealing choice, for it fits with the work of George Sand in its women's rights orientation. An epic satirical poem written by Samuel Butler and published in three parts, starting in 1663, it was set in the last couple of years of the Interregnum. Its principal character, Hudibras, was a Presbyterian, a knight, and a colonel in the parliamentary army who was regularly defeated, often by the skills and courage of women, including a rich widow whom Hudibras wanted to marry for her money. The poem ends with a detailed and humorous account by the widow of how and why women were superior to men. The editor of the leading current edition opines that, "like *Gulliver's Travels*, [it] is an unique imaginative work, capable of shocking, enlivening, provoking, and entertaining the reader in a peculiar and distinctive way, vigorously witty and powerful in its invective." The book was continuously in print in both Britain and North America throughout the nineteenth century.[26]

Eliza and Gordon placed the time of Gordon's departure much earlier than the listeners, although on the exact time they were not consistent. It was variously 1:15 a.m., between 1 and 2 a.m., and "after 1."[27] Both evinced surprise when they discovered it was so late; they had not kept track of the time. Jane Newsom had gone to sleep while Gordon was still there, at about 1, but said she had been woken up by a noise at 3 and heard someone call out that it was 3 and that Gordon was still there. Finally, Eliza also said on a number of occasions that she had heard someone in the yard and on the veranda, and assumed it was James Campbell because he was in the habit of "prowling" about the house. This assertion, if true, both made it much less likely that she would have had a dalliance with Gordon knowing her brother-in-law was right outside, and at the same time allowed her to depict James as "sneakish," prone to "prowling about," someone who had it in for her.[28]

While Eliza and Gordon simply denied that much of the alleged conversation had taken place, on some points they gave their own versions of things said, which portrayed the listeners' versions as misunderstandings, not outright lies. The references to eloping to California were to an old joke between them which stemmed from a conversation at a gathering in the Campbell house some three years previously at which Robert and other family friends were also present. Eliza had said that if she had a "fortune" she would like to travel, and mentioned California as a place to go because she had a brother there. Gordon said he would do the same thing, as he too had a brother in that state. So they had joked about going together. The conversation had also been about a story of elopement in a newspaper, so the two topics were conjoined. To similar effect the apparent reference to Eliza's navel was a result of them talking about Gordon's militia service and her asking him if he would rather be an ensign or a naval officer. Talk of "naval services" was prompted by the "Pirates" Serenade' song. The point was that the listeners had thought they heard "navel" when in fact they had heard "naval."

Finally, Eliza acknowledged saying that Gordon should move closer to her, but that was so that he could see the stereoscopic views better. Moreover, when she told him not to "put it in too far" she was talking about the stereoscope, which was broken at one end. She warned him not to put the slides in too far lest they came out of the instrument at the other end.

The stories told by Campbell and Anderson, on the one side, and Gordon on the other, about what transpired after Gordon left the Campbell home were as much at variance as the accounts of what happened inside the house. I will again provide the Campbell/Anderson version first. They finally left the yard of the Campbell house when it was clear that Gordon was about to depart, at 3 a.m., intending to go to the Campbell brothers' store, about 400 metres from the house (see street map in figure 3.2). When they got about 275 metres, to Thomas Lawler's grocery store, they heard the Campbell residence gate shut and then Gordon's steps behind them coming in their direction.[29] They waited for him to come up to them and James Campbell accosted Gordon, calling him, depending on the sources, either a "Blackhearted scoundrel" and a "villain," or a "black-hearted and double-dyed villain," or a "black-hearted and double-dyed scoundrel," or a "black scoundrel" and a "lying villain."[30] He then said to Gordon, again with variations from source to source, "You have had criminal intercourse with that woman this night," and that he would "put him through for seducing his brother's wife." Campbell and Anderson heard Gordon reply, "It was not my fault; I could not help it."[31]

Gordon's version was different in two key respects. First, as noted above, he said that he had left Eliza much earlier than 3 a.m., somewhere between 1:30 and 2 a.m. Second, and more importantly, he claimed that James Campbell had not accused him of having sex with Eliza but of attempting to do so. He said that he replied by denying the attempt, let alone its consummation, calling James Campbell "a d – n liar" and challenging him to a fight.[32]

The last act of the drama was James Campbell's return to his brother's house, accompanied by Anderson. He went to tell Eliza she had been caught in the act. By that time Eliza had gone upstairs, and Campbell shouted at her bedroom window and told her to come down as he had something to say to her. She ignored him, at which he fetched a ladder and climbed to the window. Eliza still ignored him, according to her because she could not understand what he was saying, and he shouted that "there was no use of Foxing" as he had heard everything, had "heard Gordon ask repeatedly to let him do it," had "heard all your criminal conversation" which would be reported to Robert.[33] When Eliza continued to ignore him Campbell went down and got a stick heavy enough to break the window, but Anderson dissuaded him, because it would alarm the neighbours. James Campbell claimed that he did not get home until 4 a.m., at which time he told his wife, Rebecca, about the goings on. He could not sleep properly, and was up at 6 a.m., writing an account of the evening, some of it at home and some in the office. This statement was later altered, and the change made would become important in the later court cases.

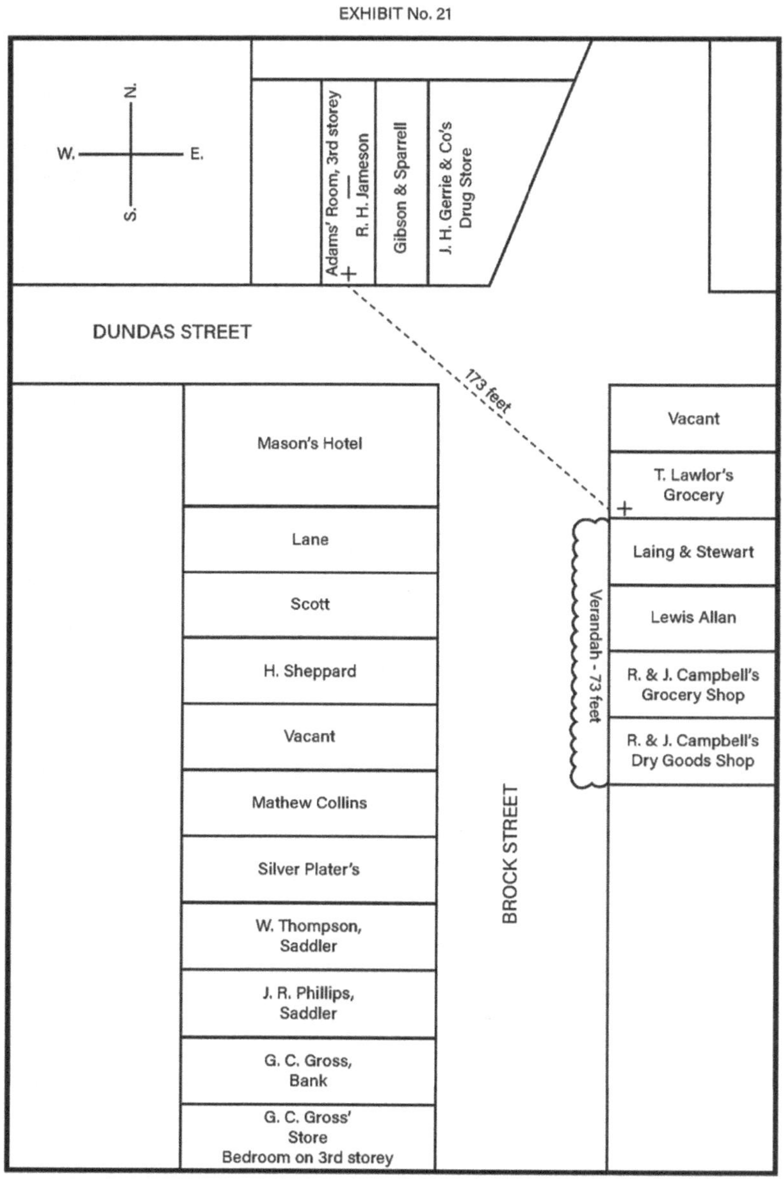

Figure 3.2. Downtown Whitby, showing the location of an altercation between Gordon, Anderson, and James Campbell

Source: Drawn by Alyssa Mintzberg, from Minutes of Evidence taken before the Senate Divorce Committee, Senate Journals 1876, Appendix A, 210.

Robert Campbell Carries Through on a Final Separation

Early in the morning of Wednesday, 27 August, James Campbell telegraphed Robert and told him to return immediately. He then went to see Martha Newsom at her sister's house in Taunton. His purpose was to gather more evidence about Gordon's visits to the house in July and the first half of August. Martha told him what she knew about Gordon's visits after Robert had gone to the UK, as recounted in chapter 2. She also said that on one occasion Eliza had talked to her about Gordon, saying he was "a fine looking man," and on another, presumably guessing that Newsom would find the lateness of his departures odd, that he was also someone who "never knew when to go away." While Martha Newsom had found all of this suspicious, she had not seen or heard anything that was "improper." She also said that she once heard Eliza go to bed "shortly before day light."[34]

For her part Eliza was up early, 6 a.m., the following morning, which surprised Jane Newsom, who had only once or twice seen her up so early, her usual time being 8. We know in general what happened over the rest of that week and the weekend, although the sources are unclear as to the precise timing of various meetings and other events. Robert arrived back in Whitby at about 8 p.m. on Thursday, 28 August or Friday, 29 August. James met him at the station, and they went first to James's house and then to the Campbell store. James told him what he believed had happened on the Tuesday night. Robert's response was not to confront Eliza but to tell her family. He asked her parents and brother James to meet him at the Campbell store. The family urged Robert to see his wife and get an explanation from her. Robert refused to do so. He insisted that he had made up his mind to separate and that "he considered his wife an impure woman," and had separated his children from her in consequence. This "last misconduct confirmed his former suspicions," which had been aroused by finding the Parks correspondence and Eliza's other writings.[35] Robert said it would "break him down" to see Eliza. He had been suspicions of her for nearly a year and had suspected George Gordon since the spring evening when he had come to his house at teatime.

Robert also had James Campbell and Anderson tell their stories to the family. In doing so, at one point James Campbell, whom the Byrnes thought seemed to be the spokesman, urged James Byrne not to "look upon this matter as a conspiracy against his sister." This was exactly what the family thought given their knowledge of the bad blood between James and Eliza and their unwillingness to believe the worst of Eliza. Indeed James Byrne went to see Eliza as soon as he had finished at the Campbells. He found her in the garden with her mother, sister, and niece, and told her what the Campbells were alleging. She denied the accusation, exclaiming "what an ungodly charge." The Byrne parents questioned both Eliza and Gordon "closely" on the Friday or Saturday, and were "satisfied as to [Eliza's] innocence." James Byrne rode down to see Gordon at the family farm on the Sunday, who responded to Byrne's news by saying: "May God Almighty strike me dead if I am guilty of that vile charge." Gordon then gave James an account of the evening which tallied with Eliza's. Gordon also tried to talk to the Campbell brothers the next day, but they snubbed him. Gordon's attempt must have been noticed, and must have involved harsh words, for a rumour went around Whitby that he and James had had a fight in which the latter's coat was torn.[36]

The Byrnes also enlisted the help of one of Robert's fellow Whitby businessmen George Conrad Gross, a hardware merchant. At James Byrne's request Gross went to see Robert to persuade him to see Eliza. Robert refused. If he did so "she would only hang around his neck and cry, and he would forgive her." As it was, "they had commenced and would go through with it." The meeting lasted about an hour and a half and ranged over a variety of issues. I will have much more to say about this meeting in a later chapter when I deal with the hearing before the Senate divorce committee. At the time Gross was in a quandary; as he testified at the later defamation trial, he did not think the Campbells would make the story up, but at the same time "he could hardly conceive it possible that a woman like her would be so indiscreet." He also "did not believe that a woman who was enceinte would allow young men to take liberties with her."*[37]

In all these conversations James Byrne thought James Campbell was influencing Robert too much. He was "prejudiced against my sister," and had "misconstrued her conduct." At one point he said to James Campbell: "You charge my sister with having had criminal connection with Mr. Gordon; did you see it?" Campbell replied that he had not, but from what he had heard, he believed that sexual intercourse had taken place. He also told the family that he had a sheet of paper containing notes of what he and John Anderson had heard, and he read the notes to them. Both Campbell and John Anderson had written down accounts of the evening in question: James immediately after he went home in the early morning of the 27th and Anderson a day or two later

---

* "Enceinte" is a French word meaning, among other things, in an advanced stage of pregnancy.

at James Campbell's request. Their written accounts would incite some controversy later, for both were altered. The conversations between the Byrne family and the Campbells concluded with Robert asking Rev. Byrne to take Eliza away to his own house. Robert must have sounded like he was returning defective goods to their supplier. Byrne refused to do so.

While Robert was talking to the family he refused to meet Eliza. There is some uncertainty about when Eliza knew of the accusation against her. If one believes James Campbell's and John Anderson's versions of the evening, she must have known that James Campbell was going to accuse her of having had sex with Gordon because he had shouted the accusation from the ladder in the small hours of the Wednesday morning. If, conversely, one believes Eliza's version, then it is also reasonable to believe her later claim that she did not know of the accusation until she was told of it by her brother James, who heard it from James Campbell.[38] In any event, as noted above, when she knew what James Campbell was saying she denied the story to her family. She also tried to see Robert, but he refused to talk to her. She saw James Campbell when she went to the Campbell store, and he told her, untruthfully, that Robert was not there. Subsequently the subterfuge was dropped in favour of an outright refusal to see her other than in James Campbell's house with James present. On her part she would not meet under those terms. She asked for a meeting with Robert alone, at the Campbell family home, or at her parents', or at the Campbell store. But she would not meet with both Campbells alone; presumably she felt, like her brother, that James held sway over Robert and her denials would not get a fair hearing. Husband and wife did not meet for eight months, until April 1874, when Chancery Court Judge Samuel Hume Blake cajoled them into a private meeting during the taking of the evidence in the alimony case, an event discussed in chapter 7.

Robert did not sleep in his own house after his return from Southampton, living with James instead. Indeed he did not occupy the family home again until after he threw Eliza out of it, an incident discussed in the next chapter. Nor did he speak to her or acknowledge her presence in the street. Likely for moral support Eliza persuaded her niece Hettie Ham to move in with her. That was the day that Jane Newsom left the Campbell house and went back home, having been ordered to do so by Robert.

Not able to see Robert, Eliza resorted to letters, written on 28 and 29 August, both asking him to see her and listen to her explanation. In the former she acknowledged that she had been "imprudent," but insisted "I have not been guilty of the charge James has imputed to me, that of having criminal conversation with that man, or any approach to it." She expressed surprise that he had not come to see her to discuss his suspicions. She must have suspected that he would not listen, for the letter reminded him of his duty if he chose to leave her: "If you do not meet me, remember you have to make an allowance for me and your unborn child."[39] Robert did not answer. In fact Eliza did not have much hope of a return to normalcy, if Jane Newsom was to be believed. She said later that Eliza had told her on 28 August that there was a "difficulty" with Robert and that "she did not think they would ever live together again." She nonetheless thought that "they could prove nothing against her."[40]

Eliza was unwavering in her public denials. The adultery allegation was the main item of local gossip, and she "demanded vehemently to be confronted with her accusers, and refused to leave the house, asserting that the stories ... were untrue, that she was an innocent and a faithful wife..., and that the whole case against her was a vile conspiracy got up by the brother."[41] Eliza stayed in the Campbell family home, with various members of her family living with her at different times, principally Hettie Ham. Robert consistently demanded that she leave the house; she had violated her marriage vow and had no right to remain there. Robert was legally right and wrong on this point. He owned the house and could decide who lived there. But he also owed his wife a duty of support, and in telling her to leave without otherwise providing for her he was ignoring that duty. He could do that legally if she had broken her marriage vow, but he had to prove that fact or Eliza had to admit it. He was in the process of proving it in a court of law, having initiated a suit for criminal conversation against Gordon, an action in which the sole factual issue was whether Gordon had had sex with Eliza. But that case, discussed in chapter 5, was not yet determined, and until then Eliza had a right to remain in the house. In the immediate aftermath of the separation Eliza could not be legally made to leave; if Robert wanted her to go he had to take the law into his own hands and eject her which, as we will see in the next chapter, he did in late September.

Robert also took steps to prevent Eliza from being given goods on credit in several of the town's stores. He and James did the rounds of their fellow merchants telling them he would not be responsible for any debts she incurred with them. As with his demands that Eliza leave the house, he was right and wrong in law in this. He did not have a duty to support an unfaithful wife, but unfaithfulness had not yet been proved in a court of law. On this issue he had the practical upper hand. If storekeepers refused to give her credit there was nothing Eliza could do other than rely on the generosity of her friends and family while using the law to try to force Robert to support her. She did both. James Byrne and her parents helped her out, and according to Conrad Gross there was enough sympathy in the town to set up a fund by subscription to assist her. Indeed Gross also said rather later, before the Senate, that "the whole town of Whitby" did not believe that "a respectable woman like her could have acted in such a manner."[42]

She also launched two related lawsuits in the fall of 1873. One was for defamation against James Campbell for statements he had made to shopkeepers about her conduct, discussed in chapter 6, the other was against Robert for alimony, discussed in chapter 7.

In the short-term Robert and Eliza worked with their lawyers to prepare for the criminal conversation case, which was heard in mid-October. Aware of what the evidence against her would be, and presumably on the advice of her lawyer, Eliza did what she could to prepare a defence. She took advantage of her continued occupancy of the house by having her female relatives – her mother Henrietta, sister Bethiah Ham, and sister-in-law Mary Byrne – conduct a "trial" of what could be heard inside the house by anybody outside in the yard. Eliza and her mother sat and conversed in the parlour while Bethiah Ham and Mary Byrne were variously outside and inside the house but outside the parlour. That evidence was presented at the criminal conversation case when it was heard in mid-October. Eliza's time in the marital family home ended on 24 September, when Robert went from demanding that Eliza leave to direct action, forcibly ejecting her from the house.

4
Eliza Campbell's Ejection from the Family Home, September 1873

Robert made good on his threats to remove Eliza on Wednesday, 24 September.[1] He later said that he had previously asked his lawyer, Robert Harrison, if he could do so, and Harrison had said that he had "a perfect right" to do it.[2] This conversation probably took place on Monday, the 22nd, when Harrison was in Whitby to argue cases on circuit and had a "long consultation" with Robert about his forthcoming suit against George Gordon.[3] In the morning Dr. John Robert Gunn, Whitby's longest serving medical practitioner and the Campbell family doctor, went to see Eliza, asked to do so by Robert who wanted to assure himself that his wife, some five months pregnant, was fit to be moved.[4] He did not tell the doctor what he intended to do. Gunn examined her "and found her complaining of a cold and cough, and a pain in her back," but in good spirits. He signed a certificate attesting to her health, and recommended a walk in the grounds. Gunn was visited by Robert between 7 and 8 that evening, who read the certificate and said he intended to remove Eliza that night. Gunn cautioned him that "nothing should be done to agitate Mrs. Campbell, ... that he had better let her alone quietly – that agitation in her condition must prove serious to her health."[5] Robert assured him that he did not intend to use any violence. This was a lie, as his subsequent actions made clear.

Robert immediately went to the house, taking with him two constables, Robert Danford and Donald Campbell. In 1873 Whitby had a small police force of just four men: the chief constable and three constables, one for each of the town's three wards. The force was under the command of the newly appointed Chief Constable Jacob Bryan, a full-time salaried appointee.[6] Danford and Donald Campbell and the other constable were part-time officers chosen to serve annually by the town's justices of the peace (JPs) and remunerated by the fees they could charge for various services.[7] Constables' duties were to keep the peace and carry out orders given to them by the local JPs or the chief constable. They had no authority to intervene in a private domestic dispute, and they knew it. There was no breach of the peace and Robert, who had recruited them for the occasion, was the only person likely to cause one. Robert was not a JP, just a wealthy prominent citizen who had decided to take the law into his own hands. The constables had presumably been persuaded by Robert to help him because Robert was one of the town's leading citizens.

Robert's party was met at the door at about 7:45 p.m. by Henrietta Byrne and Bethiah Ham. He told them he was there to put Eliza out and do the same to anybody else living there. Henrietta told him it would be a difficult task. Robert responded by telling the constables either to "do their duty" or "do their work." Robert, Danford, constable Campbell, Henrietta Byrne, and Bethiah Ham went upstairs to the main bedroom where Eliza was lying fully clothed on the bed. Constable Campbell hung back and told Henrietta "that he came to help Mrs. Campbell and not Mr. Campbell." Somebody went to fetch James Byrne, who got there a short time afterwards. In the main bedroom he saw Eliza lying on the bed and Robert standing next to her. Robert told Eliza she had to leave, and she responded by asking "what have I done, am I not your wife?" Robert's answer was that she was no longer his wife because of her adultery. Eliza retorted that Robert was a liar and that he should bring her accusers to her. A struggle ensued in which Robert tried to raise her up from the bed and she physically resisted, squirming away from his grasp and flailing with her hands. Robert asked the constables to move her, but they refused to do so, presumably aware of their lack of legal authority. Danford and Campbell did not have to wait more than a minute or two before the situation became worse for them, and for Eliza. Robert literally took matters into his own hands, seizing Eliza and lifting her up from the bed. She resisted and hit him in the chest, at which he let her fall back on the bed. She said she was his "lawful wife and would not go out," and "it is my house as well as yours." Eliza seemed to her mother to be very weak, so she stepped forward and held her hand, and Robert struggled with her to pry her grip loose. At one point he took off his jacket as if preparing for an even greater struggle, but then immediately put it on again, as if he had thought better of it. After a short while he decided that it would be better for him to continue unobserved by members of the Byrne family; he told them all to leave the bedroom. When James did not immediately do so Robert seized him by the coat collar and told him to leave the house altogether. Byrne said, "I would defend my sister," and threatened to hit Robert but then thought better of it and left as asked.[8]

It took Robert at least another half hour before he was able to get Eliza off the bed. He repeatedly raised her up only to have her fall back when she resisted. He eventually got her off the bed by pulling her legs to the side and hauling on them so that they made contact with the floor. He then raised her torso so that she was in a sitting position, and it took a number of attempts to get an increasingly tired Eliza to stand up. Neither constable helped. At some point during his efforts to move Eliza, Robert asked the constables to leave the bedroom and tell Bethiah Ham and Henrietta Byrne that there was no use in Eliza resisting. They did so, probably because they did not want to be involved in any violent coercion and thought the best way to avoid that was to have her relatives persuade Eliza to go quietly.

The constables re-entered the bedroom after some 5–10 minutes absence. Eliza was again lying on the bed and now complained of feeling sick. Robert continued to insist that she get up and go, saying he would give her 15 minutes, and then 5 minutes more. Then he did get her partly off the bed by moving her legs in the manner noted above, and asked Danford to take one arm and help him get Eliza on her feet. Danford could not take her arm because she was wrapped in a shawl, but he supported her by putting his hand under her elbow, and with Robert holding her other arm they got her standing and then moving towards the head of the stairs. Constable Campbell, who stood and watched this, later said that Eliza "walked and was pushed at the same time. There was one at each side of her, and she resisting." Eliza complained of a pain in her side as she was taken downstairs, and when she got to the bottom of the stairs she lay down on the sofa in the hallway. Bethiah Ham came forward and put some pillows under her. Eliza stayed on the sofa for more than 20 minutes. At some point she must have had a conversation with one of the constables about her personal and household effects; the constable assured her he would have them sent on after she had left.[9]

All this time James Byrne was waiting outside, at the bottom of the steps from the veranda. He was there about an hour, until somebody opened the front door. When they did so Byrne saw Eliza being supported and half-dragged along the hall to the front door by Robert and Danford. According to Byrne she was "utterly powerless." At the front door the two men lifted her over the doorstep and onto the veranda. They continued to move her forward to the edge of the veranda, "not in a condition to resist at all," at which point James Byrne rushed forward and took her in his arms. Robert shouted out that she should be put in a buggy that he had arranged to be there, but Byrne was determined to take his increasingly distressed sister home himself. With the aid of his wife Mary he got Eliza to his house, at about 9:45 p.m. – a full two hours after Robert had first entered the house. He sent for Dr. William Eastwood, who gave Eliza something to take and told the household to let her rest. Perhaps concerned that some injury had been done, Robert sent Danford to Dr. Gunn to ask him to go and see Eliza. Gunn said he would go only if requested to do so by James Byrne.[10]

Eliza had to recuperate in bed for a week. She was "incapable of being removed, except with serious consequences to her health."[11] When Eliza was able to leave her sick bed and go out there was only one place she wanted to go; to a JP to swear an information (a formal complaint) against Robert for assaulting her. Robert did not immediately move back into the house, continuing to reside in James's house until after the crim. con. trial, discussed in the next chapter, in mid-October. But he did immediately let Jane Newsom go, dismissing her via a note delivered by Danford telling her to "go away." She was replaced by her sister Martha when Robert did move back. It is not known when Martha left, but she was not the family servant in 1876 when Robert's application for divorce was heard by the Senate. She had gone to live with another Whitby family called Salkeld.[12]

Eliza Campbell Prosecutes Robert Campbell for Assault

Just less than a week after he had removed his wife from his house, on Tuesday, 30 September, Robert appeared before a bench of three of the Whitby JPs to answer a charge of assault contained in the information sworn by Eliza the previous day before one of them, John Hamer Greenwood, a local lawyer and businessman, albeit a not very successful one. He had been the mayor of Whitby, serving in that post from 1872 to 1875.[13] The other JPs on the bench were Chester Draper, a wealthy entrepreneur and, in the 1860s and 1870s, the owner of Whitby Harbour, and J.S.M. Willcox, a local farmer.[14] The information sworn by Eliza on 29 September stated that Robert "did unlawfully assault, beat, and ill-treat, and did other wrongs to [her]…, occasioning her actual bodily harm by forcibly removing [her] … from her bed, and dragging her down stairs, and putting her out of doors, whereby she was put in great terror, and made sick."[15]

The proceedings took place in the town hall on Tuesday, 30 September and Wednesday, 1 October. They were a preliminary inquiry conducted under the provisions of an 1869 federal statute, the purpose of which was to decide whether there was a case to answer at the next Quarter Sessions, the county criminal court for cases not serious enough to be tried before one of the Toronto-based superior court judges who visited the county annually on the assize circuit.[16] It was at the discretion of the JP or JPs presiding at the inquiry whether it be held in public or not, and obviously these JPs did so. Among those present was John T. Farewell, the county attorney, who "watched the proceedings on behalf of the Crown." He would likely prosecute the case if it was sent on to Quarter Sessions, although some prosecutions at Quarter Sessions were still privately conducted, as most had been before the establishment of the county attorney system in 1857.[17]

Because the trouble in the Campbell marriage had been much talked about, and because it involved one of Whitby's leading families, a sizable crowd turned out. It included Eliza's relatives, but Eliza was not there, being too ill to attend as the result, said the *Whitby Chronicle*, of her treatment at the hands of her husband. The prosecutor and the accused were entitled to be represented by counsel at the preliminary inquiry, and both availed themselves of this right. Eliza was represented by James Keith Gordon, George Gordon's older brother and a Whitby lawyer. Another Whitby lawyer, George Young Smith, a former Whitby school teacher who had then trained for the bar, represented Robert Campbell.[18] Robert, as well as Smith, cross-examined the witnesses. That Robert chose to do so is revealing. He was very confident in the rectitude of his position regarding Eliza, and equally confident in his ability to cross-examine in court even though he had no experience in doing so. It was a misplaced confidence. He asked a number of questions which allowed the witnesses to make telling points.

There were no legal arguments about whether Robert had the right to eject Eliza. It is possible that the JPs did not want to get into that. But it is more likely that everybody knew that he did have the right to resume possession of the house by telling Eliza to leave, if she had broken her marriage vows.[19] The evidence presented and the questions to witnesses were largely about whether he had used more force than necessary in getting her out, not about whether she had a right to stay in the circumstances. Had James Gordon argued that Eliza had the right to stay, and had the JPs thought she did, the case would have been an easy one. In those circumstances any amount of physical force would have been an assault. A subsidiary issue raised at the inquiry was whether the constables should have been there to assist.

James Byrne was the first witness for the prosecution and recounted the events of the evening in question.[20] The cross-examination by Smith elicited the fact that in the bedroom Byrne had told Eliza that she had a right to stay in the house and should not leave unless and until she was removed by force. Smith then asked whether in James's opinion Robert had used more force than was necessary, to which he replied, "He did. He violently wrenched her up from the bed; her arm was sore the next day. I did not hear Mr. Campbell ask her to get up and go before he caught hold of her." Smith moved to whether Byrne thought Eliza would have resisted had he not told her to do so. "Decidedly she would, her mind was made up not to leave the house until she was put out by force." Robert then took over the questioning, asking Byrne if he thought that "unnecessary violence" had been used. This gave Byrne the chance to say, "You suddenly jerked her from the bed." Robert then asked what "better method" he could have adopted, to which Byrne was able to reply, "You had no right to put her out at all." Smith weighed in again by asking Byrne why he thought more violence than necessary had been used, to which Byrne said, "By not lifting her more gently."

The next prosecution witness was Dr. Gunn, who in direct examination stressed that he had told Robert that if anything was done to agitate Eliza her health would likely suffer. He was cross-examined by Smith, who elicited the fact that Robert had said in the interview at Gunn's house "that he did not intend to use any violence." Smith must also have asked a question about whether Eliza was in a fit condition to leave the house, and that backfired, because Gunn replied: "If it was a voluntary act of her own she might have been removed without danger. It would all depend upon the state of her nervous system how she might have been affected by the compulsory removal." Gunn was re-examined by James Gordon who got him to drive home the point that Eliza was not fit to be moved other than voluntarily: "Even asking Mrs. Campbell to leave the house in a peremptory manner might be dangerous. I so considered it. Mrs. Campbell is now pretty far advanced in pregnancy, and of course in that state a female cannot bear as much excitement as under other circumstances."

The next witness was constable Donald Campbell. Under direct examination he said he had gone to the house at Robert's request, and that Robert had told him there was "no danger of anything" because Eliza would leave when asked. The constable asked Robert if he wanted him to "put her out," and Robert had said no, he was asking the constable to accompany him "to see that no violence was used." He then recounted his version of what happened in the bedroom, making it clear that it was Robert, and not he or Danford, who had manhandled Eliza. He said he had advised the Byrne family women not to resist. Although Campbell had fingered Robert as the one who had done the literal "heavy lifting," Gordon must still have asked him what authority he had to be there at all. "I was acting under no legal authority. I was acting under no warrant." Gordon must also have asked about the degree of force used, and Campbell defended Robert: "I do not think he could have taken her out of the house with any less violence than was used. I did not see him strike her in any way. I saw no weapon in his hand. No more violence was used than was necessary to put a party out against their will."

By this time it was close to 7 p.m., and constable Campbell was the last witness for the day. There is no indication in the newspaper report that he was cross-examined by Smith, but Draper took the opportunity to press him about the reason for his presence. Draper clearly had misgivings about the legality of this aspect of the evening's events, as captured in this exchange, a rare occasion on which the newspaper report reproduced questions and answers:

DRAPER: Why were you and Danford selected for this duty?
CAMPBELL: I don't know any more than I have told you.
DRAPER: In what capacity were you and Danford there?
CAMPBELL: Being told by Mr. Campbell.
DRAPER: Did you consider you were present as a constable?
CAMPBELL: I appeared because, (here witness became somewhat confused.)
DRAPER: Did you appear as a constable?
CAMPBELL: I did in case any riot took place. I was determined to see no violence done.
DRAPER: Do you consider you have a right to go on such business as a constable, because Mr. Campbell or any one else tells you to do so?
CAMPBELL: I went there as a constable to see the peace kept.

This was an effective line of questioning. It established that Robert had asked or told the constables to accompany him, and that Campbell at least had been, and presumably still was, unsure about the legality of his presence. Campbell was right to say that it was his duty to prevent violence, but with the exception of James Byrne's threat to prevent Robert from continuing his attempts to remove Eliza, any violence that occurred, or indeed was likely to occur, was precipitated by Robert.

After this exchange the court adjourned until the next day, Wednesday, 1 October, at 3.30 p.m. Henrietta Byrne, Bethiah Ham, James Byrne's wife Mary, Robert Danford, and Hugh Ross, one of the Campbell brothers' employees who had driven the carriage that Robert had arranged to take Eliza away that night, all testified.[21] Henrietta Byrne was the first witness, and recounted essentially the same story of struggle and resistance that James had told the day before. But she told it more fully and dramatically. She had demanded to know by what authority Robert was making Eliza go, and Robert's answer was Dr. Gunn's certificate. But of course this was not really an answer to her question. Dr. Gunn had only said that she could be moved; by no stretch of the imagination could it be construed as permission to move her against her will. Henrietta told Robert he should be ashamed of himself, to which Robert replied that it was Eliza who should be ashamed. Henrietta described Eliza as "much exhausted" and "scarcely able to stand" by the time Robert had pulled her about trying to get her up and out.

Smith's cross-examination elicited from Henrietta the fact that she had not been in the bedroom during the whole time that the struggle was going on. But she also used his questions to say that she could hear what went on – she heard Robert talk in a "menacing manner" and Eliza say that she was kicking at him when he was pulling her off the bed. She also declared that Robert had used more force than was necessary, and when Smith presumably asked or stated that Robert could have been more violent, she rather neatly stated, "Of course he might have used greater violence than he did; he might have kicked her dead." She also used another question, presumably about Robert's demeanour, to say that he was in "a towering passion," had at one point "pulled off his coat to fight his wife" but then checked himself. As he had the day before, Robert also took a hand at cross-examination, but by asking Henrietta about her claim that he had been violent gave her the chance to provide details of his actions and Eliza's consequent condition: "You got your arm around her waist. and held her hard by the wrist; she felt you grasping her; ... Part of the time she was lying on the sofa she was not sensible of what was taking place; she was very much distressed in body and mind."

The last part of Henrietta's time on the witness stand was taken up with Robert and all three JPs interrogating her, principally as to whether once she was downstairs Eliza had walked out of the house or been pushed out. This was not an issue taken up at any length with James Byrne the day before because he had been outside the house, whereas Henrietta was in the hallway. Henrietta initially insisted that Eliza had been pushed out, but appeared to retreat somewhat when Wilcox said that "[t]o take hold of a person and lead her is not pushing." Robert asked her a second time if Eliza walked or was pushed, and Henrietta must have hesitated to answer because Greenwood interjected to demand that she answer. Her answer was evasive, addressed to Robert: "I think you used violence all the way through." Draper took up the questioning about the degree of force used, to which Eliza's mother responded: "Mrs. Campbell manifested no willingness on her part, at any stage, to go out of the house; she said, on the contrary, while on the sofa, that she would never go out of the home; she resisted all through, as far as she was able." Draper then probably asked her a question previously asked

– was unnecessary force employed? Henrietta's answer was, "I cannot say whether he used more force than was necessary." This last sentence prompted further questions, although the newspaper did not say who asked them. Henrietta was likely flustered by this point, because she gave a confusing response. She repeated her statement that she could not say whether Robert used more force than necessary and added that Robert had walked Eliza "gently" to the door. She then reverted to depicting Robert as having acted basely: "My opinion was that it was a very cruel, unkind act, and (unjusti)fiable." But she ended by reversing field again: "I do not know how Mrs. Campbell got from the bedroom to the head of the stairs. She was led out of the hall door. I will not say she was pushed."

The next witness was Bethiah Ham, who told essentially the same story as her mother. She added that she thought Danford was very reluctant to help when called on by Robert. She also claimed to have heard Eliza cry out "don't let me fall" when Robert and Danford got her to the top of the stairs. On the crucial question of how Eliza was propelled from the downstairs sofa to the door she said that Eliza was in agony, was lifted forcibly from the sofa by Robert, was "almost powerless," and was "dragged" to the front door, "impelled forward, pushed ... along." Smith's cross-examination elicited the fact that both she and James Byrne had told Eliza not to leave the house, and that she had replied that such advice was unnecessary because her mind was made up. Smith questioned her about the extent of the violence used, allowing her to say that Robert had "jerked" Eliza to get her off the bed. Smith asked her if Robert was a "very strong man," and she flashed back with "I don't know – I think that a very unnecessary question to ask." She continued: "I will persist in saying that he used more strength than was necessary. He used all his strength. He pulled her violently.... There was unnecessary violence used; he was in a great passion – he looked like a demon. I was terrified; we were all terrified."

Robert cross-examined her, asking if he and Danford had lifted Eliza from the bed, and Bethiah said it was him alone. He had done so violently, had put Eliza on the floor and only then called Danford. Robert asked if Bethiah thought he had done so "in a violent manner," and she replied yes. Robert tried another tack, asking her if she was excited at the time, inferring that she was a typically hysterical woman who had over-reacted. She had a good answer – "I was not so excited but that I could see what was taking place." Robert then went back to the "pushing" question: Did he push Eliza? She had been pushed from the bedroom to the top of the stairs; Robert had "pushed her along." He and Danford were on each side of her, but it was Robert who had his arm on her back. Robert tried again: Had he "urged" Eliza on, or had she not been "allowed her own time?" He had "urged" her several times.

James Byrne's wife, Mary, was then called but only briefly, because her testimony, according to the *Whitby Chronicle*, was the same as her female relatives. The final witness called by the prosecution was Robert Danford. He recounted Robert calling at his residence and saying that he wanted to get Eliza out and believed that she would go if he took the constables with him. Campbell, who Robert had recruited first, was waiting outside. After Danford told how he had gone upstairs with Robert and his colleague, James Gordon got to the nub of the matter: Why had Danford intervened in the bedroom? He said that Robert tried to lift Eliza up, "and just then a breach of the peace was about being committed, and I had to interfere." The person about to breach the peace was James Byrne, who had a stick and was about to strike Robert with it, having said something "to that effect" when Robert approached the bed. Danford's contribution to preventing a breach of the peace was to take the stick away from Byrne.

Smith's cross-examination focused on minimizing the degree of violence used. Danford "positively declared" in an answer to one of his questions that Robert "used no unnecessary force." He also said that it was "a very disagreeable duty," but given that Eliza had resisted it could not have been done with less force. He then somewhat contradicted himself by saying that after the Byrne family had left the bedroom his "impression" was that there was no further resistance from Eliza, and that everybody had "made up their minds to leave as quietly as possible." Smith asked him if there was an "arrangement" to that effect, and Danford said again that it was his "impression" that there had been. Draper interjected to say that Danford's impression about an arrangement was not evidence, and asked Danford to confirm that Eliza had not resisted after he entered the bedroom for the last time. He swore positively that that was the case. On re-examination James Gordon continued to press him on the point, but Danford stuck to his story. After he had re-entered the bedroom Eliza "went of her own accord." There was "no force used"; "she was not pushed or shoved"; and "it appeared to me that she had made up her mind to be put out."

Before he left the witness stand Danford was questioned by Draper about the presence of the constables that evening, just as constable Campbell had been. Why had Robert chosen him, and "in what capacity" had he been there? The JP was still obviously concerned about the legality of the constables' presence. He received a contradictory and somewhat evasive answer: "I considered that I was in Mr. Campbell's employ, and that I attended there in that capacity, and also as a peace officer." He was there "at Mr. Campbell's service" and "expected to be paid," yet at the same time he "considered [himself] a peace officer," although Robert "did not say anything to me in reference to my being a constable." He only "considered himself" to be a peace officer. His answer must have caused the bench some concern.[22]

Danford was the final witness for the prosecution. Smith called only one witness for the defence, Hugh Ross, a clerk employed by the Campbell firm. He had driven a horse and buggy to the Campbell house and waited there to take Eliza to wherever she chose to go. He testified that he saw Eliza "led to the door" by Robert and that no violence was used. As she was at the door of his buggy she was intercepted by James Byrne who said she should go with him to his house. She walked away with her brother under her own steam. His evidence may have been true, although he was a little distance away, but it was certainly also consistent with what a loyal employee would say.

With that the proceedings were over. It was 8 p.m. The magistrates deliberated for about half an hour and then announced that they would give their decision three days later, on Saturday. In fact it took a week for them to decide, and on Tuesday, 7 October, it was announced that they had ruled 2–1, Wilcox dissenting, that the case, one of "premeditated assault," should be heard at the next Quarter Sessions. Robert had to provide bail of $200 guaranteeing his appearance, plus two sureties to put up $100 each. Obviously Draper and Greenwood thought that a *prima facie* case had been made out that Robert had been unnecessarily forceful in how he ejected Eliza, and it is also reasonable to think that were troubled by the role played by the constables. The *Whitby Gazette* thought that was the case.[23] They had been summoned to help Robert in a private dispute, and not wanting to offend a leading citizen, had gone along with it. There is no record of any further proceedings, and the case must have been dropped. It is not mentioned in the *Whitby Chronicle's* reports of the December sitting of the Quarter Sessions and the County Court for Ontario County.[24] As importantly, the case was nowhere mentioned in the long and detailed Senate divorce committee investigation of 1876. The committee took evidence about every aspect of the Campbell scandal, including Eliza's ejection from the house. It is inconceivable that either a conviction or an acquittal would not have been mentioned by one side or the other.

Opinion in Whitby

Not surprisingly the Campbell marriage scandal was the talk of the town. The *Whitby Gazette*'s editor, James Campbell, no relation to the

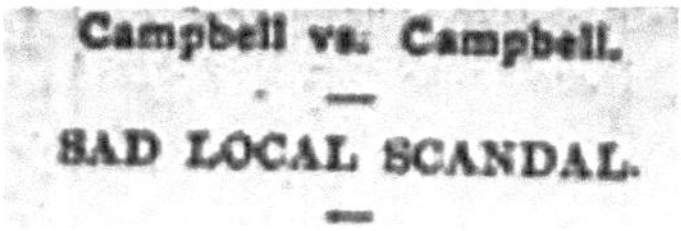
Campbell vs. Campbell.

SAD LOCAL SCANDAL.

Figure 4.1. "A Sad Local Scandal"
Source: Whitby Chronicle, 2 October 1873

Campbell brothers, said that "the matter had been largely talked of in Whitby," but he did not say that at the time or in his newspaper, but in giving evidence in the defamation case in 1874.[25] The *Whitby Chronicle* was self-admittedly deliberately reticent about commenting on the scandal, but changed its policy of not saying anything in early October when it reported the proceedings before the JPs under the heading "Campbell v Campbell. SAD LOCAL SCANDAL." Because the assault case had brought the whole affair into the public eye, there was no longer any "impropriety" in writing about it. Indeed the paper regretted that its silence had been "misconstrued" and that it had allowed "many mis-statements and exaggerations" to circulate.[26]

It then gave a brief résumé of the affair, starting with Robert's arrival from the United Kingdom, at which time stories circulated of Eliza's infidelity. The paper was careful to say that "whether true or not remains to be ascertained." It noted that the principal accuser was James Campbell, and that Eliza "demanded vehemently to be confronted with her accusers, and refused to leave the house, asserting that the stories told him [Robert] were untrue, that she was innocent and a faithful wife to him, and that the whole case against her was a vile conspiracy got up by the brother." The newspaper probably knew this because James Byrne had circulated some kind of statement on her behalf before the ejection from the family home.[27] On the surface the *Chronicle* avoided taking sides, characterizing the matter simply as "an unhappy and sad one." But there were subtle differences in the ways it talked about the Campbells, which suggested that it believed Eliza. She was "a refined, well-educated lady, very much admired for her beauty and accomplishments," who "has resided from her earliest childhood in the town, and never before has the breath of scandal whispered aught against her good name." Robert was characterized in a subtly different way, as "a highly respectable businessman," a characterization that said little or nothing about his moral character. His actions in "bringing such a charge against his wife and breaking up his household" must emanate from his "believ[ing] himself to be grievously wronged." Reading between the lines, Robert was sincere but misguided in his beliefs. The *Chronicle* then returned to Eliza, noting that people in the town had taken sides and sympathized with one or the other, but "the greatest sympathy, as is usual on such occasions,

[was] being given to the woman." This, the article implied, was right, because her "fair fame and reputation, whatever the result of the pending trials, must suffer most."

The article continued with a further plea for Eliza and for forbearance while more facts were established. Her relatives "are naturally plunged into the deepest distress" while "she herself, in her delicate condition, is reported as suffering torments of body and mind inconceivable." And the townsfolk should "turn a deaf ear to all the lying gossip" and "act the part of charitable, kindly, good neighbourhood – reflecting how they would feel were such a calamity to befall themselves." "In the absence of the positive proof," people should "refrain from pronouncing opinions" or accepting "injurious hearsay reports" as facts.

Among those who we know took Eliza's side were an unnamed group of people from nearby Oshawa who were rumoured to be planning to "make a demonstration" in Whitby against the Campbell brothers. From the *Whitby Chronicle*'s response to the rumour of the "demonstration," it was probably some kind of charivari, a folk tradition found in many parts of Europe and North America in various guises. Often a jocular mock serenading of newly-weds, featuring "rough" or "discordant" music, which could be nothing more "musical" than the banging of pots and pans, it was also used to show disapproval of, or even to threaten, people of whom the community disapproved but against whom no legal action could be taken. In its more extreme and violent manifestations it was also known in North America as "whitecapping," and could involve tarring and feathering to drive people from the locality. It is highly unlikely that anything like this was intended by the Oshawa residents. They simply wanted to show their disapproval of the Campbells because they had, in the eyes of those planning such an event, offended against a moral code even if they had not broken any law.[28] Echoing the attitude often displayed towards this phenomenon by the respectable middle classes, the *Chronicle* warned those contemplating what it termed an "outrage" that it would not be tolerated, and the authorities in Whitby would "put down with a firm and vigorous hand any such shameful conduct." Its short report ended with an admonition against extra-legal action: "No matter what the merits of the case may be, it is not for individuals to take the law into their own hands."[29]

As for Robert and Eliza, for the former it was soon business as usual. From late October through the rest of the year the *Whitby Chronicle* carried advertisements for the Campbell brothers and the Glasgow warehouse, now stocked with a larger-than-ever supply of goods which Robert had acquired in the United Kingdom that summer.[30] At some point in October Eliza moved back into her parents' house where she resided for some time. She gave birth there to her and Robert's fourth child, Francis (Frank), on 12 December.[31] Robert must have been told of this but it made no difference to him. Indeed he later, before the Senate divorce committee, professed not to know whether Francis had been born in December 1873 or January 1874.

Throughout the next few years Robert and Eliza both continued to live in Whitby, separate and apart, he in the family home with the three children, who at some point returned to Whitby from Southampton. Although there is no direct evidence of it, the day-to-day duties of housekeeper and surrogate mother were likely performed by Robert's older unmarried sister, Elizabeth, a not untypical role for a single woman if her brother was without the services of a wife.[32] Eliza lived briefly with her parents, then with her brother James, and then, after her father died in late 1874, with her mother. It seems impossible that they never saw each other in the street, for the various residences were some 185 metres apart, and Eliza had many friends who took her side and welcomed visits from her. In a letter published in both the *Whitby Chronicle* and the *Ottawa Citizen* in 1876, Eliza's lawyer in the Senate divorce proceedings, William McDougall, provided a vivid if perhaps slightly exaggerated description of the contrast in the Campbells' material circumstances. Eliza and her young child lived with her mother, "a widow in straightened circumstances," while Robert "filled her former home – a comfortable mansion – with … relatives, whom he supports in luxury" while denying Eliza and Francis "the price of a loaf of bread."[33]

While the Campbells lived separate and apart in Whitby, they remained intimately connected, because they fought each other in three lawsuits, discussed in the next three chapters. At some point soon after he had moved back into the family home Robert carried out the same test that Eliza had earlier – seeing what could be heard of conversations inside by people listening outside. The same *Whitby Chronicle* editorial on which this section is largely based announced on 2 October that the first lawsuit resulting from the scandal would be heard at the Toronto assizes in mid-October. In a comment that has a familiar ring to today's reader, it asserted that the only winners would be the lawyers, who, "as they usually do, will reap a plentiful harvest from the misfortunes of their neighbours."[34]

5

The Campbells Go to Court I: Robert Campbell v. George Gordon for Criminal Conversation, 1873

Introduction: The Ontario Civil Court System

Three lawsuits involving the Campbells were started in September 1873, before Eliza had been ejected from the house, although all were heard after her ejection. Two were tried in the Court of Common Pleas, one of two common law superior courts, the third in the Court of Chancery, which administered equity, a set of doctrines different from the common law. This chapter and the next two examine each of these cases in turn. Although each involved different causes of action, they all turned on the same factual question: Had Eliza committed adultery? Each case involved questions of substantive law and procedure, and to understand them we need to know about the structure of the Ontario civil court system in the 1870s. Until 1837 the colony's sole superior court of civil jurisdiction was King's Bench, afterwards changed to Queen's Bench, which administered only common law.[1] In that year a Court of Chancery was established, with jurisdiction in equity. The distinction between common law and equity had a centuries-long history in England, and for current purposes the salient point is that most legal disputes were decided according to the common law rules, while the Court of Chancery both exercised jurisdiction over areas not covered by the common law, or evolved supplemental rules to reduce the formality and rigidity of the common law rules.[2] In 1849 the court system was reorganized, creating an additional superior trial court of common law, the Court of Common Pleas. Common Pleas had identical jurisdiction to Queen's Bench, and from 1849 a plaintiff could choose to sue in either court. In 1853 this system was changed because most plaintiffs chose Queen's Bench, perhaps because of its perceived higher quality and/or prestige. Henceforth there was only one clerk's office, not two, and when common law suits were filed the clerk assigned them to each court in alternate batches of 12.[3] Each of the trial courts, including Chancery, had three judges, but trials were conducted with only one judge presiding.[4] Almost all suits in the two common law courts were decided by a jury, but Chancery did not use juries, findings of both fact and law being made by the presiding judge. All three trial courts sat in Toronto in each of the four regular terms of the English court calendar: Michaelmas (from October), Hilary (from January), Easter (from April) and Trinity (from June), and in the various county towns on assize (sometimes called circuit) in the fall and the spring.

In 1873 the stark divide between courts of common law and the Court of Chancery was reduced by legislation to make the two types of courts "auxiliary to one another," so that actions previously exclusively the preserve of one could now be commenced in either. Ontario Premier Oliver Mowat described this measure as a "transition scheme," a step on the road to the abolition of the separate Court of Chancery, which occurred in 1881. The 1873 reform was bolstered by another in 1874, which allowed judges to sit in any of the superior trial courts, irrespective of which one they had been appointed to. None of these changes affected proceedings involving the Campbells. Criminal conversation and defamation actions had always been tried in common law courts, alimony had always been a matter for Chancery, and the actions were tried in the same courts they would have been tried in before 1873.[5]

If a litigant in one of the superior courts was not satisfied with the jury verdict or the judge's decision, there were two avenues of recourse. One was to apply for a new trial, alleging some defect in the jury's verdict or in the judge's rulings. This application would be heard by a panel of three judges, usually from the same court in which the trial had taken place. The bench therefore often included the trial judge. The second recourse was to appeal to the Court of Error and Appeal, which had been established in 1849 when the trial courts were reorganized, or, after 1874, to the newly created Court of Appeal. None of the cases involving the Campbells went to the Court of Appeal, but two of them, including the crim. con. case, involved applications for a new trial.

The Action for Criminal Conversation

In early September Robert sued George Gordon for criminal conversation (crim. con.) claiming $3,000 in damages. Despite its name this now defunct action (except in a few American states) was a tort, a civil wrong, an action for damages that a man could take against another man for having sex with his wife. Although an action for crim. con. was not a criminal action, the name matches the popular view of adulterous sex, the most serious "offence" against the sanctity of marriage. An adulterous affair was often called a crime, a person who engaged in extra-marital sex was often said to be "guilty" of doing so. Crim. con.'s origins are obscure, but it was well established by the seventeenth century, and it was seen as a way of compensating the husband for the loss of honour that being a "cuckold" entailed and for loss of consortium, the right of comfort and fellowship that married couples had in each other.[6] It was one of three common law actions that could be taken relating to marriage, the other two being for breach of promise of marriage, an action in contract, and for alienation of affection, a tort action a spouse could take against a third party who interfered in the marriage.

There were a number of famous crim. con. suits brought in the English and American courts in the eighteenth and nineteenth centuries, famous because of the personalities involved. In both England and the US crim. con. cases were extensively reported in the newspapers and produced a substantial pamphlet literature, for they had everything the popular press wanted – well known, wealthy, and often powerful people involved in titillating and scandalous affairs. In 1769 Lord Grosvenor won a £10,000 damage award from Lord Cumberland, King George III's brother. In 1836 George Chapple Norton sued Lord Melbourne, the prime minister, for criminal conversation with his wife, Caroline. The jury found against Norton, but the publicity almost brought down the government.[7]

The action was abolished in England by the UK *Divorce and Matrimonial Causes Act* of 1857, but not in North America, where it was received with the rest of the common law in the seventeenth and eighteenth centuries. In the early 1870s the United States was riveted by a case which New York editor and author Theodore Tilton brought against the "national symbol of morality" and the country's most famous preacher, Henry Ward Beecher, for adultery with Tilton's wife. The case came to nothing legally because the jurors could not agree. But, as an editorial in the *Nation* put it, it left a "permanent blot" on Beecher's reputation and threatened to "considerably diminish if not destroy his influence as a moral teacher."[8]

Crim. con. was received in Ontario with the rest of the English common law by the 1792 reception statute.[9] There were no (in)famous cases like those in the UK and the US in what is now Ontario, but while nobody has carried out a study of the action in Ontario there were cases in both the pre- and post-Confederation periods.[10] Such suits were also brought in other common law provinces, and one in Nova Scotia in 1820 was written up as a pamphlet for those titillated by scandal.[11] We know about a small number of lawsuits brought after Confederation in Ontario because they appear occasionally in the law reports and because male applicants for parliamentary divorces were expected to sue the man accused of adultery, the sole ground for divorce, for crim. con. before they applied for a divorce. John Robert Martin, for example, a Hamilton barrister, won $2,000 in a suit against another barrister, William Lount, for criminal conversation with his wife Sophia and then successfully petitioned Parliament for a divorce.[12] There were those in the legal community who agreed with Featherston Osler, a judge of the Ontario Court of Appeal from 1883 to 1910, who wrote in 1897 that the action was "a blot upon English jurisprudence and social manners,"[13] but the action was never statutorily repealed. Nor did the courts or legislature ever make it an action that could be taken by a wife against her husband's paramour, even after married women were granted largely the same civil status as single women and married men. One decision did so in 1893, but the case was overruled by the Court of Appeal four years later.[14] Crim. con. suits were pursued into the 1970s, in all provinces. The action was ruled to be obsolete in Ontario by the Ontario Court of Appeal in 1977. In that case Dubin J.A. held that the *Family Law Reform Act* of 1975 had comprehensively abolished all distinctions between men and women, but this did not mean that the action should be made available to wives. Rather, it should be seen as obsolete because it was the product of "common law rules or doctrines which placed the wife in an inferior position, and which have now ... been removed."[15]

Going to Law

On 1 September, the Monday after he had returned to Whitby from Southampton, Robert went to Toronto to consult a lawyer, the eminent and highly successful Robert Harrison, and instructed him to bring the action. Harrison was one of Toronto's leading lawyers. He was variously a bencher of the Law Society, and chief clerk in the Crown law office under John A. Macdonald when the latter was attorney general of Canada West. He left that position to go into private practice with Featherston Osler and Thomas Moss, both later appointed to the bench, and was frequently chosen to conduct crown prosecutions. Harrison was also the MP for Toronto West, and an expert on municipal law. He authored the leading text on that subject and also published guides to procedure. An indication of the status he had in the profession is that in 1876 he was appointed chief justice of the Court of Queen's Bench directly from the bar.[16] Harrison, who thought the story Robert told him "a very painful case," must have also told Robert that he had a very good chance of succeeding with a divorce petition, both because of the

e010939099

Figure 5.1. Robert Harrison
Source: LAC

evidence he could bring about 26 August and because of the various supposed writings of Eliza he had found.[17]

We do not know what advice Harrison gave Robert, but we can make a reasonable assumption about what it was from our knowledge of the law and Robert's subsequent actions. Robert obviously wanted to sue Gordon and receive a substantial damage award. But that was just a secondary motivation. It is likely that Robert asked Harrison how he could get a divorce from his wife and be free of any responsibility, financial and otherwise, for her. Harrison would have told him three things about divorce for Ontario residents in the 1870s. Divorces could only be obtained by private Act of Parliament; they could only be obtained on one ground, adultery, and male applicants for a parliamentary divorce were expected to have first sued the man they accused of adultery for crim. con. This had been the procedure in the United Kingdom before 1857 when divorces there were only available through an Act of Parliament, and the Parliament of Canada in the early years after Confederation based its divorce procedure on that which had governed the House of Lords.

Events moved rapidly thereafter. The suit was filed in the Court of Common Pleas for York County (Toronto) in early September, Robert claiming $10,000 in damages.[18] Although most people in Whitby would have known about the scandal, the *Chronicle* reported this without naming the Campbells, saying rather that "an engrossing local topic" was "an action for crim. con. brought by a husband, a senior partner in a Whitby dry goods firm." Later in September Robert Harrison was at Whitby to argue cases on circuit, and had long conversations with Robert, John Anderson, and George Young Smith, Robert's Whitby lawyer, as well as visiting the Campbell family home which, of course, was now occupied by Robert.[19]

The case came on for trial in Toronto on 15 and 16 October 1873, just seven weeks after the fateful evening. It was not held in Whitby because the fall assizes for Ontario county were scheduled to begin on 22 September, apparently too soon after the case was filed for the parties to be ready for trial.[20] It was tried by jury, as the vast majority of civil trials were in the nineteenth century. Although the jury was increasingly criticized in this period because of its lack of expertise and its favouritism, there were no serious recommendations that its use be discontinued, even though the federal Parliament passed legislation to move many criminal cases to trial by judge alone or, even better for those who wanted to economize, to guilty pleas.[21] We know only the names of the jurors, but they would have been respectable men from at least the upper working and lower middle classes because the property qualification for jury service excluded only those at the bottom rank in the socio-economic hierarchy. The process by which men were chosen to actually serve each year was complicated and not relevant to us here. What does matter is that to be included on the lists of those eligible to serve a juror had to be between 21 and 60 years old, male, "in possession of his natural faculties and not infirm or decrepit," and "assessed for local purposes upon property, real or personal, belonging to him in his own right or in that of his wife." There was no minimum property requirement; a man had simply to be the owner of assessed property for the purpose of local taxation. From the assessment lists "selectors," municipal officials, were to draw up lists of "such persons" whom they considered to be "from the integrity of their characters, and the soundness of their judgments ... the most discreet and competent for the performance of the duties of Jurors." Many classes of people were exempt from jury service, from the lieutenant-governor to judges, lawyers, priests, and physicians and down to millers, telegraph operators, and firemen "belonging to any regular Fire Company." Between them the minimal property qualification, the exemptions, and the discretionary power of selection given to municipal office holders meant that juries comprised men who belonged to the "respectable" working and middle classes. Three peremptory challenges for each side as well as challenges for cause were allowed in civil trials, and Harrison used all three of his peremptory challenges.[22]

The trial judge was Thomas Galt, who had been on the bench since 1869. The older brother of Alexander Galt, (who was a leading financier and John A. Macdonald's first minister of finance after Confederation), Thomas Galt emigrated to Upper Canada in 1833. He took up the study of law in 1839 and articled with William Draper, later chief justice of Ontario, receiving his call to the Bar in 1845. He was both a corporate solicitor and crown prosecutor before he was appointed to the bench in 1869. He was knighted in 1888 shortly after being appointed chief justice of what by then was the Common Pleas division of the High Court. Perhaps more importantly for current purposes, he did not idolize women, his views shaped in part by his experience presiding over the 1872 trial of a Mrs. George Campbell who was convicted of murdering her husband and executed. He was also a high Tory and a pillar of the Anglican Church and thus likely to disapprove strongly of any form of marital misconduct. As it transpired Galt made it clear in his summation to the jury that he did not believe a word of the defence offered on Gordon's behalf.

Robert Campbell's principal counsel was Harrison, who was assisted by George Young Smith of Whitby, who had been Robert's lawyer in the inquiry into Eliza's assault allegation before the Whitby magistrates. Gordon was represented by another pillar of the Toronto legal establishment, Matthew Crooks Cameron, and by his brother James Keith Gordon. James Gordon was very likely a man with enough knowledge of the profession to engage Cameron, one of Toronto's leading counsel. Cameron was from a well-connected family.[23] His father was the chief clerk in the House of Assembly and then went to work for the Canada Company in its Toronto office. He sent Matthew to Upper Canada College where his education was marred by an accident which led to a leg being amputated. According to one contemporary this changed his attitude and approach to his studies. From being "lively, fond of sports, and not particularly studious, he became of a serious turn of mind." After a period of convalescence and adjustment to the use of crutches and an artificial limb, he decided not to return to the college but to pursue a legal career as his two older brothers had done.

He was called to the bar in 1849 and over the next two decades became acknowledged as one of the best trial lawyers in Canada West/Ontario, taking cases in Toronto and on circuit, and winning most of them. He was successful even against such luminaries as John Hillyard Cameron, treasurer of the Law Society and solicitor general for Canada West, Philip VanKoughnet, a future chancellor, and John Hawkins Hagarty, a future chief justice of Common Pleas who presided over the second Campbell case, discussed in the next chapter. He had "a commanding presence and impressive manner of speaking," as well as "a tremendous capacity for work despite his physical disability." His abilities later secured him appointments to the chief justiceship of the Common Pleas Division of the High Court, in 1884. He often found himself pitted against Harrison in court, and the two men were reasonably close friends.[24]

Cameron was also heavily involved in politics. He became a Conservative member of the Province of Canada assembly for Ontario North, the constituency adjacent to Ontario South which contained Whitby, in 1863, defeating the incumbent William McDougall who would become Eliza's lawyer in the later parliamentary proceedings. After Confederation he remained in the assembly and was provincial secretary in the coalition government of John Sandfield Macdonald. In 1871 he was defeated for the now federal seat of Ontario North but won the Ontario assembly seat of Toronto East. A formidable debater, he became the chief spokesman for the Conservative wing of the coalition. He left office in 1871 when the Liberals under Oliver Mowat ousted Macdonald, and in 1873 was leader of the now opposition Conservative party in Ontario. He was an ineffective politician, too high Tory for the age. In

PA-028639

Figure 5.2. Matthew Crooks Cameron

Source: LAC

taking Eliza's case he may simply have been neglecting politics for his profession, something he was accused of doing by members of his own party. But he may also have been motivated by an aristocratic noblesse oblige that on previous occasions had led him to take on unlikely briefs. While serving as a cabinet minister he accepted a retainer as one of the lawyers representing Patrick James Whelan, who was tried in 1868 for the murder of Thomas D'Arcy McGee, the foremost spokesman for the Irish Catholic interest and a member of John A. Macdonald's federal cabinet. The spectre of a minister of the crown defending a man being prosecuted for murder by the crown was heavily criticized, and Cameron was not on Whelan's defence team when he was tried.[25] The same belief in defending the underdog, this time a "wronged" woman, may have persuaded him to take the Campbell case. Whatever the reason, obtaining the services of Cameron demonstrates that the Gordon and Byrne families were not without means. Eliza's principal financial backers in all the litigation were her parents and her druggist brother James, but other members of the community likely contributed to her defence for her to be able to afford a high-priced lawyer like Cameron.[26]

The courtroom was packed for the trial, which started on 15 October, so much so that after a long day in the close confines of the courtroom Harrison was "so covered with perspiration that I had to change all my underclothing."[27] It was a month after Robert had thrown Eliza out of the house. The trial lasted two days. Many people travelled in from Whitby, including reporters from the town's two newspapers. One of the reporters was George Bengough of the *Whitby Gazette*, who later left the paper and opened a bookstore in the town.[28] George was the older brother of John Wilson Bengough, who worked briefly for the *Gazette* before moving to the *Globe* in the early 1870s. He is well known to Canadian historians as the founder and long-time proprietor of the satirical magazine *Grip*, which featured his own cartoons and caricatures, principally of John A. Macdonald. George Bengough was later a partner with his brother in the enterprise.[29]

The trial, said the *Globe*, was of "very great interest" in Toronto, likely because it involved the scandal of adultery. It described both parties as well-known Whitby residents who, "up to the present," were of "entire respectability." The *Whitby Gazette* simply noted that "[i]t is unnecessary for us to dwell at any length upon the high social positions heretofore occupied by all the parties to this case, as they are personally known to most of our readers."[30] Every seat on the main level was occupied, and many watched from the gallery, "where they might, by good fortune and a little straining of necks and ears, hear something of the conversation."[31] The trial was reported on extensively in four newspapers, the Toronto *Globe* and the Toronto *Mail*, and the *Whitby Chronicle* and the *Whitby Gazette*,[32] and less extensively but still in some detail in other newspapers, in Toronto and Montreal, which picked up Toronto reports.[33] The *Globe* and the *Mail* were dailies, their reports coming out only a day after the events reported. The Whitby papers were weeklies, being sent to the press on Wednesday afternoons and appearing every Thursday, and their reports were published after the trial had ended.[34] What follows is an amalgam of what was reported in these four newspapers, whose accounts were very similar. The quotations are mostly from the *Whitby Chronicle* and are not footnoted. Only those from the *Globe*, the *Mail*, and the *Whitby Gazette* are specifically footnoted. In this and the succeeding two chapters I have sought to avoid repeating the events described in chapters 2 and 3. I have, however, referred to them when necessary for an understanding of how each side presented its case.

The Case for the Plaintiff Robert Campbell

The trial began with an opening address from Harrison as counsel for the plaintiff, the moving party. He introduced the parties, pointing to Gordon as "the young man with the dark vest and light blue necktie" sitting at a table. He then expressed pleasure that crim. con was an action rarely tried in Ontario, following this by contrasting the characters of the Campbells. Eliza was a very attractive young woman, but one whose "good looks" had been "the ruin of herself and her husband." In contrast Robert was a husband whose business required him to risk his life on the Atlantic every year "in order to support and make happy his wife and dear little children." And it was while he was risking his life that his friend, a man who had "shared the hospitalities of his house," had taken advantage of that hospitality "to bring ruin and desolation on his house."

Harrison then reviewed the essential elements of the story recounted in chapters 2 and 3, with some considerable exaggerations. While Robert was away Gordon walked out with Eliza "night and day," and in August he visited her "night after night." When Robert returned from the United Kingdom, he was told of Eliza's infidelity, and refused to live with her, "and she knew why." In fact, she had no idea at that stage of how seriously Robert viewed the situation. Nor was it exactly accurate to say, as Harrison then did, that when Robert went away to Saugeen "a couple of his friends" decided to watch Eliza. Harrison concluded by praising Robert for not exacting private revenge. He had "restrained his feelings" and looked to the law for "redress" rather than use violence.

Harrison then called six witnesses, the first two being the Newsom sisters. At this stage Cameron would have known the general outline of what Harrison's witnesses would say, because his junior counsel, Gordon, had interviewed Eliza, the Byrne family, and George Gordon, and Rev. Byrne and James Byrne had had meetings with the Campbell brothers. In the absence of detailed knowledge about what the evidence would be, Cameron would have to rely on undermining the credibility of Robert Campbell's witnesses on cross-examination. He knew he could not call either Eliza or George Gordon to the witness stand as part of the defence case, because the law of evidence did not permit it. The common law had long provided that spouses could not give evidence against each other, a rule based on the public policy enunciated in one treatise: "The happiness of the married state requires that there should be the most unlimited confidence between husband and wife; and this confidence the law secures by providing that it shall be kept for ever inviolable; that nothing shall be extracted from the bosom of the wife which was confided there by the husband."[35] The parties to a lawsuit were similarly not competent witnesses because they were "interested" in the outcome and thus susceptible to committing perjury. It was not simply that the jury might be misled by false evidence. The "party witness disqualification," as it was known, harked back to a period where the sacred nature of the oath, sworn on a bible, meant that those who might be tempted to give false evidence were also risking their immortal souls. The bar on parties testifying was removed in the UK in stages in the mid-nineteenth century, and in Ontario in 1869.[36] The bar on spouses testifying was repealed in 1873, with the exception that spouses still could not be made to testify about communications between them "during coverture."[37]

However, there was one caveat to both these evidence law reforms. Parties and spouses were not competent to give evidence "in any proceeding instituted in consequence of adultery." Thus the witnesses for Robert could not be refuted by the only two people in a position to do so. George Gordon was a party, and Eliza was Robert's spouse. Robert was also, as a party, unable to testify, but that did not matter. He had been in Southampton on 26 August and could have said nothing about what happened in Whitby. He had James Campbell and John Anderson to make his case.

The first witness, Martha Newsom, testified to Gordon having visited the house "frequently" when Robert was away and staying late, although she had not heard any improper conversation between Eliza and Gordon or seen anything untoward. The one notable thing she had heard was Gordon telling Eliza that he "would be sincere." Martha also said that she did not approve of Eliza's conduct, and that the friendship between her and Gordon was "talked about among the servants." On cross-examination Cameron got her to say that the Campbells "lived on good terms." Robert was suspicious of Gordon, who visited when he was at home, but the Campbells and the Gordons were "intimate." Cameron then went after Newsom's statement that Gordon had visited "frequently." What did that mean? "Very often." What did very often mean? "I think your own idea will tell you. He called once or two a week." Did she call once or twice a week often? "Yes." Cameron had made his point and shifted to Newsom's statement that the friendship between Eliza and Gordon was talked about among the servants. After some initial evasion this turned out to mean that she had talked about it once with her sister Jane. Cameron shifted to asking Newsom about whether and when she had talked to the Campbell brothers about her observations and elicited that she had not talked to them until after 26 August, suggesting that neither she nor the Campbells had seen any need to discuss Gordon before then. Cameron concluded by asking about the relationship between Eliza and James Campbell, because he wanted to play up the animosity between them and thereby suggest that James was likely to have lied. Newsom said that when Robert was away James only came to the Campbell home to feed and water the horse. He never made a social call on Eliza. All in all Cameron must have been pleased at how much he had reduced the impact of Newson's testimony. On re-direct Harrison only got her to repeat her statement that Gordon did not stay after midnight when he visited when Robert was at home, a useful point to stress to the jury.

Jane Newsom was on the witness stand for much less time than her sister because she had only taken over as the live-in servant on 15 August and could say little or nothing about July and much of August. Harrison concentrated his questions on the night of 26 August, but Jane did not contribute much. Gordon and Eliza had arrived at the house at about 9:30 p.m., had sat in the parlour and were still there when Jane went to bed at 11:45 p.m. She did not hear anything that was said before or after going to bed, although in the morning she heard someone say it was 3 o'clock. Cameron's cross-examination covered a range of issues, starting with having Newsom describe the layout of the house. He continued: On the night in question were the doors closed? The parlour door was open and the front door was on the latch and partially open. The point of this was obvious; people engaging in adulterous sex would have kept the doors closed. Where would someone outside have to be in order to hear conversation in the parlour? On the veranda that led up to the front door. There was a side window with sand or gravel or tanbark covering the ground below it, but someone standing there would be mostly below the window sill.* Again, one can discern the purpose of the question, assuming that Cameron thought Campbell and Anderson would testify that they had heard things from below the window. If so Cameron could cast doubt on the reliability of their evidence.

Cameron then briefly took Newsom back to 18 August and Robert's return. Were Robert and Eliza cordial the night he returned from the UK? They were. She did not know why Robert took the children to Saugeen. Cameron switched back to 26 August. Did she see James Campbell around the house on that day? She did, earlier in the day before Eliza went out, a fact Cameron could later use to establish that Campbell was a frequent visitor to the yard if not the house and that this was well known. Cameron then asked if a person outside could see what went on in the parlour? Newsom gratifyingly answered that nothing could be seen; there were shutters on the windows that did not open. Cameron followed this by asking when and how Jane Newsom had been dismissed by Robert. In September, via a written notice given to her by Danford. Finally, did either of the Campbell brothers ask her any questions about Eliza's "conduct" while Robert was away? They did not. Jane Newsom did not provide very helpful evidence for either side. Harrison got her to attest to Gordon's arrival on 26 August and to his staying late, while Cameron had principally established that she had heard and seen nothing of consequence.

The principal witness for Robert, James Campbell, was next. He was first led by Harrison through a detailed account of the evening of 26 August. This included what the *Globe* called "conversation which showed the guilt of the parties" but which it declined to print.[38] The direct examination also dealt with the altercation in the street between him and Gordon. Campbell said he angrily called Gordon out and accused him of seducing Eliza, and that Gordon replied, "It was not my fault I could not help it." He had then turned to Anderson and asked him to "bear testimony" to the words Gordon had used, which Anderson agreed to do.

The *Globe*'s report of Cameron's cross-examination stated simply that "the witness did not vary in his testimony."[39] The *Whitby Chronicle* and the *Whitby Gazette* reported the cross at some length. Cameron knew that the law of evidence would prevent Eliza or Gordon testifying and

* Tanbark is the bark of certain species of trees, traditionally used for tanning hides into leather.

thereby denying what James Campbell had said, and thus his questions were largely aimed at discrediting James Campbell as a witness who had perjured himself. Cameron began with asking how often he had visited Eliza and his nephews and nieces while Robert was in the United Kingdom, a question no doubt designed to illustrate the poor relations between James and his brother's wife. Campbell was evasive but had to ultimately admit that he did not visit:

> During your brother's absence in England were you in the habit of visiting Mrs. Campbell frequently? I was in the habit of going about the house.
>
> That is not an answer to my question. (Question repeated)
>
> I've been at the house. (Question repeated)
>
> I've always gone to the house when I had an errand to do.
>
> That is not an answer (Question repeated) Have you ever been in the house?
>
> I have been in the house.
>
> You have been skulking around the house, did you ever visit your sister-in-law?
>
> I called once.
>
> How was it you did not call more frequently?
>
> I had my business to attend to. I was about the house and could see her almost every evening, she used to come about.

On further questioning Campbell insisted that he was on "friendly" terms with Eliza, adding that his wife Rebecca had visited her once while Robert was away, hardly evidence of familial closeness.

Cameron then asked a series of questions about the Parks letter and about whether it had been James Campbell who told Robert about the friendship between Gordon and Eliza. On the letter Cameron followed up by asking James whether he had advised Robert to talk to Eliza, and he said he had not. He said that it had been him who told Robert about Eliza and Gordon. He had heard from his wife, who had heard from Mrs. Anna Jameson "the stories going around about George Gordon going to the house and coming out so late." All of this, it subsequently became clear, was intended to paint James Campbell as the villain of the piece, dissuading Robert from asking Eliza for an explanation and planting suspicion in his mind about Gordon. To the same effect Cameron asked about the brothers' meetings with the Byrne family, which drew from James a denial that he had been the "spokesman" for his brother with the family. Campbell did admit that he did not want Robert to talk to Eliza, but denied that he was engaged in any "conspiracy" against her, and he also agreed that Robert had decided to separate from Eliza before the 26th, an admission that Cameron later used to argue that even if the jury found against Gordon the damages should be reduced.

A good deal of Cameron's cross-examination was about the exact words Campbell and Anderson had heard, and the noises which convinced them that sexual intercourse had taken place. Campbell was ready enough to repeat "Robert might suspect"; "has Robert had any connection with you since his return"; and discussions about going to California. But he resisted Cameron's repeated attempts to give more explicit details. When Camerson asked him exactly what he had told Rev. Byrne he declined, saying that "the words he heard passing between Mrs. Campbell and Mr. Gordon were of so filthy a character" that he would rather not repeat them. He did say that he had heard the "smacking of lips," Gordon saying "Come, my dear Eliza, I want to kiss you," and Eliza asking Gordon "if he would come half way" towards her on the sofa if she "went the other half." But he resisted saying more, until Cameron pressed him again towards the end of the cross-examination, challenging him by asserting that "we say it is false from beginning to end." That made Campbell say more, most of which the newspapers would not print: the *Whitby Chronicle's* version reads: "During the carrying on heard Mrs. Campbell ask which way (the vile language said to be used is of the most filthy and disgusting character, and unfit for publication)." This was what Cameron wanted, for it allowed him to challenge Campbell on the unlikelihood of a clergyman's daughter from a "highly respectable" family saying such things. Cameron kept goading Campbell on this point by repeating the words himself: "Did you tell Rev. Mr. Byrne that you heard Mrs. Campbell say to Gordon: 'Don't push ****.' (words unfit for publication)?" These exchanges produced one obvious untruth, although the *Whitby Chronicle* reporter might have been the cause. He had Campbell saying that he had told the Brynes that he saw Gordon feeling Eliza's breasts. Given that on no other occasion did either Campbell or Anderson claim to have seen something rather than heard it, and that Cameron did not pursue the inconsistency, Campbell surely did not say that.

The cross-examination covered other issues – the stereoscope, the issue of "naval" and "navel," and the late-night altercation, and Campbell stuck to his story as recounted in chapter 3. The only other significant questions were about the accounts of the evening written down by both Campbell and Anderson the next day. Campbell admitted that he had written two versions, the first of which he destroyed and the second he had given to Harrison. But both were essentially the same.

Anderson had also written an account, which he, Campbell, had seen but made no attempt to compare with his own.

Harrison briefly re-examined Campbell, on three issues.[40] Campbell confirmed that the words he had quoted from Eliza and Gordon were "exactly as he related," and insisted that he had no animus against Eliza – "on the contrary, he and his wife were on the best of terms with her – visiting terms." Harrison also asked about Campbell's written memorandum of the events made very shortly after he had got up the following morning. It had been correct, but "very rough, so rough that no one but himself could read it." That was why he had written a better version and destroyed the original.

Harrison's next witness was the other "watcher," John Anderson. Like James Campbell he recounted what he had seen and heard on the evening of the 26th, adding nothing to what was discussed in chapter 3. His account agreed with Campbell's on the words said in the street altercation – Campbell had said that Gordon "had criminal conversation with his brother's wife" and Gordon replied that it was not his fault – and with what they had heard from outside the house. The *Whitby Chronicle* used asterisks for the "filthy" words used while the *Whitby Gazette* avoided choosing between the words and asterisks by reporting that Anderson said that he "heard enough to satisfy me that criminal connection had been going on." Anderson was cross-examined by Cameron, the *Whitby Chronicle* reporting the cross in some detail, although its account mirrored much of what had already been said. Cameron extracted from Anderson the fact that when Robert told him of his marital difficulties, he had Parks in mind, not Gordon. As he had with James Campbell, Cameron insisted that Anderson provide exact details on what he heard said and done, which produced more asterisks from all the newspapers. Anderson did say one thing that Campbell had not – that "I think" that Eliza and Gordon had had sex twice.

When Cameron got to the altercation in the street, he pointed out that the statement he had made at the request of George Young Smith on the Sunday following Tuesday the 26th had been altered. The words first written were "*You have been in my brother's house from nine to three o'clock, and have attempted to seduce his wife, if you have not already done so.*" The words substituted were "*You have been in my brother's house from nine to three o'clock, and have had criminal connection with my brother's wife.*"[41] Cameron put it to Anderson that "the first statement was the correct one," and the second "an afterthought" written "to suit the evidence required to be given." Anderson explained the change by saying that the statements had been written "from recollection" and "the last recollection was the best." On re-examination Harrison, not surprisingly, returned to this issue, getting Anderson to tell the jury that "the correction was the truth; struck out what I was not certain about." There is obviously a world of difference between "attempted to" and "did so," and Anderson's admission must have harmed Robert's case although, as we will shortly see, not enough to affect the verdict.

Harrison concluded his case by calling two other witnesses, George Cameron and Walter Henry Fagan of Whitby, who gave the evidence of seeing of Gordon and Eliza together that was recounted in chapter 2. Cameron cross-examined them both about when these events occurred, hoping to cast doubt on their memories and therefore on the veracity of their stories. George Cameron could not give the exact date or the time of the day, he knew only that it was about two months previously and in the evening. Fagan, who had told the story of the two at the gate of the Campbell home, "remembered this was in August, because he got his hands hurt at that time."[42]

The Case for the Defendant George Gordon and Rebuttal Witnesses

With Cameron and Fagan the case for the plaintiff closed, and at 4:10 p.m. the defence put on its witnesses. Knowing that he could not call Eliza or George Gordon, Cameron's only recourse was to try to undermine the evidence for the plaintiff, especially by portraying James Campbell as prejudiced against Eliza. His first two witnesses were James Byrne and Rev. Byrne, who went over the conversations they had had with the Campbell brothers. The younger Byrne repeated James Campbell's comment that he hoped Byrne would not see the whole thing as a "conspiracy." He said this at least twice in his testimony, and he also said that he had long known that there was "a bad feeling" harboured by James for Eliza. When James Byrne talked to Robert he told him that "his brother James was influencing him too much." Rev. Byrne similarly averred that James Campbell was the "spokesman" for the brothers and "the instigator of the whole trouble." Cameron then used the testimony of Byrne père and fils and of all the defence witnesses to provide an alternative narrative to that given by Campbell and Anderson. The Byrnes recounted what the Campbells had said to them, and what they had said in response – that Eliza was a good woman, that Robert had made up his mind to leave her before the 26th and refused to listen to her explanation, and that the Byrne and Gordon families were old friends. The implication was that Robert had an incentive to have the house watched to garner or, if necessary, fabricate the additional evidence that would be needed to get a divorce. As he had with Campbell and Anderson, Cameron made his own witnesses repeat the words used and the sounds allegedly heard on the 26th, by recounting what James Campbell had said to them. The purpose was the same as with his cross-examinations – to later argue that a respectable wife and mother and daughter of a clergyman would never use such "disgusting language."

After James and Rev. Byrne had given their testimony, Cameron tried to call first Eliza and then George Gordon, even though he knew they could not testify. Presumably he wanted to drive home to the jury the fact that they were being prevented from hearing the other side. Naturally Harrison objected and Galt sustained the objections. There was nothing else Cameron could do other than call Bethiah Ham and Mary Byrne to talk about the "sound trial" conducted before Eliza had been ejected from the house. Bethiah Ham had been outside and said that even though one window was cracked slightly open she could not clearly hear conversations that took place in the parlour. This was at about 7:30 p.m. on a calm evening, but despite that and despite the fact that Eliza and her mother in the parlour "appeared to be speaking in an ordinary tone of voice," she "heard very indistinctly" what was said. Mary Byrne said the same thing. Harrison cross-examined both women, asking Ham if there were any men inside. This was presumably meant to contrast their experience with that of James Campbell and Anderson, who had heard a male voice, Gordon's. Harrison also got Ham to say that she did not know where in the parlour her mother and sister had sat during the test, and to acknowledge that she was at the southwest window and not the window at the end of the house, which was too high for her but was the one that Campbell and Anderson had stood below at some point. In answer to further questions from Harrison, Ham admitted that she could hear well enough to know who was speaking at any point. But she insisted that she could not discern what they were talking about. Mary Byrne also said that she had good hearing, but, like Bethiah Ham, she nonetheless could not make out the words. The only word she identified in 10 or 15 minutes of listening was "unexpectedly."

By this point it was 5:40 p.m. The evidence was not quite all in. Cameron had one more witness to call, and Harrison had witnesses to call in rebuttal on the question of what could be heard from the parlour. The court adjourned, but not before Galt told the jury that they were not to speak to anybody about the case. News of what had happened that day must have spread very quickly, arousing a good deal of public interest, because during the afternoon Harrison had called Galt's attention to the fact that "a newspaper in the city had been commenting upon the evidence in a manner likely to affect the case prejudicially."[43]

The trial resumed at 10 a.m., on 16 October. The courtroom had been very full the day before, but with word of the sensational testimony having got around it was now "crowded to the very door," and many people were turned away. The atmosphere was "crammed and suffocating." "It was one dense, closely packed mass of humanity," Harrison confided to his diary.[44] The first witness of the day was the defence's final witness, Henrietta Byrne. She gave testimony about three things. First, that Eliza had been at her house in the evening of 26 August, and that Gordon had come by with Annie Byrne and Henrietta's granddaughter Hettie, the daughter of Bethiah Ham, who had been visiting with the Gordon family. Gordon had escorted them home, and then walked Eliza home at about 9 p.m. This was presumably to make the point that Gordon had done the gentlemanly thing: He was not at the Campbell house at 9 by a pre-arranged assignation. Second, Henrietta had been present at the test of what could be heard by those outside the Campbell house and said that she was one of those inside and had "talked naturally" and "rather loud." Third, she said that the Gordons had known the Byrne family for 22 years, and she had met George Gordon at Eliza and Robert's house when Robert was also present.

Henrietta Byrne was cross-examined by Harrison, who asked her only about the "noise trial." She and Eliza had been inside and had talked about "this business which mostly occupied our minds." This concluded the evidence for the defence. Cameron's witnesses must not have been very persuasive when stacked against the evidence Harrison had presented. None of them was able to say that Campbell and Anderson had not heard what they claimed to have heard for the simple reason that they had not been there on the night in question. And the result of the noise "trial" could not have counted for much. All the witnesses were Eliza's close relatives.

Despite the very limited value of the defence evidence, Harrison called five rebuttal witnesses on the question of what could be heard from outside of people speaking in the parlour. The Campbell brothers must have heard about the experiment undertaken by Eliza's family and arranged their own once they had control of the premises. It took place on Wednesday, 3 October.[45] The rebuttal witnesses – James Campbell again, Charles Scott, James Fraser, a salesman who worked for the Campbell brothers, John Tweedie, brother of Rebecca, James Campbell's wife, and Michael O'Donovan, carriage maker and, in 1873, reeve of Whitby – must not have occupied much time. Not surprisingly they claimed they could hear from the outside what was said inside.[46] When they were finished all the evidence was in. One person, George Conrad Gross, the Whitby hardware merchant, had been subpoenaed by James Gordon and was on the list of witnesses given in the *Whitby Chronicle*, but was not called. As we will see in the next chapter, his testimony would have directly contradicted one part of Campbell's and Anderson's evidence, the time at which the altercation on the street in the small hours had happened. Cameron probably did not call him because he had not told James Gordon anything more than that he had seen Robert to try to persuade him to meet Eliza but was unsuccessful, and Cameron did not know about his version of the time of the street argument. He would be called in the subsequent defamation and alimony cases, because he came forward with his story about the time when he read the testimony in the crim. con. case reported in the newspapers.[47]

Counsels' Speeches to the Jury

The defence made its closing arguments first. Cameron was up against it. His witnesses had only been able to say that their daughter/sister would not have done such a thing, or that James Campbell and John Anderson could not have heard what they claimed to have heard. His address was therefore an attempt to convince the jury that Campbell and Anderson had lied, and that is what he said up front. After referring to "the exceedingly painful" nature of the case, he expanded on what made it so painful – a "conspiracy had been got up between the plaintiff and his brother for the purpose of ruining the wife of the former." In fact "the whole testimony was false, and not one circumstance connected with the charge was true with the exception of the fact that Gordon was at the plaintiff's house at a late hour of the night." And the mere fact of his being there did not support an allegation that there had been "an impropriety between him and a lady." In addition, the lady in question was someone whose "conduct heretofore has been irreproachable" and was the daughter of a clergyman. Here Cameron reminded the jury that he had called Eliza and Gordon to testify, but the law of evidence had prevented him doing so, and thus the "only two persons in the world who must know about the matter were excluded from giving their evidence." This suited Robert, who wanted to prevent his wife "purging herself from the foul stigma cast upon her" by declaring her innocence on oath. Eliza and Gordon were nonetheless ready at any time to give their side of the story, to show that their behaviour had been innocent. Galt interrupted Cameron at this point, stating that the evidence referred to was inadmissible and upbraiding Cameron for making an "inappropriate" reference to it. But Cameron had made his point, even if his tactic would likely be considered unethical today.

Cameron then returned to the theme of the Campbell brothers' duplicity and provided a motive for Robert to behave as he had. He wanted to get rid of his wife and had determined to do so as soon as he read the letter from Parks, which was before he had been told about the alleged "improper intimacy" with Gordon. About that letter, which had not been produced in court, there were "very suspicious circumstances." Whether such a letter had been written by Parks "was much to be doubted," although Cameron did not say who he thought had written it, or when. He knew only that it provided an excuse for Robert to take the children away and to tell James to "set watch on her actions." Anticipating an obvious objection to this idea, Cameron noted that it was "a matter of wonder" that "a man who possessed as accomplished and beautiful a wife" should want to be rid of her. But it was not possible to know what went on in his mind.

With that Cameron turned to the testimony of James Campbell and "his friend the butcher," who "went prowling around the ... house for the purpose of entrapping his wife into an indiscretion." Cameron tore into their evidence, which made no sense. They said that they had listened from 9:30 p.m. to 12 a.m., while those inside must have been talking, and yet "not one word they said during that period could be heard." Then for the next three hours they could hear everything that was said and done. But if Eliza and Gordon were waiting for Jane Newsom to go to bed before they engaged in sexual conduct they would have spoken more loudly "in order to satisfy the girl's mind that they were not suspicious." Cameron also very much doubted that Eliza had used the words James Campbell attributed to her. "[N]o woman of respectability, education, or refinement could [possibly] have uttered" such "coarse vulgarities." Moreover, when James Campbell got into the witness box and said what he had told Rev. Byrne, he did not initially remember what he had said and had to be reminded of it by Cameron. This was an unreasonable characterization of the cross-examination. James Campbell had been reluctant to give details until Cameron pressed him to do so; he had to persuade Campbell, not remind him.

James Campbell's fetching of a stick to break the window was also raised. If he wanted to "protect his brother's family and children and the honour of his house" he would have carried through with it; he would not have stood by and allowed the adultery to occur. A "man of honour," a "gentleman," would have intervened to prevent the disgrace of all. But Campbell and Anderson were not there to stop it; they were there to catch Eliza and Gordon in the act. James Campbell wanted to destroy the "virtue and untarnished name" of a sister-in-law he disliked. The falsity of the watchers' statements was illustrated by the fact that Anderson's initial written statement had said "attempted to seduce" Eliza; how could someone write that if he and Campbell had indeed heard what their testimony had recounted? "Great importance," said the *Whitby Gazette*, "was attached to the word 'attempting.'"

Having dismissed much of the evidence given as fabrication, Cameron also provided alternative explanations of the mention of Eliza's navel and of the stereoscope discussion. It was not navel, but naval, and was said during the time Eliza was singing and the two of them were talking about different kinds of songs. There was a need to adjust the stereoscope to get a better focus. Regarding both issues James Campbell had "interpreted" the words in a "dreadful manner." Cameron conceded that it was "indecorous" for a young married woman to entertain a young man until the small hours of the morning, but argued that the explanation was innocent; they had spent a long time playing draughts. At this point Cameron ignored Galt's previous admonition and slipped in another reference to the exclusionary evidence law: "The jury would understand that the parties implicated were excluded from giving evidence, and they would therefore have to take all this on suspicion and bring disgrace on a Presbyterian clergyman, one who stood well in the eyes of the community."[48]

Other parts of the evidence given by Campbell and Anderson were assailed as contradictory or inconclusive. Anderson had testified that he heard Eliza say that she wanted to go to California but would not go unless Gordon accompanied her, while James Campbell had told Rev. Byrne that Gordon had solicited Eliza for sex "thirty or forty times," and she only gave in when he promised to go west with her. The testimony about the "noise trial" was unreliable because Robert's witnesses were all men and while "no doubt ... respectable gentlemen" they had gone to the house when summoned by the Campbells "for the purpose of sustaining the evidence." The Byrne family ladies, in contrast, had conducted their trial with "no design, no teaching, no plan." In fact it was very unlikely that anybody could have heard what was said on the night in question because people who talked about and engaged in sex would have been quiet .

Nearing the end of his speech Cameron returned to his theme of a scheme concocted by the Campbell brothers to ruin Eliza, beginning with the instantaneous decision by Robert to leave Eliza and the haste with which James had been sent to Toronto and Vaughan to have a facsimile of the letter made and sent to Eliza. On the night of the 26th James Campbell, intoxicated after he and Anderson had drunk whisky at the store, had returned to the house and "taunted" Eliza. She, "no doubt, had been imprudent in remaining alone" with Gordon for "so many hours." "But the fact of her being imprudent did not make her a criminal." James Campbell "had entertained a feeling of hatred and uncharitableness" towards Eliza for some time. It was he who had talked of a conspiracy against Eliza; "and why should he have thought that unless he was conspiring as a cowardly dastard?" Cameron ended by reminding the jury of the unlikelihood of Eliza saying the words alleged and of their chivalric duty to protect an innocent woman. The words she had allegedly spoken would not have been said by even "the greatest strumpet on the street." The jury should discredit the evidence on that point, for "as men they were bound to protect the woman unless the evidence that attacked her chastity was of the most unmistakeable character."

For all that Cameron's speech was an "able address" according to Harrison,[49] he ended it very weakly. After stating that Campbell and Anderson were "men who, like prowling hounds, scenting for their prey, hunted a defenceless woman to her ruin," he said that if the jury nonetheless believed in the adultery the fact that Robert had previously decided to separate from his wife would be sufficient reason to substantially reduce any damages award. In quibbling over the damage award Cameron conceded that the story might be true, and he characterized Robert's decision to separate not as the reason why he had set up his wife so that he had the proof of adultery needed to get a divorce, but as a mitigating factor in that adultery. He also, again weakly, complained about the trial being held in Toronto and not Whitby where people know Eliza's true character.

Harrison replied in a speech as long as Cameron's and one which he judged to be as "equally able." He had to make exactly the opposite principal points to Cameron – Campbell and Anderson had no reason to lie and had not lied, and Eliza, daughter of a clergyman or not, had engaged in adulterous sex. He began where Cameron had ended, with the venue. There was not enough time after the suit was filed "to complete the necessary arrangements" for a trial in Whitby. Given that the suit was filed very early in September, that the parties and all the witnesses were from Whitby, and that the Whitby fall assizes began on September 22nd this does not seem a convincing explanation. Cameron was surely right that Harrison did not want a home-town jury. Harrison followed this by telling the jurors that their verdict should be based on the evidence and not "the eloquence of counsel." Like Cameron he believed that some of the parties concerned "were entitled to the fullest sympathy" – the Campbells' children, "deprived of a mother," Robert, "deprived of a wife," the friends and relatives of both parties who must feel the disgrace even if they themselves had nothing to do with it. But there was one man for whom there would not be much sympathy, Gordon, towards whom he aimed all his invective. In line with prevailing views of women's agency, he largely blamed the man, not Eliza. Gordon was "the author of all this disgrace and ruin." He had "stolen the virtue of a wife and mother," and Harrison's only regret was that the law was "defective" in making it a criminal matter to steal 10 cents but not punishing, beyond a fine, a man who "stole the virtue and fair fame of an honest matron."

Harrison knew he had to respond to Cameron on the question of the exclusion of Eliza and Gordon from testifying, and he first said that Cameron's references to it were "all done for effect." Cameron knew well what the law was, and he knew why it was the way it was:

> If a man were base and bad enough to visit and dishonour a woman in her own house he would not stop to add perjury to the crime of adultery. And the woman who harboured the adulterer would … not shrink from the same…. For when virtue leaves a woman truth generally follows. When a woman becomes lost to all … that is due to her husband, to her friends and to society, she would not be baulked by the tender of an oath.

With that Harrison returned to Gordon. The jury could judge human nature, and would any of them leave Gordon alone in a house with their wife until 3 a.m.? There were young men who would view such conduct as "good fun," and Cameron had said Gordon was there to sing; but "singing was not his forte." What therefore was his purpose? Saying nothing about Parks Harrison insisted that as early as the spring of 1873 the "attentions" of Gordon to Eliza gave Robert "grave cause for uneasiness." He could do nothing about Gordon at that time for lack of proof, but he sensed that Eliza "showed a greater fondness for another than for her husband." The situation became more serious when Robert went to the United Kingdom. This left the field clear for Gordon, who might have been "one of those good men who when the husband was away undertook … to comfort the wife." Gordon and Robert were friends, and maybe the visits were a way for Gordon to help his friend Robert, "but he (Harrison) did not think" so. The evidence showed that Gordon came more often and stayed later once Robert was away. Gordon and Eliza had been seen walking in the streets with his arm around Eliza, which showed that "at that time Gordon's intercourse with Campbell's wife was so open and so frequent that people noticed it and talked about it." This was a rather exaggerated summary of the evidence of just two men, but it set Harrison up to discuss the crucial evening.

"What took place between them" that night? Harrison began. The evidence showed that they were not singing or painting or talking about naval officers or looking at a stereoscope or engaged in some other "innocent amusement," the explanation Eliza would have given had she been allowed to testify. There was no evidence to show that there had been any singing that night, nor that Gordon was a singer. It was also well established that Eliza was "entertaining a young blood" until 3 a.m. If Eliza had been a virtuous woman she would not have entertained Gordon at all. But she did, "and when the baser passions in our nature are aroused they overcome all the dictates of reason, prudence, and virtue." Eliza's story might just hold water if this had been the only occasion that Gordon had visited while Robert was absent. But the servant's evidence showed that Gordon came frequently after Robert had gone to the United Kingdom.

Harrison then turned to other matters. The discovery of the Parks letter showed that "the finger of Providence was visible in this matter" because it led Robert to watch his wife. James Campbell had acted honourably by going to Toronto in the place of his "crushed and prostrated" brother. He had exhibited brotherly affection in agreeing to watch the house and did not deserve to be labelled a "prowler." He did not visit Eliza much because he had business to attend to; he was not like "this idler Gordon." If the jury believed either his or Anderson's testimony the case was made out. Both were honourable and respectable men, and it was not in their interest that scandal should attach to their own families.

Cameron had said that it was "incredible" that Eliza would use such coarse language, but "it was astonishing how swift was the downward progress when a life of vice had once begun." He, Harrison, could say that there were in Toronto young girls in brothels who were accomplished in many respects but who used disgusting language because they associated with low characters. As for Eliza being the daughter of a clergyman, "[i]t was a common saying that the sons and daughters of ministers were in general no better than those of other people." No doubt because they were brought up "under restraint," when they got more freedom "they did not know how to use their liberty." One wonders how Harrison knew such things about Toronto's brothels and wayward ministers' daughters; but that is a question for another time and place.

In conclusion, Harrison asserted that Campbell's and Anderson's evidence "proved the case completely." Had they wished to perjure themselves they could have said that they had seen Eliza and Gordon in the act. If Gordon were innocent he would have said so when confronted by James Campbell, but instead, like the "coward" he was, he had said it was not his fault. When Eliza was also confronted by James Campbell when he returned to the house, she skulked off to bed without offering an explanation. Thus both were guilty, and the one confessed in words and the other by conduct. The only issue was damages. The law required "full compensation." But what did that mean? If Gordon had offered Robert $10,000 "for the use of his wife," what would he have said? Damages for the loss of a cow could be estimated, but not for "the loss of a wife's virtue." Robert was a "broken-hearted" husband who had lost his wife, because even if Eliza returned to the house she was no longer his wife. A "great wrong" had been done to him and the jury should "render such a verdict as would satisfy their consciences and at the same time mark their disapproval of such criminality." They would then be "discharging their duty towards the plaintiff, themselves, and society in general."

As he finished Harrison was confident that he had won. "I felt, as I proceeded with it, that I was carrying the jury with me," he confided to his diary. Some jurors were in tears, and others "nodded assent' to what he was saying."[50] He was right.

Justice Galt's Summing Up and the Verdict

Robert had two advocates speaking for him that day, for Galt made it very clear what he thought in addressing the jury. The case "rested entirely on the weight and credibility they attached to the evidence," he began, and he immediately went on to say what he thought of that evidence. If they did not believe that James Campbell and John Anderson had come into court and "foully and knowingly perjured themselves," a proposition for which there was "no apparent motive," they had to find for Robert. Moreover, if they believed the evidence that Gordon had confessed and said that "he could not help it," that was conclusive. They need not trouble themselves about the exclusionary rules of evidence. Even had Harrison not objected to the attempt to call Eliza and Gordon he would have prevented it as clearly prohibited by statute. As for any small points of difference in the details of Campbell's and Anderson's evidence, he offered an analogy to the Bible: "They were well aware that one of the great arguments for the authenticity of the Holy Scripture was the fact that while seemingly at variance on some details, it all agreed on the great and fundamental points."

With this clear admonition to find for Robert Campbell, the jury retired. Cameron knew what was coming, but he asked for the jury to be recalled so that Galt could tell them that Robert had decided to leave his wife before the fateful evening. Galt did so, and also made it clear that this fact was "merely to operate in the mitigation of damages." For all the one-sidedness of the evidence the jury took about an hour to find for Robert and awarded him the full sum claimed of $3,000. Robert never collected on the debt, unable to satisfy writs of execution against Gordon's property.[51] But that was not important. Robert had a verdict that his wife had committed adultery, a powerful weapon in his forthcoming attempt to persuade a Senate committee of the same thing. In fact, Robert did not petition Parliament for the divorce until more than a year and a half later, probably because he wanted to get all the litigation resolved first. Eliza's suits for defamation against James Campbell and for alimony against Robert, discussed in the next two chapters, were still in progress, and the crim. con. case was not over, because Cameron immediately applied for a new trial, discussed in the final section of this chapter.

Opinion in Whitby

Not surprisingly in the small town of fewer than 7,000 people, the crim. con. trial was, in the words of Yeoman Gibson, a local storekeeper, "the topic of conversation all over the town."[52] According to a Port Perry newspaper it was the talk of the county, and "the interest manifested in it by men, women, children threatens to rival that of the famous Tichborne trial," a reference to a cause célèbre in England of the same time that was reported on at length in the *Whitby Chronicle*, as well as, no doubt, many other newspapers. The Port Perry editorialist had some fun with the story about a prominent businessman in the county town. Gordon had tried, without Robert's consent, to "enter partnership with him in the conjugal part of his business," and Robert had retaliated against the "impudent trespasser."[53] The case was reported on in nearby Oshawa and other towns in Ontario, and, as noted earlier in this chapter, in Montreal, in ways that made it clear that people were familiar with it and took a keen interest. The London *Daily Advertiser* called it "The Whitby Scandal Case," and the *Ottawa Free Press*, in a story a year later on the application for a new trial, discussed below, referred to it as "the Whitby Crim-Con case."[54]

Robert was "triumphant."[55] But despite his win, opinion in Whitby shifted decisively in Eliza's favour. As we saw in chapter 3, from late August attitudes in Whitby were mixed, but in the immediate aftermath of the crim. con. trial that had changed somewhat, as exemplified by an editorial in the *Whitby Chronicle*, published on the same day that the newspaper printed its account of the trial. The overall tone was decidedly non-committal on the surface, but the editorial reminded its readers that the jury had not heard both sides because of the exclusionary rules. That would come "in the other proceedings still pending," a reference to Eliza's defamation suit, which is discussed in the next chapter. In the meantime it was not for journalists to provide *ex cathedra* opinions. What William Higgins could say was that "friends and partisans of the accused ... remain as incredulous and as unconvinced as ever." He also thought that "to assert that Mrs. Campbell is guilty of the vile language and conduct attributed to her is something so incredible, so monstrous, that no one who knows the lady and can speak of her refined manners and gentle nurture [sic] can bring himself to believe." On the other hand the Campbell brothers and John Anderson were respectable citizens whose veracity had never before been doubted. What is significant is what Higgins did not say. The editorial did not refer to partisans of the Campbell brothers, and did not say that it was unbelievable that they could commit perjury in pursuit of a conspiracy to ruin Eliza. It simply said that "it is for the public to draw their own conclusions" from the evidence given in court. As importantly, Higgins thought it was "much to be regretted ... that the state of the law is such as to have precluded" Eliza and Gordon from "obtaining a full hearing." Harrison thought the editorial, which he pasted into his diary, was "non-committal" because local opinion was "divided," but it was not.[56] It was a carefully worded assessment designed to give that impression, while at the same time making a statement in Eliza's favour.

Two weeks after the trial a large advertisement appeared in the *Whitby Chronicle* announcing that the stock that Robert had bought in the UK in the summer had arrived, a collection "larger than ever" and bought at very advantageous prices because Robert "searches more diligently that the buyers from Montreal or Toronto to find the manufacturers who are hard up for money or who ... have an overstock."[57] Yet at the same time that the Campbells were celebrating their win and success in business, there was a strengthening of pro-Eliza sentiment in Whitby. It came about because James Campbell's testimony about his meeting in the street with Gordon after they had left the Campbell house was called into question by some residents of the business district who remembered the incident differently. These people had not been called to give evidence in the crim. con. trial, probably because nobody in Eliza's camp knew exactly what Campbell and Anderson were going to say or that there were people in Whitby who had a different memory of the altercation in the street. But they would be called on Eliza's behalf in the next case, discussed in chapter 6. In the interim they talked about it in the town and Eliza's lawyers heard about this new evidence, directly or indirectly. Now they had evidence that James Campbell's story was untrue in one important particular. One of those people was George Conrad Gross, a hardware merchant who lived above his store in Whitby's business district, in which he owned a large double store and a three-storey block.[58] He had gone to Toronto for the trial and, when he returned, had told people that James Campbell had not told the truth about the time the street altercation had occurred. As a result James Campbell wrote to him saying that if Gross continued with his statements he would sue him for damages.[59] Robert had been disapproved of for his refusal to listen to Eliza's explanations, his adamant insistence that the marriage was over, and his forcible removal of his pregnant wife from the marital home. James Campbell now joined him in the rogues' gallery of public opinion by his "spying" on the fateful night, and his place as the biggest villain of the piece was confirmed by a belief that he had perjured himself.

Robert could do nothing to stem the tide of local gossip and conjecture, but he could sever his relations with the Gordon family. In December 1873 he asked the benchers of the Law Society to relieve him from the bond he had posted as surety for James Keith Gordon. The benchers agreed, requiring Gordon to find another surety.[60]

Eliza was not content just to know that many people in Whitby were on her side. She also tried to get her story in the newspapers, but Higgins would not print a letter she submitted in late October or early November. He refused, he said, with "much reluctance," and despite the fact that her letter was an "affecting … explanation of her unfortunate position." But the editor did not wish to be subjected to a contempt finding by courts "very jealous of their authority," or to become liable for defamation.[61] The tone of Higgins's editorial was apologetic that Eliza could not be given a "hearing before the public," just as he had regretted her inability to testify in the crim. con trial. But he might have had more reason than fear of litigation for refusing to publish. He perhaps simply did not want to overtly take sides, to offend the wealthy and influential Campbell brothers.

Application for a New Trial

Cameron moved almost immediately for a new trial in the crim. con. case, his motion being heard over two sittings a year apart, on 21 November 1873 and 27 November 1874.[62] This was not an appeal. A motion for a new trial asked the court not to give a different verdict but to order a new trial on a variety of grounds, including a procedural error or a verdict contrary to the evidence. The motion for a new trial had long been the principal way of overturning a jury verdict in common law jurisdictions and was available in both civil and criminal cases. As a contemporary article in the *Canada Law Journal* put it, quoting an eighteenth-century decision by Lord Mansfield:

> Trials by jury in civil causes would not subsist now without a power *somewhere* to grant new trials. If an erroneous judgment be given in point of *law*, there are many ways to review it and set it right. Where a court judges in fact upon *depositions in writing*, their sentence or decree may … be reviewed and set right. But a general verdict [by a jury] can *only* be set right by a *new trial*, which is no more than having the cause more deliberately considered by *another* jury, where there is a reasonable doubt that *justice has not been done.*[63]

Cameron moved for a "rule *nisi*" for a new trial in November 1873. A rule *nisi* was a rule or order upon condition that it becomes absolute unless "cause is shown" to the contrary. The rule *nisi* was issued, and confirmed a year later, but the court did not rule on whether it should be made absolute, that is, whether there would be a new trial, for almost two years, until September 1875, an unusually long delay, which is explained below.

The motion was heard in Queen's Bench by three judges – William Henry Draper, chief justice of Ontario, and Joseph Curran Morrison and Adam Wilson, judges of Queen's Bench. Cameron argued three grounds. First, that the verdict was contrary to law and the evidence. One of his arguments to this effect was that Galt's summation for the jury was one-sided, and in that, as we have seen, he was correct. In support of this ground he had Gordon and Eliza swear affidavits before James Gordon giving their version of 26 August. His second argument was that he had fresh evidence. He had an affidavit from Wellington Adams, the young Whitby dentist who had established his practice in the town in 1871 and who had lived on Dundas Street in a third-floor room over the Robert Jameson store (see figure 3.2 above). As noted in chapter 2, he knew Gordon and had been a visitor at the Campbell home with other young people. He swore that he had heard the conversation between Gordon and James Campbell in the street in the small hours of the morning. He said it took place rather earlier than the 3 a.m. claimed by Campbell, and that far from admitting the act, Gordon had denied it and threatened James Campbell with violence if he repeated the accusation. Adams came forward when he read the report of the crim. con. trial in the newspaper and concluded that James Campbell had committed perjury.[64]

Cameron's third argument, the least important of the three and one that did not go to the finding that Eliza had committed adultery, was that the damage award was excessive. Robert had told his brother to watch the house, and James Campbell had spent hours listening when he could at any time have prevented what happened. This should reduce the damages, Cameron argued. All we know of Harrison's arguments on the other side is that he questioned the credibility of Eliza's and Gordon's affidavit evidence, submitting at least one affidavit of his own, from James Fraser, who worked for the Campbells as a salesman and lived above their store. He had heard a row in the street and James Campbell come into the store at around 3 a.m. He thus refuted Gordon's claim of having left Eliza much earlier.[65]

No decision was given until September 1875. The reason for the delay was likely that the judges were waiting for the results of two other cases involving the Campbell marriage breakdown, the defamation and alimony cases, discussed in the next two chapters. The *Campbell v. Gordon* crim. con. case was mentioned in Chancery chambers proceedings on 2 March 1875, in what context is unclear. But what matters is that the case having been raised, the (unnamed) presiding judge said that as two other trials had taken place arising out of the same events, "the Court preferred to wait until the judgment in those cases was given."[66] Eliza won the defamation case in March 1874, but lost the alimony case when judgment was rendered in mid-September 1875. The defendant in the defamation case, James Campbell, immediately applied for a new trial, and was granted one in December 1875. Two days after the judgment in the alimony case was issued Justices Morrison and Wilson (Draper's name is not mentioned) denied the application for a new trial in the crim. con. case, without costs, but did reduce the damages to $1,500.[67] The point is that seven judges, six who decided the two new trial motions and one who decided the alimony case, all of whom were based in Osgoode Hall, heard three cases, all turning on one factual question, likely discussed the cases with each other, and then issued three judgments in fairly short order having sat on them for some time. The three judgments, one refusing a new trial in the crim. con. case, one allowing the motion for a new trial in the defamation case, and one rejecting Eliza's application for alimony, all went against Eliza by deciding, in effect, that she had committed adultery with Gordon.

6

The Campbells Go to Court II: Eliza Campbell (Robert Campbell *et ux*) v. James Campbell for Defamation, 1874

Introduction

The second lawsuit resulting from the breakdown of the Campbell marriage was, like the crim. con. case, started in September 1873, at about the same time that Robert sued Gordon and before Eliza had been ejected from the family home.[1] Eliza accused James Campbell of defamation. The case was not heard in Whitby but in Toronto, for presumably the same reason that the crim. con. case had been tried in the provincial capital. Eliza was again represented by Matthew Cameron and James by Robert Harrison. There were two counts: that James Campbell had slandered Eliza by saying that she "had had criminal intercourse" with Gordon, and that he had told various persons that Eliza was not to be provided with any goods because she was "under a criminal charge" and as a result Robert would not be responsible for her debts. As a result of the latter statement, people who heard what he said assumed that Eliza had committed a criminal offence for which she would be prosecuted. The statements were made to shopkeepers and other people in Whitby. At common law Robert was responsible for supporting Eliza, and it was common practice for married women to get household goods on credit and for the husband to pay the account. A husband who no longer wished to do so was obliged to advertise the fact, either through local newspapers or in person.[2] A husband could only do this if his wife had broken her marriage vows, by deserting him or by, as in this case, allegedly committing adultery. I have not been able to find any such advertisement in either Whitby newspaper, but that was not important in the case. James Campbell did not defend the case on the basis that the accusation had not been spoken or written. He defended on the ground that the statements he made about Eliza's adultery were true.

As a result of James Campbell's statements Eliza, in the words of her pleading, had been "greatly injured in her good name, fame, and reputation, and brought into public scandal and disgrace." She had also been "shunned and avoided by divers persons and otherwise injured," and "deprived of the society of friends … who now refuse to associate with her." As we saw in the previous chapter, that was not altogether true; some people had come down on her side. She had also been forced to support herself and claimed $10,000 in damages.[3] George Gordon also filed suit against James Campbell for defamation, although the case seems to have gone nowhere.[4] The plaintiff in the case against James Campbell, albeit only nominally, was Robert. In 1873 a married woman had the right to hold her "separate property" free from the liabilities of her husband, but had only limited rights to launch legal actions in her own right. She could sue to recover property that was her "separate property," and could be sued "in respect of any of her separate debts, engagements, contracts or torts." But fully equal civil status was not conferred on her until 1884.[5] Thus the style of cause was *Campbell et ux v. Campbell*, with the first-mentioned Campbell being Robert, and *et ux* meaning "and wife."

Cameron must have seen the defamation suit as a way to effectively relitigate the central factual issue in the crim. con. case, the adultery, this time with Eliza and Gordon being competent witnesses, because this was not an action "instituted in consequence of adultery," in the words of the statute of 1869 discussed in chapter 5. It was, to refigure the statutory language, an action "instituted in consequence of defamation." Cameron knew that the best defence to defamation was to prove that the words spoken were true, and Harrison would have to defend on that basis. As a leading English text cited in reported defamation cases in Ontario at this time stated, "it is now perfectly well settled, … that the truth of defamatory matter is a bar to an action."[6] Thus the case would turn on whether the jury believed that intercourse had taken place, the same factual issue as the crim. con. case. The reader familiar with recent events will note the similarity to the defamation suit launched by E. Jean Carroll against Donald Trump. At the time she was unable to prosecute him for sexual assault because the limitation period had expired, so she simply publicly accused him. He responded by calling her a liar (and of course other things, this is Donald Trump we are talking about) and she sued him for defamation. I am not the only person to make a joke about this case. The editorialist in the *North Ontario Observer* who had employed the "partnership" metaphor in commenting on the crim. con. case continued with it. Eliza launched the suit because she insisted that "Gordon never took an active part in running the conjugal department of R. Campbell's business"; thus Eliza "challenged Mr. J. Campbell to a legal duel."[7]

Pre-Trial Motions

Harrison tried to have the suit thrown out in early October 1873, filing a motion before Robert Gladstone Dalton, Q.C., master, to set aside Eliza's writ because it had been issued without Robert's leave.[8] James Campbell was represented on this motion by one of Harrison's partners, Featherston Osler. The Oslers were a prominent and very successful Toronto Anglican family, Featherston's brothers being Britton Bath Osler, arguably the foremost trial lawyer of his time and the man chosen as the lead prosecutor of Louis Riel; Sir Edmund Boyd Osler, financier and later Conservative MP for Toronto West; and Sir William Osler, a leader of the medical profession and later co-founder of the Johns Hopkins Hospital. Featherston Osler had been called to the bar in 1860 and practised for some years with future judges Thomas and Charles Moss. In 1879 he was appointed to Common Pleas, and in 1883 was promoted to the Court of Appeal.[9] Eliza was represented by Newman Hoyles, who was very much a junior lawyer at the time. From a wealthy Newfoundland family and educated at Upper Canada College, King's College in Windsor, Nova Scotia, and Trinity College Cambridge, he was newly called to the bar, in 1872. Hoyles later became a prominent lawyer, in partnership with, among others, a group of similar young men who later all became leading lights in the profession and who practised as the firm of Bethune, Osler, and Moss, with Hoyles later joining the partnership. They included James Bethune, Q.C., a leading member of the Toronto bar in the 1870s and 1880s, who was formerly in partnership Edward Blake and James Kirkpatrick Kerr and the Liberal MPP for Stormont. He died at the age of 44 in 1884. The other partners were Charles Moss, who was appointed to the Court of Appeal in 1897 directly from the bar, and William Glenholme Falconbridge, appointed to the Queen's Bench Division of the High Court in 1887. In 1894 Hoyles became the head of the Law Society's law school at Osgoode Hall.[10]

Osler argued that Eliza's case should be dismissed with costs to the Campbell brothers because Robert had not agreed to the suit being filed. Hoyles responded by asserting that the action could proceed because Eliza had given her assent to it doing so, and also offered to indemnify Robert against any costs for which he might be found liable should the suit go in James's favour. Dalton reserved judgment, and the following day found for Eliza.[11] In February 1874 Cameron filed his own motion,

Figure 6.1. Judge John Hawkins Hagarty
Source: Dictionary of Canadian Biography Online

applying to change the venue from Toronto to Ontario County, that is, Whitby, obviously because he believed that a Whitby jury would be much more favourable to his case. But Osler opposed, arguing that a fair trial could not be had in Whitby. Given the way opinion there had coalesced in favour of Eliza after the revelations that James Campbell may have lied in the crim. con case, he was surely right about that. The attempt failed.[12]

The defamation case was heard in Toronto on 26 and 27 March 1874, before John Hawkins Hagarty, chief justice of Common Pleas, and a jury. Hagarty was one of the leaders of Toronto's Anglican Irish community, having been educated at Trinity College, Dublin, before emigrating to Upper Canada in 1834. After apprenticeship he was called to the bar in 1840 and built a very successful practice while also teaching law at Trinity College. He was appointed a puisne judge of Common Pleas in 1856, moved to Queen's Bench for six years, and then was made chief justice of Common Pleas in 1868. He served for a decade in that capacity before moving back to

Queen's Bench as chief justice. When he retired in 1897 as the president of the Court of Appeal and chief justice of Ontario he had been on the bench for 41 years.[13]

We have three lengthy newspaper reports of the trial – from the *Globe*, the Toronto *Mail*, and the *Whitby Chronicle* – and notes of the evidence given made by Hagarty, although those notes do not add anything to the newspaper reports.[14] The *Chronicle* story was rather longer than that in either of the Toronto newspapers, providing a more detailed account of the lawyers' speeches, especially Cameron's. Unlike most other newspaper reports of cases used in this book it also sometimes printed the questions and answers rather than simply reproduce a narrative summary of the testimony. The account which follows is an amalgam of the three newspapers' reports, with quotations from the *Whitby Chronicle* unless specifically referenced otherwise. The *Globe* story was headlined simply "DEFAMATION"; the *Mail* led with "The Whitby Slander Case"; and the *Whitby Chronicle* with "THE GREAT SLANDER CASE." All three newspapers started their stories with dramatic opening sentences, the *Mail* and the *Chronicle* referring to "the great Whitby slander case of *Campbell v. Campbell*," and the *Globe* stating that its readers would remember "an exciting trial that took place at the Toronto Assizes in October last," the crim. con. case. The *Globe* also reminded its readers of the "sensation" created by that case, which was now "renewed" by the defamation suit. The Campbell case was also briefly reported on in the Toronto newspaper *The Union*, in other Ontario newspapers and, the first time that the Campbells' story was reported on outside Ontario, by the Montreal press.[15]

As with the crim. con. case, every seat in the courtroom was filled throughout the two days of trial, but when Eliza went into the witness box in the afternoon of the first day, and was followed by George Gordon, "the crowd far exceeded the designs of the architect of our Courthouse."[16] Both parties successfully challenged some of the jurors. We do not know who was challenged or why, but it could not have involved many jurors because only three peremptory challenges were allowed in civil cases. For this trial we know who the jurymen were, their names, occupations, and residences being listed in one of the Toronto newspapers. They were all upper working-class or lower middle-class men, with only two of them, John Brewer, a foreman who lived on Simcoe Street, and William Walsh, a wood dealer from Queen Street, being residents of the city of Toronto itself. The other ten were from other parts of York County – three from King, two from York, two from Markham, and one each from North Gwillimbury, Etobicoke, and Vaughan. Two were farmers, one was a merchant, and five were described as yeoman, a catch-all term for a person above the status of labourer but below that of an independent professional or farmer.

Matthew Cameron's Opening Address

Matthew Crooks Cameron's opening statement first explained that the suit had been brought by Eliza and the fact that it named Robert as the plaintiff was a formality. Cameron then enumerated the "very grave injuries" that Eliza had suffered from the defamation. She had been "deprived of the association and protection of her husband; her children had been wrested from her; she had been turned out of house and home; and finally had lost name and reputation, and everything that was dear to a woman, in consequence of the slanders which ... were made by the defendant against the woman whom it should have been his duty to protect." Cameron then reviewed the Byrne family history, stressing that they "were held in a very high estimation in the community," and that "there never was the slightest intimation or breath of suspicion uttered against" Eliza.

This was just a warm-up for Cameron to turn his ample rhetorical guns on the Campbell brothers as the villains of the piece, especially James. Robert had been away in the UK, and while he was away Eliza and James Campbell had hardly seen or spoken to each other. The purpose of this was no doubt to plant in the jury's mind the idea that James Campbell did not like his sister-in-law. Eliza knew this was so, but there had been "no overt act" to show the community that "envy, hatred, or uncharitableness existed in his heart towards his brother's wife." Hatred was a strong word, and no doubt Cameron chose it carefully to impress the jury. Cameron then recounted Robert's return to Whitby in August and immediately cast doubt on the authenticity of the letter from Parks. Parks had apparently written Eliza care of the firm in order that it would "come into the possession" of the Campbell brothers before it reached Eliza. But why would a letter that actually was from Parks be sent to the Campbell store unless the purpose of doing so was to have Robert read it? Thus it likely did not come from Parks. Cameron did not discuss the letter's contents more than saying that "there was nothing in it whatever that would indicate there had been any criminal conduct" on Eliza's part. But it did give James Campbell, on whom Cameron turned all his rhetorical accusatory guns, a chance of "venting his ill-feeling" against Eliza to Robert, to "poison" Robert's mind.[17] In his turn Robert, without saying anything to Eliza about why, took the children to Southampton, a "pre-concerted design" to take her children from her.

Cameron then described James Campbell's and Anderson's activities on the evening of 26 August, in the most unflattering terms possible, repeating some of what he had said in the crim. con. trial. James Campbell "made himself … a spy," and the two of them "prowled about the house like thieves in the dark." They claimed that they "heard language of so disgusting a nature that one would have supposed it could have proceeded only from a common prostitute," but in fact they were supposedly the words of "a lady, the daughter of a clergyman, who could scarcely be acquainted with such language." James Campbell had then fabricated a 3 a.m. conversation in the street between himself and Gordon in which Gordon had admitted the sexual tryst; this was "a tissue of falsehoods." It was true that they had met in the street, but rather than admitting anything Gordon had denied it and said he would "thrash" Campbell and Anderson if they repeated their accusations. And yet "these men had sworn in a Court of Justice" that Gordon had confessed.

Far from there being anything to confess to, Eliza, who was fond of music, had played music for Gordon and "nothing improper occurred between them." Yet James Campbell had told Robert and others his false story, and dissuaded Robert from communicating with Eliza. If the story he told were true, what kind of a man would not intervene to protect his brother's honour? If he thought beforehand that something was likely to happen, he should have told Eliza that she should not be entertaining a young man during Robert's absence. If he really had heard the things he claimed to have heard, he should have gone into the house and interrupted them, but instead he chose to "listen[ed] patiently to a man soliciting his brother's wife, time after time." This was not the act of a brother but of "a viper trying to destroy this woman's happiness." Cameron finished with a reference to the evidentiary problems of the crim. con. trial. Eliza wanted an opportunity of confronting her "traducers" in court, to "declare in the witness box that the charge was untrue." When she did so the jury would believe her and believe also that "a conspiracy had been formed against his client for the purpose of destroying her reputation."

The Witnesses for James Campbell

Harrison chose not to make an opening statement, and as the plaintiff Eliza put her case on first. But this part of the trial was short-lived. Cameron began with witnesses to prove that the defamatory words had been spoken. His first witness was James A. Campbell of Whitby, not a member of the Campbell family but the former editor of the *Whitby*

Gazette. He had had a conversation with James Campbell after the JPs' hearing on Robert's alleged assault, and James had told him that Eliza was enceinte. James also said that Robert had not co-habited with Eliza for more than nine months. By "co-habited," James must have meant "not slept with," because they had cohabited for the first half of 1873, and James followed this statement by saying he therefore "suspected something" because of the pregnancy. That is, he suspected that the father of the child was not Robert. In addition, James "spoke of Gordon in connection with the matter," although the newspaperman could not remember exactly what was said. Campbell may or may not have been cross-examined,[18] but if he was it was short. Harrison, after conferring with his client, announced that he was admitting that the defamatory statements had been made, and was pleading justification. In the circumstances there was no point in Cameron calling more witnesses on the question of whether the words had been said, and the court then allowed Harrison to call defence witnesses to prove the truth of the words said.

Harrison called seven witnesses – John Anderson, James Campbell, the Newsom sisters, George Cameron, Charles Scott and William Fagan, who had all testified at the crim. con. trial – and Robert Campbell, who had not. He began with Robert, perhaps surprisingly because Robert was nominally the plaintiff and, in any event, could not say anything about the night of 26 August. Harrison began by asking him about his marriage, which may have been a mistake, because although Robert knew he had been married in April 1862 he was imprecise about his children; he and Eliza had "several" children, the last one born before the separation "about six years ago." These answers were a clear if subtle indication that Robert's interests were in his business not his family; how many people when asked about their children say they have "several" of them, can provide only an approximate birth date for one, and do not acknowledge the existence of another? Moving to his relationship with Eliza, he said they "lived happily" until about a year ago, the spring of 1873. In early 1873 Parks and Eliza began a correspondence. Then came some visits from Gordon. Despite this recitation of apparent suitors, Robert was certain that Eliza had not transgressed before he went to the United Kingdom. He then told of the discovery of the letter in his office, and it was read out in court, as were the various writings found in Eliza's secretaire. The rest of his evidence in chief reviewed his decision to take the children to Saugeen and his return to Whitby after receiving the telegram from James. This was all that Robert could testify about.

Cameron's cross-examination dealt with every aspect of Robert's testimony, seeking throughout to show that his rapidly arrived at conclusions were misguided. Did Robert know that Eliza read a great deal and noted down passages from books? Robert could not say. Did he know that she often wrote down things on scraps of paper? Robert did not know, nor did he know that she intended writing a book. Indeed on this topic he showed his general inattention to her by adding that he "paid no particular attention to her writings and readings." Moving on to her alleged interest in young men, Cameron got Robert to admit that he had said nothing to her about Pugsden on board ship, only after landing, "after all danger had passed." Robert added that the problem was that she was with Pugsden all the time, so that "I could not get a word from her." This answer drew laughter from the crowded courtroom. But Robert surely was not laughing when Cameron got him to admit that he knew Pugsden well and was a friend of his. Cameron continued with a question that was not a question, but a statement that allowed him to cast Robert as overly jealous and influenced by James: "And yet it was because your wife walked and talked with him [that] you found fault with her! I don't wonder at your believing all that your brother told you about your wife under these circumstances!"

Cameron's principal line of questioning had to be about Gordon, specifically about the long relationship between the Campbells, the Byrnes, and the Gordons, and the fact that Gordon and Eliza were childhood friends. He knew there was evidence aplenty that Gordon had visited the house, and stayed late. This had to be made to seem the innocent result of a long acquaintance. His first question to Robert was about how long he had known Gordon, and Robert not only said it was 28 years but also that he knew Gordon's lawyer brother James, and had been "security" for him. Cameron drove the point home, confirming that Robert was referring to the $500 bond he had signed to allow James Gordon to enrol in the Law Society. Cameron followed this with questions about Gordon's visits to the house, and Robert admitted that there was nothing wrong with them, that there was "no reason why his wife should shut the door in his [Gordon'] face." Indeed, sociable fellow that he was, Robert "had not an aversion to all mankind coming to the house" and had never complained about anybody else doing so. But Robert also got into his answer that Gordon had never been invited by him to come to the house alone. Cameron then moved to the evening when Gordon had called at teatime, and asked why Robert had characterized his being shown into the parlour as Eliza acting imprudently? There was no reply. Cameron must have sensed he was doing well on this point, so he asked the same question again in a different way: "You think she acted wrong because a young man you and she had known from boyhood comes to your house to spend the evening, and she entertains him?" Again, no reply. Cameron kept on – "Was he not a young man of respectability?" – but this time Robert managed some pushback. He did not think so, "at least not now." Cameron's final question about Gordon was why had he stayed that evening until Robert returned from his store; would he not have left earlier if there had been something going on? Robert either answered obliquely or Cameron asked further questions about subsequent visits; Robert had seen Gordon on other occasions when he visited, but he "never looked at me in the face after that time."

Cameron next led Robert through the few days after his return from the UK, expressing feigned surprise that, having found the letter at his store, Robert immediately sent James to Toronto for a detective, and said not a word to Eliza. Robert's reply was that he knew the letter was from Parks because he had a sample of his handwriting to compare it to. Cameron's further questions elicited Robert's almost immediate decision to separate and his duplicity in saying nothing to Eliza about the letter, her other writings he had found, or the real reason he was taking the children away. He had "made up his mind that he would part from her without getting any explanation," and the only person he told was his brother. Cameron rephrased this bluntly: "You wanted to get rid of your wife?" One thing Cameron did not do was ask about where the various things Eliza had written down were copied from. Had he done so he would have made Robert look foolish for not knowing they were from literary works and precipitate for jumping to conclusions. It is possible that Eliza had not told him.

Cameron came back to Gordon, asking Robert to confirm that James had heard from a woman that Gordon had been going to his house. Whether Cameron meant Mary Jameson or James Campbell's wife Rebecca, to whom Jameson had given the information, Robert objected to the word "woman," and said the information came from a lady. This led to some repartee between counsel. Cameron said, "A woman sometimes embraces a lady" and Harrison muttered sotto voce "And a man sometimes embraces a woman." Much of the rest of Cameron's cross-examination took Robert through his journey to Southampton and return, his meetings with Eliza's family, and, probably most important as far as Cameron was concerned, his refusal to see Eliza or to answer her letters.

Cameron ended with questions about Robert denying Eliza credit and throwing her out of the house. Presumably in an effort to show that Robert was a wealthy man who could afford to support his wife, he then pressed him on his income and net worth, but Robert not only would not answer, he also "appealed to the protection of the court" to affirm that he did not have to. All he would say was that he was in business and owned his house and other real estate in Whitby. It was not an "extensive" business, and rumours that he was worth $75,000 were untrue. Cameron got him to say that he knew that Eliza would be entitled to a dower right in his real estate "unless it was proved that she had misconducted herself." As discussed in chapter 13, Robert did later clandestinely have an amendment made to the province's *Dower Act* that enabled him to try to take away Eliza's dower right.

Harrison's re-examination was very brief. He asked only one substantive question: Was Gordon a frequent visitor to the house before Robert went to the UK? Robert said he was not, making the point that Gordon's visits increased considerably when he was absent.

The next witness was Martha Newsom, who had returned to Robert's service and moved back into the Campbell home after the crim. con. trial. She gave very similar testimony to what she had said at that trial, but with some additions. She did say that Eliza had told her at one point that Gordon "never knew when to go away," which could not have pleased Harrison because it made Eliza a less willing participant in the late-night visits. Newsom talked about her suspicion on one occasion that the two had been drinking wine, about the pinning of the curtains to keep them closed, and about finding Eliza's boots in the parlour, which she attributed to her not wanting to make a noise when she did go upstairs. Cameron's cross-examination began with asking why her memory had "brightened a good deal," a reference to the fact that she had not said what she now said about the curtains and the boots in the crim. con. trial. Newsom said that she had not referred to them because she "did not think it of any consequence." That was a weak response, raising the question of why she now thought they were. Cameron then asked her about other young men who visited, and she gave the names of local dentist Wellington Adams, and a John Mitchell, the former having come with Gordon on just one occasion. This was presumably meant to make the point that Eliza entertained a variety of people, but its effect was undermined by Newsom also saying that while other gentlemen called, they did not spend time alone with Eliza. Cameron then asked her what time she went to bed, and when she said she did not go early, he chafed her about having her beau visit and keeping her up late. Newsom probably got a little testy about this, retorting that one Bob Harding used to visit the house with her sister, not to see her, and nothing improper took place. Cameron got a laugh from the spectators when he responded: "There was nothing improper in what was done by the maid in the kitchen, but when done by the lady in the parlour it was improper."

Cameron finished with two more lines of questioning. First, he asked Newsom where she lived, and she said she had been living at the Campbell home, as servant to Robert, since after the crim. con. trial. It was from speaking with him that she "might have learned from him that the evidence she had just given was important." Thus Cameron secured an admission that she had in some way been coached by Robert, even if it was coaching that brought on a genuine recollection about the pinned curtains and the boots in the parlour. Second, he returned to Harding, asking if she recalled telling Bethiah Ham and James Byrne that Robert had threatened to "expose you and Bob Harding." The problem with this question, of course, was that Newsom had an effective rejoinder, reminding Cameron that Harding had not come to see her but her sister Jane.

Newsom was followed on the witness stand by John Anderson, but the report of his testimony was short because, as with the crim. con. trial, the newspapers did not print the salacious details. Anderson described his watching and listening with Campbell, according to the *Whitby Chronicle*, "detailing at length the criminal conduct alleged to have been witnessed by him, and also the disgusting language which he said he had heard." The *Globe* was similarly reticent, stating that the alleged conversations between Eliza and Gordon "were unfit for publication."[19] Anderson also described the meeting in the street afterwards, stating that when he was accused of seducing Eliza, Gordon had said "it was not my fault" and had not denied the accusation of adultery.

Cameron's cross-examination concentrated on three things – the relationship between Eliza and the James Campbell and John Anderson families, the focus of Robert's initial suspicions, and Anderson's written account of the evening of 26 August. On the first issue Cameron had Anderson admit that he was an infrequent visitor at the Campbell house, and that there was "no great intimacy" between Eliza and James Campbell's wife Rebecca. On the second issue Anderson stated that when Robert had told him about his problems on the evening before he went to Southampton, he had suspected someone who did not live in Whitby (obviously Parks) and had not mentioned Gordon. Anderson did not know anything about Gordon being suspected until James Campbell asked him to go with him to watch the house.

The third issue was what Anderson had written down the weekend after the 26th of August. His statement must have been produced in court and, as described in the previous chapter, Anderson had originally written that James Campbell had accused Gordon of "attempt[ing] to seduce" Eliza, "if you have not already done so." Those words were later crossed out and instead Anderson had James Campbell saying, "You have been in my brother's house from nine to three o'clock, and have had criminal conversation with my brother's wife." There is obviously a significant difference between the two in the use of the word "attempted" in the original version. There is perhaps an equally significant difference between "seduce" and "criminal conversation." "Seduce" was a word that everybody would understand as referring to sexual intercourse; "criminal conversation" was a legal term for an action that could be taken following that intercourse. Anderson might have altered his memorandum after Robert had seen Harrison and heard about the action for crim. con. The newspaper reports do not say what, if anything, Cameron said about these alterations, but he must surely have said something. He had exposed for the jury that Anderson had changed his written statement when told by someone that he needed to do so to make it consistent with James Campbell's evidence and with the legal action taken by Robert.

James Campbell was the next witness, but while the newspapers reported that he was examined and cross-examined at "considerable length" (the *Globe*) and "much length" (the *Whitby Chronicle*), few details of his examination in chief were reported by any newspaper. His evidence was "substantially the same" as Anderson's and the same "as given on the former trial." The only new thing he said on direct examination was that Eliza had once said, presumably to him, that Robert "had married her for her beauty, and that she had married him for his money." He was "severely cross-examined" by Cameron about his story of the night of the 26th, but all we know about the cross-examination was that Cameron must have asked him when he wrote his statement of the evening's events, to which he replied that he had done so shortly after he got up the following morning, at 7 a.m., and that he had written the statement twice, first in pencil and then in ink.

The next witness was Jane Newsom. The newspaper accounts of her testimony were very different. The *Globe* had her saying that Gordon had been at the house alone with Eliza on several occasions during the short period between when she started as a live-in servant on 15 August and the 26th, and that he had stayed until 3 a.m. on the 26th. The *Whitby Chronicle* reported none of the testimony about Gordon's visits before the 26th, and said that Newsom stated that she had "either dreamt or heard" that Gordon left at 3 a.m. It also reported Newsom saying that she had had a conversation with Eliza "the day after the difficulty" – Wednesday, 27 August – in which the latter said that "she and Mr. Campbell could scarcely ever live together again." Cameron's cross-examination was reported as asking only one substantive question – whether the parlour doors were left open while Eliza and Gordon were in the room. Newsom said they were. The final witnesses for the defence were the men who had told the Campbells in August that they had seen Eliza and Gordon walking together. They said what has been recounted in chapter 5, and there is no report of any cross-examination.

The Witnesses for Eliza Campbell

Although Eliza was the plaintiff, the fact that James Campbell had not contested that the words were spoken and instead moved immediately to justifying them as true meant that she presented the bulk of her evidence second. Her witnesses were there to show that the defamatory words were untrue, that there had been no adultery. She herself was the first witness, testifying as she had not been able to do in the crim. con. case. Cameron led her through her childhood friendship with Gordon, his visits with her family, and her version of the night of 26 August. She denied any intimacy and said Gordon left between 1 and 2 a.m. She admitted that Gordon had been at the house five or six times during Robert's absence, but she saw nothing wrong with that because she always thought Robert and George Gordon were friendly. Cameron also had her talk about her limited relationship with her brother-in-law and his wife; James had only visited her once, and that was to make a complaint about her children.

Harrison's cross-examination began with questions about Eliza's relationship with James Campbell. She said she had had a "misunderstanding" with him over "profane language" directed towards Robert about nine years previously, when she and Robert had been temporarily residing at James's house while theirs was being renovated.[20] They had another disagreement six months later when she and James's sister Elizabeth had had words, and James called upon her to say that "he would not have any more of her d– nonsense." They had another disagreement in the late winter of 1872–73. Harrison may have been trying to elicit the fact that this was a flimsy basis for her claim that James had enough animosity towards her to want to ruin her marriage and reputation and to perjure himself to do so. He also asked about her alleged flirting with Pugsden. Eliza said this was the first argument she and Robert had had, and she did not understand its cause. She had been showing Robert affection, and he accused her of thinking more of Pugsden than of him. She had only met Pugsden the one time, and her only communication with him after the voyage had been a letter he sent giving his compliments to them both.

Harrison then moved to more dangerous ground for Eliza – the Parks correspondence. Very little had been said about this at the crim. con. trial, and we must assume that Harrison devoted time to it on this occasion as a way to paint Eliza as a loose woman, one prone to infidelity even if she was not accused of it with Parks. She said she had met Parks in the fall of 1872, and had corresponded with him since then. She was "not ashamed" of that correspondence, though she "regretted" it because it had "caused so much trouble" between her and her husband, who was "inclined to be jealous." At this point the *Whitby Chronicle* report changed from narrative to question and answer. Why did she give her husband cause to be jealous by corresponding with a young man about whom she knew nothing? It was a piece of thoughtlessness on her part. There followed questions and answers about the pieces of writing found in her secretaire. Were they in her handwriting? Yes. Was she going to write a book? I think I was. What was the subject? I don't know. I collected a great many expressions of thought. Harrison then asked her if her views were "liberal in matters of thought." They were "in church matters." Note that, as with Cameron's cross-examination of Robert about Eliza's habit of writing her thoughts down, there was nothing about where these writings came from. For some reason Eliza and Cameron must have decided not to provide this evidence, or perhaps Eliza still had not told Cameron.

At this point Harrison gave her a copy of the letter signed "book-keeper," which had been found in her drawer, and asked if it was something she wrote for a book? It might have been a letter she intended to send to Parks; she was not in the habit of keeping copies of her letters. Did she send the letter to Parks? No. Did she intend to send it to him? She could not say. She had a habit of writing her thoughts on scraps of paper and afterwards changing her mind. What does "book-keeper" mean? She did not know, she supposed she was writing "thoughtlessly." Harrison read out the sentence from the letter that said the writer had been remiss in answering "your letters," and asked Eliza what letters they were? Eliza said she "may have meant Parks's letters." He asked her what she meant by writing that "incognito came safely to hand." Eliza said, "It may have been a letter I received from Mr. Parks." Did he address you as "Dear Maria"? No, "he called me Marie, that is my second name and the name I used to sign letters to him."

Harrison was relentless:

Q. You thank him in this scrap for the interesting letter. Did you get many interesting letters?
A. Sometimes.
Q. What does "a great deal might have been thought, but I've never heard anything of the past?"
A. I don't know. Perhaps I referred to my walks. I don't know of anything improper.

Q. Whom do you mean by the "Guardian" in this letter?
A. My husband. I used to term him my guardian and guide.
Q. What journey of your guardian do you refer to here.
A. I suppose his trip to the old country.
Q. Why do you assure him on your honour that no one else had given you a walk after service. Was he jealous?
A. I don't know. I never sent this letter.
Q. Well, you say further on, you don't forget so easily those whom you like.
A. He always treated me in a gentlemanlike manner and therefore I liked him.

Harrison then switched to questions about one of the "scraps" found in her drawer.

Q. What do you mean by "I don't know whether I shall stop here or stay?
A. Perhaps it was part of the romance.
Q. Oh! then it was a romance you were going to write?
A. Just for my own amusement.

Harrison returned briefly to the writings in general.

Q. And you intended to make these young men leading characters in your romance? Was this second scrap part of the romance?
A. Yes. It was written two or three years ago.

The questions then focused on another piece of writing found in Eliza's drawer, the very romantic paragraph:

Q. What does this mean, "our last fond meeting so soft with bliss?"
A. I don't know for what it is intended.
Q. On your oath did you not intend to write this letter to the young man at Concord?
A. No. It was a letter to be written by the heroine of the romance I intended to compose.
Q. Where was your hero to live, in Concord?
No answer.

Then the questions went back to the letter from Concord.

Q. Do you know this writing?
A. It looks like that of Mr. Parks.

Q. Did he generally address you as "Dear Marie?"
A. He addressed me that way sometimes.

All in all Eliza did not respond well to these questions. Her answers were sometimes evasive, sometimes entirely unpersuasive, and sometimes she did not answer. One wonders why she and Cameron, or one of them, did not simply admit the letter received from Parks and explain the origins of other things she had written down. There was no allegation that she had committed adultery with Parks, and, as we shall see in both this case and later before the Senate, nobody was persuaded that she had not had a flirtatious correspondence with him, which was perhaps foolish but had nothing to do with the alleged adultery with Gordon.

From this point the *Whitby Chronicle* report reverted to the standard narrative format. When asked about the argument following Gordon coming to the house in the spring of 1873 when Robert and the family were at tea, Eliza could not remember the incident. She denied telling Martha Newsom that she thought Gordon "a fine young man"; she was not in the habit of talking to her servants. She also talked about Gordon's visits while Robert was away, depicting them as unplanned – she met him on the street and he came in for the evening – and not always spent in the parlour – one evening they sat for an hour in the summer house, with the children; on another they were in the drawing room. On yet another occasion, in August, Gordon had walked from her house with her unmarried sister Annie and her niece. She also insisted that her evenings with Gordon at her house were innocent, spent playing music and singing. She denied pinning the curtains together, or putting footstools on them to hold them down, or on any occasion leaving her boots in the parlour. Gordon was never in the house past midnight, except for the night of 26 August, when he left at 1:15 a.m., and she was in bed by 2. She had been aware that someone was moving quietly around outside on the night of the 26th into the 27th. She thought it was probably James Campbell, who had been "prowling about nearly two months nearly every night." She denied that she went for walks with Gordon by appointment, rather their meetings were unplanned. She denied much else – Gordon putting his arm around her, her promising not to tell Robert anything, going for drives with Gordon while Robert was away. She also recounted that one of the topics of conversation on the night of the 26th was about the army and the navy. Cameron re-examined Eliza when Harrison had finished, but mainly to elicit denials on small points. The most important thing she said was that when she had said that she was "liberal in church matters," she had meant that she preferred a "plain" church service.

Eliza was succeeded on the witness stand by George Gordon. He told the same story of 26 August that Eliza had. He had left between 1:15 a.m. and 1:30 a.m., well before 3 because his walk home was three kilometres (two miles), and he got home at 2:30 a.m. There was "no criminal intercourse between him and Mrs. Campbell that night or at any other time." On his way home he saw James Campbell and Anderson on the street corner near Lawler's store. They "made for him on the run." James Campbell called him "a black-hearted villain," and said: "You have been trying to seduce my brother's wife, if you have not done so already." Gordon told Campbell he was a "d– liar." He had not admitted what he was accused of, nor did he say that it was not his fault. Thereafter the three of them walked down the street together until they got to the Campbells' store, where James Campbell said: "I will make it hot for you in the morning"; and Gordon replied: "If you come out on the sidewalk, I will make it hot for you." Campbell's rejoinder was: "The morning is time enough for you, my boy; I will attend to you in the morning." Cameron moved his witness to other matters to elicit a series of denials. He had called at the Campbell house five or six times while Robert was in the United Kingdom but never stayed later than midnight before 26 August. He had walked with Eliza on the street a few times, but never alone and never with his arm around her. He knew George Cameron, one of Harrison's witnesses, but "did not believe he bore a first-class character." He denied taking any "improper liberties" with Eliza, and said she never used "improper language."

Harrison cross-examined Gordon, and at this point in its report the *Whitby Chronicle* reverted to the question-and-answer format. I have not reproduced all the questions and answers, but the salient ones are as follows:

Q. Did you ever hear Mrs. Campbell speak of her husband as "the guardian?"
A. No.
Q. Why did you stop up so late?
A. It is not unusual.
Q. What, with another man's wife?
A. I did not say that. …
Q. Did you look at your watch [when you left the house]?
A. Yes; it was half-past one by my watch.
Q. You have, I believe, made an affidavit for a new trial of the suit brought against you last fall by Mr. Robert Campbell for the seduction of his wife, in which damages were returned against you for $3,000?

A. Yes.
Q. What time did you state in the affidavit you left Mrs. Campbell's house?
A. I think from a quarter past to half-past one.
Q. Now you use these words in your affidavit – "time passed unconsciously away, and was much astonished on rising to depart to see it was a quarter to two." Did you swear to this?
A. Yes.
Q. Why did you swear to it?
A. I did not make it out. [Meaning he had not written it.]
Q. Who did?
A. Mr. J.K. Gordon.
Q. Was it read to you?
A. Yes.
Q. How do you explain this discrepancy in time?
A. I suppose I passed it over.
Q. Well, taking your own time, how was it you remained so late at Mrs. Campbell's?
A. I don't know; time passed unconsciously.
Q. Very agreeably, no doubt?
A. Yes, I think it did.
Q. Did she read and sing to you?
A. She read out of the "Language of Flowers," and sang three pieces. She read a piece that was rather light. I cannot remember what it was, or even the subject.
Q. Was it the "Jumping Frog?"
A. No, it was not. (Laughter.) She read other pieces out of the scraps book.
Q. Where was Mrs. Campbell sitting?
A. We were sitting by the table. Am not certain whether she was on the sofa or not. I was sitting on the sofa at that time. Don't remember her reciting pieces to me on any such occasion.
Q. Now, was not Mrs. Campbell on the sofa?
A. If she was on the sofa, she was at one end and I at the other. Don't recollect her asking me to come nearer.
Q. Do you remember the songs she sang?
A. I think she sang "Kathleen Aroon" and "You Will Not Forget Kathleen." The last thing she did was to read.
Q. Was anything said about California?
A. Yes, there was a conversation about California. She said if she had a fortune she would like to travel, and the first place she would visit would be California. I said I was fond of travelling, and if I

had the means would travel also. It is all a joke. The joke came in about three years ago. I was at Mr. Campbell's house, and we made arrangements in fun to elope. Mrs. Campbell then turned round to her husband, and asked him how he liked the program. He replied, "I am quite satisfied, if you are." It was carried on in joke ever since.

Q. It seems to me that you have carried the joke a little too far. What do you mean by saying it was carried on ever since!

A. It was often referred to.

Q. Do you know Fraser?

A. Yes.

Q. Do you remember saying to him that you did not like to call at Mrs. Campbell's because her husband was jealous?

A. No; I don't remember.

The *Chronicle* report then reverted to the narrative style. In answer to further questions Gordon said that he did not know that Robert had returned until he went there on Saturday, 22 August to return some books Eliza had lent him. He denied that he had ever told anybody that he went to the Campbell house to try and seduce Eliza, but until then had not succeeded. He went to hear Eliza sing and play. Cameron's re-direct was short. He asked Gordon something about the crim. con. case, allowing him to respond that "I was not examined in the previous case, neither was Mrs Campbell." Cameron's final question elicited a simple but probably strongly stated denial that anything improper had occurred. At this point it was 6 p.m. and the court adjourned.

When proceedings resumed promptly at 9:30 the following morning, Friday, 27 March, there were, according to the *Globe*, a "goodly number of spectators in the gallery," and the *Whitby Chronicle* made the same point more dramatically: The court was "densely crowded" and "the greatest interest manifested in the proceedings." The morning was taken up with more witnesses for both sides. Cameron went first, calling a series of people to say what they knew about two matters – the time that the early hours altercation took place on the Whitby streets and what was said on that occasion.

Hardware merchant George Gross was first. He testified that he had been woken up by a row in the street at about 1:30 a.m. on the night of the 26th into the 27th. There was "no doubt in his mind" that it was between 1 a.m. and 2 a.m. Although he could not clearly see who was doing the shouting, he did see various people going into and out of the Campbells' store. Gross did not claim to have heard what was said in the street that night; he thought he heard the word "liar" or "fire." He did not know Eliza, although he did know Rev. Byrne. He recalled notice being given that Eliza should not be extended credit. He also recounted his calling on Robert after 26 August and them talking for about an hour and a half, with James Campbell and Anderson also present. James Campbell told Gross that Gordon had "denied the charge." But then, "what would he say?" James Campbell added.[21] This was evidence that James Campbell had lied in his testimony in the current case and the crim. con. trial. The issue of Eliza's "condition" also came up, and Gross opined, as recounted in chapter 3, that he did not believe that a woman well advanced in pregnancy would have sex with a man not her husband. Anderson replied that women in that condition "were prone to forget themselves in that way."

Harrison's cross-examination elicited the fact that Gross had been subpoenaed to give evidence at the crim. con. trial and had been present in court but was not called. He did not say by whom he was subpoenaed. Although he claimed that he was still on friendly terms with the Campbells, he had told people after the crim. con. trial that he thought that James Campbell had not told the truth about the time the street altercation had occurred, and as a result he had been threatened with legal action by James Campbell.[22] Pressed by Harrison about whether he might be wrong about the time, Gross insisted that he "would not say what was untrue." He "had certainly made some observations upon the evidence of the Campbells; he did so because before the trial, they had acknowledged that the time was half-past one when the Gordon difficulty took place; and he observed at the trial that they swore it was about three o'clock before Gordon left the house."[23]

Gross also said that one Mowbray had come to see him, sent by the Campbells, and Gross told Mowbray "that he did not believe Mrs. Campbell was guilty." Harrison was not doing well with this cross-examination, and moved on, testing Gross's testimony about the night of the 26th and 27th. He woke up because Whitby was a quiet town and the noises had disturbed him. He woke at about 1:30 a.m. by his watch, and the row must have started before then because it woke him. Because he thought he heard somebody say "fire" or "liar" he was frightened into full wakefulness. The "liar," if that was the word he heard, was a reference to Gordon calling James Campbell a liar. Harrison's final question did get Gross to admit that he had called Gordon a scoundrel in the conversation with the Campbells, "because the way the story was told made him think that there was some truth in it." Gross's evidence must have affected the jury. Here they had a respectable businessman, an acquaintance of the Campbells who thought they were "fine men," tell a plausible story about the time that contradicted what they had heard from James Campbell and what James Campbell had said at the crim. con. trial.

Two other witnesses cast similar doubts on James Campbell's account. Mrs. Jane Allin (Allen), who lived above the book and stationery store she ran with her husband next door to the Campbell store, said that she had been reading, and at around 1 a.m heard James Campbell speak very loudly. She also heard the door to the Campbells' store shut and a few minutes later heard it slammed closed.[24] Cross-examined by Harrison she said her window had been open. It was common to hear noises on the street, but it was unusual to hear James Campbell's voice, which was "distinct" and "would be easily recognized by anyone acquainted with it." In response to another question from Harrison she said she was confident that when she heard the noises it was not yet 2 a.m. Cameron had a final question – where was she sitting? – to which she replied that she was in the dining room in the front part of her house.

Even better for Cameron's case was Wellington Adams, the dentist, who lived about 69 metres (75 yds.) from the Campbell store. His office was above Robert Jameson's store on Dundas Street, and the men he heard arguing were in front of Lawler's grocery store. Jameson was the husband of Mary Jameson, the woman who had supposedly told James Campbell's wife about Gordon's visits to Eliza. In direct examination Adams said he recognized the voices of Campbell and Gordon and heard Campbell say "you can't deny it George," to which Gordon's reply was "you're a d– liar if you say so." He also heard Gordon threaten to "thrash" Campbell and dared him to come out of his store after he had gone in. Adams's window had been open. He did not know what time this was exactly, but thought it was between 1 a.m. and 2 a.m., and could not have been as late as 3 o'clock. Harrison cross-examined Adams, but all he got was confirmation that the house where he lived was 69 metres (75 yds.) from Lawler's grocery store, a distance he and James Byrne had carefully measured.

Cameron called four more witnesses, including Rev. Byrne and James Byrne. The former was asked about his conversations with James Campbell, but the press reports of his account of what James Campbell had said were contradictory. The *Globe* had him saying that James Campbell "made no distinct statement about what Gordon had said," and that he "had given him to understand that Gordon had admitted the criminal conduct."[25] The *Whitby Chronicle* had him saying that the Campbells "made no statement that Gordon admitted the charge"; indeed James Campbell had given Rev. Byrne "rather to understand the reverse." Harrison cross-examined him on whether he knew that Robert and Eliza "lived unhappily," but he said he did not know.

Figure 6.2. Wellington Adams and family, 1910. Adams is standing far left.
Source: Whitby Archives Photograph 19-062-01

In response to another question Byrne said that he knew that James Campbell "was not friendly" towards Eliza. Further questions elicited a denial that Bethiah Ham had warned Eliza about her conduct. He was asked about the writings by Eliza he had been shown, and replied that "he considered them only as romances and quite harmless."[26] In his turn James Byrne was clear that when he went to see the Campbells very shortly after 26 August, James Campbell had told him that Gordon had denied the accusation of adultery, and that he had first said that his altercation with Gordon happened at 3 a.m., but then later said it might have been at 2 a.m.

Cameron's final two witnesses were George Warner and James Davidson. Warner, a railway worker resident in Whitby, was asked about a conversation he had had with George Cameron, the man who had testified in the crim. con. trial to having seen Eliza and Gordon walking closely together. Cameron had said he knew nothing of the local scandal, but he wanted to go to Toronto, and he knew of somebody else who was going to get $7 in witness expenses. George Cameron told Warner that he had told Robert that if he was called to testify he would say that he saw Gordon walking with his arm around Eliza. Warner was surprised to hear that Cameron had sworn to this in court, given that he had previously said that he knew nothing about Gordon and Eliza. Davidson was a student who roomed with Adams.[27] He said he was woken on the night in question by voices in the street but could not distinguish anything that was said. This was at about 1 a.m. When he woke up he saw Adams at the window. Harrison asked him if the window of the room he shared with Adams was open, and he said it was.

At that Cameron announced that he had completed his case. Harrison had another chance to call witnesses in rebuttal. He called the Campbell brothers and John McGillivray. McGillivray knew Adams and had talked to him in his office before the crim. con. trial. Adams had told him that he did not hear all of the conversation in the street, only part of it, and that he did not know who had spoken. On cross-examination by Cameron he said he was not positive about his evidence; it was "to the best of his recollection." James Campbell said he had talked to Adams before the crim. con. trial and Adams had said that he knew nothing about what was said in the street and did not want to know. Harrison's last witness, Robert, said that as far as he was aware James had always had friendly feelings towards Eliza and had visited regularly. Eliza had never complained about those visits, although "he knew that his wife did not like his brother." This ended the taking of evidence. A number of Whitby residents had been subpoenaed to give character evidence on each side, but according to the *Whitby Chronicle*, after the testimony of Gross and Adams both counsel decided not to call any of them, as "the evidence as to character … would have been given pro and con."

Speeches to the Jury

Harrison addressed the jury first, a 2-hour long speech that started at 11 a.m. and went to 1:10 p.m. He began in sarcastic mode. In his opening Cameron had explained everything. Eliza was "the daughter of a clergyman, and was moral and virtuous," while James Campbell "was a bad man, bent only on the destruction of his own brother's wife." But even Cameron would admit that there were "irregularities" that needed explaining. James Campbell was in fact "influenced by a sense of duty to his brother, … and it was a strong sense that would make him say something that would cover two families with disgrace, including his own."[28] For her part Eliza was not what Cameron had tried to make her out to be, and Cameron ought to concede that she had been guilty of "indiscretions" and "most unbecoming conduct." In the "modern cant" Cameron might even say that she had committed "some business irregularities," but she had not broken the law. Juries were known to favour women, for they saw women as "the weaker vessel" and were more ready to believe a woman's oath than a man's. This was not right. Invoking Eve in the Garden of Eden, he reminded the jurors that "from the earliest ages of the world woman had erred."

Harrison then reminded the jury that in the crim. con. case the question of adultery had been tried, and Robert had won $3,000 in damages. Cameron would no doubt say that this was because Eliza's evidence was excluded, and Harrison conceded that there had been fresh evidence in the current trial. But Eliza's evidence had been excluded for very good reason, the law having done so in such cases as "the temptation to commit perjury would be almost irresistible." Eliza had told her story this time, but the jury should put little weight on it because "when virtue left a woman's breast, truth rarely remained long after it." It "might easily be believed that whoever would commit adultery would not hesitate to commit perjury." The same objection pertained with equal force to the person accused of being the adulterous partner, and thus he also could not testify before. A man like Gordon, "a man who was bold enough to enter a friend's house and afterwards destroy its peace would not stop at an oath." In the current case the rules of evidence were different, but the temptation to give perjured evidence was the same. Eliza could now testify, but nonetheless the underlying accusation was adultery, and "it was reasonable to suppose that the woman who would be guilty of committing the crime ... would not hesitate to perjure herself in order to cover up that crime."

Harrison spent some time contrasting the characters of the principal protagonists. He mocked the idea that James Campbell had a motive to lie in "the gratification of some personal spite against" Eliza, and criticized Cameron for his earlier remarks about him "prowling round the house." He had not watched the house to manufacture a case. Rather, "what was discovered that night was but a confirmation of what had been approximately guessed at before." Cameron had made much of the "prowling about," but he forgot that this was the only way that Eliza's guilt could be brought home to her. "If a man suspected that his house was about to be broken into he would prowl about the premises until the burglar had effected an entrance and would then confront him." But according to Cameron "the burglar would have to be let off because he had been detected by means of prowling about." Adultery was a greater offence than burglary, and under the circumstances James Campbell's action was only just and right.

Harrison's principal theme was Eliza's lack of wifely virtue. She had behaved badly with Pugsden, and the correspondence that was discovered showed that she had another man besides Gordon who could have been her lover. To judge the events of the night of 26 August it was necessary to look at Eliza's history, to consider "whether she was a person likely to entertain a young man in the manner or under the circumstances, alleged." Eliza had tried to explain away the letters as part of a novel she had been writing, "but it was a strange thing that the hero of the novel should be a young man residing at Concord in the county of York." She was not a flighty young girl but a "staid matron," a clergyman's daughter, and the mother of three children who had lost affection for her husband. She knew well what impropriety was, and the difference between right and wrong. The letter to Parks, which had never been sent, showed her true character. It was "not the letter that a virtuous, decent, respectable woman would write, and if she were the daughter of 50 clergymen it would not save her, for it was not the letter of a pure woman." "Witnesses might lie," said Harrison, "but these letters told a tale that was true." Lest the jury think that daughters of the clergy could not behave badly, which Cameron had suggested, Harrison repeated what he had said in the crim. con trial: "Clergymen's sons and daughters were no better than other peoples."

There was much more on Eliza's character. The husband who had married her for love was referred to in her correspondence with young men as the "Guardian." Harrison asked the jurors "as sensible men" whether any woman of propriety would have called her husband such a name? In 1870 there occurred the "flirtation" with Pugsden, which "gave her husband great offence." But her indiscretions did not stop there. In 1873 she "took a fancy to this young man" Parks. She tried to get him a job at the Campbell store, so that when Robert was away "the book-keeper and his lady patron would have had a nice time of it." Robert refused to engage him, and so he moved to Concord, but neither forgot the other. The letters that had been produced contained "references, expressions, and inuendoes" that should not have come from a faithful wife. Eliza was "no doubt a clever woman," so "she at once discovered that she was an authoress and that these letters had been written for the purpose of adorning a novel." This "showed the resources of the woman" when she realized that the letters would be used against her. Harrison picked out phrases and cast them in an unfavourable light. "You were so enchantingly persuasive that I could not help but yield" could not have been written by a "prudent woman" or a "virtuous heroine," assuming it was "virtue that was yielded." And if it was merely part of a romance, "what strange thoughts must have been passing through her mind." Again it seems that nobody other than Eliza seemed to know the genesis of some of the things Eliza had written down.

Harrison then switched to the period after Robert had left, and recounted the evidence of the Newsoms that whenever Gordon came to the house the curtains were pinned, and the parlour door was left open to give the impression that nothing improper was taking place. Eliza also took off her boots to "creep up to bed unheard" Servants had no reason to invent things and were "admirable detectives." Everything culminated on the night of the 26th, when Robert was successful in getting the conclusive evidence he needed. James Campbell and Anderson had no reason to perjure themselves, and the two versions of Anderson's written statement were essentially the same. He had been hurried when he first wrote, and said that James Campbell had accused Gordon of having attempted to seduce Eliza, instead of having in fact seduced her that night, as he afterwards, "on reflection," wrote.

Coming to the end of his speech, Harrison stressed that the jury had the sworn testimony of James Campbell, Anderson, the Newsoms, Cameron, and Fagan to set against that of Eliza and "the man Gordon." There was a strong motive for the latter two to commit perjury, while there was none in the case of the other witnesses. Harrison dealt very cursorily with the strongest evidence against his client, the inconsistent accounts of what took place in the street. They were unimportant in themselves, and irrelevant if the jury believed what was alleged to have occurred inside the house. As to times of departure, it was admitted that Gordon left the house very late and he himself was "in some confusion" about the time, at one point saying 1:45 and at another 1:15. Harrison ended his oration by telling the jury that much more was at stake than this one case. Eliza's conduct should be censured, which would show that a woman's virtue "deserved careful guarding." If the law was not to be "paramount" in policing the boundaries of proper marital conduct, Canada would become like the US, where "the pistol was so swiftly called in to punish an offender." But the primacy of the law "could only be secured by the courage and intelligence of juries."[29]

Cameron rose to address the jury "amidst breathless silence, and the deepest attention," the courtroom "packed to its utmost capacity with an expectant audience." He spoke for about half as long as Harrison, and a consistent theme in his speech, which he came back to time and again, was that the Campbells, Robert in particular, had not lived up the standard of manliness expected of them. Rather than love and support his wife, Robert had treated her cruelly for his own selfish ends. Much of the evidence was irrelevant, said Cameron, because it was about Parks or other incidents prior to the evening of 26 August. James Campbell had not brought Parks from Concord to testify because, had he done so, Parks would have said that, "like Gordon, … he had never been criminally intimate with" Eliza.[30] (Presumably nobody knew at this time that Parks had joined the NWMP.) Cameron noted Harrison's statement that he was lucky to have a woman for a client because juries favoured women out of "sympathy." Not so. What mattered were the facts, and these were that throughout the Campbells' marriage Eliza had never shown any "inattention or neglect" to the children, and until Robert's return from the United Kingdom "no fault as a woman, or levity of conduct, had been established" against her. Even the shipboard incident was of no importance, for Robert had said nothing about it at the time.

With that Cameron turned to the week or so after Robert had returned from the UK, casting his behaviour in the worst possible light. A letter was found addressed to Eliza but which was delivered to the Campbells' store. Robert decided it had come from Parks; whether it had or not, Cameron "could not undertake to say," but he cast doubt on its authenticity by noting that it was dated 14 August in Concord and should therefore have reached Whitby on the 15th; yet it was not received by Robert until the 19th. James Campbell denied tampering with it, yet it was not delivered to Eliza. The Campbell firm had received one letter from Parks asking for a job, and from that Robert and James jumped to the conclusion that it was Parks's handwriting, and also that Eliza was corresponding with him. Cameron then upbraided Robert for searching his wife's drawers and finding, among "a hundred others," the few "scraps of paper" that had been read out at the trial. As a result "this *man*, this husband, who desired to protect his wife and her children, determined, there and then, as he himself tells, to be separated from that wife, and to disgrace his children, before he was aware that she had committed any act of criminality." Cameron reminded the jury that "a lady may flirt without being guilty of a criminal act." The law was clear that "so long as a woman did not commit the one act charged against the plaintiff, she was innocent, no matter how thoughtless or giddy her conduct might have been."

Thus, Robert Campbell had "determined to separate from his wife without proof." He consulted with his brother, and they recruited their "worthy brother-in-law, Anderson." According to Anderson Gordon was never mentioned in connection with Eliza until the night the two watched the house, and that mention was only "on the suspicion expressed by Mrs. Jameson of seeing him visit the house." Why was it, Cameron asked, that Mary Jameson was not called to prove Gordon's visits? Harrison had said that female servants made good detectives. This might be true, but the two Newsoms could not "prove anything wrong," and if they had suspected anything they would have watched when they knew Gordon was in the parlour with Eliza. Indeed Martha Newsom "did not discover anything suspicious until after Mrs. Campbell was turned out of doors like a dog." Only when she went back to live in Robert's house did she remember matters like the lace curtains being pinned together the morning after Gordon had been at the house. "Her memory," said Cameron, "had perhaps been refreshed by the Campbells."

Cameron referred at this point to the crim. con. trial, at which Robert's "determination to have a separation were kept in the background" because it "would not have served his purpose then." Now, when he thought it would help, Robert made the most of Eliza's past indiscretions. In general "it seemed as if the desire to ruin Mrs. Campbell had been first determined on, and then the conspirators had set to work to devise the means."[31] As for James Campbell, he had acted the part "of a skulking viper and a sneak," and "in a cunning, designing manner, ... conspiring with his brother to get rid of [Eliza] ... in order to be relieved of the burden of maintaining her." As to what took place on the night of the 26th, it may have been "indiscreet" and "unbecoming" given the lateness of the hour, but it involved nothing more than singing, reading, and draughts playing: "No matter how indiscreet that might have been, ... Mrs. Campbell was not guilty of the charge made by the defendant so ruthlessly and with such determination and persistency." The fact was that Campbell and Anderson were looking for something "criminal." They watched and listened at the windows, and "pretended they could distinguish nothing that was said inside until after 12 o'clock." James Campbell, "who came there as a detective," said it was a still night but that the noise of the omnibuses, cars, and farm wagons prevented them from hearing up to 12 o'clock. The girl's story was that she could hear better upstairs than in the kitchen, "and yet she could hear nothing." Campbell and Anderson had learned their parts by rote: "They had all the dirty story of the pretended conversation heard between Gordon and Mrs. Campbell."

Cameron then addressed the question of the time. Both Campbell and Anderson said they left at around 3 a.m. They both recollected minutely the words Campbell addressed to Gordon, which they said were – "You black-hearted, you dyed villain, you had this night criminal intercourse with my brother's wife." They stated that Gordon had replied: "I could not help it; it was not my fault." But Anderson had written down that Campbell said: "You have attempted to seduce my brother's wife, if you have not already." And this was what Gordon himself swore was actually said to him. Why did Anderson alter his original statement? Perhaps they talked the matter over, and thought it would be better for their case to change the words. Gross, who was a disinterested party, swore it was a little after one o'clock when the altercation took place in the street, and that he was aroused by hearing the words "fire" or "liar." Gordon had sworn that he had called Campbell this and, if Gross had been truthful, James Campbell must have lied. If he lied about this, no credit could be given to his and Anderson's evidence on other points.

Cameron stressed the connection between one lie and the other salient parts of James Campbell's story. The jury had heard both Eliza and Gordon swear that no sex ever took place. She had brought the action to clear her reputation. The jury should pay special attention to the words that had been struck out in Anderson's statement. He would not read out the statement because of its indecent language, but he asked them to take the struck-out words into consideration with the other evidence. His client was the daughter of a respectable clergyman, who wanted to bring husband and wife together, but the husband had "steeled his heart against her whom he had pledged to cherish and protect." He had also taken his children away while giving her a "Judas kiss," and refused to listen to Eliza's explanations.

Cameron then analysed the contradictions in the evidence about the evening in question. It began with "the accidental circumstance of Gordon's accompanying Mrs. Campbell home"; it was not a pre-arranged assignation. The jury had to consider the "improbability" of the "vile language" attributed to Eliza. How could Campbell and Anderson hear things from outside that the servant upstairs did not? They had the testimony of Mrs. Allin and Adams as to the lateness of the hour, and Adams had also given evidence that Gordon had threatened to "thrash" James Campbell. They also had Gross's testimony. It was for the jury to compare the evidence for both sides. If they believed that Gordon had not admitted to the seduction, then James Campbell and Anderson were "scoundrels" who had concocted their evidence. He reminded the jury that it was given unchallenged in the crim. con. trial. But the moment an account of the trial was published, Mrs. Allin, Adams, and Gross had come forward and said it was not true. Cameron also reminded the jurors of the intimidating letter written by James Campbell to Gross when he discovered that Gross had said that he had not told the truth.

In what the *Whitby Chronicle* described as "eloquent terms" Cameron compared the treatment Eliza had received from the Campbell brothers with her own explanations and admissions. She "admitted everything except her guilt." He reminded the jury of James Campbell's unfriendliness towards Eliza, and "in a most eloquent and pathetic appeal" he asked the jury to decide between the veracity of the two parties on each side, with one side being "the two dastards, Campbell and Anderson, whose conduct he warmly denounced in no measured terms." This part of his speech brought loud and sustained applause, and an intervention from Hagarty, who said that he admired counsel's oration as much as anyone, but he could not allow anybody to disturb the proceedings. The audience's approbation seems to have only encouraged Cameron in his rhetoric, adding Robert Campbell to the mix, a man whose smirking and smiling in the witness box showed his "callous heart." The Campbell brothers had not lived up to their social and moral obligations as men. Their conduct was "unmanly," and no damages were sufficient to mark the jury's "disapprobation" of it, to show that the jurors disapproved strongly "of the unmanliness displayed by those men towards this woman." The Campbells deserved "public execration."

Cameron knew that Robert's ultimate objective was divorce, and he knew what that would mean for Eliza's future, because she would lose all support if he obtained one on the grounds of adultery. But if he had cared for the honour of his family, for his wife, and the future of his children, his conduct would have been different. He would not have taken the "dastardly" advice of his brother; he would not have taken the children away from Eliza. He would not have said nothing to Eliza while he and his brother were playing conspirators without the slightest indication that he had made up his mind to disgrace her and separate from her. The man who was guilty of all this had not done the right thing. He wanted to destroy the woman. Base as the conduct of James Campbell had been, Robert's had been equally so. Cameron continued on his themes of James Campbell's perfidy and Robert's unmanly behaviour:

> referring in terms of bitterest reproach to Jas. Campbell's prowling around his sister-in-law's house like a burglar, to the conduct of the husband, worse than that of a burglar in seeking to deprive his wife of that virtuous good name which could never be restored to her again, the man who had never put out a helping hand to save and support her in her trouble, but who cruelly joined in the inhuman acts of his brother in hounding her down.

At this point some of the jury were "melted to tears," and there were tears streaming down Cameron's own face as, "with choked voice," he implored the jury for a favourable verdict. "Had Robert Campbell the feelings of a man, he would have said to himself that for those children's sake he would not have the notoriety of this scandal go to the world and have the mother of those children branded as a person of infamous misconduct, and the child – his child – then unborn, pronounced illegitimate."

Cameron returned to the legal question at issue, although hardly in dry and dispassionate terms. The charge was defamation. The "devilish" James Campbell had defamed Eliza's good name and "outraged her virtue." Robert Campbell's complaint was minor – that Gordon visited the house upon one occasion and remained there for a couple of hours until Robert's return. Robert was supposedly Gordon's friend, "and yet this *man*, because his wife acted a hospitable part and endeavoured to entertain his friend, goes into the witness box and has the meanness to proclaim that he refused to sleep with his wife that night because she happened to entertain his friend!"* The greatest publicity, he reminded the jury, had been given to this case, and yet no incriminating word beyond the testimony of Campbell and Anderson, and the "dastardly contemptible charges" of Robert, could be brought against Eliza.

Cameron ended by telling the jurors that the defence had failed. It had failed with regard to the time things happened, "and the men who would misrepresent in one respect would not hesitate to misrepresent in another." Robert Campbell was determined to separate from his wife before he had evidence of her guilt at all. The only question for the jury was one of damages. The statement that Robert Campbell had been prostrated by the shock he had received at his wife's conduct was "hypocrisy" most "shocking." They had seen Robert Campbell's demeanour on the witness stand, where his relaxed attitude showed him to have a "callous heart." The Campbells may have lost business, and no wonder – people were very susceptible when confronted with conduct like theirs. No damages that the jury could award would be sufficient to mark their disapprobation of the conduct – the "unmanly conduct" exercised towards a woman – the outrage upon a wife and mother's feelings, and he appealed to them to award such "substantial damages" as would "stamp the conduct of the unmanliness displayed by those men towards this woman to future courts and juries as well as to" the public.

Hagarty's Summing Up and the Verdict

Chief Justice Hagarty's summing up was fair; it might even be said to have favoured Eliza. He began with a lengthy review of the evidence and by explaining what had happened at the crim. con. trial, especially

* Emphasis in original.

the effect of the evidence laws that had been largely determinative of that case. He himself did not agree with the witness prohibitions, but that was the law, and what he termed the "seduction case" had been decided on the evidence of one side only. The current action was brought by the accused lady in the former case. It was a straightforward case because James Campbell had not denied the defamatory statements. The case, therefore, turned on the evidence of Eliza and George Gordon on one side, "who swear positively that no act of criminality ever took place between them," and Campbell and Anderson on the other, who swore that they had been witnesses "to such conduct as must place the crime of adultery beyond dispute."

The only two things that one could be sure about was that Eliza had been "most unfortunate in her behaviour," which was "the height of imprudence," and that "black, very black perjury" had been committed by someone. Hagarty then reviewed the history of the Campbells' marriage down to the Parks correspondence. Assuming, he said, that correspondence to have taken place, and to have been of an innocent character, it was certainly unfortunate for a married woman to have taken part in it. Anything more indiscreet or more calculated to excite suspicion Hagarty did not know. Nonetheless "so long as there was nothing in it the wife must be held innocent," and the husband, "although he might have reason to find fault, had no claim." It was clear that Robert, after his arrival from the United Kingdom, had become "much affected" by what he was told about Gordon, especially so given that he was "perhaps of a jealous nature." Before going to the UK Robert had been bothered by something about Gordon, but it was a small matter of which he took little notice. What really got his attention were the letter and the other writings. Without telling his wife his purpose, or that it was to be a final separation between them, he took away the children, telling his brother to watch the house. Then came the night of the 26th. It was quite unnecessary to "pain the ears of the jury with what they said they had heard; he would not offend their ears by even a reference to the filthy language." If their stories were true, the offence with which the woman had been charged had been committed beyond doubt.

Hagarty then recapitulated the evidence of the witnesses. It was abundantly clear that Eliza had been indiscreet, but there was "a great gulf between indiscretion and guilt." Gordon's remaining in the house so late, and Eliza not making him leave, was "a most unfortunate, unwise, and foolish thing." He hoped that this case would be a lesson to others. But there was "a vast gulf between … utter folly, and … the crime of adultery." The court was not trying Eliza's frivolity, or whether she had lived "a correct and careful pattern of married life." Nor were they trying Robert's responsibility and his "duty" to "ton[e] his young wife down to the duty of a respectable matron." What mattered was the evidence of adultery, and whether James Campbell was right. And that was a question for the jury, who had to decide whether to accept Eliza's and Gordon's denials, or the assertions of Campbell and Anderson. He hoped the trial would show how easy it was for a woman to lose her reputation, but he was glad that he had the jury "between him and the verdict." The jury had been addressed by "two of the most distinguished ornaments of the bar," and it was their decision; they were not to interpret anything he said as offering an opinion one way or the other. But having said that, Hagarty dwelled a little on James Campbell's role and Robert's apparent motive. It was alleged that James had a deep dislike of Eliza, that he had poisoned Robert's mind against her, and that Robert wanted to get rid of his wife and of her dower right in his land. If the jury believed that there was a conspiracy against Eliza, that Campbell and Anderson had invented their stories, a more "black and diabolical" piece of business had never come before a court of justice. It would be the most "blackhearted piece of villainy" he had ever known. Hagarty concluded by saying that he "earnestly prayed that their verdict might be led to a righteous decision." As to the question of damages, that rested with the jury. With that he told them to retire and consider their verdict. Before retiring some of the jurymen wanted to know the birth date of Francis Campbell. It is possible that they wanted to know exactly how many months pregnant Eliza was in August 1873, because they saw that as relevant to whether she had had sex on 26 August.

The trial ended at 3:50 in the afternoon.[32] The Toronto *Leader* dramatically captured the emotions of those left in the courtroom after the jury departed. There was a "general buzz" as the spectators speculated about the result. Opinion was "a good deal divided, but generally in favour of Mrs. Campbell," in part because people thought that Cameron's speech was "one of his best efforts." Harrison himself knew there was "much speculation" as to the verdict, and he was aware that he was up against it. By 6 p.m. the jury was not able to agree and told Hagarty there was no chance of their doing so. He sent them back nonetheless and at 8:30 p.m. they delivered, on Hagarty's instructions, a sealed verdict. The next morning, when the court resumed sitting at 9:30, Hagarty opened the envelope, revealing that the jury had decided for Eliza, with damages set at $1,000, only 10 per cent of the amount she had sued for. According to the *Whitby Chronicle* the damages award was the cause of the lengthy jury deliberations. The jury had no trouble finding for Eliza, but two of the twelve wanted to award her the full $10,000 demanded, a very large sum. This may not have been correct, and in any event it would have been very unusual for someone to know that much about the jury's deliberations.[33] Harrison was disappointed but not surprised, as he had "anticipated an adverse verdict."

Despite the failure to get the full award, the verdict was nonetheless a signal victory for Eliza. The London *Daily Advertiser* saw it as "a complete vindication of Mrs. Campbell's honour."[34] She now had a jury decision that directly conflicted with that given in the crim. con. case, the result of her being able to testify this time around and of the new evidence that cast doubt on James Campbell's and John Anderson's veracity.

Whitby's Reaction to the Verdict

When the verdict was announced there were celebrations outside the courtroom among the people from Whitby who had travelled to Toronto to hear the case. But they were relatively muted, because it was just a small group of people in the big city, and it was 10 a.m. Matters were very different when Eliza got back to Whitby later that day. A torchlight procession headed by the Whitby band paraded through the main streets and halted in front of James Byrne's house, where Eliza was staying. There "hearty cheers" were given for Eliza, James Byrne, and Cameron, and a fireworks display followed. James Byrne was the local hero, for having stood by his sister emotionally and financially. For his part James Byrne thanked the *Chronicle* for its "kind remarks" but took pains to point out that it was not just him willing to "make a sacrifice" to defend his sister. Other members of his family had "stood shoulder to shoulder" with him in resisting the "hellish" attack, the "moral murder far worse than a physical one."[35] There is no evidence of whether Eliza's sister Bethiah had also supported her, but she may not have done. She made no public statements and soon after, in May 1874, she remarried, wedded to Thomas Johnston, a man more than 20 years her senior and with four children of his own. Johnston worked as an assistant commissioner in the provincial crown lands department, and Bethiah left Whitby to live with him in Toronto with their blended family of seven children.[36]

The Byrne family's and the general townsfolks' celebration of Eliza's win was not wholeheartedly reflected by William Higgins, editor of the *Whitby Chronicle*. His editorial criticized both sides.[37] It was "a sad and most unfortunate episode in the married life of the parties" concerned, and "[t]here is little room indeed for exultation on either side."

Hagarty's charge had been "a reprimand" to both parties, and he had not refrained from "condemning the lightness and frivolity of character which in great part led to the sad consequences which ensued." Those consequences were "saddest of all to the wife and mother," and the "poor children." It was to be hoped that the trial would be a lesson to "giddy people disposed to romantic nonsense," and the "unpardonable, unmatronly, and indefensible offence of the mother of children, and lady of a respectable household, flirting with, corresponding with, and keeping company with young gentlemen of leisure."

Higgins had equally harsh words for the Campbell men and Anderson, for their lack of true manliness. They "had no charity in their hearts," were willing to "swear away a woman's reputation." Making every allowance for them, they had displayed a "want of Christian Charity." They looked for evidence of guilt rather than try to prevent "a crime." They cared nothing for "the woman whose reputation and character should have been considered sacred in their sight, and whose chastity it was their duty to protect." Higgins continued: "Had they punished the man whom they believed to be a seducer, like men, instead of acting the part of miserable cowardly spies – worse – looking on at the consummation of the infamous act, as they swear they did do – there is not a jury in the Dominion that would not have held them harmless." Similarly, Robert had not "acted a manly part" in "imprinting false kisses upon his wife's lips (while he was surreptitiously taking her children away and conspiring with his brother for a separation from her)." If he had instead "upbraided her with her conduct, called upon her for an explanation, told her plainly of his intention, and sent for her father or protector to come to his house and hear his accusations," then even if he had "then spurned her and all her explanations," there would at least have been "some manly pride in his conduct." Robert should have tried reconciliation. The Bible said that a husband should "cleave to his wife." The trial showed that he was "too hasty in condemning his wife," and the result was the "deplorable consequence[s]" of public exposure.

The defamation case, like its predecessor, was reported in Ontario newspapers outside of Toronto and Whitby. The jocular editor of the *North Ontario Observer*, who had previously made fun of the alleged "conjugal partnership" of the Campbells being joined by a third party, Gordon, now decided to make the Campbell marital breakdown a sporting event. The first "heat" had been won by the Campbell brothers, the second by Eliza. It was "not known yet whether the legal race is to be best two in three or the best three in five," although he thought the latter more likely. Whoever won would be tired and dirtied by the competition, because the fight had involved, and would involve, accusations of blatant perjury.[38]

In fact the score was not tied. Eliza's win was to be overturned by a panel of three judges, as discussed in the next section. In the interim Eliza's position in the town was strengthened by the verdict. Not only was there a public celebration, it seems that the Campbell brothers somewhat withdrew from the public eye. They did not place a single advertisement for their business in the *Whitby Chronicle* between 7 May 1874 and 1879. In 1875 they advertised a substantial part of their premises for lease, including "the large double shop, suitable for a dry goods, hardware, or grocery store."[39] There is no affirmative evidence that there was some kind of boycott, but the disappearance from the public prints of a hitherto mainstay business of the town is revealing of at least the fact that the Campbell brothers thought it advisable to keep their heads down.

A Successful Motion for a New Trial

James Campbell moved for a new trial in May 1874. Harrison was his counsel and Cameron represented Eliza. The bench comprised three Common Pleas judges, including Hagarty, who had been the trial judge. This would never happen today, but it was considered not just acceptable but desirable in the nineteenth century, because the trial judge had the best knowledge of the case. The other two judges were Galt, who had presided over the crim. con. trial, and John Wellington Gwynne. Gwynne had been variously a railway speculator, corporate lawyer and, in the 1850s, one of Toronto's leading barristers and a prominent crown counsel. He had been appointed to Common Pleas by John A. Macdonald in 1868, and in 1879 Macdonald's patronage also got him a seat on the Supreme Court of Canada bench. He was well respected for his legal acumen but not always liked because of his crotchetiness. He was also a devout Anglican and likely to have little sympathy for Eliza, and that proved to be the case.[40] James Campbell's cause was also likely substantially aided by having Galt on the panel.

Harrison summoned James Campbell to come up to Toronto to attend the hearing, which was a success. On 21 May 1874 he won a rule *nisi* for a new trial, Galt not surprisingly having shown himself "very favourable" during the argument, although Hagarty, the trial judge, was "hesitating."[41] Almost exactly a year later, on 26 May 1875, Cameron "shewed cause" to set aside the rule *nisi*, but the court did not deliver its judgment confirming the new trial until December 1875.[42]

It is not possible to know exactly what arguments the parties made on each occasion that the motion was argued, because they are only briefly reproduced in the final judgment. But we can assume that in both May 1874 and May 1875 Harrison and Cameron made the same arguments. Harrison's principal point was that the jury verdict was against the weight of the evidence.[43] He also argued that the damage award was excessive, in part because special damages had not been proved. Special damages in tort law are awarded to compensate successful plaintiffs for actual pecuniary losses, as opposed to general damages that compensate for non-monetary injury, such as pain and suffering or loss of reputation. Harrison argued that the loss of the society of friends and neighbours and the danger of losing her dower right were not heads of damages, and there was no loss of income. Finally, he asserted that the words spoken were not actionable because they were about Eliza and under coverture the damage had been done to Robert, not Eliza, and Robert had not claimed damages.

Cameron was able to successfully refute the special damages argument with a very recent English case, *Davies and Wife v. Solomon*,[44] which held that the kinds of heads of damages claimed by Eliza, loss of the "hospitality" of friends and the support and companionship of her husband, were sufficient to maintain a claim for special damages. The three-judge panel also agreed with Cameron on the argument about coverture. Having agreed that the action was Eliza's and being allowed to testify as a result, Robert could not now use Eliza's coverture to nullify the damages award. Indeed the argument, opined the court, "comes now with ill grace" from Robert.

More importantly, the judges, including Hagarty, unanimously confirmed the rule for a new trial on the basis of the unreasonableness of the jury's verdict. It was a verdict "attributable to sympathy with the wife, rather than to an intelligent and impartial appreciation of the evidence." No doubt Galt had his own view of whether adultery had occurred from having sat through the previous case. The judgment, however, did not say anything about why the verdict was unreasonable, it simply said that the jury's verdict in the crim. con. trial was "conclusive" on the issue of adultery, as was that of Chancery judge's Samuel Hume Blake similar verdict in the next case, discussed in the next chapter, on Eliza's application for alimony.[45] But the verdict in the crim. con. case had been given by a different jury on different evidence, and in law it was in no way "conclusive" of the issue. The court was wrong to treat the prior jury's verdict as determinative, especially as at the time the *res judicata* doctrine required mutuality of parties; a verdict in one case only decided a future case if the parties were the same, and here they were entirely different.* Gwynne's reference to the Chancery decision is also instructive. As we will see in the next chapter, the Chancery judgment in the alimony case also turned on whether Eliza had committed adultery, and the judgment was released in September 1875. The Common Pleas judges, therefore, sat on their decision in the defamation case for seven months after hearing argument in May 1875, and during their wait Samuel Hume Blake, the Chancery judge, issued his judgment. Three months after he had done so the Common Pleas panel released their judgment, referring to Blake's decision as conclusive. As discussed in chapter 5, Gordon's application for a new trial in the crim. con. case was also delayed until after Chancery had given its decision. The conclusion that the judges discussed all three cases to ensure that they came up with consistent rulings is inescapable. Eliza never proceeded with the new trial. By the time the Commons Pleas judges gave their judgment, she and Cameron must have been clear about one thing: No judge in Ontario was going to find in her favour, even if one jury had.

* *Res judicata* is Latin for "judged matter" – the matter has already been adjudicated. I thank Robert Sharpe for pointing out the importance of mutuality in the past. The modern law is not so insistent.

7
The Campbells Go to Court III: Eliza Campbell v. Robert Campbell for Alimony, 1874–1875

Introduction and Preliminary Proceedings

Eliza Campbell sued Robert for alimony before she had been thrown out of the family home, James Gordon filing suit on her behalf on 10 September.[1] Alimony was a remedy available to a married woman whose husband failed to fulfil his common law duty to support his wife. In the United Kingdom it was awarded by the ecclesiastical courts before 1857, and by the Court for Divorce and Matrimonial Causes thereafter. No Canadian colony had ecclesiastical courts, but in Ontario alimony was considered to be within the jurisdiction of the Court of Chancery once that court had been established in 1837, even though the relevant statute did not expressly say so. When the court's jurisdiction over alimony was challenged in 1851 then Chancellor William Hume Blake simply asserted that as it "had been assumed and exercised" from its establishment, the practice would continue until corrected by a higher court.[2] Women who applied for alimony, women who had either been deserted by their husbands or who had been subjected to violence, and/or other treatment that, according to the common law, entitled them to no longer live under the same roof as their husbands, were invariably successful. Elite men who had no truck with any suggestion that the fundamental inequality of husbands and wives in marriage should be changed, the equity judges were nonetheless usually tough on men who did not carry out their side of the marital bargain. Women were less successful in collecting on their awards, but they did win most cases – provided they had not themselves committed adultery, which justified a husband refusing support.[3]

It would take time for the case to go to trial, and until then Robert was required by the law of husband and wife to pay Eliza interim alimony, the standard amount being $50 a month. Not surprisingly he did not pay, and in November 1873, following his success in the crim. con. suit, Robert tried to relieve himself of his obligation to do so. The motion was heard by George Smith Holmested, a barrister of seven years' call who had been appointed referee in Chambers in the Court of Chancery at the end of 1872.[4] Eliza was represented by John Hoskin, Q.C., and Arthur Godfrey Molson Spragge, both lawyers who specialized in equity in the period before the courts of common law and equity were "fused," combined in one Supreme Court of Judicature. Spragge was very well connected, the son of John Godfrey Spragge, the chancellor (chief judge) of the Court of Chancery, but a very recent admission to the Law Society (1869) and the junior on the case. Hoskin had been called to the bar in 1863 and the firm he founded became, in 1882, the still existing Toronto megafirm Osler, Hoskin, & Harcourt.[5] Thus yet again Eliza was represented by elite lawyers, albeit on this occasion ones early in their careers, one of whom was more from an elite legal family than he was an elite lawyer. On the other side was William Alexander Foster, called to the bar in 1861. Common law expert Harrison was not involved, this being an equity case. Foster was a successful lawyer, but his main interest was politics. He was an ardent nationalist and one of the founders of the Canada First movement.[6]

Foster argued that alimony was awarded because the common law rules about married women's property presumed that a wife had no means of support and therefore needed it from her husband. But statutory changes to the law of married women's property, most recently the *Married Women's Property Act* of 1872, had done away with the presumption that a wife had no property to support herself as she was now allowed to hold her "separate property," property that had been hers before she married or that she had acquired by her work since then, "free from any … claim of her husband."[7] Thus interim alimony should not be granted "as of course," and refused "if it appears that the wife's conduct is such as to disentitle her." Foster suggested that it did so in this case and wanted to be allowed to put in affidavits to show that Eliza had committed adultery.[8] Holmested found for Eliza. He rejected the idea that the 1872 Act had eliminated the common law duty of a husband to support his wife, likely relying on the presumption that statutes did not change the common law unless they did so expressly, and the equitable principle that interim alimony was always granted by the court pending a full hearing on the matter. The merits could not be decided on an application for interim alimony. Holmsted referred the question of the amount to the master at Whitby, who set it at $50 a month. Robert did pay the alimony for almost two years.[9]

Chancery had always operated with different procedures than the common law courts, most importantly in not using juries. For a long period of its history in England, Chancery also did not take *viva voce* (oral) evidence, using written depositions instead, but that changed in the nineteenth century, in both England and Canada West/Ontario. This change was one of a series of reforms in both jurisdictions that responded to critiques that Chancery was a rich man's court, inaccessible to the ordinary person and inordinately slow, and also to arguments that it made no sense to have two different kinds of courts operating with different procedures and different substantive rules. For our purposes this meant that the Court of Chancery was allowed to appoint local masters and deputy registrars in the various county towns in 1850, and its judges began going on circuit in 1857 to hear cases, just as the common law courts had long done. As there were no juries, the evidence could be adduced in the county towns with legal argument and judgment delivered later in Toronto.[10] Transcripts of what was said in Whitby were made for later review by the judge.[11]

The Court of Chancery on Circuit in Whitby

When the Chancery court arrived in Whitby as part of its semi-annual circuit in late April 1874 it was only a month after the jury had found for Eliza in the defamation case. She and her counsel must have felt confident. Although she had been found to have committed adultery in *Campbell v. Gordon*, the defamation case had come to the opposite conclusion, because she had been able to give evidence in the latter and had witnesses to cast doubt on Campbell's and Anderson's stories. The same would be true in the alimony case, and she was having part of the case heard in her hometown, where she remained popular. It would not be decided by a home-town jury, but she must surely have thought that the venue was to her advantage. Her hopes turned out to be ill-founded.

The court was presided over by Samuel Hume Blake, one of two vice-chancellors on a three-judge court, the head of which was Chancellor John Godfrey Spragge. Blake was the son of William Hume Blake, the architect of the court reforms of 1849 which had established the three courts discussed in chapter 5. He was called to the bar in 1860 and practised with his famous brother Edward, justice minister in the Liberal government of Alexander Mackenzie and founder of the still existing Blake's law firm, one of modern Toronto's megafirms. In 1872 one of the vice-chancellors, Oliver Mowat, resigned to become leader of the provincial Liberal party and premier, and John A. Macdonald

Figure 7.1. Vice-Chancellor Samuel Hume Blake

Source: Dictionary of Canadian Biography Online

chose Samuel Hume Blake to replace him despite the fact that, like his father and brother, he was an avowed Liberal. He was only 37 when appointed to the bench, testament to his sterling reputation as a lawyer. Blake was prominent in the evangelical wing of the Anglican establishment. He had married the daughter of Bishop Benjamin Cronyn of London, Ontario, was a life-long temperance advocate, a Sunday-school teacher for decades, and spoke out on a variety of social and religious questions, including prison reform. He was dubbed "Psalm Blake" as a result. He received a good deal of adverse comment and was the subject of complaints to the federal government about his apparent lack of impartiality derived from his social reform commitments. In 1881 he resigned from the bench and devoted himself to his very successful law practice and his many and varied public campaigns. He turned out not to be the best judge Eliza could have drawn.[12]

Cameron again acted for Eliza, Thomas Moss, not Harrison, for Robert. Moss had been one of the best students at the University of Toronto, was called to the bar in 1861, and a decade later was a leading equity practitioner, appointed equity lecturer for the Law Society. In 1871 he went into partnership with his brother Charles, later chief justice of

Ontario, and others, a partnership that Robert Harrison joined in 1872. Harrison obviously thought it was better for an equity lawyer to take the case in Chancery, despite his own familiarity with it. Moss was a Liberal federal MP when he argued the Campbell case and, like his brother, later became chief justice of Ontario.[13] The same two local lawyers as in the other two cases, James Gordon and George Young Smith, were their juniors. Cameron had double-booked himself, and was only present for the first two days, Wednesday, 23 April and Thursday, 24 April, because he had to appear at the Welland Assizes. His place was taken by Dr. Daniel McMichael, yet another leading counsel. He had been called to the bar at the age of 33 in 1849, was a bencher of the Law Society from 1863 to 1891, and had been made a Q.C. by both the Canadian and Ontario governments in 1872. In the 1860s he was a member of a law firm headed by Matthew Crooks Cameron, and the latter obviously had a high regard for his abilities. McMichael had handled at least one case involving adultery; he represented lawyer William Lount when he was sued by another lawyer, John Martin, for criminal conversation in 1870.[14]

Yet again the case turned on whether Eliza had committed adultery, with the same principal witnesses on each side. While much of what was said was familiar from the two previous trials, more new witnesses had been found by Eliza's family and counsel to cast further doubt on the story told by Campbell and Anderson. This time around the *Globe* did not report the proceedings, presumably not considering them important enough to send a reporter to Whitby, although in September 1875 it did publish a brief summary of Blake's judgment.[15] A very brief account of the proceedings was printed in the 23 April issue of the *Whitby Chronicle*, and there was a much longer report in the issue of 30 April.[16] There is a more detailed account of some of the evidence, especially that of James Campbell and Anderson, which included their depositions, reproduced in Blake's judgment delivered a year and a half later in September 1875 and reported in *Grant's Chancery Reports*. Robert Campbell also swore a deposition for this case, reproduced in part by Blake.[17] What follows is an amalgam of these sources. As with previous chapters, I have not footnoted quotations from the principal source, the *Whitby Chronicle* of 30 April, but I have footnoted quotations from the other sources.

The Witnesses for Robert Campbell

Moss presented witnesses on Robert's behalf first, because Robert was the "moving party," Eliza having won her case for interim alimony.

There were six witnesses for Robert, all people who had testified at the two previous trials. In order of appearance, they were the Newsom sisters, William Fagan, George Cameron, John Anderson, and James Campbell. The *Whitby Chronicle* very briefly summarized what they said as the same as the evidence they had given in the other two cases, with some "slight additions and variations."[18] The *Oshawa Reformer* was altogether less prosaic, referring to Campbell's and Anderson's accounts of what they had heard as "painful," "disgusting," and "foul."[19] One notable point about both of the first two days was that women substantially outnumbered men among the spectators, and they were collectively rebuked by Blake for their "prurient curiosity" about the evidence given. The *Whitby Chronicle* received two "indignant letters" about the behaviour of these Whitby women, but did not print them because it did not wish to "subject our townswomen to the humiliation of publishing" comments on "the impropriety of their attendance."[20] There were men in attendance also, but no suggestion that they should not have been there. While the Whitby townsfolk knew all about the scandal of the Campbell marital breakdown, many would not have been able to attend the two trials in Toronto. This was therefore their first opportunity to hear the evidence that the newspapers would not print.

The first witness was Martha Newsom, whose evidence, while not reported in the *Whitby Chronicle*, was summarized in Blake's judgment. She said in chief what she had said in the defamation trial. Cameron cross-examined her, getting her to confirm that the parlour door was not closed on any of Gordon's visits. On re-examination Newsom said she thought Gordon coming there so often was "strange," and "not proper." Martha was succeeded by her sister Jane, whose evidence was again reproduced in part in Blake's judgment. She recounted the events of 26 August, with the only noteworthy thing she said being that Newsom had asked Eliza "if her beau had left," and Eliza replied, "No." Cameron cross-examined her on this, asking if she thought her question to Eliza impertinent, and Newsom said she did not think so "because Mrs. Campbell had been very free in asking me questions."[21]

The next witness was John Anderson. He gave *viva voce* testimony and the statement he had written of the alleged events, discussed in previous chapters, was also presented in court as an exhibit.[22] He was cross-examined by Cameron, his answers, reproduced by Blake in his judgment, telling a familiar story. Cameron tested him as best he could under cross, asking whether he was hard of hearing. His main line of attack was about the statement he had written. This time it was brought out that he had initially written the statement on Sunday, 31 August, at his own house, and then showed it to the Campbells. After he had done so he "made an alteration in my statement in regard … to what Campbell said to Gordon." Cameron asked, Who had struck out the original words? Anderson. Cameron asked, Why? "Because I afterwards recollected the correct words used."

The last witness for Robert was James Campbell. What he said on direct examination was extensively reproduced by Blake in his judgment.[23] Moss led him through the by now familiar story of the evening of 26 August, and anticipated a question that had come up before: Why did Campbell not intervene and stop what was happening? His answers were a mixture of his inability to do so and his desire to catch them in the act, the latter coupled with an inconsistent assertion that he was not there to gather evidence:

> I don't think I could have prevented what I saw taking place when I went there, for I thought Mrs. Campbell and Gordon were so intimate that it would be useless to do so. I did not want to get evidence as to my brother's wife's criminal actions. I could not go in without ringing the bell. I could have gone in by the kitchen. I wanted to satisfy my mind as to the position of my brother's wife.… I wanted to satisfy myself by going to the window and listening.

Campbell testified to two further things. First, he had written out two statements of what had occurred. The first was written on "rough tea paper," and later he made a fuller statement, presumably on better paper, for Harrison. Second, on re-examination he was asked about Anderson's drinking habits, something Cameron presumably raised although Blake did not reproduce any part of the cross-examination. Anderson may well have been known as a "drinker." In July 1875 he was convicted by the Whitby magistrates of being drunk and disorderly.[24] On this occasion Campbell asserted that Anderson did not drink "once in six months," and neither of them had had anything to drink before going to the house on the night in question.

The Witnesses for Eliza Campbell

On the second day, Thursday, 24 April, Cameron had his turn, and he began with six witnesses who had not appeared at the previous trials: Yeoman Gibson and his wife, Mary Jameson, William Calvery, John Stanton, and Walter Coulthard. He also called four people who had previously testified: Wellington Adams, Jane Allin, James Davison (or Davidson), who roomed with Adams, and George Gross, but there was no report in the newspaper about their appearances or what they said.

We know they testified only because Moss briefly reviewed their evidence in his arguments later in Toronto. However, it is reasonable to think that Adams, Allin, and Gross told much the same stories that they had given in the defamation trial, stories adverse to James Campbell's account of the time the altercation in the street occurred. Cameron finished the day with George Gordon.

Yeoman Gibson was the most important of the new witnesses. Born in Ebberston, Yorkshire, a village near the English Whitby, he had emigrated to Canada West in 1847 at the age of 19 and took up residence in the town of the same name. He had been a clerk and bookkeeper, went into business as a produce dealer with William Laing and Robert Yarnold, and then set up on his own. He was a successful and sufficiently well-respected businessman to be elected to the town council and to be chosen by his fellow councillors as mayor when John Hamar Greenwood resigned in 1875. A pillar of the Methodist Church and the Masonic Lodge, his obituary described him as "noted for his social manner, open heart and liberal views."[25] He was called by Cameron to testify to the fact that he and his wife Belinda had passed by the Campbell house between 11 and 11:15 p.m. on the 26th and heard Eliza playing music and singing. He said to Belinda, "That's Mrs. Campbell playing," and she remarked, "She must have company." Gibson also said that Eliza was a "beautiful singer and player" and that he had stopped to listen to her on many occasions when passing the house. The Gibsons also saw two figures under the veranda, one wearing a white hat, which seemed to confirm that it was the 26th. This was clear evidence that Campbell and Anderson had lied when they had repeatedly claimed that they had not heard any music or singing. It was also entirely new evidence, the Gibsons not having testified in either of the previous two cases. Cameron asked Gibson why he had not come forward with his story before, and Gibson explained that he had not noticed when reading the newspaper report of the crim. con. case that Campbell and Anderson had sworn they did not hear singing, but he had picked up that point from the press reports of the defamation trial. When he did so he had said to those around him at the time in his store, "That's confounded wrong."

Gibson was cross-examined by Moss, whose initial questions tried to establish that the singing and playing could have occurred on a different evening. Gibson was adamant that it must have been the 26th because that was the only night that he had been out walking that week, and his wife was with him on that occasion, and they discussed the singing. Moss moved to other questions designed to cast doubt on where the music came from. Gibson could not distinguish the voices, he was too far away, which seemed to contradict his statement that

Figure 7.2. Yeoman Gibson, c. 1880
Source: Whitby Archives Photograph 31-009-015

he distinctly recognized Eliza's voice, although he then repeated that statement. He only listened for about a minute and a half, and the singing and playing stopped when he moved away. He had talked with his wife about what he saw and heard that night, and they had talked about it more when he came home from a trip to Montreal, as his wife informed him that "there was trouble in Robert Campbell's house."

Moss then asked him questions about his relationship with the Campbells and any conversations he had had with them or others. He had talked to James Campbell about the problems in the Campbell household in the street one day in late August, and he had also talked about the same subject to John Stanton, who was the mechanic and typesetter for the *Whitby Chronicle*.[26] He had conversed with James Byrne the day after the defamation trial. Having read a newspaper account of Campbell's evidence in that trial Gibson had decided that Campbell had been "wrong" about the singing, although he considered himself "as good friends as ever with the Campbells." He denied telling William Laing, a former business partner and a successful grain dealer and the treasurer of Ontario County, that the Campbells were interfering with his business; he was not in the same business as the Campbells.[27] Gibson was followed to the stand by his wife, who corroborated what he had said. She was sure that the night she had heard singing was 26 August, and equally sure that the music could not have come from another house. Moss cross-examined her at length but could not shake any part of her testimony. The Gibsons must have been very effective witnesses, casting grave doubt on an important aspect of the evidence of Campbell and Anderson.

Belinda Gibson was followed by Mary Jameson, the woman said to have told James Campbell's wife Rebecca about Gordon's evening visits to the Campbell house. She testified that before the defamation trial Robert Campbell had asked if she could confirm what was written on a sheet of paper that he had, as the information she had given to Rebecca Campbell. She said that she could not because those were not the words she had used, and that Rebecca Campbell was "a very mean woman to say so." Moss cross-examined her, establishing that she and Rebecca Campbell had talked about the Campbell marriage as "unhappy" before 26 August. Moss asked her about her "mean" comment, and Jameson responded that she did not think it mean to write down what she said in these conversations, "if she did so correctly." Although she lived only a short distance away from the Campbell house, she never saw Gordon going there nor had she seen Gordon and Eliza together. She had heard of Gordon going to the house while Robert was away from her sister, who had seen it once, but had not witnessed it herself. Jameson's evidence was somewhat helpful to Eliza, for it cast doubt on how many times Gordon had visited in the summer.

Jameson was followed by three more witnesses called by Cameron. William Calvery, described as a solider (presumably a member of the militia), and John Stanton testified to what James Campbell had said at the defamation trial, which they had both attended.[28] Overall the witnesses called by Cameron, opined the *Whitby Chronicle*, had given new evidence favourable to Eliza. Cameron also called Wellington Adams, James Davison, Jane Allin, and George Gross. But we know very little about what they said beyond the fact that they talked about the time at which they were woken by the ruckus on the street, and that Adams actually corroborated James Campbell on the issue of what he said to Gordon, although he said the words were spoken much earlier than 3 a.m.

The next, and obviously a crucial, witness was George Gordon. All we know about his examination in chief is that his evidence was the same as he had given in the defamation case, and that he denied "in positive terms" any sexual intercourse with Eliza. He was subjected to a long cross-examination by Moss. His answers were invariably a mix of positive assertions – for example, he definitely did not visit Eliza more than three times when Robert was away – and a refusal to be specific about details – he could not recall when the visits occurred. Dates "made no impression on him." Whatever the date, he went there to return some books he had borrowed. Gordon was clearer about how long he stayed. The only time he stayed after 12 was the night of the 26th, but there was another occasion when it was "pretty near" 12. He was "not in the habit of sitting up with married ladies until after twelve o'clock." Moss then asked him when he knew that Robert was going to Southampton? He was trying to make it seem that the two had arranged something for Robert's absence. Gordon's response was that Eliza had told him at church on the Sunday that Robert was going away, and on Tuesday the 26th she said that he had gone. It came up in casual conversation the first time, and either when he walked her home on the 26th or after they had gone into the house. He could not recall whether he knew if Robert was in the house when he entered. He certainly did not know before or after he entered the house that Robert had taken the children.

Moss then honed in on the night of the 26th, asking which songs had been sung, and Gordon gave the answers he had given previously. He did not know the pirate song so he did not join in. He did not know how many songs there were but he could remember the three mentioned in chapter 5, and as he had heard "Kathleen Aroon" before, Eliza having sung it on other occasions, he knew the words and joined in. Moss asked him about his evidence about the songs in the defamation case, and he said that on that occasion he had referred to "two or three songs" but the newspaper report of the trial was wrong, because he had mentioned the pirate song and had said it was the first one sung. The questions about singing ended with Gordon saying that it stopped about 11 p.m., although of course he could not be sure of the exact time.

The next subject covered was Eliza's reading to him. Gordon could remember very little. Eliza read several pieces out of a "scrap book," and extracts from three books, but he could not remember how many. He could remember two of the book titles, but not what she took from them, although some of the pieces were funny and he laughed. He could not recall how long all the reading took; it might have been half or three quarters of an hour, he did not look at his watch. Nor could he recall whether she was sitting on a chair or at one end of the sofa; he thought it was a chair; he was sitting at the other end of the sofa, if it was the sofa. The overwhelming impression a listener would have had was of someone listening politely while entirely uninterested or even bored. Gordon remembered more about the games of checkers that followed the reading. They played two or three games, with him sitting on the sofa and Eliza on a chair in front of him with the checkerboard on her knees. He won all the games. He left immediately after the checkers, having checked his watch and discovered that it was 1:15 a.m. He was not "horrified" to find what time it was, but he was surprised. At some point in the evening, Gordon could not remember when, Eliza said that "she supposed James Campbell would be outside watching."

Moss pressed Gordon on what time he had left the Campbell house, pointing out that an affidavit Gordon had signed as part of the application for a new trial in the crim. con. case said that he had left at 1:45 a.m., not 1:15. Gordon's explanation was that the affidavit had been prepared by his brother James, with whom he had talked about the matter many times, and Gordon had read it over in a great hurry. So great was the hurry that the statement about 1:45 "never caught his ear." He only found out what it said when he read a copy two or three days before the defamation trial. Whether Moss had any more to say on that is not reported. He moved back to the conversation after the singing. Although Gordon did not remember all, or much, of what was said, he did recollect a mention of going to California. It was all "mere playfulness and joke." Moss then revisited the issue of Gordon's visits to the Campbell house. Gordon said he had been there on one Saturday night during Robert's absence, but he could not recollect if he was the only guest. He had heard two Saturdays were sworn to by a previous witness – but then "a good deal had been sworn to that never took place." This was a good riposte, and Gordon followed it by "positively" denying that he had been alone with Eliza on two Saturday nights. Moss then went at him from all sides: He did not know when the servant went to bed; he had not heard her go to bed on the 26th; Eliza read pieces to him, she did not recite them; he could not recall whether she had read to him on any other occasion; when he finally got home on the 26th it was 2:45 a.m.

Moss's final set of questions returned to the time in the parlour and then to the events in the streets after Gordon had left the house. Moss asked if he requested Eliza to come closer to him while he was on the sofa. One might have expected a denial, but he said only that he could not recollect doing so. He did recall her asking him to "come up nearer" or to "come here to see the stereoscopic views." On the events after he had left, he said that he walked briskly from the Campbell house on Dundas Street as far as Gibson and Sparvel's store and then cut across the street on an angle to Lawler's store. He was about 9 to 14 metres (10–15 yds.) from the corner when he saw James Campbell and Anderson "on the run for him," going down Brock Street. The night was not dark, but he could not easily see people across the street. Not until he got as far as Jameson's could he see them clearly; they were standing behind the telegraph poles at Mason's tavern. There ensued a good deal of "loud talk" between him and James Campbell, but Anderson said nothing other than to identify Gordon when Campbell asked him to. When they got opposite the Campbells' store Campbell and Anderson went in, Campbell shouting out, "I'll have you arrested in the morning. I'll make it hot for you in the morning, my boy." The feisty Gordon gave as good as he got: "If you come out on the sidewalk I'll make it hot for you just now." He followed this by telling Campbell to "bring out his long-legged mate too, [Anderson]," he could deal with both of them. After a few more questions Gordon's testimony ended, and with it the court day.

Vice-Chancellor Blake's Intervention to Urge Reconciliation

When the court opened the following day, 25 April, McMichael had replaced Cameron and called Eliza to the stand. But before any questions could be asked Blake said that he wanted to make some remarks, which turned out to be a plea for reconciliation.[29] He had listened "with extreme regret" to the "painful recital of facts" for two days, and he was sure that no "right feeling person in court" would not agree with him that it would be better if a settlement was reached. He thought Robert in particular would want this, having already seen his wife giving evidence in previous cases and being subjected to a "painful examination." Robert should "consider well all the consequences before again putting her through the ordeal." Blake stressed that he was not taking sides. Robert had no doubt suffered because of Eliza's "levity of conduct" and "folly." But then, putting away the even hand, he sounded a note of warning. Although he disapproved of Eliza's behaviour, he had not yet been able to conclude that she had been guilty of the "gravest charge that a man can bring against his wife." Moss's great skill and eloquence "has failed to establish the charge against the plaintiff to the satisfaction of my mind." He therefore could not at this point conclude that he could "stamp Mrs. Campbell with the indelible stigma which must attach to her should I find in favour of" Robert.

This was a strong and surprising intervention, but it was not motivated solely by sympathy for Eliza. He was as much concerned that Robert had failed in his manly duty to give Eliza a chance to explain and to not do something he was threatening to do – break up a family and deprive the children of the love and guidance of both parents. Hence he appealed to Robert not to submit Eliza to another 'ordeal," for his "feelings as a husband" would mean that nobody would feel the pain of what she would go through more than him. Blake referenced Eliza's "appealing" letter of 28 August, which had been read by counsel and in which she "so beseechingly" asked for a chance to explain, and to remember 10 years of married life "passed in comparative happiness."[30] This last was a carefully chosen phrase. The evidence did not permit Blake to refer to 10 years of marital bliss, but bliss was not required or expected. Marriage was duty and stability.

Blake also invoked the children, who could not "plead for themselves." If the parents were again united they would be blessed. But if they remained separated the children "may grow up to regard with aversion" one or both of their parents. Thus Blake invoked Robert's "tenderness as a father." True to form "Psalm Blake" also brought in the Almighty. Both parties had only a "short span" to live, and "looking also to the light of the great Hereafter, to which we are all so rapidly hastening," he appealed to Robert "to spare his wife and himself this ordeal." Eliza had already gone through great misery, and surely Robert could now "rest assured" that "warned by the fearful ordeal she has undergone" Eliza would doubtless behave better in the future, would "cultivate that spirit of obedience to his wishes, which it is her duty to exhibit." She would more carefully look after the children and her household duties, be "a good wife and mother." Blake finished by returning to the fact that if he was not heeded, he would have to render a decision one way or the other, a decision that must ultimately be "fallible." If he found Eliza guilty when she was innocent, it would be Robert who would be responsible for "inflicting on her the greatest injury that can be done." Robert must "feel strongly the improbability of the truth of the grave charge made against her." He concluded by insisting that it was not too late to end things now, to allow the matter to conclude in "happiness" before a decision was made that "may do an irreparable wrong."

As he was making this speech the crowded courtroom in the small town was hushed, people hanging on to every word and some moved to tears. Whitby residents had been consumed with the Campbell matrimonial dispute for months, and this presaged a possible end to it. William Higgins's editorial in the *Chronicle* praised Blake's "eloquent and pathetic" intervention, which did honour to his "head and heart as a Christian judge." Blake had appealed to the parties "by every tender tie that could bind man and woman together." The brief silence that followed Blake's speech was then interrupted by Moss, anxious to clarify exactly where Blake stood. He presumed that Blake was "disposed to give … full credence" to the evidence of James Campbell and Anderson, "so much so" that he was not "foreshadow[ing] what conclusion he would come to." He had nonetheless understood Blake to say that at this point he saw the case as one "amounting only to … grave suspicion" against Eliza. The vice-chancellor wanted the couple to meet and resolve their differences, "without at the same time casting the slightest doubt upon the credibility of the witnesses on one side or the other." Moss's questions were delicately phrased to the point of obfuscation, because they were hard questions to ask. Had the judge made up his mind? If not, was he leaning one way, and if so, how far one way? Did he not find Campbell and Anderson to be credible witnesses? Moss wanted to know as much as possible about Blake's views, because he was going to have to advise Robert on the strength of his negotiating position.

Blake did not give Moss a lot of comfort. He said that while he had not concluded that James Campbell had acted in bad faith, he also did not think he had behaved in the way that he, Blake, would have. Blake did not want to say that James had any "bad purpose" in view when he went to the house; he should get credit for going to see how matters stood, and he acquitted James of "intentional wrong," which left open the door to finding that he had been unintentionally wrong. Tellingly Blake concluded by saying that were he to find against Eliza it would have to be "upon the most distinct and clearest evidence." English case authority required that there must be proof beyond doubt of the wife's guilt in such cases. Moss could not have been pleased with this answer, but there was nothing more he could do than suggest that the court move on to other cases while the attempt at a reconciliation took place.

Robert and Eliza met later that morning for about half an hour in a room at the courthouse. It did not effect a reconciliation, although the content of the conversation did not become public for another two years, when they both testified about it before the Senate divorce committee.[31] According to Robert Eliza asked him if he believed the adultery claim, and he responded that he did or he would never have taken the actions he did. Robert then asked her to explain the Parks letters. Eliza said they were "not proved," and he replied with obvious incredulity that she was surely not denying her handwriting? He asked her: "Eliza do you say that you did not write those letters?" She did not respond but asked him again if he believed the adultery allegation, and again he said that he did. According to Robert Eliza did not admit or deny the allegation of an affair with Gordon, she merely asked him if he believed it. Eliza remembered the conversation similarly. She insisted that Robert take back the accusation of adultery, but he would not. He was prepared to take her back into his house, but not as his wife. She would be in effect an unpaid housekeeper.

Thus neither of them gave an inch. Eliza perhaps believed that she would win the case and require Robert to support her and any of the children she could gain custody of. But an equal part of her perhaps did not care about that as much as she cared about her reputation. She was firm in her denials of any adultery, and she would not return to her husband unless he accepted that. The *Whitby Chronicle*, so laudatory of Blake's intervention and so much wishing for it to work, could only comment that whoever was responsible for the failure in the courthouse that day would live to regret it. Blake, out of "the kindness of his heart," had opened a door through which they could both walk out in peace, "leaving behind them further litigation, exposure and heart-burning," and go on their life's journeys "in quiet and happiness together." Instead they had chosen "the way of strife and misery, … to the regret of their neighbours and all right-feeling people." Higgins was naive. He did not understand Robert's adamantine insistence on his own rectitude and his fury at being, as he saw it, betrayed, and was equally unable to comprehend the strength of Eliza's conviction that, even if she had behaved foolishly, she had not abandoned her womanly virtue and honour.

The Taking of the Evidence Resumed: Eliza Campbell

When the court opened on Saturday, 26 April, Eliza was the first witness. She was likely on the stand for some hours. McMichael took her through her direct examination. Gordon had been at the Campbell home on a number of occasions, with Robert there, and she had met him at socials in other people's houses, including her father's. She had always seen Gordon as "on friendly terms" with Robert as well as with her, and when she was alone with him the drawing room door was always open. When asked about 26 August she acknowledged that that was one of the occasions he had visited, but insisted that neither on that occasion or any other had there been any "improper intimacy" between them. "Never (emphatically)" wrote the reporter. The only other point McMichael touched on was her relationship with James Campbell: "We have been on speaking terms, never on intimate terms."

Moss then launched into his cross-examination with a familiar issue – how many times was Gordon at her house when Robert was in the UK? She gave two different answers to this, "five or six times" and "three or four times," but only the latter included the phrase "alone with me." The former included occasions Gordon was there with others, thus her evidence matched Gordon's on this point – he had stuck to no more than four. Moss also asked the same questions that had been directed at Gordon and got the same mix of definite answers and cannot recalls. Was he there on the 2nd or the 9th of August, consecutive Saturday nights? He was there on one of those nights, but she could not recall which one. When Gordon first visited her house when Robert was away was it at her invitation? Eliza could not say. She had been standing at the gate with the children, Gordon walked by, they talked, and she asked him in. And what was that occasion? She could not recall the date, but she did know he came by between 8 and 9 in the evening and definitely did not stay as late as 12. Nor did she know whether the servant had gone to bed when he left. Newsom was in the habit of going to bed late; there was "no stated time" for her. When was the next time that Gordon visited after the chance meeting at the gate? Eliza could not recollect, she "kept no account." she did not know whether he came by invitation or not. Nor did she have any recollection of when he came next, or of when he left when he did come, although she did know that he once stayed after 12 but not when that was.

Whether Moss decided he had made his point, or that further questioning about Gordon's visits was pointless, he moved to Eliza's correspondence with Parks. He started with how and when she knew him, but she had, as usual, little to say that was precise beyond the fact that she did not know him before his arrival in Whitby. She could not say when he arrived beyond the fact that it was in the fall of 1872, or when he left other than that it was in February 1873. She also did not remember whether there had been any arrangement made as to whether they would correspond after he left, or whether she had told him he could write. Nonetheless she was not surprised when a letter came from him, although she would also not have been surprised had no letter come. She could not say when the first letter arrived; it was a week or two after he left and might have been in February. She surely strained Blake's credulity when she said she also could not remember sending Parks envelopes with her address written on them, although of course she also could not state positively that she had not done so. She acknowledged that his letter of 14 August 1873, did mention her sending envelopes and asked for more; she just did not recollect anything about them. Nor could she remember how many letters had passed between them; it might have been five or six; there certainly were "a number." She did not keep notes of what she wrote, nor make a draft, although "there may have been [notes] on some things written down by me."

Given all this vagueness it is not surprising that Moss went more directly at one of the two seemingly solid pieces of evidence, the draft of the letter found in her secretaire, that began: "I have been very remiss in answering your letters." "That may have been a letter to Mr. Parks," she replied, but it also may have been to "a lady correspondent." She had "an impression" it was to Parks, but she could not say for sure. She had not been writing to anybody else signing herself as "incognito" at that time. Moss "severely cross-examined" her "at length" on some expressions in this letter, which were read out in court. He asked especially about the sentence that talked of her going to Toronto to meet someone, but for some reason the reporter did not record her answer. He did, though, provide other answers to other questions. She had never spoken disrespectfully of Robert to Parks, although she did call him "the guardian." She had not seen Parks since he left Whitby. The papers found by Robert in her drawer were "memos" to be used in a romance she intended to write. She had wanted the correspondence with Parks to end and had written to him to that effect.

Moss changed tack, back to Gordon. Eliza had seen him on the Sunday before the 26th, while Robert was still in town. She "probably" told him that Robert was going to Southampton the next day, but she could not remember doing so. She thought she asked him in after he had walked her home on the 26th. They spent the next few hours in the parlour, until after 1 a.m. She left the parlour only once, to tell Jane Newsom to bring in a jug of water but did not go into the kitchen because there was a young man unknown to her sitting there. The time was spent in conversation and singing and looking at the stereoscope. She did not remember at what time they moved from one activity to another, or whether she got up from the piano between songs. She could remember telling Gordon that she thought James Campbell was outside on the veranda; she had twice heard noises from outside, one made by the lattice gate, as if someone had gone through it. She assumed it was

Campbell who had been in the yard because she knew that "he was in the habit of watching the house." Overall Eliza was not a persuasive witness. Far too many of her answers were that she could not recollect this or that, and listeners would surely have wondered how she could be so vague about an evening that had dominated and fundamentally changed her life ever since. She may, however, have been advised to stick to this approach because it was consistent with what she had said in the defamation trial. Moss would have seized on any inconsistency between then and now.

Moss's next set of questions were about James Campbell's actions on the evening of the 26th. Eliza was not surprised that James Campbell would do something harmful to her, but "did not believe he would make so vile a charge against me." She knew he had been watching the house for some time; she first noticed him while she and Gordon were playing checkers. The final questions on cross-examination covered a miscellany of issues, most of which had already been addressed, and produced answers as imprecise as those she gave throughout. She could not remember how long she had read to Gordon ; she may have sat on the sofa with him in the early part of the evening; she thought that she had proposed the checkers game; the game may have lasted an hour and involved "two or three" games; she could not "remember distinctly" whether she sat on the sofa next to him to play or on a chair in front of him. She was a little more sure that Gordon left a few minutes after the checkers, and thought it was 1:15 or 1:20 a.m. She could remember asking him what time it was and was "astonished" to find it was so late.

Eliza was briefly re-examined by McMichael, who had a few more questions about Parks. She had never been intimate with him. She had many "scraps" of writing in the drawer in addition to those Robert had taken, and she had broken off her correspondence with him. Blake interjected with a question about when her fourth child had been born. Perhaps he wondered about the connection between that child and the alleged tryst with Gordon. Eliza must have thought that was what lay behind the question, for she answered, "My child was born about four months after the 26th." Moss was then allowed a few more final questions. He asked about any discussion with Gordon on the 26th about elopement. Eliza said there were "allusions" to a conversation that had taken place "a long time before." Robert was present when the conversation took place. It derived from a newspaper story. Moss asked her about other topics discussed that evening. They included the army and navy, a subject prompted by her singing of "The Pirate's Serenade." Eliza's testimony concluded with a smattering of inconsequential questions, and she was then allowed to step down. As we will shortly see,

Blake's judgment concluded that she had committed adultery with Gordon. We cannot say if his change of mind, from not being persuaded on Friday, was in whole or in part a result of her unconvincing performance on the witness stand. All we can say is that it was unconvincing. Many of her answers were evasive, some frankly impossible to believe.

Moss called four more rebuttal witnesses, none of whom had much to say except for David Smith, Jane Newsom's young man. He gave his brief evidence mixed in with giggling "over the fun of the thing." He had walked home with Newsom on the evening of the 26th and spent some time in the kitchen with her. At one point Eliza had come out of the parlour to ask for a glass of water, and Jane had asked her, "Has your beau gone yet?" Eliza said no. It may have been the fact that his girlfriend had asked her married employer about her "beau" that made Smith giggle. The proceedings ended with Blake telling counsel that he would hear argument at a time convenient to them, and which he assumed would be after the summer vacation. Eliza and Robert would be in limbo for some months yet.

Local Reaction, Family Tragedy, and Legal Delay

As matters turned out it was over a year before Blake heard arguments from counsel, on 14 May 1875, and an additional few months, until 15 September, until he issued his judgment.[32] While everybody was waiting for the case to conclude another tragedy befell the Byrne family. The Rev. Byrne died at the age of 64 in November 1874 in Albany, New York, on his way home from a visit to the US. According to his obituary he died from a broken heart and shame at the scandal that had engulfed his favourite daughter. He had never been the same man since the crim. con. trial, the publicity accompanying it having brought his "venerable grey hairs ... to a premature grave." He had devoted his life to his calling and his causes and eschewed the things of this world. He left his widow and son James less than £600.[33]

People in Whitby were keen to know the result and puzzled by the delay. "AN ENQUIRER" asked the *Whitby Chronicle* early in 1875 if the case had been settled, prompting Higgins to say that many others had asked him for information. He blamed the delay on the lawyers, who had "dilly-dallied" and proved unable to agree on a date for the argument. Higgins expressed the frustration of Eliza and her family. She was "wasting away" with the anxiety, as was her "true-hearted brother," and her mother had been unwell since all the trouble started. The most victimized, of course, was Eliza's now deceased father, who had "died ... from the effects of the shock to his system."[34] Higgins hinted at dark forces at work. Was the delay wilful, an attempt to drag out the case to the benefit of "those with the longest purse?" This was an obvious reference to the Campbells, yet Robert was still paying interim alimony until the court ruled in his favour, if it did, and he likely felt unable to pursue proceedings for a divorce until the case was settled – a matter discussed in the next chapter. So Robert had no incentive to encourage his lawyers to delay. As argued in chapters 5 and 6 it is probable that the six common Pleas judges who still had the two new trial applications before them, and Blake, discussed their respective cases. They knew that all three cases turned on one factual question, and that two juries had decided that question inconsistently. They may have decided to delay their judgments to ensure they arrived at a consensus; thus delay in any one case meant delay in all three.

The Campbell brothers may have sunk even lower in public esteem during the wait. There had only been a few weeks between the torchlight procession celebrating Eliza's victory in the defamation case and the holding of the Chancery circuit, and now people had heard more of the locals cast doubt on their veracity. And when the neighbouring *Oshawa Reformer* discussed the Campbell case in a manner adverse to Eliza, Higgins's editorial in the *Whitby Chronicle*, entitled "Making a Bad Use of His Columns," told his fellow editor not to do so "in opposition to all the merchants, traders, and business men, … and even the women, of the town of Whitby."[35]

The Campbells seem to have taken it all quite badly, judging by attempts they made in 1875, while everybody was still waiting for Blake's verdict, to have the tax assessments of 13 of their fellow merchants raised in the local Court of Revision. Their reason for appealing other people's assessments was, they said, because they thought they had themselves been assessed too highly. The *Chronicle* was scathing in its denunciation of their actions. If they thought their own assessment wrong, they could and should have appealed that and try to have it lowered. But instead they "spitefully turn on their neighbours and seek to do them all the injury in their power." Higgins made a connection between this behaviour and the brothers' treatment of Eliza. "There is a vindictive meanness displayed" over the assessments, he editorialized, that was "quite characteristic" of them, and consonant with their other actions. In fact the Campbells did claim that they had attempted to appeal their own assessments, but had missed a deadline for doing so. When they asked to be allowed to proceed anyway, the court turned them down, twice.[36]

Robert likely did not care much about community disapproval. He was committed to one thing and one thing only – getting rid of his wife and divesting himself of any financial obligation to her. To that end, while he waited like everybody else for Blake's verdict, sometime in 1874 Robert ensured that Eliza was cut out of the will of an elderly wealthy Scottish relative of his and James, James Bremner. Bremner's will, originally made in 1867, had nine codicils, some of which left money to James and Robert and their sister Elizabeth. One of the codicils, added in August 1874, specified that the cash legacies to Robert were for the use of him and his children only. It also stated that "the same shall not be taken into account in any way or in any question between himself and his wife Mrs. Eliza Campbell or in any claim she may have against him in consequence of their marriage." Bremner would surely only have made this codicil if he had been told about the marriage breakdown by Robert and asked to ensure that Eliza had no claim on anything left the Campbell family in the will.[37]

On the other side of the community divide, George Gordon also remained somewhat in the local spotlight, though not in a good way. In March 1875 he was convicted in the Whitby magistrates' court of assault and battery on one Eliza Cross, a servant on the Gordon farm, for apparently striking her in the face when chiding her for disobedience for leaving the stove door open. His father William defended George in the press, arguing that he had only taken her by the shoulders and given her a "shake," while conceding that he should not have done even that. William Gordon blamed the legal trouble on a local JP, Wilcox, who had dissented in the proceeding which sent the assault charge against Robert to the Quarter Sessions. Wilcox had apparently persuaded Cross to lay a charge when she did not want to, and thereby "converted a molehill into a mountain" and "acted the part of a one-sided partisan magistrate."[38] It was really all a storm in a teacup, but it may have played some role in persuading Gordon that small-town life did not suit him, for in the spring of 1875 he followed the example of Godfrey Parks and went west, to Manitoba, as many Ontarians did in the 1870s.[39]

Legal Arguments in Toronto, 14 May 1875

The arguments of counsel in the Chancery courtroom in Toronto began with Moss, who pointed out that in cases involving adultery it was very difficult to obtain eyewitness accounts and that courts therefore did not require such direct evidence.[40] It was enough if it could be shown that the parties had been alone together and the opportunity arose to have "criminal intercourse." Given that Eliza and Gordon were alone together, the only explanation that was consistent with the circumstantial evidence was that they were guilty. Moss enumerated that evidence, highlighting the improbability of the story told by Eliza and Gordon. He started with the correspondence with Parks, which showed that Eliza was "a very fit subject for any seducer." She had not "kept her purity of mind unstained," had behaved with "great … impropriety." The claim that the evening had partly involved playing and singing was contradicted by Jane Newsom. There may have been reading and checkers, but it should be noted that the board was placed on their knees even though there was a table in the room. Eliza's claim that she told Gordon that James Campbell was "on the watch" could "hardly be credited," because if she had done so Gordon would not have stayed so late. The fact that Campbell and Anderson could not hear what was said early in their vigil had a simple explanation; Eliza and Gordon had spoken low while Newsom was downstairs. After she had gone to bed they spoke loudly enough that those outside could hear. In the alternative, the later the hour the stiller the night, enabling those outside to hear if the parties spoke at the same volume. Moving to the other side of the equation, Campbell and Anderson had no reason to try to destroy Eliza's character. No evidence had been produced to that effect.

Moss then reviewed the evidence tendered on behalf of Eliza. She had tried to establish that music had been played, but the weight of the evidence was against that. Eliza and Gordon had both claimed he left at 1:30 a.m., but Gordon in his affidavit had earlier sworn that it was 1:45. No importance could be attached to the evidence of Davidson and Allin about the time, and Gross's story was "extraordinary." As for Adams, his testimony corroborated that of Campbell and Anderson about what Campbell had said to Gordon on the street.

Cameron's reply took issue with Moss's characterization of the standard of proof when dealing with circumstantial evidence. Such evidence "must be such as would lead to the conclusion of improper conduct." This was not the case here. Gordon and Eliza were childhood acquaintances, and Gordon had been "intimate" with Robert and a frequent visitor at his house. If Gordon was to be found guilty of "impropriety and impudence" in seeing a married woman home, and accepting her invitation to come in, then "people of the utmost respectability" commit such improprieties every day. Cameron then "very strenuously" argued that the evidence of James Campbell and Anderson "cannot be accepted as worthy of credit." The weight of the evidence supported the claim that there was music and singing on the night in question; the Gibsons could not be mistaken about that, and Jane Newsom was too much absorbed with her "lover" to be reliable on the point. Cameron also cited Adams's evidence as being in his favour, because it showed when the altercation between Campbell, Anderson, and Gordon on the street had taken place.[41]

Moss replied with three shortly stated points.[42] First, there was no evidence to support the claim that Robert had dispatched his brother and Anderson to "get up evidence" of Eliza's adultery. Second, with reference to the evidence that had been given about Gordon being "intimate" with the Campbell family, it was a very different kind of "intimacy" while Robert was at home compared to when he was away. Third, there were plenty of cases where juries had found adultery based on circumstantial evidence.[43] Moss cited one Canada West case, *Frank v. Carson*, an 1864 decision given by Justice Adam Wilson in a crim. con. suit that involved Robert Harrison, Matthew Crooks Cameron, and Daniel McMichael as counsel.[44] It certainly supports the proposition that not only could adultery be proved by purely circumstantial evidence, but also that the evidence needed only to be strong, not overwhelming. Mrs. Frank and her husband were separated, and she lived at a boarding house where her bills were paid by Carson, who also supplied her with a bedstead and mattress. Carson visited her at all hours of the day, although there was no evidence that he stayed the night. They were often seen walking and driving together, and at one point she sent a telegram to her husband telling him she had money, a telegram she signed "Loo (short for Louisa) Carson." The jury found for Mr. Frank, and Carson applied for a new trial on various grounds including that the verdict was contrary to the weight of the evidence. Justice Wilson dismissed the application, noting that "looking at all these facts and circumstances, it is impossible to say that they are not evidence against him, more or less cogent, of the fact of adultery having been committed."

Blake's Judgment: 15 September 1875

Blake's judgment was released on 15 September, a year and a half after the evidence was taken, and published in *Grant's Chancery Reports*, the law report series dedicated to Chancery decisions. It must have been both a surprise and a bitter disappointment to Eliza and her lawyers given what Blake had said when he urged the parties to reconcile. It was later vigorously assailed by Eliza's lawyer in the Senate divorce hearing not only for that inconsistency but as fundamentally flawed in its reasoning.

Blake began with a recitation of the uncontested facts of the marriage and its breakdown, and then turned to a review of the applicable principles governing proof of adultery, which derived from the decisions of the English ecclesiastical courts that had dealt with matrimonial offences prior to 1857 and the establishment of the Court of Divorce and Matrimonial Causes.[45] His discussion of the English law took up some six pages in *Grant's Reports*. He began with John Aylife's text, *Forms of Ecclesiastical Law*, first published in the early eighteenth century but updated and republished a number of times thereafter, most recently in 1844.[46] The passage he cited read:

> Adultery being an act of darkness and of great secrecy, can hardly be proved by any direct means; therefore in relation to the proof of adultery, by reason of such difficulty, it happens that presumptive evidence alone is sufficient proof; and this presumptive proof is collected and inferred *ex actibus propinquis*, that is to say, from the proximity and nearness of the acts; and thus adultery may be proved by such inferences as are received and approved of either by law or nature.

Blake reinforced this point with quotations from other cases to the same effect. "[D]irect evidence of the fact is not required, as it would render the relief of the husband almost impracticable," and thus "there must be such proximate circumstances proved, as by former decisions, or in their own nature and tendency satisfy the legal conviction of the Court, that the criminal act has been committed." In adultery cases the court should rely as much as it could on precedents, but ultimately "it must find its way, as well as it can, by its own reasoning on the particular circumstances of the case." Blake followed these general principles by citing cases that had involved the parties being alone in a house together. In some the particular circumstances had led to a conclusion that adultery had occurred, but not all. Thus while such meetings were "highly improper," more was necessary to convince the court that "the woman has transgressed not only the bounds of delicacy, but also of duty."[47]

Having offered this caveat, which seemed to favour Eliza, he cited a further case, *Loveden v. Loveden*,[48] which cautioned against the use of "remote and artificial reasoning," and said that the court should employ the "guarded discretion of a reasonable and just man" in deciding whether circumstantial facts proved adultery. This was followed by a further three cases where a man and a woman were alone in a house, which compelled the same finding.[49] He then seemed to offer a further note of caution drawn from Thomas Poynter's *Marriage and Divorce*, which warned that "the same presumption of probability is not in every case to be drawn from the same facts."[50] But the real thrust of this contention was that an important circumstance was "the rank and condition, the situation and habits of the parties." One could not expect the same thing from people "in different ranks of life, and in different countries, different modes of education, and different notions and manners." Class and culture mattered, those of a "humble life" could behave in innocent ways but the same behaviour by the higher classes, people "of a more refined education," would naturally lead to a very different conclusion. This did not bode well for Eliza; she was not of the English gentry or aristocratic classes that Poynter had written about, but she was from a very respectable middle-class Christian Canadian family and was a reasonably well-educated and refined lady. She was not going to be given any benefit of the doubt based on ignorance and lack of upbringing.[51]

With that Blake turned to the Campbell marriage before 1873. He asked whether Robert and Eliza had an affection for each other, whether each was satisfied with the marriage, or whether, in the alternative, they "sought, beyond their own immediate circle, for pleasure which they did not find there." Eliza was a well-educated daughter of a clergyman, and a good musician. Robert was a man of "good business habits," but he took "little, if any, interest" in things that pleased her. They were not well-suited. The depositions and the *viva voce* testimony of each, which Blake reviewed, were consistent with that conclusion. This was the state of things when Robert left for the UK, and when he returned he found the letter of 14 August from Parks, which Blake reproduced, as well as the other scribblings by Eliza.[52]

Blake next extensively reviewed the written and *viva voce* evidence of Anderson and James Campbell about what they had heard. He took the opposite approach to the newspaper editors, providing many explicitly salacious details. He was reluctant to do this because of the unsavoury nature of the evidence, he said, but did so because Cameron had relied strongly on that evidence to argue that what the listeners' reported was not true. This meant that "any feelings of delicacy" must yield to the need to establish the facts on which the whole case turned. Eliza's correspondence with Parks, as well as the evidence in general, showed "beyond doubt" that Eliza's affections were "alienated from her husband." It was "plain that feelings were entertained by the wife for the young man with whom she corresponded, which no wife could have … unless her moral nature were more or less depraved." She had an "undue regard" for Parks, and the content of her writings "shew that her mind had been very considerably warped" prior to August 1873. In addition, the evidence clearly showed that Gordon had visited her often. On 26 August he left no earlier than 1:30 a.m. They sat side by side on the sofa for hours, playing backgammon "with their knees for their table."* The blinds were drawn, and sometimes an "extra precaution" was taken, pinning together the curtains and placing a footstool to hold them in place. Among other things they talked about eloping.[53]

There was only one conclusion to draw from all of this. Were they there "to repeat their pater-noster?" Blake rhetorically asked. It would be "more in accordance with everyday experience, to find that during these hours spent in such close proximity advantage had been taken of the opportunity afforded to give free course to their passions." As a general rule, where both parties had a "disposition" to commit adultery, and an opportunity arises to do so, "the act will also there be found." "Is it to be believed," he said, "that no inclination, which such circumstances ordinarily produce, was gratified?" Eliza in particular must have known that in spending hours alone with a young man she was "outraging her husband's feelings, and giving up all claim to anything in the shape of delicacy and decorum." There must have been "some object to be gained by such a course of conduct," and "no legitimate one was assigned even in argument." They did not have enough in common to otherwise explain "these constant and lengthened nightly meetings." It can only have been for "the gratification of her animal passions, or surrendering up her body to her paramour, in order by her compliance with his wishes … to retain him as her friend."

Blake turned next to the testimony of James Campbell and Anderson. It took the case from "one of the very gravest suspicion" to one in which "legal proof" was present. Their evidence had been assailed for James Campbell's animus and for discrepancies, and Blake agreed that as a result his evidence should be "narrowly scanned." Campbell had suspicions about Eliza and Gordon, which he dwelt on. He had a "ready tongue," which he used to tell Robert of his suspicions. And he made no attempt to warn Eliza, or to ask somebody else to do so. If he had taken the same trouble to prevent what happened as he took to procure proof of it, he would likely have succeeded. He and Anderson "were willing to play the spy and eavesdropper, with the expectation of being able to catch a wife … in the act of adultery." That having been said, it was one thing to consider their evidence "in a most guarded manner," but "quite another to reject it" in total. Blake did not think that they had manufactured their story. If they had "sunk so low as to conspire to ruin an unfortunate woman," they would have produced an agreed-upon statement, one that did not refer to the difficulty of hearing what

* The reference to backgammon was presumably an error caused by Blake not understanding the difference between board games.

was said and what went on. They would have both said that either the sofa or the floor had been used. They would not have said that they were listening from different places and that Campbell could hear better than Anderson as a result. There would not be a difference between them as to how many times Gordon and Eliza had intercourse. Despite the differences between their evidence, both agreed on the main issue – "the act of adultery had been committed." This was therefore in the class of cases where the evidence is strengthened by a difference in details and agreement as to the main points. The differences show that "the testimony has not been manufactured."

As for the argument that their evidence should be discredited because of the "improbability" of a woman like Eliza saying the things she said, it must be remembered that Campbell and Anderson were "shrewd enough" to know that some people would think Eliza could not possibly have said such things, and yet they reported them anyway. That was a factor that must be taken into account in deciding what weight should be given to their testimony. If they had sat down and decided beforehand what words would have led to the conclusion of adultery and been easily believable, they would have come up with different language. Moreover, while it was difficult to believe Eliza would talk the way they said she did, in such cases "judgment gives place to the passions," and words are spoken without much thought. Blake himself could hardly believe that Eliza had talked to Gordon about when she had last had sex with Robert, or that she would commit adultery when five months pregnant. But in the circumstances he could only conclude "that the process of rendering the mind impure had been going on for a longer time than might otherwise have been thought." This was a more reasonable conclusion than any other. Blake bolstered this assessment by a short diatribe on "impure literature." At the trial he had been shown books by George Sand, to prove that some of Eliza's writing were just extracts from Sand's novel *Monsieur Sylvestre.* Blake opined that if this was the case he could understand "how speedily her mind would be contaminated." It was not so much the novel in question that was corrosive, but Sand's earlier works that advocated "infidel and highly immoral views."

In the remainder of his judgment Blake dealt with two evidentiary issues about which he was less than entirely certain, both of which could have favoured Eliza. The first was whether Eliza had played and sang that evening. If it could be established that she had done so that would have cast into very serious doubt all of Campbell's and Anderson's testimony, for this was not one of those minor discrepancies that enhanced the veracity of the major points in their testimony.

It was a large and important difference between the accounts given. Blake resolved the question by concluding that the Gibsons, the only witnesses other than Gordon and Eliza to testify to the music, had got the evening wrong. They had seen two people in the grounds wearing white hats, but they were probably Jane Newsom and David Smith, who had walked in the grounds the evening of the 27th. The white hats would not have been visible on the 26th, because Campbell and Anderson had removed theirs, and their heads would have appeared black in the moonlight.

The other issue Blake was even less certain about was the hour at which Gordon, Campbell, and Anderson had left the house. He was unable to reconcile the testimony of the principal witnesses, nor that of the other people who lived on the main street. Wellington Adams, James Davidson, Conrad Gross, and Jane Allin all said it was earlier than Campbell and Anderson claimed. Jane Newsom's story of being awakened and hearing the words 3 o'clock supported that as the time but only "to a certain extent." Blake concluded that Campbell and Anderson had probably told the truth on this point, but even if they had not there was no reason to discredit their evidence on the main issue, and the time they all left did not matter. According to Campbell and Anderson the adultery had been committed by 1:30 a.m., and the case against Eliza was not made stronger or weaker by the time that Gordon left. There was no reason for Campbell and Anderson to have said 3 unless they, in good faith, thought that was the time when they left the house.[54]

Thus the facts overall supported the accusation of adultery. Should Blake "displace" this conclusion because "the persons implicated solemnly pledge their oaths to its falsity?" The answer was no. The case against Eliza had been proved by the evidence presented, and he could not conclude otherwise because of her denials. A wife accused of adultery will go to "almost any length" to deny it. Adultery was a "crime" that "at all times the parties are too apt to deny." This had been the case, the biblical expert Blake said, from the time of Solomon, and he cited the Book of Proverbs as support: "Such is the way of an adulterous woman; she eateth and wipeth her mouth, and saith, I have done no wickedness."[55] Blake explained why:

> The heinousness of the crime, the breach which it is almost sure to cause between the husband and wife, the injury to the children, the disgrace cast upon relatives and friends, the loss of social standing, combine to lead one, placed in this terrible position, to make any statement which may have the effect of freeing her from the impending calamity. The accusation

> made is so disgraceful in its character, and so dire in its results, that one feels justified in adding almost any other sin to it, in order to free one's self from the punishment so much dreaded, and to escape detection.[56]

The same could be said of Gordon, a man who "by falsehood and a system of duplicity, utterly irreconcilable with the conduct of an honest man, steals enjoyment regardless of the laws alike of God and man." Nothing would prevent such a man from lying in the witness box. Moreover, people of his "loose class" have a "code of honour" that requires "the protection of the female, even to the extent of perjury." In addition the evidence showing Gordon to be complicit was ample. When Robert went to the UK, his "back was turned," and Gordon's visits became frequent. Blake had no doubt that Eliza had told Gordon of Robert's proposed visit to Southampton, and that on the Sunday they made plans for an assignation on the 26th. He also thought that the story about naval and navel was manufactured between them once they knew that Campbell and Anderson would testify to having heard the navel discussion. Blake's inevitable conclusion was that "adulterous intercourse" had taken place. The case had caused him "very great pain," because it was "deplorable to witness the ruin which has been brought upon a household" by a lack of self-control. But then the social reformer on the Chancery bench showed himself. He "deeply sympathize[d]" with both parties and greatly regretted the failure of his attempts at reconciliation. Perhaps surprisingly he then observed that he did not see why the admittedly "grievous crime of adultery" should be viewed as "the unpardonable sin." He did not see that "an unfortunate woman" who "once becomes … a sinner" should be condemned forever by her "fellow sinners, … shunned by all earth's dainty clay." If she repented she and Robert should be able to come together, for that is what God, who always tempered justice with mercy, would want. Blake ended by reference to the difference between his role as a judge and his faith, having, of course, just injected the latter into his judgment. It was not "within my province to enter into the discussion of these questions; my duty ends with the dismissal of the bill."[57]

Blake's judgment must have come as a bitter surprise to Eliza. Her lawyer before the Senate in the divorce committee hearings in 1876 captured its tortuous reasoning well when he said that Blake had "argued himself out of his doubts in her favour, by a laborious process, which required 17 months to reach an adverse conclusion."[58] The *Whitby Chronicle* mentioned the Campbell family scandal as a major event in the town in its "1874 – A Retrospect" editorial at the beginning of 1875, but surprisingly did not report Blake's judgment.[59] However, an opinion piece in another local newspaper, probably written by a Whitby resident in the early months of 1876 as Robert's divorce petition was making its way through the Senate, stated that the "impression prevalent in Whitby" was one of sympathy and support. Eliza had been "extremely foolish" but was not guilty of adultery. It was "a very serious indiscretion" to have written "love letters" to Parks, and she was "excessively foolish" to have entertained Gordon when Robert was away. But that was the extent of her transgression. Indeed Whitby opinion attributed some of the blame to Robert, who was "much her elder in years" and cared only about his business.[60] Similar views were expressed in another piece in the *Hamilton Weekly Times* in 1876, which backed up its assertions by citing Jane Allin, who had just testified before the Senate divorce committee. She "affirmed that no lady or gentleman in Whitby believed that the charge had any foundation in fact."[61] Thus, as we will see in the ensuing chapters, many in Whitby continued to support her morally and, to the extent possible, financially, through the next few years as she fought her case in Parliament by opposing Robert's application for a divorce and in seeking a legal separation. In the immediate term Eliza not only did not get a larger monthly alimony award than the $50, she stopped getting even that. Blake's judgment, noted the *Whitby Gazette*, "opens the door for the husband to apply for a divorce with some chance of success."[62] This book now follows Robert through that door.

8
Robert Campbell Petitions Parliament for a Divorce, 1876

Canadian Divorce Law in the 1870s

Canadian divorce law in the 1870s was a complex mosaic of different provincial and territorial jurisdictions and cannot be fully understood without knowing something about the history of divorce law in England. Three provinces – Nova Scotia, New Brunswick, and Prince Edward Island – had divorce courts that had been created before Confederation, in 1760, 1791, and 1835 respectively. The Prince Edward Island divorce court was comprised of the governor and executive council, and it only ever granted two divorces. It was effectively moribund long before the 1870s. Like many aspects of their law Nova Scotia's and New Brunswick's divorce law was a product of their European settlers' New England heritage, and thus reflected the low Protestant view of marriage as a contract and not a sacrament.[1] Although "marriage and divorce" were heads of the federal Parliament's jurisdiction under section 91 (26) of the *BNA Act*, the federal Parliament did not legislate nationally in the area of divorce until the 1968 *Divorce Act*, and thus the maritime provinces' pre-Confederation divorce law stayed in force under section 129 of the *BNA Act* until it did so.[2] British Columbia's Supreme Court also had jurisdiction over divorce in the 1870s by virtue of its reception date for English law being 1858, the year after the UK Parliament passed the 1857 *Divorce and Matrimonial Causes Act*, which established the Court for Divorce and Matrimonial Causes.[3]

Neither Ontario nor Quebec had a divorce court before Confederation. The reception dates for Quebec and Ontario were 1763 and 1792 respectively, long before the 1857 UK Act. Quebec's law was, in any event, the 1866 *Civil Code of Lower Canada*, which mirrored Catholic doctrine in providing, in Article 185, that the only thing that ended a marriage was the death of one of the parties. The Upper Canada legislature passed one Act for a legislative divorce in 1838, and the Province of Canada passed four such Acts, although one was disallowed in London.[4] Thus, to the extent that it can be said that Ontario had a divorce law in 1867, it was that only legislative divorce was available. There were also no divorce courts in Manitoba or the Northwest Territories, because it was accepted in the 1870s that the 1857 UK Act was not in force in the prairie region. In 1919 the Judicial Committee of the Privy Council, the highest court of appeal for Canada, would decide that the 1857 Act had been part of the law of both Manitoba and the Territories (and therefore of the successor provinces to the Territories, Alberta and Saskatchewan) because it had been enacted before 1870, the reception date, and this made judicial divorce available.[5] But that was far into the future. In the 1870s residents of the prairie provinces and territories were in the same position as those of Ontario and Quebec. The only way to get a divorce was by private Act of the Parliament of Canada, which exercised the jurisdiction to grant divorces that the House of Lords had had in the United Kingdom before 1857. In the 1870s Canada was one of only two countries in the empire where at least some of the residents had to go to Parliament for a divorce. The other was Ireland.[6]

Robert Campbell had, therefore, to apply to Parliament. Despite the fact that Parliament passed no general legislation establishing a divorce court and delineating the grounds on which divorces could be obtained, it was quickly generally accepted that section 91 (26) gave it the power to pass private Acts of divorce.[7] Indeed, the oft-cited reason for divorce being in section 91, federal powers, and not section 92, provincial powers, was that Catholic Quebec would never enact a divorce law, and an avenue for divorce should be made available for Quebec Protestants. The new Dominion Parliament's first private divorce Act was passed in 1869 for Joseph Whiteaves, the curator of the Museum of the Natural History Society of Montreal. Three more divorce Acts, all for Ontario residents, were passed between 1870 and 1875.[8] Had Robert Campbell won his divorce case in 1876 he would have been the fifth person divorced by an Act of the Canadian Parliament. One other person applied for a divorce in this period, but his petition was rejected.[9] All of the divorce Acts passed in the early years of Confederation were for male petitioners; the first one for a female was not passed until 1878, when Mary Bates of Mitchell, Perth County, was divorced from her adulterous and bigamous husband.[10] It was not easy to get a divorce bill through Parliament. One of those who had succeeded, John Robert Martin, twice had his bill rejected before succeeding on the third attempt. The Senate, noted a Toronto newspaper, passed divorce bills "only on the clearest evidence."[11]

A parliamentary divorce was like any other Act of Parliament. The bill divorcing two people had to pass three readings in both Houses. A parliamentary divorce was, at the same time, also a judicial proceeding. The bill would be given a pro forma first reading in the Senate – divorce bills were always introduced in the Senate – and then a vote would be taken on second reading on the general principle of the bill. If the bill passed that vote it would go to the Senate divorce committee, which conducted what was effectively a trial. The parties were represented by counsel who adduced evidence from witnesses and presented arguments. If the Senate divorce committee found the evidence of adultery sufficient and the Senate as a whole adopted the divorce committee's report, the bill would go to third reading. If the Senate passed the bill it went to the Commons and underwent the same three readings. The Commons did not hold a hearing and receive evidence; MPs voted on the basis of the evidence adduced in the Senate, which was printed and distributed to all senators and MPs. Canadian parliamentary divorce law, unlike divorces granted by the English court, were gender neutral. Under the 1857 English Act a male applicant had only to prove adultery, a female applicant had to prove adultery plus some other aggravating matrimonial offence – incest, cruelty, bestiality, bigamy, or desertion. The Canadian Parliament granted divorces to either spouse on the sole ground of adultery.

Robert Campbell's Petition to Parliament

The Senate rules on bills of divorce required that notice be given by the party applying by publication for six months in the *Canada Gazette* and in two local newspapers.[12] This long period of notice was required because divorce was not seen simply as a matter that concerned the divorcing parties. The public interest was concerned because, as noted in chapter 1, marriage was viewed as a bedrock institution, crucial to social stability. Thus, married couples could not simply agree to be divorced and to satisfy the legal requirements by a collusive action. The long period of notice, and the requirement that it be advertised in two local newspapers, allowed third parties to know about the petition and to alert a senator or MP if they had evidence of collusion. Robert first advertised his intentions in June 1874, when the alimony case was still undecided, but did not carry through with a petition to Parliament.[13] The *Whitby Chronicle* claimed that "the unwarranted language" employed in that notice, presumably its reference to adultery, aggravated the decline in health of Eliza's father, who had already suffered greatly from the notoriety of the scandal, and he died of a heart attack in

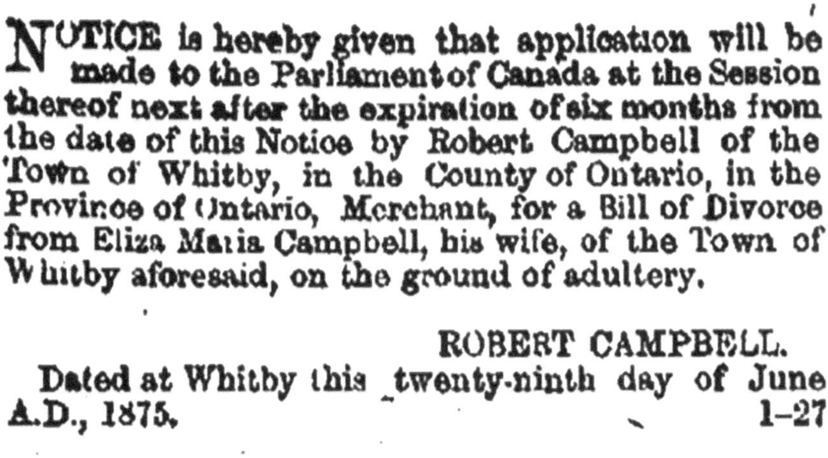

NOTICE is hereby given that application will be made to the Parliament of Canada at the Session thereof next after the expiration of six months from the date of this Notice by Robert Campbell of the Town of Whitby, in the County of Ontario, in the Province of Ontario, Merchant, for a Bill of Divorce from Eliza Maria Campbell, his wife, of the Town of Whitby aforesaid, on the ground of adultery.

ROBERT CAMPBELL.

Dated at Whitby this twenty-ninth day of June A.D., 1875. 1–27

Figure 8.1. Robert Campbell's divorce notice

Source: *Canada Gazette*, 3 July 1875, and *Whitby Gazette*, 9 September 1875.

November 1874.[14] Robert may have decided not to petition Parliament for a divorce because of his father-in-law's death. In any event he advertised again in July 1875 and for the ensuing six months (figure 8.1).[15] The notice in both cases was dated 29 June 1875. By this point the Campbell marital breakdown was well enough known that Robert's divorce notice was reported on in the Ottawa newspapers.[16] The rules also required Eliza to be served with the notice (Rule 73), which Robert did, by having it left at her mother's house. The server, Erastus Howard of Whitby, reported that Henrietta Byrne "supposed she must receive it." When the six months had expired Robert paid the $200 fee and filed a petition in the Senate asking that a bill of divorce be drawn up. His petition was accompanied by exemplifications of the judgments in the crim. con. and alimony cases, as required by Rule 74.*

The Senate that Robert Campbell petitioned in 1875 comprised 77 members. The *BNA Act* specified 72, 24 from each of Quebec and Ontario, and 12 senators from each of Nova Scotia and New Brunswick.[17] The total had increased to 77 by 1876, with the addition of two from Manitoba and three from British Columbia. Prince Edward Island also joined Confederation in the early 1870s, but its four senators replaced two of the Nova Scotia and two of the New Brunswick senators so as to keep

* An exemplification was a copy of the official record, accompanied by the seal of the court.

the Maritimes contingent at 24, the same as Ontario and Quebec. Senators were appointed by the governor-general, that is, the federal government, for life, not elected, and had to possess $4,000 in real estate. As John A. Macdonald put it in 1864, the Senate was not to represent the popular will, that was the role of the House of Commons. It was rather to be "the representative of property,"[18] comprised of men who had a substantial stake in the community but were not representatives of an entrenched ruling class like the House of Lords.

The original 72 senators were all former legislative councillors from the three confederating colonies in 1867. This had been a formal requirement in the Quebec Resolutions of 1865 and the resolutions passed in the London conference of 1866, and although it was not specifically included in the *BNA Act* it is generally assumed that section 127 is an implicit requirement that only legislative councillors were to be named to the Senate in 1867.[19] The same was not of course true for later appointments, including those for the provinces that joined after 1867, but senators appointed after 1867 were invariably members of the provincial political elite and supporters of the party in power in Ottawa. In the late 1860s and early 1870s the Senate had a substantial majority of Conservatives, including Liberal-Conservatives and independent Conservatives, over Liberals, Reformers, and independents, the result of the make-up of the legislative councils in 1867 and of Macdonald being able to make all replacement appointments up to late 1873.[20]

Robert's divorce petition had to be presented by a senator, like all petitions to the Senate. The senator asked to do this was customarily from the same region of the same province as the petitioner.[21] The only and invariable exception to this was that no Catholic would participate in any way in a divorce proceeding. Robert asked David Reesor of Markham, whom he did not know but who was the senator for King's Division, Ontario, which included the County of Ontario. Reesor was a successful farmer and prominent local politician from Reesorville, a village north of Toronto established in 1825 (now Markham), and the editor of the *Markham Economist*, who had been elected to the province of Canada legislative council in 1860. Although he favoured an elected Senate and was a Liberal, he accepted the appointment as one of the 24 Ontario senators chosen by Macdonald in 1867.[22] Reesor was married to Emily McDougall, sister of prominent Ontario politician William McDougall, who turned out to be Eliza Campbell's counsel in the Senate hearings, and although he did agree to present Robert's petition, Reesor proved to be Eliza's staunchest supporter in the Senate. Presumably if Robert had known of the connections among Eliza, Reesor, and McDougall he would not have asked Reesor to present his petition.

a026434

Figure 8.2. Senator David Reesor

Source: LAC

He also would not have done so had he been aware that Reesor knew something about the case beforehand, and that his sympathies lay with Eliza. News of the Campbell scandal had reached Markham, only 40 kilometres from Whitby. Reesor may also have known about the Campbell scandal from his eldest daughter Marion, who was married to an Oshawa physician. Testament to the notoriety the Campbell case had attracted Reesor claimed later that he was not optimistic about Robert's chances of success, telling him, "frankly and distinctly, that from what he had heard outside" he had doubts as to whether Campbell could make his case.[23]

Robert's petition was presented on 21 February, along with a certificate of service on Eliza, and a motion that it be "read and received" passed "on a division."[24] This was not a real division, with a vote taken. It had been the practice in prior cases to include the statement that there had been a division on a vote involving a divorce in order that Catholic senators would not be criticized by their constituents and the church for not actively opposing a divorce. Many Catholics also did not wish to stand in the way of Protestants whose religion did not prevent them from getting divorced. Sir Frank Smith, an Ontario Catholic and one of the richest men in Canada, had expressed this sentiment in a debate over second reading of a divorce bill for William H. Peterson of Guelph the year before. On that occasion three Quebec senators – Joseph-Hyacinthe Bellerose, Pierre Baillargeon, and François-Xavier-Anselme Trudel – stated that they opposed divorce on religious grounds and would vote against the bill. Smith found himself in a quandary. His religion told him that divorce was wrong; therefore he could not vote for one. But he also thought it "improper" for a Catholic to deprive a Protestant of the right to obtain a divorce. To do so would be to interfere with the law of the land and to force his religious opinions on others. Thus he would not vote for or against.[25] The practice of recording a division when none had occurred continued for decades. In 1876 Trudel, having changed his views from the year before, argued that a division that did not happen should be recorded as having done so, and all agreed.

Immediately after the motion to receive the petition passed, Erastus Howard of Whitby was called to the bar of the Senate to testify to service. Reesor examined him, bringing out not only that he had served Eliza but that he was well acquainted with the Campbell and Byrne families. He had known Robert for about 25 years and Eliza since she was a child.[26] Robert was in town for these preliminary stages, staying at the Windsor Hotel, having arrived there on 19 February.[27] We do not know if he sat in the Senate's public gallery, but given how keen he was to rid himself of his wife it is possible that he did.

The Campbell divorce bill was read for the first time on the following day, 22 February, and Reesor moved that it be read a second time on 8 March, at which time Robert Campbell would be examined. Again this passed "on a division."[28] The two-week delay between first and second reading was required by Rule 76. On 8 March the bill came forward again in the Senate as scheduled, and Reesor moved, seconded by fellow Ontario Senator Elijah Leonard, that it be read a second time and then referred to a committee to investigate. The first motion, for formal second reading, was actually voted on and passed 33–14, but the second passed "on a division."[29] Seventeen of those in favour were from Ontario, 12 were from the Maritimes, two were from British Columbia, and one from each of Manitoba and Quebec. All 33 were Protestants, including the one Quebec senator, Methodist James Ferrier who was one of the richest men in Montreal.[30] The 14 votes in opposition were all cast by Catholics: 13 from Quebec and Marc-Amable Girard from Manitoba. This was typical in the 1870s and for a few decades thereafter. When there was a recorded vote on first or second reading of a divorce bill the petitioner invariably won, but never without a significant minority voting against, all or most of them Catholics.

Having passed second reading the bill was referred to a select committee of nine: Reesor and eight others whom he chose.[31] Because he had introduced the petition Reesor was considered the sponsor of the bill, even though, as we have seen, he was less than optimistic about its chances. Not until 1888 was there a standing committee on divorce, which heard all the cases in the session. Before then a separate committee was formed for each case, chosen by the bill's sponsor. The committee was to consider all documents already presented to the Senate, plus the documents from the court cases, and take *viva voce* evidence for and against. The identity of these nine men is important to this story, for they made the decision to reject the claim of adultery and give Eliza her own unique remedy. Reesor chose four fellow Ontarians: James Cox Aikins, Elijah Leonard, Walter Dickson, and Benjamin Seymour, of whom only Dickson was trained as a lawyer, although he had not practised for decades. Aikins joined Macdonald's cabinet in 1869 as secretary of state. He remained in that post until Macdonald's government fell and regained it in 1878 when Macdonald came back after the 1878 election. He was a conscientious administrator, a devoted Methodist, a firm supporter of temperance, and generally thought of as dull and reliable. Perhaps ironically his son, leading Winnipeg lawyer James Albert Manning Aikins, was the first Manitoban to be granted a divorce by private act, in 1892.[32] Elijah Leonard was a foundry owner from London who made a substantial fortune from manufacturing items for the Grand Trunk railway and diversified into a variety of other businesses. Although not a party man, he broadly sympathized with reform and Liberal principles and was the only senator who used the label "reformer." Walter Dickson was a Niagara lawyer, businessman, and a Conservative. The final Ontario senator on the committee was Benjamin Seymour, a Conservative and a merchant from Bath.[33]

The two men on the committee from Nova Scotia were both lawyers: Robert Dickey and Henry Kaulbach. Dickey was a Conservative, a native of Amherst, and a former member of the Nova Scotia legislative council. He had attended both the Charlottetown and Quebec City conferences leading to Confederation. Kaulbach, from one of Lunenburg's founding families of the 1750s, had extensive landholdings in that county and was also a shipowner and a Harvard-educated lawyer with considerable experience as a crown prosecutor. He had a reputation both for harshness and sharp dealing in business, and he represented Lunenburg in the Nova Scotia assembly from 1863 to 1867 as a Conservative. He ran unsuccessfully for the Commons in 1867. His brother, Charles, was a Conservative MP, and perhaps he influenced Macdonald to appoint Henry Kaulbach to the Senate in 1872 at the comparatively young age of 42. Kaulbach will feature largely in this story. He turned out to be one of only two of the nine senators on the divorce committee who believed that Eliza had been proved to have committed adultery, and in all the ensuing debates said so often and vociferously in language that on more than one occasion angered his colleagues.[34]

The final two members of the committee were Prince Edward Islander Robert Poor Haythorne and Clement Cornwall of British Columbia. Born in the United Kingdom to a prosperous family, Haythorne emigrated to PEI in 1841 to manage the 10,000-acre estate the family had acquired. He was unusual among the Island's landlords, supporting tenant rights in the bitter dispute over the land question. By the mid-1860s he had abolished leasehold tenure on his estate and sold land to the tenants at $2 an acre. He was elected to the Island legislative council as a Liberal in 1867, and when the Conservative government of James Pope fell, he joined the cabinet of the new premier, George Coles. When Coles resigned due to ill health in 1869 Haythorne became premier. His government was defeated and then regained power in the early 1870s, and through these years the central issues were Confederation and the land question. Haythorne was long a sceptic about whether the island should become part of Canada, but it was he who negotiated the "better terms" arrangement that took the island into Confederation. He lost the provincial election soon after, to Pope's Conservatives, but that did not change the outcome of the Confederation decision. Macdonald appointed Haythorne to the Senate as a reward. Cornwall had been born in England, was educated at Cambridge, and called to the bar in 1862. He immediately left for British Columbia and made money from stock raising and practising his profession. He was elected to the colonial legislative assembly and appointed one of the province's first three senators in 1871. He devoted time, energy, and money to the "gentlemen's sports" of racing horses and "fox" hunting – coyotes were used

e010942764

Figure 8.3. Senator Henry Kaulbach

Source: LAC

rather than foxes. He was the other senator, in addition to Kaulbach, who thought Eliza guilty of adultery.[35]

Although the committee had four lawyers, it was a relatively inexperienced one at this work. Haythorne, Kaulbach, Leonard, Reesor, and Seymour had not previously served on a divorce committee, and

Aikins and Cornwall had served on only one. Only two of the members had a lot of experience: Dickson had served on 5 of the 7 prior committees, Dickey on 6. Dickey was chosen as the chair.[36]

Two days after the selection of the committee Reesor presented a petition from Eliza, asking for an order to compel Robert to provide money for a defence. This was not unusual. In part it was because divorce proceedings were expensive for both parties. Both had to pay for counsel, for their own travel to Ottawa, and for accommodation in the capital, and the same expenses for any witnesses. While the reforms to married women's property law discussed in a previous chapter had improved the financial position of many women, having the right to keep your own money, including earnings, was only beneficial for women who had money in the first place. Eliza had been living since 1873 on her alimony payment until it was stopped in 1875, and on the largesse of family and friends, which presumably continued. In addition to many women involved in a divorce proceeding needing financial help to equalise the assets of the parties, making the husband pay was a way to ensure that divorce petitions were defended, not collusive proceedings. Divorce was seen as a necessary evil, but an evil indeed. It should never be easily attained, and thus the parties needed to be seen as actively prosecuting and defending the case. The Senate referred the petition to the divorce committee, which granted Eliza $500 to be paid by Robert.[37] As will be discussed in chapter 13 below, Robert resisted paying Eliza's lawyer McDougall, who had to take Robert to court to obtain the money.

Counsel in Parliament

Throughout these preliminary stages both Robert and Eliza had been represented by counsel, who would continue to represent them before the divorce committee. Robert's lawyer was 37-year-old William Henry Walker, who had been called to the bar in 1867 at the age of 28 and practised in Ottawa in the firm of Walker, McIntyre, and Ferguson. He had a good reputation as a lawyer and was made a Q.C. in 1889, although this was his first divorce case. In the mid-1890s he gave up law to start a graphite mining company, but that enterprise was a disaster and he went bankrupt in 1897. Testament to the connections he made during his years in Ottawa, his investors/creditors included Senators Richard Scott and Francis Clemow.[38] Another member of the Walker firm, Alexander Fraser McIntyre, represented John Anderson. McIntyre was a 29-year-old junior partner in Walker's Ottawa firm and the son of Dr. Daniel McIntyre, sheriff of the United Counties of

Glengarry and Dundas. He had articled with James MacLennan, Q.C., a future Court of Appeal and Supreme Court of Canada judge, and with Edward Blake, and been called to the bar in 1872. He had been elected for Cornwall in the Ontario assembly in 1875, but his election was overturned, and he was defeated in the subsequent by-election. A follower of Edward Blake in politics, he was twice unsuccessful as a Liberal candidate for the federal riding of Ottawa. He was made a Q.C. in 1890 and died in 1914.[39]

Eliza Campbell's lawyer was a man much better known to Canadian historians. William McDougall, 54 years old in 1876, was educated at Upper Canada Academy in Cobourg, a Methodist school that later became Victoria College of the University of Toronto.[40] The Liberal reformist values he imbibed there stayed with him more or less throughout his life. He qualified as a lawyer in 1847 and practised intermittently as a solicitor, but did not join the bar until 1862, a political favour arranged by Law Society Treasurer John Hillyard Cameron when McDougall was a Province of Canada cabinet minister and Cameron a political ally. In the 1840s and 1850s he devoted the bulk of his time to journalism, as a newspaper owner and editorial writer advocating agricultural reform and colonization. He became a member of the Clear Grit faction of the reform party, arguing for a broadening of the franchise to manhood suffrage and its concomitant political ideology of "common sense democracy," including secularization of the clergy reserves. He was a follower of George Brown and especially Brown's demands for representation by population in the Province of Canada. The *Act of Union* of 1840 had entrenched equal representation for the former Upper and Lower Canada in the Province of Canada assembly, and as Canada West's population outstripped that of Canada East Brown and his followers increasingly denounced the constitution as undemocratic.

Like many Canada West Liberals McDougall's support of representation by population was at least partly the result of resentment of Catholic influence in the assembly, which he saw as an anti-modern and anti-British, "a religion which is not the religion of the empire," inimical to popular democracy. Like other Ontarians from the mid-1850s he also believed in the assimilation of Indigenous people to Western values, and supported the idea of the annexation of the Hudson's Bay Company (HBC) lands west of Canada West. Elected to the Province of Canada assembly in 1858, he earned a reputation as a maverick, dubbed "Wandering Willie" for the inconsistency of his views and his ability to make personal enemies.

McDougall somewhat surprisingly obtained a ministerial post in 1862 as Commissioner of Crown Lands, and in this role encouraged

a027387

Figure 8.4. William McDougall
Source: LAC

northward colonization by selling off crown lands and repossessing reserves on Manitoulin Island on the ground that they had not been put to "proper" agricultural use and were an impediment to further white settlement. He followed George Brown into the "Great Coalition" in 1864, whose aim was to solve the political deadlock in the Province of Canada by a separation into two polities under a federal system. He became provincial secretary and took part in the Charlottetown, Quebec, and London conferences that led to Confederation. He was made Minister of Public Works in John A. Macdonald's first administration after winning a seat in the Commons in the first federal election. His principal interest became the absorption into the Dominion of the HBC lands. In 1867 he steered through Parliament the resolutions for Canada's acquisition of the HBC territories, and he accompanied Cartier to London in 1868 to negotiate the transfer, which took place as of 1 December 1869. The apogee of his career was being named lieutenant-governor designate of the Northwest Territories, which in 1869 comprised all the Prairie West including what became Manitoba. But he reached his nadir when he was prevented from entering Red River in November 1869 by the Métis under Louis Riel. The Métis were keen to join Canada, but by negotiation and as a province, not by unilateral annexation as a territory ruled from Ottawa. Angered by McDougall's refusal to negotiate with the Métis, and his general lack of understanding of the complicated politics of the Red River settlement, Macdonald recalled him to Ottawa in disgrace. Although he carried out a few commissions for the federal and Ontario governments in the 1870s, and was elected to the Ontario assembly in 1875 and to the federal Parliament in 1878, he never again held office.

McDougall resumed his still-born law practice in the 1870s after the collapse of his political career, and in 1876, according to his biographer, founded the firm of Campbell and Gordon. It is very likely that Gordon was James K. Gordon, George Gordon's brother, and that the Campbell divorce was the only case that "partnership" worked on. McDougall's involvement was most probably the result of his sister Emily being married to Reesor.[41] Although McDougall was bigoted about the French and about Indigenous people, he was a more than able lawyer, and he certainly proved to be that when representing Eliza through three years of debate in Parliament. He was remarkably successful, not only convincing the Senate divorce committee to refuse Robert's bill for divorce but also persuading Parliament to grant Eliza a unique legislative remedy – separation, support, and the custody of her youngest child.

9
The Senate Divorce Committee I: The Case for Robert Campbell

Introduction

The Senate divorce committee began its hearings on Monday, 13 March in Committee Room 17 in the Senate. It was eagerly anticipated by one Ottawa newspaper as "likely to be of interest to those who like scandal."[1] A Toronto newspaper, *The Union*, had been more sanguine two years before when reviewing the three court cases. Perjury had been committed by someone, which meant that in the event of a divorce petition a "very complicated case" would confront the Senate.[2] Reporters and other members of the public were allowed into the committee room, so if scandalous testimony were given many people would hear about it. The committee met on the 13th and on every day thereafter until Tuesday, 28 March, except for Sundays, 19 and 26 March, and Tuesday, 21 March, a total of 13 days. The Senate as a whole started every day at 3 p.m., and as a result committees met in the mornings and early afternoons.[3] All nine members of the committee were present every day. When all the evidence had been adduced, there followed two days, 29 and 30 March, of speeches from both counsel, deliberation by the committee, consideration of a petition by Eliza asking for amendments to the draft bill submitted by Robert, and the preparation of the committee's report. Thus 15 days in total were needed. The committee presented its report to the full house on Friday, 31 March. A verbatim transcript of the proceedings was made by a team of four reporters and later, after the end of the session, published as a 254-page appendix to the Senate *Journal* for 1876.[4] All senators and MPs could vote on divorce bills and thus the evidence was always printed and made available to them. On this occasion the publication of the transcript later in 1876 brought a rebuke from a newspaper in Sorel, Quebec, because there was "so much filth in one volume,", printed at public expense.[5]

APPENDIX

TO THE

TENTH VOLUME

OF THE

JOURNALS OF THE SENATE

OF

CANADA.

SESSION 1876.

Printed by Order of Parliament.

OTTAWA:
PRINTED BY MACLEAN, ROGER & CO., WELLINGTON STREET.
1876.

Figure 9.1. Minutes of Evidence Title Page

Both parties were represented by counsel, who took each of their witnesses through their direct examination and cross-examined the other side's witnesses. The key question before the committee was whether Robert could "prove the preamble" in his draft bill. The preamble of all divorce bills provided the names of the parties, the date and place of the marriage, and the allegation of adultery, with varying degrees of detail about with whom, where, and how often. If a male petitioner had been successful in an action for crim. con. that was also stated. The rest of the always short, one- to two-page bill, the operative provisions, simply stated that the parties were divorced and could marry again. "Proving" the preamble, that is, persuading the committee that Eliza had committed adultery, did not formally require more than the usual civil burden of proof in court – the balance of probabilities. But informally it meant that the divorce committee had to be well satisfied by the evidence. The fact that a male petitioner had won a crim. con. case was not by itself enough. Given that divorce was seen by many senators and other Canadians as a necessary evil in unusual cases, it was not something that should be easily obtained. Thus the informal standard of proof was something like "clear and convincing evidence," less than beyond a reasonable doubt but more than a mere balance of probabilities.[6]

The Senate divorce committee proceedings made the Campbell marriage breakdown somewhat more notorious than the three court cases had. Those cases, as we saw in chapters 5 through 7, riveted Whitby and, to a lesser extent neighbouring communities like Oshawa and Port Perry. They also attracted attention in Toronto in part because they were heard by Toronto juries in Toronto courtrooms. Once the scene shifted to the Senate the *Globe* printed short summaries of the preliminary stages and, once the hearing proper was under way, of the witness' evidence.[7] The *Ottawa Citizen* ran a short item in February, the news that Robert had arrived in the city and was residing at the Windsor Hotel, and followed this a little later with the news that Eliza had arrived and was staying at the Russell Hotel.[8] But perhaps surprisingly the *Citizen* did not follow the case closely until after the divorce committee proceedings on Robert's case were finished and Eliza petitioned for her own divorce bill, a development discussed in chapter 12. Even more surprisingly, the *Whitby Chronicle* did not report on the divorce committee proceedings while they were going on, even though it had a section on "the Dominion Parliament" in the issues of 16 and 23 March. Its first mention of the divorce proceedings appeared on 30 March, under the heading and sub-heading "The Campbell Divorce. What the Papers Say," which, as its title indicates, consisted of unattributed extracts from other newspapers. The other Ontario newspapers that reported on the case included the *Guelph Mercury*, which noted that as a result of the Senate proceedings the Campbells' matrimonial breakdown "is an item in the conversational world once more," the *Ingersoll Chronicle*, the *Kingston Daily News* and the same city's *British Whig*, the *Acton Free Press*, the *Hamilton Times*, and two Ottawa papers, the *Times* and the *Citizen*.[9] Unlike the court cases, the parliamentary proceedings attracted attention outside of Ontario, in Montreal, Quebec City, Manitoba, and across the border in Chicago, Dayton, Ohio, Springfield, Massachusetts, and Jefferson City, Missouri.[10] While the press coverage was not as extensive as it was in a later Ontario cause célèbre, the trial of the aristocratic Englishman John Birchall for murder in 1890, it was substantial, testament to the considerable reach of news wire services in the later nineteenth century.[11]

The Testimony of Robert Campbell

In this and subsequent sections on the witnesses I will not go into detail about the content of the evidence given, for that has already been reviewed in previous chapters. I refer to the evidence only when necessary to capture the cut and thrust of examination and cross-examination. As the petitioner Robert presented his evidence first. Eliza was not in Ottawa for this stage, remaining in Whitby until she was called for.

The first day of the committee hearing, Monday, 13 March, began with formal evidence to prove the Campbell marriage. James Campbell, John Anderson, and Robert Campbell, in that order, all gave testimony to having been at the wedding, and an extract from the marriage register was entered into the record.[12] Robert remained on the stand after this formality had been concluded, and told his story from the first decade of marriage through the discovery of the Parks correspondence and all the litigation. Walker put all this evidence in even though he had been told, presumably by Chairman Dickey, that none of it would "influence" the committee's decision because it was irrelevant when the issue was whether Eiza had committed adultery with Gordon.[13] Given that Walker would have known that Blake had likely been "influenced" by the evidence of a relationship with Parks, it is not surprising that he ignored the admonition.

Thus the correspondence between Eliza and Parks and the other writings by Eliza were quickly introduced as exhibits.[14] Various other exhibits were put into evidence as well – a photograph of a portrait of Eliza, the executions issued against Gordon's land and personal property, the decree issued by the Court of Chancery, a floor plan of the Campbell home, and six photographs of the house, exterior and interior, showing different views.[15] Occasionally a committee member interjected with a question on mostly minor points. The only one that might have raised eyebrows came from an unnamed committee member, after Robert had answered a question about when his fourth child had been born. His answer was "I think, either in December or January after I separated from her. I think it was some time in December 1873." The senator interrupted with, "You do not know at what date in December?", and Robert replied "I do not."[16] It likely came as a surprise to those listening that a man would not know the date his child was born.

Less than half way through the session on the first day Walker completed his direct examination and McDougall took over.[17] His cross-examination went over the same ground, and my best judgment from the questions asked is that his main purpose was to paint Robert generally as a harsh and unfeeling husband and as one who had decided to leave his wife before the alleged adultery with Gordon took place. If he had simply separated from Eliza, he would have been responsible for supporting her. The only way to be relieved of this legal obligation was to show that she had been adulterous. Thus Robert had an incentive to manufacture evidence of that adultery. McDougall began with a series of questions about whether Robert had communicated with Eliza after the initial discovery of the letter from Parks or at any other point, especially after 26 August. Robert first evaded answering, saying that he had read the Parks letter to Rev. Byrne and James Byrne, and given them copies. McDougall pursued the point, and Robert had to admit that not only had he not contacted Eliza, he also had not replied to her letters or made any attempt to see her. His answers showed him in a bad light, as someone who never gave his wife a chance to explain, or to ask for forgiveness.

Robert compounded the bad impression in response to further questions. He did not know when he received letters from Eliza, and he "could not say" if they were delivered by post or by hand. When asked how long one letter was, he said, "It was two or three pages, I dare say." When asked if Eliza's letters had been read out in a court proceeding, he said one letter was read in Court, "and I dare say that would be an example of them all." A few minutes later, when asked the same question a different way, he said there was a letter read, "but I will not undertake to tell" which one. McDougall had other questions about Eliza's letters to him in the few days after 26 August, and he was either pointlessly evasive or answered in a resentful way, as if Eliza deserved no consideration. When asked if he had any of Eliza's letters with him in Ottawa, he "could not say." When asked if she had written more than once he acknowledged that she had done so three or four times, but then added that "that was all I got from her," as if there was something else she could or should have done with a husband who had immediately made up his mind to leave her and did not respond to her letters or see her.[18]

McDougall also questioned Robert about the settlement meeting in the Whitby courthouse during the alimony case. He focused on whether Eliza had denied the alleged adultery. Robert insisted that she had neither admitted nor denied it, she had merely asked him if he believed it. Asked if Eliza had asked him to forgive her and take her back on that occasion, Robert replied "I cannot say that she did." Interpreting this as "I don't know," McDougall seized on the answer to again paint Robert as uncaring. His follow-up question posed as an assertion was: "It was so unimportant a matter that you have forgotten all about it?" McDougall continued with the theme of Robert's overly hasty conclusions about Eliza when he asked about the Parks letter dated 14 August. Although the letter was in a "disguised hand," and although Robert had just one short note from Parks to compare it to, and although it was signed J.H., how was he able to be sure it was from Parks? Robert's answer was that there was "sufficient resemblance" between the two letters that he could "easily" identify it. McDougall took a similar tack with questions about Gordon, showing Robert to be somebody who jumped to conclusions. He had him admit that he had no suspicions regarding Gordon until the day after he returned from the UK, and James or Rebecca Campbell told him that a neighbour had told them that Gordon had visited the house in his absence. When McDougall then asked him what inquiries he had made in consequence, he could not have obtained a better answer if he wanted to paint Robert as prone to precipitous decisions: "The inquiry I made was this; I had three children … and the feeling that came over me was this – that under such circumstances my wife could not be a proper guardian for these children; and I took the children away." Robert then likely compounded the bad impression he had given by his answers to further questions about his actions before he went to Southampton. He waited to go until after the weekend but said nothing to Eliza; he did not tell her why he was going. He lied to her about the reason, and he kissed her goodbye as if nothing had happened.[19]

McDougall continued with questions about Robert's return from Southampton and subsequent actions talking to members of the Byrne family. From there McDougall moved to Robert's "next step," which was to consult Harrison in Toronto. After a few questions the lawyer turned to Eliza's removal from the house, painting his actions as cruel and again stressing the limited evidence on which Robert had decided that Eliza had committed adultery. The exchange was as follows:

Q. How long [did Eliza occupy the house]?
A. I should say she occupied it about a month.
Q. That was after the discovery of the alleged offence?
A. Yes.
Q. How did you put her out?
A. I went with two constables and put her out.
Q. Did you turn her out on the street?
A. No, I did not turn her out on the street, but I drove a carriage to the door and led her down to it and had a man to drive her to her brother's or anywhere she liked. Her brother was there to take her to his house.

This was, of course, a very much sanitized version of the events of 24 September 1873. McDougall then asked what evidence Robert had had about Eliza before 26 August, taking the opportunity to describe the removal from the house quite differently:[20]

Q. From the time of your suspicions having been aroused to the time the constables drove her from the house, had you any evidence of misconduct on her part except the letter of Parks and the statement of your brother of what he heard on the night of the 26th?
A. And what the girls told me, that was all.
Q. How many girls were there – there were two of the Newsoms?
A. Yes. Martha and Jane....
Q. Which was there on the 26th?
A. Jane.
Q. Was it the evidence of Jane that corroborated the suspicions in your mind?
A. In the first place it was Martha, and afterwards Jane.
Q. But Martha was not there?
A. I saw her in town.
Q. But she was not in the house. I want to know what other evidence of criminality there was that affected your mind besides the letter of Parks and the statement of your brother of what took place on the night of the 26th. What other evidence besides that induced you to turn your wife out of the house and take legal proceedings?

A. It was just the fact of the girls telling me of Gordon's visits to the house in my absence and remaining to late hours.
Q. Was that all the evidence you had?
A. That was all.

The questioning moved to Gordon, and McDougall got Robert to state that Gordon had been to parties at the house, that he was a childhood friend of Eliza's, that he came from a respectable family, and that he was "one of the social circle of the neighbourhood – a family acquaintance." Robert was questioned at length about the evening when Gordon had visited for tea and Robert had gone back to work afterwards and found Gordon still there when he returned. The purpose was likely to have Robert admit his coldness towards Eliza. Robert said he had "chafed" her for Gordon still being there, and she had admitted that she had been "imprudent" and cried. She had also asked him to forgive her and to sleep with her that night "to be good friends." He replied, "No, Eliza, this thing seems to be serious, and I will not." It was an answer that revealed a cold and censorious disposition. McDougall's last two topics for the day were Eliza's pregnancy and support payments. Robert agreed that Eliza must have been some five months pregnant when the adultery occurred, and he admitted that he had not provided Eliza with any support since the decision in the alimony case, and as far as he knew she had no other means of support.[21]

The day ended with two questions from committee members. Henry Kaulbach of Nova Scotia asked if Robert "was in the habit of taking offence" at Eliza's conduct before the night he refused to sleep with her. Robert said that had been the only occasion he could recall, and in answer to another question from Kaulbach said that he had not alluded to it again. Aikins asked more pointedly if he usually opened letters addressed to his wife. Robert said he did not, but on this occasion "I thought it so strange to see a letter in a man's hand that I opened it."

It is not possible to say precisely how many hours were taken up by the first day's proceedings. As noted above Senate committees sat in the morning when the House itself was not in session, and the session proper always began at 3 p.m. and usually ended at 6.30 p.m. There was therefore plenty of time for committee meetings. Divorce committee members were on other committees, although all were present this day. The minutes of the first day took up just over 18 pages in a question-and-answer format in the printed appendix to the Senate *Journal*, and I would estimate that it took about three hours to complete the testimony.[22]

Robert Campbell testified for the entirety of the next day, Tuesday, 14 March, starting it still under cross-examination by McDougall, who began by casting doubt on the authenticity of the Parks letter. It had been postmarked on August 15th and discovered by Robert lying on his desk on the 19th. Did this not make it likely that James Campbell had obtained it earlier and detained it? Robert gave evasive and non-responsive answers while insisting that James had nothing to do with it. McDougall did not let him off the hook, asking why he had never made inquiries about why the letter took so long to get to Whitby and how it was simply found on his desk. Robert shot back: "The contents of the letter appeared to be of much more consequence than that." McDougall shifted to the other writings by Eliza, and to Robert's direct testimony. He had told Walker that from reading the letter and the "scraps" and from hearing Eliza's testimony in court that he knew they were all letters from Parks. What testimony was that, McDougall asked? From the Chancery case. But the newspaper reports of that and prior cases have her saying that the "scraps" "were mere memos to be used in a romance she had intended writing for her friends and her own amusement." McDougall and Robert then argued over what Eliza had said in the lawsuits, especially the Chancery case, about the writings found in her secretaire. Robert insisted that Eliza had admitted that some of them were drafts of letters to Parks, but he was wrong about this according to the accounts we have of the trials. She always maintained that most of them were things she had written for herself or for possible publication in a magazine.[23]

That completed the cross-examination, and Walker had an opportunity to re-examine. He knew what parts of the cross-examination could have hurt Robert's case, and he hopped from one topic to the other. He started with whether Eliza was in the habit of writing romances. Robert did not know anything about such a pastime until it came out in the litigation. Had she ever contributed stories to the local newspapers or the *Ladies Journal*?[24] Not that Robert was aware of. Do you know the name of the romance Eliza was writing? Robert did not. All of this was obviously an attempt to cast doubt on the existence of any literary ambitions and to suggest that they had been fabricated to explain away drafts of letters to Parks. Walker then devoted a number of questions to the fact that "[g]reat stress has been laid on your not having seen your wife" after the 26th. To counter the impression of Robert having not been willing to see Eliza, Walker had Robert explain that he had wanted to do so, but only at James Campbell's house because he was very upset and "quite unfit to bear the scene I knew would happen if I met her in her mother's house," or in his own house. Walker then established that Eliza had not responded to an invitation to meet at James Campbell's house.[25]

Perhaps because he did not know what had happened in September 1873, Walker allowed Robert to give a demonstrably false account of Eliza's removal from the house. Having allowed Robert to say that Eliza had packed all her belongings and was ready to move, the first part of which may have been true, this followed:

> Q. Then she was not driven off by two constables?
> A. No. I had a carriage at the door, and I led her gently down stairs and out of the door.... I merely had the constables there to see that there was no rudeness or anything improper done; and these men were able to testify that my conduct at that time was all that was right.

As we saw in chapter four, Eliza was definitely not "led gently downstairs." Why Robert and/or Walker phrased things this way is unclear; they must have known that a very different account would be provided later.

Further questions followed about what Eliza had taken from the house. Robert claimed initially that "[m]y house was completely stripped; I had not sufficient left to furnish a bed," although he had to concede that "[o]f course the carpets and furniture were not taken." Members of the committee piped in with questions on this issue, Kaulbach, Reesor and Aikins all asking for clarification of what had been taken and how things had been removed. Robert was forced to retreat a bit from his house being "completely stripped" to answering yes when he was asked if Eliza had "confined herself to wearing apparel and bedding," and answering no when he was asked "[n]ot your wearing apparel?" More importantly Robert said that the things were packed up before she left and the trunks taken away the following day. Eliza had not, therefore, moved her things out before she herself was moved. Reesor was intent on getting Robert to agree that he had not objected to the removal of things from the house, asking that question twice. Aikins asked if it could be said that Eliza took things that "she ... very justly ... considered ... [as] belonging to herself as part of her marriage portion," and Robert replied that she took a "large number of things" that could not be described as such. As we will see in the next chapter, Eliza's version of what was taken from the house was very different.

After Walker's questions McDougall had the opportunity to "re-cross-examine" Robert. He began with a number of questions about Eliza's accomplishments and abilities. Did she read and write a lot and was she a person of "superior education?" She was, said Robert, someone of "moderate" education, not superior. She read a lot. She played the piano and sang well. "Was she not rather superior to the ordinary young women of the neighbourhood when you married her?" "I suppose I thought so when I married her." After a number of related questions McDougall asked Robert about the relative talents of Eliza and Rebecca Campbell, James's wife. The purpose was presumably to plant the idea that James resented her because he had the less accomplished wife. Robert conceded that Eliza was a better singer but insisted that Rebecca could sing even if not as well as Eliza and was otherwise generally as accomplished. The questions shifted to why Robert was so sure that the letters to and from Parks, which did not mention that name, were what he claimed them to be. Robert answered these questions well, using references in them to him and to specific events as well as Eliza's admissions in court that she had written to Parks.[26]

With no preamble McDougall moved to much more difficult ground for Robert – Eliza's ejection from the house. His first question was aggressive: Robert had told Walker that he had not taken the constables in their official capacity, "but to see that you were courteous to your wife." Robert ignored "courteous," and said he took them as witnesses and to provide any assistance needed. One of the committee members interjected to ask if he had taken a lawyer's advice, the answer being that Harrison had told him that he had a right to remove Eliza, by force if necessary. McDougall then asked if Harrison had advised him to take the constables and got the evasive reply: "As to that I am not prepared to say." There followed an exchange in which Robert was forced to give a very different picture to the one he had painted for Walker only minutes before:

Q. In point of fact, did she not refuse to go out? Did she not lie on the bed and refuse to move?
A. Yes
Q. And in point of fact were you not two or three hours in getting her out of the house – constables and all?
A. Before I went to put my wife out, I requested the family doctor to come and see if she was well – to see what state she was in. I did not tell him what my object was. He said that he went in and found her perfectly well and active, and that she seemed to enjoy herself with her friends. Then I thought that if she was really well –

Mr. McDougall at this point suggested that the witness should confine himself to the facts. The chairman ruled that these should be more closely followed.

Q. I wish to know whether on that occasion she went away voluntarily, or only after two or three hours of discussion and resistance?

A. She at first refused to go.
Q. At what hour of the day was that?
A. I went to put her out at between seven and eight o'clock in the evening.
...
Q. At what time did you put her out?
A. I could not say.
Q. Give an approximate idea?
A. I should say that two hours elapsed between the time I first went to her and the time she left the house.

That ended both Robert's testimony and the second day of the hearing.

The Testimony of the Newsom Sisters

The third day was taken up with evidence from the Newsom sisters, first Martha and then Jane. Their evidence was not reproduced in the same question and answer format as Robert's and later witnesses, but as two continuous narratives with their signatures at the end. I have thus had to guess what the questions were from the answers, as in previous chapters. The Newsoms said nothing under direct examination that has not been recounted in those chapters. McDougall cross-examined Martha at some length, but did not shake her testimony in any way.[27] Indeed, she said more than she had under direct examination. For example, she said that on one occasion Eliza and Gordon were in the summer house when the children called out to ask their mother to put them to bed. Eliza "told the children to be good children and go to bed" themselves. On another occasion Gordon and Eliza had offered the children "coppers" to go to bed, which Martha thought "a remarkable circumstance" because Eliza "was not in the habit of bribing her children to go to bed." A little later, in response to her statement that Gordon "had been there long enough to leave," McDougall pressed her on her own male friendships. She acknowledged that she also had visitors, sometimes young men, but added that "I had no husband to dispute it." In any event her young men only stayed until 10 or 11. McDougall must have asked her if she was aware that Gordon and Eliza were childhood friends, and she acknowledged that she had not known that until she heard or read the evidence in the crim. con. trial. But that did not change her mind about his visits, which she still thought were a "matter for suspicion."[28]

On another occasion, again in response to a question, she recounted one of Gordon's visits, which took place just as she was going out.

Eliza was singing and Gordon opened the door and walked in saying, "I heard you singing and thought I would come in." She thought it "remarkable" that he would do so. Newsom used another question to talk about a July evening when Eliza had gone out to a party at her mother's and Gordon had accompanied her home at between 1 and 2 in the morning and then stayed with her for a time. McDougall must have asked her how long he stayed, and she admitted that "I will not swear that he stayed longer than ten minutes." But she added that she "thought it very strange and improper for a gentleman to come in so late after accompanying a lady home from a party."

McDougall must have asked Newsom about James Campbell's evening visits to the field next to the house to look after his horse, probably to set up the oft employed characterization of him "prowling" about the house. But if so this backfired because it gave Martha an opportunity to declaim on what she thought was Eliza's guilty conscience. She said that on 13 August she was sitting on the back kitchen steps waiting for her sister when Eliza came out and asked if James Campbell had come in through the gate from the road. In answers to follow up questions Martha said he came most evenings to take care of the horse, that he never went to the house, and that she did not consider that he was "prowling about." In addition, she said that she thought it was "very remarkable" that Eliza had asked her the question: "I thought that a guilty conscience needs no accuser." When asked what she meant and in answer to other questions she said:

> I did not think that she was guilty further than she did not wish anyone else to know that Mr. Gordon came to the house; I thought that her conscience was troubled with regard to that; my conscience does not trouble me when there is no guilt, but I think that if I had any person in the house, and did not wish any person to know it, my conscience would trouble me a little then.... I thought that Mrs. Campbell was guilty as far as this; she did not wish that anyone else should know of Mr. Gordon's visits.

McDougall had succeeded in bringing out two points. That James Campbell was frequently around the house in the evenings and that he rarely, if ever, visited Eliza, despite how easy it would be to drop in on his sister-in-law. But he had also shown the senators that James had a good reason to be there, and that Eliza did not want him to know that she had entertained Gordon alone.[29]

Towards the end of the cross-examination McDougall did get Newsom to say that Eliza had never told her not to say anything about Gordon's visits, but she put that down to Eliza knowing that she could rely on a loyal servant not to tittle-tattle. On the whole Newsom proved to be a strong witness for Robert's case, albeit only to the extent of establishing that Gordon visited often and stayed late. As in the lawsuits she could say nothing about whether adulterous behaviour had taken place on any occasion.

The other witness that day was Jane Newsom, who by 1876 was living with a family called Salkeld in Whitby. Her direct examination, like her sister's, did not elicit anything much that had not been said in the previous cases. Only one statement she made had not been said before, that Eliza had said at various times that "she did not love her husband." McDougall's cross-examination brought out nothing new, nor did it get her to change her story in any way. Asked about singing on the night of the 26th she said that she had heard that some person said there was some, but "I know it is not true, there was nothing more than the running of fingers over the keys of the piano."

The Testimony of James Campbell

James Campbell had made a brief appearance on the first day of the committee hearing, for the simple purpose of proving the marriage. His next appearance was the day after the Newsoms, Thursday, 16 March. He was on the stand for nearly three days. His testimony comprised 40 pages of the printed evidence. The first three pages, Waker's direct examination and part of McDougall's cross-examination, were in the continuous narrative format, the remainder in question-and-answer style. The direct examination took up all of Thursday, 16 March, but that must have been a shortish session, because it was only three pages, albeit in the continuous narrative format, the equivalent of about six pages of question and answer. Walker only had Campbell talk about the night of the 26th into the 27th, and he said nothing different than in all the court cases. Kaulbach asked him one question at the end: Was he sure that there was no light in Eliza's bedroom while Gordon was there? Campbell affirmed that that was the case.[30]

The next day and a half, Friday and Saturday, 17 and 18 March, were taken up with McDougall's cross-examination of James Campbell. Both men would have had ample opportunity to prepare, because this was now the fourth time that James Campbell had stood up in public and told his version of events. McDougall knew that there was no point in trying to set up an argument that there had been some kind of misunderstanding. Either Campbell and Anderson had lied and were continuing to do so, or Eliza and Gordon had lied in the past and she would do so again. McDougall needed to at least cast enough doubt on

Campbell's testimony that the senators could decide that the preamble had not been proved.

He began with many questions about what seems an unimportant matter: did Campbell and Anderson talk on their way from Anderson's house to Robert's residence and, if they did not, how did James Campbell know that Anderson was "astonished" (Campbell's word) to hear that Eliza might be playing fast and loose with Gordon? McDougall did manage to make Campbell seem a little silly with his statement that Anderson was "astonished" because he also said that he and Anderson had not exchanged a single word of conversation on their way to the Campbell home or when they got there. While this was not relevant to the main issue, it might have had some senators wondering about Campbell's veracity.[31]

After asking about other matters McDougall moved to the time when the watchers were in situ, listening at their stations. Did Campbell say anything to Anderson when he left him at the parlour window to go to the veranda? Campbell could not recollect. "Then, although you were the chief party in this affair, you went away without saying anything to your co-listener?" McDougall must have deliberately chosen the words "chief party" because he wanted to paint James Campbell as the principal witness against a woman he disliked and resented. James Campbell was on to it immediately: "I deny that I am the chief party in this affair; I went of my own accord, and I was merely carrying out the promise that I made to my brother." With that McDougall asked why Campbell had moved from the parlour window to the veranda. Because he could hear better. Then Anderson could have heard better from there as well? Campbell could not say. Was Anderson hard of hearing? No. Why could Campbell hear better from the veranda? Because the veranda was on the same level as the parlour, whereas the parlour window was above the ground outside it.[32]

Other questions followed about why it was easier to hear from the front veranda some way away from the parlour than from the window of the parlour, about why Campbell did not tell Anderson to join him, about how tall each man was (Anderson was taller, at 1.82 metres [6 ft.]). Campbell eventually said that he had gone onto the veranda to be warmer because the night was cold for the season. McDougall had him:

Q. Then you did not go there [to the veranda] because you could hear better than at the other window?

A. I found when I went to that window the air suited me better, and I was more comfortable.

Q. It suited your acoustic faculties?

A. Yes.
Q. You could hear as well at the other window?
A. Oh, perfectly; but it was more comfortable at the other.
Q. What is your evidence – that you heard better there or found it more comfortable?

Campbell managed an answer to this last question, saying that he had moved to the veranda to "shelter [his] head from the cold dew," but once there he found he could "hear so well that I remained." But he could not get around the fact that he had given inconsistent answers and also raised doubts about how well either of them could hear what went on inside.

McDougall next addressed the question of Campbell hearing only indistinct voices before midnight but clear words, phrases, and noises thereafter. He asked whether it was at "precisely 12 o'clock that your hearing became so acute," and Campbell said he had looked at his watch. There followed a rather confused discussion of how well he could see his watch on a dark night. He got off the veranda to see if Newsom had gone to bed and at that time looked at his watch. But Newsom had gone to bed and there was no light from her window to see his watch by? Campbell reversed field and said he had looked at the watch before he got off the veranda. McDougall pointed out the contradiction and Campbell provided a rather unresponsive answer: "I looked at it before I went round to the north-east end of the house to see if the girl had gone to bed. I saw a light in her room, and it was sometime afterwards before I heard the conversation so as to understand it." McDougall continued asking questions about the light and the watch until he presumably decided that the senators had heard enough to be confused by Campbell's inconsistencies.

There followed a number of questions about the rumours that had circulated about Eliza and Gordon in August 1873, James's nightly visits to the Campbell house, and the instructions Robert had given him before he left for Southampton. The questions about the nightly visits showed both that James went to Robert's house more or less every evening and that he hardly ever went into the house itself or spoke to Eliza. Thus McDougall was able to establish that Eliza was used to his being there and would have expected him to be around the yard and in the adjoining field on the 26th, and that she and James were not very friendly. On this last point James denied any bad relations with Eliza. He "never had a hard word with her in my life," and if Eliza said otherwise "she swears what is not so" and she would not have said such a thing "before this trouble."[33]

McDougall moved to the letter from Parks that Robert had found on his desk when he returned from the UK. Campbell readily admitted that he had put it there, and that he usually sent all letters for the family that had been delivered to the business up to the house. This time he had forgotten to do so when the letter arrived on Monday, 18 August. Had he received other letters for Eliza in the past? "Plenty of them." Had he sent them to the house immediately? "Always." Why not this one?

> On this occasion, as I was going to my dinner, I got the letter along with a lot of other letters; I opened the other letters when I was going home to my own house.... I put this letter in my breast pocket, and I never thought any more about it until towards evening; this letter came up when I was fyling the other letters, and I laid it on the desk, intending to send it up to Mrs. Campbell with her nephew, Norman Ham, who was our cash boy.

McDougall did not care for this elaborate explanation and said, "Never mind all that," leading James to respond, "I want to explain."

McDougall moved him on to who the letter was from, and of course James said it was from Parks. But was it signed Parks? No. Then how did he know?

> The way I know it is this: My brother ... called me in two hours after he opened the letter, and shut the door; I was very much surprised; he took me into his back room and said "Here James, read that".... I read the letter, and said to him: "This letter is not for you at all, Robert.... It is headed Dear Maria, and that is not your wife's name, which is Eliza." "No," he said, "my wife's name is Eliza Maria." This was the first time I ever heard of it; she never signed herself Maria, and I had not known that this was her name, although I had known her since she was a little girl.... I read it again, and says I, "Robert, who do you suspect that letter is from?" "Well," says he, "James, the only party I can think that this latter can be from is a party named Parks." "We can very easily tell that," I replied, "because you recollect that last March he sent us a letter, applying for the position of book-keeper." He said, "Then you can lay your hands on that letter?" I said, "Certainly, yes."

This statement precipitated a series of questions about how the Campbells could identify the sender from one other letter when there were differences in the handwriting. Campbell said the differences were superficial, the letter applying for a job written in a "running hand" and the letter to Eliza "feigned, and written in a back-hand."[34]

McDougall then took Campbell through the subsequent dealings with the letter, Robert's discovery of other writings by Eliza, and his decision to go to Southampton. He pressed Campbell on whether Robert had told him before or when he left that he was going to separate from Eliza, but James denied that Robert had told him. He also denied that Robert had said anything to him about Gordon before he left for Southampton. This contradicted what had been said in the previous lawsuits and what Robert had said under direct examination in the Senate. On one other small point Campbell contradicted himself. When asked about his trip to Toronto McDougall said, "And you got a detective," to which Campbell replied that "he was not a detective, he was 'someone.'" A little later he said, "I gave the detective instructions."[35]

At this point McDougall returned to 26 August. Some of the questions covered ground that had been mentioned earlier in the cross-examination, but the focus was on the time Gordon had left, specifically on how Campbell had been able to see Gordon's hand on the parlour door at 3 a.m. from his position on the veranda. After some back and forth the focus changed back to why Campbell could apparently hear better from the veranda than from below the parlour window? The answer was that early on the street noises had prevented Campbell hearing very well. McDougall then asked him about the "Robert might suspect" exchange:

Q. After you were there for a time you say you heard Mrs. Campbell say: "Robert might suspect." Was that the first expression you heard?
A. That was the first expression I heard; up to that time all had been faint and indistinct....
Q. Did it strike you that there was anything extraordinary in the expression?
A. It did.
Q. What was the reply?
A. "Has Robert had anything to do with you since his return," or "has Robert had any connection with you since his return?"
Q. Are these the words: "Has Robert had anything to do with you since his return?"
A. Yes, these are the words.
Q. And you wish them to stand as your evidence?
A. Yes, that is my evidence.
Q. You correct your evidence of yesterday very considerably?

In fact, in his direct examination the previous day James had said: "After 12 o-clock at night I heard Mrs. Campbell say to Gordon 'Robert might suspect.' Gordon asked her if Robert had anything to do with her since his return, and she said, 'Only the first night.'" It is hard to see any difference between what Campbell said he had heard, let alone to see that his evidence in cross-examination varied "very considerably" from what he had said under direct.[36]

McDougall then found a better question to ask – what did Robert "having connection" with Eliza have to do with whether or not he suspected anything? James Campbell did not know. What did Eliza reply when Gordon said that Robert could not suspect? Campbell did not know because at that point he went away for a stick to break in a window, which he did not carry through with. McDougall then asked him what Anderson had told him when he returned from the wood pile, which was that while Campbell had been away Eliza and Gordon had "got through," by which Anderson meant they had had intercourse. So, said McDougall, at that point Campbell had no evidence from his own eyes and ears about sex? Yes, only what Anderson told him. Did he get that evidence later? He did. About half an hour later someone said, "Now they're at it," although Campbell could not say if he said it to Anderson or vice versa. They were at their separate stations and both leaned out and caught each other's eye and one of them said it. Eliza and Gordon were partly on the sofa and partly on the floor at the time. Was this before someone said they were at it? Campbell could not say, he was "too much interested in watching them inside." "How could you watch them?" "I was listening."[37]

There followed a series of questions eliciting some of the dialogue between Eliza and Gordon given in chapter 3. McDougall came back to the question of where exactly they had been to perform their sexual gymnastics, receiving the answer that it was on the floor, and on the sofa, and with their feet on the floor and their bodies on the sofa: "I am not prepared to swear they had it on the floor, nor am I prepared to swear they had it on the sofa." The next exchange might have brought a smile from the committee members:

Q. Are you prepared to swear they had it at all?
A. I am.
Q. By what evidence?
A. I could hear them.
Q. You could hear the operation going on?
A. Yes, I could. I am a married man.[38]

Then there was a series of questions about other things Campbell had heard Eliza and Gordon say, and exactly when they had said these things. Campbell provided the answers in more or less the same words that he had used previously in the court cases and in his direct examination. On two occasions McDougall said the phrasing had been slightly different on those previous occasions, but the differences were very minor. On another occasion he said that Eliza had suggested Gordon stay over as he was so tired, and McDougall asked him why he had not said that the day before. "You did not ask me" was the response. McDougall accused him of not saying this at the previous trials, and Campbell replied: "I swear that this conversation took place, whether I gave it in evidence before or not; I may have given this evidence, or I may not; I am not prepared to swear." This line of questioning ended with McDougall confirming that, despite Gordon asking for it again, to Campbell's knowledge the two had only had sex the once.[39]

It was getting close to the end of the day's session and McDougall switched topics abruptly: "Was Mrs. Campbell in the habit of playing what are called drafts sometimes?" Campbell did not know, and when asked about her education and reading habits he said what Robert had said earlier in the week. Campbell denied hearing Eliza read on the night of the 26th, or the sounds of people playing drafts, and he did not know there was a stereoscope in the house. McDougall abruptly shifted again to James's improbable earlier statement that he had heard kissing, and the resulting exchange might have also raised a smile from the listeners:

Q. You said yesterday, that you heard them kissing each other?
A. Yes, frequently.
Q. They must have been kissing very loud?
A. Yes, they were good smacks.
Q. That was the kind of kissing that was going on?
A. Yes.
Q. Is that the way you kiss your wife?
A. Yes.
Q. And you give her a smack that makes a noise?
A. Yes, sometimes.
Q. On this occasion they smacked so loudly that you could hear them through curtains, blinds, windows and brick walls?
A. Yes, quite easily.[40]

Having had what he must have thought was a bit of fun, McDougall came back to Eliza's alternate explanations of how she had spent the evening, the drafts and the stereoscope. Campbell said the conversation he had heard could be nothing like instructions about how far to push slides into a stereoscope. In doing so he said something that not even the printer for the Senate would print: "There is a great deal of difference between a stereoscope, and a – , and a – , and a – ." The reader can supply his or her own words, but they must have been strong ones. McDougall was not deterred:

Q. No doubt. I am quite aware of that; but if you did not see what was going on, and merely hear a person say that something was being pushed too far, how do you know?
A. I heard too much of it; I know what was being pushed in.
Q. How do you know?
A. If you had been there you would have known.
Q. How? Give us a reason?
A. I heard them in the criminal act.
Q. What did you hear?
A. I heard them doing it. I cannot explain it.
Q. You heard them using criminal language, such as described, and you came to the conclusion that they were in the criminal act.
A. I came to no conclusion.
Q. On ordinary occasions it does not make any noise, does it? What were the indices and facts? Could they not have been looking at pictures, or playing drafts, or doing something else?
A. I hope the Hon. Committee will think that I have explained it as far as I possibly can; I cannot explain this thing any further, there is no use.
Q. There are no ladies present. It involves the reputation of a woman, and is a very serious matter. What was the additional evidence that would enable us to say how the act took place? Was there any?
A. All I can say in reply to you is this; I am a married man myself, and I have got a family myself, I cannot explain this thing any further than that.

Campbell must have been tired; he had been on the witness stand for over 3 hours without a break and had undergone a ceaseless badgering by McDougall. Yet he could have avoided the initial questions, which were predicated on a few words about putting stereoscope slides in too far, by saying he did not base his opinion on that one phrase, but on the sounds of lovemaking. That is where he got eventually but he may have not been thinking clearly before then. What he did say when he had to explain the source of his impression was reasonable enough.

Who else, even today, might not say, in effect: "You ask me how I know they were having sex? I've had sex. I know what it sounds like."

There was time enough for a few questions about the defamation case before the session ended for the day. Campbell was back on the stand the next day, Saturday, 18 March, but for a much shorter period of time – seven pages of transcript compared to 29 on the previous day. McDougall asked questions about the things Campbell had reported Eliza as saying on the two previous days. Each time he did so McDougall asked for "the exact words" or the "precise words," and when Campbell answered he asked him to repeat the words and/or asked if he was sure. On one occasion McDougall said, "You are getting into the same difficulty again"; and on another he said, "You have given altogether different statements," but neither time did he follow these assertions by saying in what way Campbell's answer had been different to a prior answer. McDougall was likely trying to sow seeds of doubt about Campbell's veracity. It is easy to stick exactly to a true story, much more difficult to tell lies consistently. As noted at the outset of this chapter, McDougall's task was to prevent Robert being able to "prove" the preamble. He did not need to disprove James Campbell's story, only to make a majority of the senators on the committee unsure.[41]

McDougall also pushed at other aspects of the testimony about what had been said on 26 August. Why would Gordon say he would go to California with Eliza when he was a young man living in his father's house and working as a farm hand? Campbell dealt quite well with this, with Kaulbach's assistance. The Nova Scotia senator interjected a question about whether the California conversation was a reference to the then three-year old joke about eloping there. There were a number of questions that seem to have been designed to get Campbell to say that he had seen things – Eliza's breasts, her navel, her state of undress – but Campbell stuck to the line that he had only heard words spoken and from those words and other noises had formed impressions about where the two were and what they were doing.

After some time McDougall moved to the last act in the drama, the confrontation on the street. Campbell stuck to his story that he had accused Gordon of having had "criminal intercourse," not of attempting to seduce Eliza. He stuck to it despite McDougall asking repeatedly about Wellington Adams's testimony in the defamation and alimony cases. Adams was simply wrong. As for George Gross's previous evidence, which McDougall also asked about, Campbell said it had been confusing, that Gross had been unsure whether he heard the word "fire" or "liar," and that Gross's statements about the time "wandered all over the place." Campbell must have expected to be asked about these other witnesses and knew that his only response was to stick to his story.[42]

McDougall's final questions were about the Campbell brothers' property holdings and Eliza's dower interest in Robert's land. James acknowledged that wives usually had dower although he did not know whether Eliza did. He also agreed that the brothers owned land together as part of their partnership, and they both owned land individually. He would not exactly say how much, nor whether he and Robert had ever discussed the law of dower, about which he knew only the general outlines. That completed McDougall's cross-examination.

Walker had the chance to re-examine Campbell and asked about things which McDougall had not mentioned. He had won a new trial in the defamation case but there had never been one. George Gordon had applied for a new trial in the crim. con. case but it was refused. James Campbell had never consulted a lawyer about dower rights. James was willing to talk to some extent about the value of the partnership's land, which he had resisted doing when McDougall asked. The "Glasgow Warehouse" had been bought for $4,400, and a block in the business district for $6,000. These were purchase prices, not current value. Current values were given for a house and lot in Whitby ($600) and some undeveloped farmland ($1,000). McDougall briefly re-cross-examined and undid some of the damage done by Eliza's failure to carry through on the new trial in the defamation case. Eliza had to provide security for costs in the original trial. And did Campbell know that she would have to do so again? He did not know anything about that. Did James know that she couldn't afford it as she was "perfectly penniless?" James didn't know about that either. His answers were irrelevant for McDougall's case, because the questions were not really questions but a way for McDougall to effectively give evidence about Eliza's poverty, in contrast to the Campbells' relative affluence. In the same vein McDougall's final questions concerned the "Glasgow Warehouse." Had it not been enlarged from one to three storeys since they bought it? Yes. It is now a much more valuable building, yet you "attempted to lead the Committee to believe it was worth only $4,000?" This was not a question, of course, but it was presumably not worth objecting to. What would you sell it for? Campbell was not prepared to say. That ended his time on the witness stand.[43]

The Testimony of John Anderson

Anderson began his testimony immediately after James Campbell, and went to the end of Saturday 18 March. He must have been on the stand for some two hours. He was not represented by Walker but by Alexander McIntyre, who took him through his own version of 26 August, which differed in only one respect from what has been recounted here and in previous chapters. Anderson said that after the altercation on the street, as he and Campbell were unlocking the door of the Campbell store, Gordon called out to Campbell "James Campbell, you're a damned shit-arse for watching."[44]

McDougall's cross-examination was for the most part unsurprising and unremarkable. Anderson's answers were terse and very often "No" or "I don't know." Anderson had not heard singing on 26 August, he knew nothing about Parks or where he now was, he had not read the Parks letter, he did not know why Robert wanted the house watched, he had heard nothing about Gordon before James Campbell fetched him, he said nothing to Campbell on the way, and so on and so forth. McDougall was perhaps trying to make Anderson annoyed or to look foolish with his questions about why Robert wanted the house watched:

Q. You were simply to watch the house; were you afraid it would run away?
A. No.
Q. Were you afraid she [Eliza] would run away from the house?
A. I think not.
Q. Were you afraid someone would run into the house?
A. I don't know anything about it.

At another point McDougall must also have been trying to goad Anderson into embarrassment. After Anderson said that Gordon had asked Eliza for more sex for what Anderson knew would have been the third time McDougall followed up:

Q. [H]e wanted it the third time?
A. Yes.
Q. That surprised you a little?
A. No, it did not.
Q. You are a married man, are you not?
A. Yes, sir.
Q. And it did not surprise you that within a short time this man should want it three times?
A. It did not.
Q. Not when this woman was five months gone in the family way?[45]

There were a number of things that Anderson said he had not heard but that Campbell had. Anderson did not recall hearing Gordon give any reason why he needed to leave, whereas Campbell recalled him saying he was tired and needed a few hours' sleep because he had a hard day's work ahead. Anderson heard no sounds of kissing. Nor did he hear Eliza suggest that Gordon stay the night. McDougall was also able to put Anderson in an awkward spot over his amended written statement. Anderson acknowledged that the statement had been written on the Sunday after Tuesday, 26 August and at the suggestion of the Campbell brothers. More importantly, he also acknowledged that he had first written down that Campbell had accused Gordon of attempting to seduce Eliza and then changed the statement. Why? Anderson's answer was hardly convincing:

A. I struck it out I suppose on looking over it afterwards while correcting it.
Q. Was this not some time afterwards when looking over it and comparing it with the other statement?
A. I could not say.
Q. You will not undertake to say that you did not reverse this first statement until you saw some other statement?
A. I do not know; I do not suppose that I saw any other statement. I am not sure; but I do not think that I did.[46]

McDougall then moved briefly to the previous lawsuits, especially the defamation case, in which, he suggested, the jury had not believed Anderson. Anderson, rightly, said he could not tell if that was the case. McDougall's final questions, as were some of those he had asked James Campbell, were vehicles through which he effectively testified to various facts: that Eliza had no means, was living with her mother, was frequently seen about town, and had "conducted herself properly." Finally, Anderson said yes to whether he knew that on her return from Toronto after the defamation case there had been a torchlight procession and "a great concourse of people to receive her."[47]

McDougall had finished and was followed by a flurry of questions from committee members. The principal ones came from Dickey, who wanted to know how close Anderson was on the outside to the sofa on the inside? About two feet [.6 m]. This prompted Dickey to observe that a person where Anderson was would have been able to hear better than a person at one of the front windows could have. That other person, of course, was James Campbell. But Anderson said he "could not say" who could hear better; "a person at the front window would be higher up, … and would have a little advantage on that ground." McIntyre had the last word. He knew he had to clear up the issue of the altered statement as best he could, but Anderson did not help him much:

Q. How came you to strike out in your statement, that to which Mr. McDougall has referred?
A. I was not sure of the words used, I suppose that those were the words; I supposed that he made the charge twice; I was not sure, and then I struck them out.
Q. You mean to say, that you thought James Campbell charged Gordon twice?
A. He made the charge once; I was not sure of the words.
Q. Will you tell us whether you made out a second statement, or simply struck out the words?
A. I struck out the words, I think, I have no proper recollection about it.

The Conclusion of Robert Campbell's Case

The committee did not sit on Sunday, 19 March, but reconvened on Monday, for what must have been a short session, producing only three and a half pages in question-and-answer format with William Fagan on the stand. He had nothing new to say, telling the same story he had told in the lawsuits. McDougall cross-examined him, getting him to admit that he had only glanced at Eliza and Gordon as he was walking by and that they had called each other Mrs. Campbell and Mr. Gordon, not Eliza and George. McDougall pressed him on when he had first told his story to anyone; it was at work and he mentioned it to a Harper and a Morris when they were all gossiping about the Campbell family trouble. He then told the story to Robert, who had come to his house to ask about it – testament to the way news travels in a small community. Shortly afterwards he was served with a subpoena to appear at the crim. con. trial.[48]

This ended the *viva voce* evidence presented by Walker. The appendix to the Senate *Journal* at this point contains Blake's judgment in the Chancery alimony case.[49] It is obvious why Walker would have wanted it on the record. It was an extended review of the evidence on the one fact needed to prove the preamble, by one of Ontario's leading judges, and Walker likely thought it might be persuasive. Walker and McIntyre were perhaps not that happy with their other evidence, the witnesses. Robert had been shown to have been unreasonably precipitous in resolving to leave Eliza, to have been totally unwilling to give his wife a chance to explain away the accusations against her, to have physically thrown her out of the house, and to have given her no support, even after his youngest son had been born. His brother had been at times evasive and inconsistent, and Anderson the same. Worse, a number of aspects of the story the two told made little sense, especially the idea that a person on the veranda at the front of the house could hear what was going on inside as well as or better than someone crouched just below the windowsill of the room in which it supposedly all happened.

The correspondent for the *Hamilton Weekly Times*, who was very much in Eliza's corner, did not think the Campbell brothers and Anderson had acquitted themselves well. James Campbell's "demeanour" was "anything but calculated to create an impression in his favour," nor did Anderson impress. Robert Campbell's "anxiety" to prove Eliza guilty "was commented upon with some severity." The reporter thought that Robert's motive in wanting to be rid of his wife was at least in part financial, true to his avaricious and parsimonious nature. He was, after all, "the man who allotted his wife $1.50 per month as pin money, during his absence in Scotland, and who told her to enclose her letters to himself in the letters to the firm, in order to save postage."[50] Having said this, the evidence for Robert was believable, especially given that Eliza had entertained a young man in the family home, unchaperoned, until after midnight. It was now up to McDougall to persuade the committee that doing so was simply inappropriate and foolish, that it had not led to what James Campbell and John Anderson claimed that it had.

10

The Senate Divorce Committee II: The Case for Eliza Campbell and Rebuttal Witnesses

Introduction

The committee heard no evidence on Tuesday 21 March, to allow Eliza to travel to Ottawa. It did hear a motion from McDougall that Robert's petition be dismissed without presentation of the defence evidence, but dismissed it.[1] Eliza brought with her a supporter, George Conrad Gross, "an elderly gentleman and a friend ... who believed in her innocence ... like many of her townspeople." They stayed at the Russell House hotel, one of the capital's most expensive and the one used by many parliamentarians and other dignitaries, and the other witnesses for Eliza did likewise. Robert complained indignantly about this to Dickey, because he was responsible for her expenses, which were said to be $4,000 to $5,000.[2] When Eliza and Gross went into the dining room of the Russell House she was recognized, and within five minutes "every one in the room was staring at her." She knew that she was "the cynosure of all eyes," but did not look much at her fellow diners as she conducted an "earnest conversation" with Gross. Then, as now, a news story about a woman had to discuss her age and physical appearance: "Mrs. Campbell is tall and very slight in figure, a pronounced brunette, with large, black eyes and pleasing, well-marked features. That she was extremely engaging, blythesome, and even very pretty in youth none would deny, for her appearance, her carriage, and lively manner at ten years distance bespoke a sufficiency of spirit."[3]

Eliza was on the witness stand for two whole days, Wednesday, 22 March and Thursday, 23 March, and for part of Friday, 24 March. Her direct and cross-examinations took up some 60 pages of the transcript.[4] She was followed on 24 and 25 March by other witnesses – Yeoman Gibson, Wellington Adams, and Gross. Walker and McDougall then both called rebuttal witnesses.

Figure 10.1. Advertisement for Russell Hotel

Source: Morgan, *Canadian Men and Women of the Time*, 1040.

The Testimony of Eliza Campbell

The committee room was overcrowded when Eliza appeared on Wednesday morning to give her evidence. She spoke in a low-key fashion, her manner "sad" and only once did she show "indignation."[5] McDougall began with the marital relationship before 1873. They had, Eliza said, lived as happily "as the generality of married people do." She explained the two occasions when they had had a tiff – the Atlantic crossing and Gordon's visit in the spring of 1873 – as not really serious disagreements, and denied that Robert had made her cry on the latter occasion. The questions soon moved to Parks. Eliza denied having had anything more than a friendship with him while he lived in Whitby. There was a brief correspondence between them after he had left, initiated by him, and lasting five or six weeks. It was "only nonsense and fun, done for a lark," and Eliza broke it off when she thought he had started to write "in rather a familiar way." She had burned the copy of the letter of 14 August from Parks that she received. McDougall then took Eliza through the papers found in her secretaire, which had been introduced by Walker as exhibits. Did the piece that began "Come when thou wilt I've a welcome for thee" refer to Parks or Gordon or any other person? No. What does it refer to? "It is my own composition." Next was one line from Exhibit 6: "Here I am vacillating between two opinions, whether shall I stay here or stray afar off – Duty says stay." Was it addressed to anybody? No. What about the apparent letter to Parks, Exhibit 5? It was a copy of a letter she had intended to send to Parks but which she then decided not to.[6]

The questions turned to Gordon. Eliza said that he had visited two or three times in the summer of 1873, had not stayed late, and they had talked and played music. Regarding 26 August, Eliza described the evening as she had done in the lawsuits. There was conversation, reading, playing, singing, looking at the stereoscope, and checkers. The conversation included the old joke about California, the warning about putting the slides too far into the "mutilated" stereoscope, and the discussion of army and naval service. The parlour door was wide open at all times, and the front door was ajar, Jane Newsom having left it that way when she admitted them both. Gordon left just after 1:15 a.m., both of them surprised at how late it was. McDougall concluded this section of his examination by questions to elicit denials:

Q. [W]as there any improper conversation between Gordon and you from the time of his coming into the house till he left it?
A. No; there was not.
Q. Was there any attempt on his part at any undue or improper familiarity with you?
A. There was not.
Q. Did he always treat you in a respectful manner, as a reputable gentleman of the neighbourhood ought to do?
A. Yes.
Q. Then the charge contained in this bill respecting Gordon you utterly and positively deny?
A. I deny it; and I always denied it.[7]

McDougall moved on to the defamation case, asking questions that enabled Eliza to say that she had not moved ahead with a new trial for lack of funds. That led to the fact that Robert had paid her nothing since he won the alimony case and nothing at any time for their youngest child. She was not under Robert's protection when the child was born, but in her brother James's house, which provided a perfect segue to McDougall's next series of questions, beginning with "[h]ow did you come to leave your own house? Did you leave voluntarily?" The story of her ejection from the family home followed, with Eliza's answers long, detailed, and dramatic. She had left with only the clothes she stood up in, and Robert had sent on only the clothing, silver, and bedding that she had brought to the marriage. The next topic was the Whitby courthouse meeting between Robert and Eliza. It had not led to a reconciliation because Robert had made it clear that he would never believe her. He was "bound to believe his brother's word in everything ... in preference to mine." He had even said "if an angel came down from heaven and told him I was innocent, he would not believe it." Once he had said that Eliza thought any further conversation was pointless, but Robert still asked her several times for her "price"; "I supposed he wished to give me so much to get rid of me."

McDougall then spent a little time calling by proxy on the opinions of Eliza's community. People treated her no differently than they had before August 1873, visited her, had her to their houses, and associated with her in public. He then moved to the Newsoms, asking about Jane's "illegitimate" child and about the characters of both sisters. Eliza spoke well of them. They were "'not perfect, of course, but they were 'upright,'" and she could say "nothing detrimental" about either. McDougall finished with James Campbell, and had two points to bring out. First, Eliza said that "we were not on intimate terms" and that James had been "bitterly opposed to my marriage with his brother." Second, James did not visit when Robert was away but was around the yard frequently, at all hours of the evening. McDougall's final question was obviously meant to suggest that it would be very unlikely for Eliza to transgress in her own house: "Then, for anything you know, he might look in at the window, or come in at the door, or come about the house at any moment at night."

This completed a wide-ranging, but not very long, direct examination. Walker's cross-examination was rather longer, going to the end of the day's session. The *Ottawa Times* called the cross-examination "vigorous," but the correspondent for the *Hamilton Weekly Times* was impressed with Walker's considerate manner. His task was a "very delicate and unpleasant one," but "he performed it with great consideration for the feelings of the witness, placed, if innocent, in so cruel and painful a position."[8] Walker began with Eliza's friendship with Gordon, getting her to admit that he had been in the house two or three, or perhaps slightly more, times before Robert left for the UK, but five or six times thereafter. The three or four times, Walker adroitly pointed out, were over 10 years of marriage, the five or six times over six weeks of her husband's absence. He then peppered Eliza with questions about whether she remembered things like Gordon coming in without knocking or Eliza giving Martha Newsom the evening off when Gordon came. Eliza answered no to all these questions. To other similar ones, about matters such as Martha Newsom having put the children to bed while Gordon was there, she did not recollect. She also did not remember Robert chastising her for having Gordon to tea in March 1873 or refusing to sleep with her that night. Her answers were invariably terse, largely because she often claimed she did not remember.[9]

After some time Walker got to the 26th of August. A number of questions were answered by Eliza saying she did not know or was not sure. For example, having elicited that Eliza had seen Gordon at church the day before Robert left for Southampton, he asked if she had told him that Robert would be out of town. "I do not remember" was her first answer, and when asked if she would swear that she had not told him, she replied "I swear I do not remember; but I will not swear that I did not tell him." The same kinds of answers were given about when the singing took place, and when Jane Newsom went to bed. She did know when Gordon left, at 1:45 a.m., but she did not hear James Campbell calling to her later. She definitely did not tell Jane Newsom the next day that there would be trouble between her and Robert. She knew nothing of the allegation of adultery until her brother James told her about it on 28 August. When asked if it had occurred to her that it was "imprudent" to be alone with a young man when her husband was absent, she said "I did not think so at the time." And she gave the same answer to the question: "Did you not think it was likely to create suspicion in the mind of your husband's brother?"[10]

When the questions dealt with the testimony of Campbell and Anderson Eliza sometimes had a ready explanation. The stereoscope was broken at one end, it was Eliza not Gordon who had talked of "naval," and references to eloping and going to California were inspired by a three-year-old conversation in which things were said in jest. Conversely when questions were asked about other damning claims Eliza simply denied such things had been said; nobody had talked about her breasts. She could remember very little about what she had read to Gordon. She had read from *The Language of Flowers* but could not remember what part and had left the book at home. She had also read from *Hudibras*, but beyond the fact that it was a humorous passage she could not recall what part. She knew George Sand's work but did not read from *Monsieur Sylvestre* that evening. She did have a book of Sand's in the house, *The Enchanted Lake*, but had not read from it except some lines of verse that she had written on one of the fly-leaves. The verses were sentimental, but she could not remember which ones, and that book had also been left at home. She only read for about 20 minutes, and while she did not know if Gordon's tastes were romantic, she did think that he had appreciated what she read.[11]

The session was nearly at an end when Walker moved to the checkers games. Eliza could not recall who suggested playing, or whether she had sat on the sofa or a chair while they played. Walker asked if she had testified previously that the board was on their knees, implying that she was on a chair and he on the sofa, she said "it was on our knees whichever way we sat." But their knees were not close together. Walker ended the day by asking how she had felt the following morning? She was "uneasy" because she knew James Campbell had been around the house the previous evening. Did that mean that she was worried that James would report Gordon's visit to Robert? Eliza had a good response to that, which reinforced her claim that James did not like her: "He had made so many reports to my husband that I had become indifferent." There the day's session ended.[12]

The following day, Thursday, 23 March, was entirely taken up with Eliza on the stand. Walker must have spent the evening comparing what she had said the day before with a transcript of her testimony in the Chancery case, and launched immediately into inconsistencies between the two. His first question asked Eliza to confirm that she had testified the previous day that Gordon's first visit was about the beginning of July. Eliza did so, and then Walker referred to the evidence she had given in the alimony case. Eliza stuck to her testimony of the previous day and said that the report of her Chancery testimony was incorrect:

Q. Then when you stated in the Chancery trial that his first visit was in the latter part of July or the first of August, you must have been mistaken?
A. It must have been a misprint.
Q. I have nothing printed in my hand; this is a certified copy of your evidence.
A. His first visit was in the beginning of July.
Q. Then, if your evidence was taken down in that way, it is wrong?
A. It must have been wrong.
Q. I will read it to you. "The first time that Mr. Gordon visited was in the end of July last or the beginning of August. So far as I recollect my husband returned on a Monday."
A. That is correct about my husband returning on Monday.

Q. But take the first paragraph?
A. It was the beginning of July.
Q. Then the evidence you are reported to have given on the Chancery trial is incorrect?
A. It is incorrect.
Q. Did you sign that evidence?
No answer.
Q. It was read over to you was it not?
A. It was not.
Q. Did you sign it?
A. I don't understand you.
Q. Was it read over to you by the officers of the court, and did you afterwards sign your name at the foot?
A. I have no recollection of that.[13]

Walker then turned to any discussions Eliza had had with Gordon since 26 August, which included talking about the evidence she would give. She had met him, but not "frequently," and she did not know how many times. Eliza was probably coached by McDougall to say as little as possible that was specific and could thus be disproved. "I do not recollect," "It might have been," "I cannot swear to that," and the like, were her answers to most questions. For example, when Walker turned to when Gordon had visited her house while Robert was absent, she "could not recollect" any date other than 9 August, although Gordon "may have" been there on the 2nd and 16th as well. Nor could she remember exactly when Gordon had left on these occasions except for one time when he stayed until "about 12." When asked where she was sitting when she read to Gordon she said "On the chair by the table, or on the sofa, I cannot say which." She had "no recollection" of who proposed playing checkers. Did she remember Gordon asking her if she was "sincere" on the night of 26 August? She did not. Would she swear that Gordon did not say that? She would not. On other matters Eliza unequivocally denied things said by Campbell and Anderson. She had not said Gordon had hurt her, she had not said that she did not wish to be tied down to one man only, and nobody used the phrase "topways, sideways, bottomways." She had "no recollection" of her asking Gordon what he would say if told that his wife entertained young men as she did.[14]

Walker then went back to Parks and the correspondence between them, and again Eliza's answers were evasive. Had they arranged to correspond before Parks left Whitby? "I don't remember that." Would she swear that no such arrangement had been made? She would not.

Had she given Parks envelopes addressed to her in her own handwriting? The same two answers were given. And so it went on:

Q. How many letters passed between you?
A. There might have been five or six, or there might have been more, but I could not say as to the number.
Q. Were there more or less?
A. I could not say.
Q. What became of these letters?
A. I destroyed them.
Q. Had you any particular reason for destroying them?
A. I do not know that there was.
Q. Did you destroy all letters you received at all times?
A. I could not say as to that.[15]

Similar answers were given to questions about the content of the correspondence. Eliza did admit that "Guardian" was her husband, a word she used in jest when speaking of Robert as her "guardian and guide." But her other answers said little. Parks had asked her to "be sure and write"; had she written? "I had written to him not to write to me again." Did you write again? She had no recollection of doing so but could not swear that she had not. What did the phrase "Tell me where the suspicion is" mean? Eliza had written that to "frighten" Parks into not writing again. What did she mean by various phrases in the draft letter? She did not send it; it was a draft. This was not an answer to the question, but Walker let it go and pressed her on whether she had sent the letter. She had not and had no recollection of saying at one of the trials that she had, although she would not swear that she had not said that. Had Eliza received letters that she picked up from the post office and that were not delivered to the business? She may have done so. Did she have a private address? This must have meant a pseudonym under which letters were posted to her care of the Whitby post office. She did have a private address. What was the name used? Improbably she could not remember – "It was some high-flown name."[16]

Walker turned briefly to the piece of paper that began "Come when thou wilt." Eliza was adamant that it was not written to anybody, it was a draft of a romance, a work to which she had not given a title. She had destroyed the rest. She then became vague again. She did not know whether the extract was from the beginning or middle of the larger work, she had not named the characters in the romance. She did know that the romance was not set in Whitby.[17]

Walker then adopted a scattergun approach, asking questions about various issues in no particular order. Did she go to Toronto to meet Parks while Robert was away? She was in Toronto but she did not meet Parks. She could not remember the date. Did she have company in the evening of 27 August? Yes, her niece. Was there singing? No, instrumental music but no singing. This was important because, it will be recalled, Blake had concluded that Yeoman Gibson was wrong when he said there had been singing on the 26th, it must have been the 27th. With the day nearly at an end, and Walker asking questions about the meeting in the Whitby courthouse with Robert, Kaulbach interjected a question: In that meeting had she denied Robert's allegation? She had. After a couple more questions from Walker Kaulbach asked his question again: "What way did you deny the charge after he persisted in believing the accusation?" Eliza's answer was unequivocal: "I positively stated it was not true." This completed the day's session and Walker's cross-examination.[18]

Eliza was on the stand for no more than an hour the following day, Friday, 24 March. The session began with McDougall re-examining her, and his first act was to proffer her letter to Robert of 28 August, discussed in chapter 3, as an exhibit.[19] The purpose was presumably to provide evidence that she had tried to talk to Robert, but he had rebuffed her, and to emphasize that the letter acknowledged that she had been "imprudent" but insisted that "in God's sight I have not been guilty of the charge James has imputed to me." McDougall went over a number of other issues. She had seen Gordon after 26 August, but always in the company of other people; Robert had told her that James Campbell used to complain to him about her; Robert had no taste for or interest in her music, thus she "had an inducement" to display her musical talents to others; the whole Campbell family was opposed to Robert marrying her because they thought she was "too fine" for him. She was also asked questions about Robert's cheapness. He insisted that her letters to him while he was away be enclosed in the firm's correspondence, to save postage, allowed her only $1.50 a month "pin money" while he was absent, and had the "reputation of being very close and careful in his business transactions."[20]

McDougall's cross-examination brought up something that had not been aired in any of the court cases. He produced a letter Eliza had written to Robert in Scotland at the end of July 1873, that referred to James Bremner, the wealthy Scottish uncle of the Campbell brothers mentioned in chapter 7. Eliza testified that she had met him in Scotland, and that in a subsequent conversation Robert had told her that Bremner had made Robert and James his principal beneficiaries and also that there was a "surplus" left to Eliza. Bremner had died in April 1875 at the age of 84, but Eliza had heard nothing about any legacy. McDougall made no further comment, but the purpose of this evidence was obviously to suggest that the miserly Robert had somehow taken the money that had been left to her.[21]

Walker took over for the last few minutes. He was clearly intent on undoing the damaging comments about Robert's cheapness and possible shady dealings. His questions elicited the fact that she knew about the supposed legacy because Robert had told her and that he had told her also that there was only a "probability" of one because a will could be changed. Also, she had written to Bremner after the separation but he had not replied. The implication was that Bremner changed his will when told of her adultery. As for Robert's cheapness, she agreed that during his absence she was able to get everything she needed from the Campbell store. McDougall then asked one further question: Had she been cut off from any source of goods after the separation? Yes. Eliza's many hours on the witness stand concluded with questions from Kaulbach about where Gordon was now and whether she had communicated with him. She had not.[22]

Reading the transcript without being able to assess her tone and demeanour suggests that Eliza's performance before the committee was not impressive. She did consistently deny that she had committed adultery, but there were two principal difficulties with the evidence she gave. First, she had admitted the flirtation with Parks. Of course Robert was not alleging adultery with Parks, but Walker had followed the line that had been so persuasive to Vice-Chancellor Blake. Eliza was flighty and flirtatious, did not abide by her marriage vows, and thus was more likely than not to commit adultery with someone. Second, while she consistently denied the worst of what Campbell and Anderson had claimed, she had also been consistently evasive on a host of matters. The standard answers outlined above – "I do not recollect" followed by "I will not swear that it did not happen" – cannot have left a good impression. Moreover, some of her evidence was highly implausible. How could someone destroy letters yet not know how or when she had done so? Was it really believable that a person could write a letter to somebody and not remember whether they had sent it?

Yet those who wanted to believe Eliza on the large and crucial question of her alleged adultery thought she had done well. The *Hamilton Weekly Times* correspondent told his readers that Walker had not been able to shake her testimony "on any one point." He conceded at the same time that while that did not damage Eliza's case it did not help her much either. Had there been no other evidence, the committee's decision would have to be based on the credibility of Eliza and her direct accusers.[23] To similar effect the unnamed reporter whose stories appeared in the *Whitby Chronicle* painted a favourable picture. Eliza had gone through an "ordeal," subjected to "the most searching questions," but had "maintained a cool composure and lady-like demeanour," which "had a favourable effect on the committee." Moreover, she had spoken in a low voice, one that would be "impossible" to hear through curtained and shuttered windows, so that Campbell's and Anderson's testimony, the reporter implied, was not true. Robert had also shown his true character, a "dyspeptic man who kills himself with business [and] has no soul for music and the pleasures of life." His character was not simply revealed by Eliza's testimony, his conduct proved it. All in attendance could hear him "energetically doing all he could to prompt his attorney to catch his wife and break down her evidence." Everybody, the reporter noted, thought that Eliza had been "indiscreet in her conduct," but that was all. Sympathy for Eliza "is openly expressed by outsiders," and it was clear that even Robert's lawyers "were thoroughly baffled and disgusted" by the Campbell brothers' actions.[24]

The Testimony of Yeoman Gibson, Wellington Adams, and George Gross

The rest of 23 March was taken up with three Whitby witnesses called by McDougall: Yeoman Gibson, Wellington Adams, and George Gross. Gibson repeated the testimony he had given in the alimony case, that he had heard singing from the Campbell home at about 11:15 p.m. on 26 August. Senator Walter Dickson interrupted and asked how far he was from the house, and Gibson estimated 37 metres (40 yds.). McDougall asked how he could be so sure of the date, a key question given that Vice-Chancellor Blake had concluded that Gibson had mistaken the evening for another. Gibson had his answer ready. He was travelling on business the next day, but because he was out late on the 26th he had overslept and missed his train to Toronto. He was cross-examined by McIntyre, who established that Gibson knew the Byrne family well; indeed, James Byrne was his next-door neighbour. McIntyre then asked to whom Gibson had first mentioned his story, and he retold the story he had given at the alimony trial about reading James Campell's evidence in a newspaper and remarking to those present that it was "confoundedly wrong."[25]

Why had Gibson not come out with his story after the crim. con. trial? Had he not read newspaper reports about that case? He did not think he had. Was there not a lot of talk about it in Whitby? Yes. "Your next-door neighbour was connected with this trial, and yet you swear that you did not take sufficient interest in the matter to read the reports of the evidence in the first trial?" Gibson had not read the newspapers in October 1873 because he had heard enough about the whole affair without doing so. This answer likely conveyed to the committee a sense that he had better things to do than to be absorbed by gossip about local scandals.[26]

McIntyre then tried to impeach Gibson's evidence by suggesting that he and the Campbells had argued over the latter "poaching" customers from Gibson. Gibson's answer was simple. It was old news because three years ago he had changed his business so that they were no longer competitors. Kaulbach interjected with a series of questions about matters that had already been discussed, such as how could Gibson be so sure of what night he had heard the singing? Since Kaulbach turned out to be the committee member most certain that Robert had made his case, it is likely that he was trying to undermine the damaging testimony Gibson was giving. When Kaulbach had finished, McDougall had the chance to re-examine Gibson, and focused his questions on a conversation Gibson had had with James Campbell shortly after 26 August, in which Campbell told him his version of what had happened. McDougall asked Gibson what exact words James Campbell had used, but all Gibson could remember was that Campbell had said "something about half way – but I cannot remember what." McDougall also tried, repeatedly, to get Gibson to say which of the two stories he believed. McIntyre did not object to these questions, even though Gibson's opinion was irrelevant. What mattered was his evidence. But Gibson would not be drawn into saying that James Campbell had lied. He would only say that his story was "inconsistent" with what he knew, and he added that he thought that Eliza had been "imprudent."[27]

McDougall's next witness was Wellington Adams. Had he been woken up on the night of 26 August by any noise? Yes; he had heard James Campbell say to Gordon, "You cannot deny it," and Gordon's reply, "You are a damned liar if you say so." This was at about 1 a.m. McDougall then took him through reading about what Campbell had said at the crim. con. trial and deciding it was incorrect. There followed questions about whether Adams or anyone else had ever suspected anything improper between Gordon and Eliza (no), and about whether Eliza was a "lively sociable person" who gave parties attended by young unmarried men like him (yes). Finally, McDougall asked whether she still maintained her "standing" in the town. "She does," asserted Adams, "among all her friends," despite "all these events."[28]

Walker's cross-examination of Adams went to the end of the sitting on Friday, 25 March and resumed the following day. He asked for all kinds of details about where in Adams's room the bed was, when he had gone to sleep, whether the window was open, and so on. He tried to make Adams seem like a good friend of Gordon's, presumably for the purpose of insinuating that he would lie to help his friend. He tried to undermine Adams's testimony by going into the relative locations of Adams's residence on Dundas Street, the block on Brock Street where the Campbells' business was located, and the place also on Brock Street where the altercation between Gordon and James Campbell had occurred (see map, figure 3.2). Given that Adams did not live opposite to the Campbells' stores, and 53 metres (173 ft) from where the altercation took place, he probed exactly what Adams could see and hear. Adams would not be shaken. Walker had his most success when he turned to discrepancies between the affidavit Adams had sworn for the new trial application in the crim. con. case and his current testimony. The former had stated that Adams had heard Campbell accusing Gordon of sex with his brother's wife, and that Gordon had denied that. There had been no mention of sex in Adams's direct testimony, and under cross-examination he said he did not hear that, only a denial of something. Similarly, the affidavit had said Adams was 27 to 37 metres (30–40 yds.) from the shouting, whereas it was, as just noted, 53 metres. Adams explained that he knew there were small errors in the affidavit, which had been read over by him in a hurry because James Gordon had a train to Toronto to catch. He had told Gordon about those errors, but Gordon had said it was all right.[29]

Walker also probed Adams's relations with James Campbell. Adams knew him, but not well. He had talked to him numerous times, usually in his store when Adams was shopping. He had not heard him speak in anger or use profanity. Had he actually seen Campbell and Anderson enter the Campbell store after the argument? He had not, by that point the angle of sight prevented him from doing so. Had he talked to anybody about the street altercation between 27 August and the crim. con. trial? Only John Mitchell. Although Adams answered some of the questions with the well-worn "I cannot recollect," Walker did not shake his evidence on the principal issues of the time and Gordon's denial.[30]

McDougall re-examined him, establishing that Adams had heard from local gossip that Eliza had been accused of adultery, and he had therefore assumed that that was what James Campbell had accused Gordon of in the street. But he had not heard those words, only Gordon's denial. Finally, some committee members asked about an occasion when John Mitchell asked Adams to go with him to the Campbell store. This had come up in direct examination to no import. The committee members wanted to know why Mitchell had wanted him there. Because John Tweedie, James Campbell's brother-in-law, wanted Mitchell to swear a statement about something. Mitchell did not say what, but Adams did say that Mitchell wanted him present because "he wanted me to go with him to protect himself." McDougall had a nice nugget of testimony: Somebody unconnected with the affair had implied that anybody who got in the Campbells' way needed protecting. Overall Adams's evidence was very significant. The time Gordon left the house was a matter of "extreme importance," said the *Hamilton Weekly Times* correspondent. If Campbell and Anderson were wrong on this point "little weight could be attached" to all the other things they had said.[31] The reporter whose stories appeared in the *Whitby Chronicle* went one step further. Gibson and Adams had given evidence contradicting that of James Campbell and John Anderson on "the most essential points," essentially "convicting them of wilful perjury."[32] Anderson was incensed by the phrase "wilful perjury."[33]

McDougall's next witness was Gross, who did not let Eliza down when he turned from chaperone to witness. He told the same story as he had in the Chancery court, adding that he could fix 1:30 a.m. as the time of the altercation because John Hamer Greenwood, who ran a clock-making business and who wanted Gross to invest in it, had lent him a clock to show him how good they were. There could be "not the slightest" mistake about the time. McDougall had more to get from Gross. He had him recount the meeting he had with the Campbell brothers after James Byrne had asked him to be an intermediary. Gross testified to Robert saying "they had commenced and would go through with it," and seizing on the "they" McDougall asked if anybody had spoken about the Campbells as "a race or clan?" The answer was that James Campbell had laid a hand on Gross's shoulder and said, "The Campbells know what they are about." Here was evidence for the brothers' oft-alleged "clannishness," which overrode any other loyalties, including those owed to wives and children.[34]

Gross had an even more damning report from his meeting with the Campbells in late August 1873. At one point Gross had contradicted James about the time. Campbell's response was, "Well, say it was only one o'clock; he asked me (Gross) if I thought it was right for a young married woman to entertain a young man to such an hour during her husband's absence." McDougall then moved to what James Campbell had said at the same meeting about whether Gordon had denied that intercourse had taken place. He told Gross that he had. Kaulbach, who almost certainly had his mind made up, tried to lessen the impact of

Figure 10.2. George Conrad Gross

Source: Whitby Archives Photograph 321-009-253

Gross's evidence about Gordon's denial by asking if Campbell had said when Gordon had uttered it. Gross did not know. Of course, Gordon had consistently denied the allegation from shortly after 26 August. The important point was that according to James Campbell Gordon had not denied it in the early hours of the 27 of August.[35]

McDougall had more to get from Gross. During his meeting with the Campbells and Anderson Gross had said that he found it very hard to believe that a woman well advanced in pregnancy would do what Eliza had allegedly done. Anderson had a crude reply. "[L]adies in that state were more prone to go with men," and he laughed at Gross and told him he should know better. Gross was offended and told Anderson that his own "experience was rather different." Anderson was thus painted as prone to making crude statements about women. Probably the most important thing Gross said was the "impression" he had taken away from the 90 or so minutes with the Campbells. He thought he had failed in his principal task, to persuade Robert to see Eliza. More importantly, he thought "Mrs. Campbell was not guilty" and that the Campbell brothers and Anderson "appeared to me as if they had come from a hunt; that they had caught – and were pleased over it."

Walker's cross-examination began with a clear indication of the line he would take: "Do you understand the sanctity of an oath?" He peppered Gross with questions, the answers to which would not have inspired confidence in his memory, although the quality of his answers could be seen as impaired by the fact that English was his second language.

Q. What day of the week [was the 26th into the 27th of August]?
A. I don't know it.
Q. What month?
A. August.
Q. What year?
A. I don't know; I did not keep trace of it.
Q. Is your memory good?
A. Not just now.
Q. Was it good at the first [crim. con.] trial?
A. Not much better than now.
Q. Is it as good now as it was then?
A. I could not say.
Q. Was it as good at the last trial as at the slander trial?
A. I don't think.
Q. Don't think what?
A. I don't think about it.
Q. What do you swear.
A. I don't swear about it.
Q. Will you swear your memory is not failing.
A. I don't observe, myself, any difference....
Q. Is your eyesight good?

A. Sufficiently good to see people.
Q. Did you have your spectacles on that night?
A. I had not; I don't wear them at night.[36]

There followed questions about small discrepancies between Gross's evidence at the defamation and alimony trials and his evidence in chief before the committee, but they were not important. For example, Walker said that at the defamation trial Gross had said he knew the time was 1:30 because he had looked at his watch, whereas that day he had said he knew by a clock. This did not, of course, undermine the main point, which was that the time was 1:30. In any event, Gross said "watch" was an incorrect transcription of his evidence; he had said "clock." After a number of other questions about not very relevant details of that night, Walker somewhat surprisingly asked Gross if he thought Eliza was guilty when he went to see Robert in late August. This gave him the opening to say, "I had no belief in it, because I was loath, like the whole town of Whitby, to believe a respectable woman like her could have acted in such a manner." The cross-examination continued for some time longer, and Walker at one point changed tack from challenging Gross's memory on details to depicting him as a knight errant, a man who had decided to be Eliza's "defender." Gross did not know what was meant by the question; Walker could call him what he wanted. Sometimes it helps to have a less than perfect command of English! On the whole Gross stood up well after a faltering start. He became adept at responding to Walker's questions about why he had not said at one of the previous trials something he was saying now. He often answered that it was because he had not been asked.[37] McDougall had the chance to re-examine and used it to have Gross stress that he had gone to see Robert having been assured by Rev. Byrne and James Byrne that they were confident in Eliza's story having examined her and Gordon "closely."[38]

Rebuttal Testimony: The Newsom Sisters and the Campbell Brothers

The last part of Saturday 25 March was taken up with four rebuttal witnesses – the Newsom sisters and the Campell brothers. Walker called Jane Newsom to establish that in the evening of 27 August, Eliza had been at home with Hettie Ham, Bethiah's daughter, and they were both playing music and singing. In addition, Jane had been in the yard with David Smith. This was, of course, for the purpose of showing that a person walking by on the 27th would have heard music and voices and seen two people in the yard. If Yeoman Gibson had been that person, he had simply got the date wrong, as Vice-Chancellor Blake had concluded. In cross-examination McDougall asked Newsom to confirm that David Smith had visited her on both the 26th and 27th, and if she were married and if she had a child. This was an obvious attack on her moral character. Martha Newsom then made a brief appearance, Walker establishing that she had never told Eliza that James Campbell was watching the house. McDougall in turn confirmed that she had left the Campbells' employment on 15 August, thus "anything that was told to Mrs. Campbell about watching could not have been by you?"[39]

The Newsoms could not have been on the witness stand for more than a few minutes. They were followed by James Campbell. Walker wanted to undermine the testimony of Gross, Adams, and Gibson. He began by asking if James had told Gross that Gordon had denied having sex with Eliza. He had not done so on the night, he had "confessed" then and only denied it afterwards. Walker moved to a conversation James Campbell had had with Adams shortly before the crim. con. trial, in which, said Campbell, Adams said he knew nothing about the scandal, "and did not want to know, or to be mixed up in it." All of this was inconsequential because it concerned a conversation that took place before the crim. con. trial and thus before Adams knew about Campbell's evidence on the time of the altercation in the street. Robert followed his brother and was very briefly examined on the conversation with Adams, to the same effect as James. That ended Saturday's session.

The Final Witnesses: Joseph Bandell, James Fraser, James Davison, Mary Jane Allin, and James Byrne

The committee reconvened on Monday, 27 March, and heard two rebuttal witnesses put forward by Walker – Joseph Bandell and James Fraser – and another witness for the defence, James Davison. The day's session must have been a short one, producing only 10 pages of transcript in question-and-answer format. Bandell, a German-born Whitby hotelier who until 1870 had been a shoemaker and retailer, was James Campbell's near neighbour.[40] He testified that he had seen James walking home at about 3:30 a.m. on 27 August, and had said hello to him. Bandell was up at that time because he had been serving two men who were going to Toronto and wanted a bottle of whiskey. McDougall's cross-examination dealt with the obvious points – how far away was Campbell when Bandell spoke to him; did Campbell say anything; did the clocks in his house work; had he had a few himself when he served the travellers? His main line of attack was whether Bandell knew what date this had occurred. He drew out that Bandell had signed two affidavits in lawyers' offices sometime after 27 August – he did not know how long after, but it was many months – but could not read. The affidavits had been written out by lawyers at the dictate of James Campbell, and read over to him before he signed them but, as McDougall took pains to point out, he did not know what he had signed. Bandell bridled: he could read figures and thus knew the date. He showed he could read figures by getting some dates right that McDougall wrote out then and there.[41]

Fraser, as we saw in chapter 5 a salesman who worked for the Campbell brothers and lived above their store, was the next witness. He had been woken up at about 3 a.m. on the 27th by two people talking in the store, one of whom was James Campbell. McDougall's cross-examination did not shake his story in any way. McDougall then called the last witness of the day, Wellington Adams's roommate James Davison, who in 1873 had been a student preparing for his entrance exams for university. He was still living in Whitby where he taught in the high school. His testimony agreed with Adams's about the time they had been woken up on the night in question.[42]

The last two witnesses were called on Tuesday, 28 March, by McDougall. The first was Mary Jane Allin (or Allen), who with her husband ran the book and stationery store next to the Campbells' store. Her evidence repeated what she had said in the alimony case – she was up reading when she heard loud voices in the street opposite, one of them being James Campbell. She then heard the Campbells' door shut, then reopen as somebody went out again and walked away towards the Campbell home. All of this was at about 1 a.m., although, she said, "other witnesses seem to have different views." Naturally McDougall asked her how she believed it was 1 or so. She admitted that she had not looked at a clock, but she was rarely up after 12 and she knew from the fact that she had stayed up reading a book she was "engaged" by that it was sometime after that. She had "always felt" that it was a little after 1, she had no doubt about that. She had "never been able to think that it was quite so late as other witnesses had said." She was "confident" that it was not as late as 2. Having established this as her evidence, McDougall asked about her relationship with Eliza – "visiting terms" still – and her view of Eliza's character. Allin thought she was an "honest woman," nothing had changed in that regard, and that was the general view of people in Whitby. "I have never met either a lady or gentleman who accused Mrs. Campbell of anything wrong," she declaimed. She knew that there were people in Whitby who accused Eliza of having done something wrong, but she had not met them, and she would not put such persons "in the category of ladies and gentlemen."[43]

McIntyre did the cross-examination of Allin. He focused on how she could be so sure of the time, and she repeated her answers on direct. He asked about differences between her current testimony and that in the two previous trials, but she responded effectively by either not recalling exactly what she had said and by correcting McIntyre about the meaning of what she had previously said. When McIntyre asked her how many conversations she had had with others about the 26th and 27th of August, she refused to say, because she had had so many conversations about it over the years. Allin was an effective witness, because she was both adamant about the time and freely admitted that she had not consulted a clock. She stood up well to McIntyre's questions and must have left a good impression with the committee members.[44] One of the reporters whose story appeared in the *Whitby Chronicle* recounted an incident during McIntyre's cross-examination in which he asked an "insulting question" suggested to him by Robert. The committee members and other senators in attendance thought McIntyre's question "vile," with Speaker David Christie, one of those in attendance, going so far as to denounce the question as "outrageous and unprecedented," for which statement he received general applause. It is impossible to even guess what the question might have been, for nothing in the transcript can be so characterized, and the question was probably not reproduced. But what matters is that, according to the reporter, the incident "had the effect of shewing the committee, as much as anything else, the character of the men who would not hesitate to outrage a woman's holiest and best feelings in order to gain their purpose."[45]

The last witness was James Byrne. He told of how he had heard of the accusation from the Campbell brothers and then gone to see Eliza. She had given him an account of the evening which did not differ in any material way from what she had said at the various trials. Gordon had told him the same version. McIntyre's cross-examination only resulted in Byrne affirming what he had said. With that the evidence was all in.[46] Ottawa's *Daily Citizen* reported that "the general impression appears to be in her [Eliza's] favour." The reporter whose stories appeared in the *Whitby Chronicle* agreed, and went further. "[F]rom a reliable source' he had learned that "'the Campbells stand little chance of succeeding... , and their conduct has disgusted all with whom they came into contact at the Capital."[47]

11
The Senate Divorce Committee III: Counsels' Speeches and the Committee's Report

Introduction

The taking of the evidence was followed, as in a court case, by speeches from counsel for each side, on 28 March. Eliza did not remain in the committee room for those speeches, no doubt McDougall's tactical choice. I assume that Walker went first, although there is no record of what he said. He would have spoken first in any civil court case because he represented the moving party, the party that had the onus of establishing that the facts met the legal claim. He could not have spoken for long, perhaps because Philemon Pennock, a solicitor in his Ottawa office and a junior on the case, died on 29 March.[1] McDougall also began his speech for the defence on 28 March and spoke for the rest of the day for what must have been some three hours. He finished his speech the next day. His remarkably effective address, a mixture of rhetoric and devastating forensic analysis, was recorded in shorthand by a member of the Senate's reporting staff and published in the *Whitby Chronicle* in 1876. It was republished in 1879 as a pamphlet when Parliament was debating Eliza's separation bill and distributed to all senators and MPs.[2]

William McDougall's Address to the Committee

One theme stressed throughout by McDougall was the standard of proof that Robert had to meet. Despite the fact that it was not a criminal case, but in line with the language always used about adultery, McDougall insistently reminded committee members that Robert had to do more than meet the ordinary civil standard of proof on a balance of probabilities. The burden of proof was that of "clear evidence," that adultery must be "clearly and indubitably proved"; "no mere

THE

CAMPBELL DIVORCE BILL.

:o:

WOMAN'S RIGHTS IN ONTARIO.

:o:

Parliament as a Court of Justice.

:o:

Speech of the Hon. Wm. MacDougall, Counsel for Mrs. Campbell, before the Committee of the Senate; taken in Short Hand.

Figure 11.1. *Women's Rights in Ontario* title page
Source: CIHM No. 09414

inferential conclusion will suffice," the senators "must be satisfied beyond any question."[3]

McDougall began, as lawyers often do on such occasions, by characterizing the issue as much larger than one affecting the interests of a few people. The decision of the committee would be read with interest throughout the country and would have "a powerful moral influence upon other families and individuals far and wide." At the same time the decision would have an especially significant effect on Eliza Campbell; it was "life and death" to her "morally speaking." A verdict in her favour meant life, albeit a "clouded and unhappy" life, but a life with her children as a respectable woman. A verdict for her husband would "condemn[ed]" her to a "living death, branded with a mark of infamy." She had been able to survive the setbacks in courts, obtained by "perjured testimony" and one in a case in which she had no opportunity to testify – "the relic of a barbarous jurisprudence." Supported by relatives and friends who knew the "motives of her accusers and the falsehoods by which they had misled the court," she was able to "hold up her head and assert her innocence." She could "point triumphantly" to the second jury verdict, rendered by men who did not believe her accusers. Then came the third case, decided by a judge who had taken seventeen months to "argue[d] himself out of his doubts in her favour." She retained throughout the "sympathy of strangers" and "hundreds of undoubted believers in her honour … among her neighbours." But an adverse verdict by the committee would be final, with no appeal other than to "that dread tribunal, where the helpless victims of human justice may look for exculpation if innocent."[4]

McDougall then took the committee through the three court cases, dwelling on a scathing critique of Blake. He emphasized the contrast between the words Blake had spoken when he tried to get the parties to reconcile and his judgment written so much later. He, McDougall, had looked very carefully into the cases Blake had cited and was convinced that he had "misinterpreted and misapplied" the law as laid down in those cases. He had done so because he did not understand "the social habits of our villagers and country people." Blake had cited a number of English cases, but in none of them was the evidence of adultery as weak as in this one. McDougall expanded on some examples, without actually naming the cases, including one where a married woman had spent a considerable time in a man's house and the surrounding circumstances made it very clear that she did not like her husband. These facts "tended to produce such a violent presumption of guilt" that the court, "treating the question as men of common sense would," had found adultery proven. In another case a married woman was seen to go into the bedroom of a young man and stay there a considerable time. McDougall referred only to reported cases from the United Kingdom, but he could have cited prior divorces granted by the Canadian Parliament. The year before Henry Peterson, a Guelph barrister, obtained a divorce from his wife Emma, the evidence of multiple witnesses showing that a local doctor, Tuck, had visited the Peterson house for hours on end when Peterson was out, and had been seen with her in two different hotels in surrounding communities where they both stayed the night having engaged separate rooms, although Tuck was seen to go into Emma's each time. Nobody caught the lovers *in flagrante delicto*, but an indignant maid at one of the hotels had entered Emma's room without knocking and saw her lying on the bed with "her clothes up to her knees" and Tuck lying across the foot of the bed.[5]

Such cases stood in marked contrast to the current one. Eliza was in her own house, in the company of a neighbour whom she had known from childhood, and who was a friend of the family. He had visited the house a number of times, and on at least one occasion her husband had left them together. The families had interacted over the years, and on the very night in question Gordon had accompanied members of the Byrne family home. This was all common behaviour in a "country village," where the social relations are "familiar and unrestrained," even to the point that a member of her social circle should be alone at the home of a married woman in the evening. There was nothing that "requires explanation or justifies suspicion."[6]

Having disposed of cases where the circumstances had compelled a conclusion of adultery, McDougall turned to the evidence in the current one. Robert's case was as follows. Eliza had shown "signs of dislike and repugnance" towards him and sought "pleasure" in the "intellectual and friendly intercourse" of others, which Robert denied her. Even if that were true "it does not prove crime." But in fact there was no testimony to support this theory about Eliza's dissatisfaction other than Robert's, and even his evidence was limited to a very few instances. He said that she had told him once that she wanted to separate from him and wished the children were dead, but she denied that. There were also two other instances of marital tension, her "frivolity" on the Atlantic crossing, walking on the deck of the ship with a fellow traveller. Everybody knows that people quickly make friends on board ship. It was only after their return home that Robert said anything, and yet this "insignificant circumstance" is now used as something relevant to a claim of adultery. Blake seems to have believed that it was relevant, but the committee members, some of whom were lawyers, knew that it was not, and ought not to be taken into account. The other instance of "alleged improper conduct" was the evening that Gordon visited while the family was at tea. At the time Robert had not accused Eliza of any impropriety, and we all initially thought, said McDougall, that she had not been guilty of anything. In fact Eliza denied the tears, and admitted only the "chaff." It was "mere banter." The committee was being asked to believe that these "two instances of proofs of waning affection" were "preparation" for an act of infidelity that took place later. McDougall had "never heard or read of a case standing upon such a flimsy foundation" as proof of "alienation of affection" leading to "improper behaviour."[7]

McDougall then moved to the Parks correspondence, which he conceded could not be treated so lightly. The letter found on his desk by Robert was supposedly written by Parks, even though it was signed "G.H." Yet Robert had decided it was from Parks and, moreover, decided "then and there" to leave Eliza because she had, he believed, committed adultery with Parks. Robert's belief derived from the phrase in the letter "where do you think the suspicion is." Robert was reinforced in his belief by the writings found in Eliza's secretaire, which

McDougall dealt with first. "You have them before you," he stated. "Look at them." All but one were extracts from books, books that can be found in the library. This was the first time that one of Eliza's lawyers had mentioned the origin of some of her writings. Eliza was a woman of "reading and cultivation," who occupied herself with books while her husband was busy with his business. The committee was asked to believe that these "disconnected passages, found on different scraps of paper" are "copies of letters written to her paramour." There was nothing to justify that belief, and the Parks correspondence could be ruled out anyway as nothing to do with the issue at stake, which was whether there had been adultery with Gordon? The contention of Robert's counsel was that when a married woman writes letters to a young man containing expressions of affection that show a "laxity of morals" and a "corrupt imagination," she is willing to commit adultery with *any one*. This conclusion was very "far-fetched."[8]

Eliza's letters and other writing had been used in the Senate to show that Robert had acted properly when he deserted her without explanation, and took his children away from her on a false pretense. A husband must show when he comes to court that he has "clean hands," had not "contributed to his own dishonour," not "neglected or exposed his wife": "if he wants equity, he must shew that he has done, and is ready to do, equity." McDougall was citing an equitable maxim that a person who seeks equitable relief must have "clean hands," must have behaved with honour and rectitude. Robert's hasty conclusions did not satisfy this standard because he immediately believed they constituted evidence of adultery and deserted her.[9]

From that McDougall moved to a related point – that all the case authorities state that "a letter *to* a person is not evidence to prove a crime committed by that person."* McDougall cited famous examples of the principle, including the case of Marshall Spring Bidwell, speaker of the Upper Canada assembly in 1837 who had been wrongly suspected of complicity in the 1837 Upper Canadian rebellion on the basis of letters written to him.[10] He had acted wisely, said McDougall, giving in to an excessive analogy, for if Blake's reasoning had prevailed in his case, Bidwell would have been "hanged beyond question." Coming back down to earth, McDougall noted that there were no letters in evidence written by Eliza and received by Parks. Eliza had admitted that she and Parks corresponded, and that after a while she broke off the correspondence because his letters were becoming "rather frequent

* Emphasis in original.

and familiar," and "likely to bring her into difficulty." She specifically said in one letter that there was "suspicion." The letter of 14 August from Parks corroborated her account. It said that he had not received a letter from Eliza for some time, asked for envelopes, and asked her where she thought "the suspicion was." This was all consistent with there having been a correspondence, with it having been broken off by Eliza because it had gone too far, and with her denial that she had sent him envelopes. Her evidence before the committee was that she had used the phrase about suspicion to frighten him off. The Parks correspondence was a "lark," and "very imprudent," but it in no sense justified an allegation of adultery or the granting of a divorce.[11]

Having assailed the cogency of the evidence about the Parks correspondence, McDougall went on to castigate Robert. When he found the letter of the 14th of August, he should have asked for an explanation. To a "fair-minded sensible man" the explanation Eliza gave the divorce committee would have been entirely satisfactory as to adultery. But Robert, "impelled by evil counsel," obviously James Campbell, jumped to the conclusion that Eliza had been "guilty." Guilty of what? Not adultery, but of writing to a young man without the knowledge of her husband – and that was not the charge in the draft bill. The committee was not here "to try or admonish people for breaches of decorum." At this point McDougall returned to the other extracts in Eliza's handwriting, and to Chancellor Blake. The extract beginning "Here I am vacillating" was word for word from a book, yet printed in Blake's judgment as if it was part of a letter or composition. Also "patched into" Blake's judgment "as a copy of a letter to Parks" was the passage beginning with "I believe there are certain men." But the passage was written by a man, or by someone pretending to write in a man's voice, and was also an extract from a book. From all this Blake had reasoned that Eliza's mind had been "corrupted," that she was "a fit subject for seduction," and that "therefore Gordon seduced her!" Blake's test for detecting adultery was one that "hundreds of women in this country, good wives and good mothers," would not be able to pass.[12]

At this point Kaulbach interrupted to say that Eliza had not denied that the letter signed "Book-keeper" was a letter sent to Parks. McDougall corrected him; she admitted only that it might have been a draft of a letter, which she never sent. He went on seamlessly to ask the "so what" question; what if she had written and sent it? It did not contain a single word about adultery with Parks. Is a discussion about attending Holy Trinity "the language of a corrupted wife to her paramour?" Was a high church/low church comparison? The letter, draft or otherwise, contained no more than gossip. In short, and concluding this part of his speech, McDougall insisted that there was nothing in the various writings "to sustain a charge of anything more than thoughtless levity – indecorum if you will – which this poor woman now confesses she committed, though at the time she had no evil intention, and was unconscious of the danger to which she exposed herself."

By now McDougall had made a very effective case for discounting the evidence relating to Parks, but it was evidence that he himself had said more than once was irrelevant. What mattered was the evidence relating to Eliza and George Gordon. Gordon, McDougall wrongfully claimed, was not even in Robert's mind when he told James Campbell to watch the house, it was Parks he suspected. In fact, as we have seen, Robert had been told about Gordon's visits once he had his suspicions aroused by the Parks letter. Whatever the truth on this point, McDougall ridiculed the assumptions at the centre of Campbell's and Anderson's evidence:

> [W]hat is the story? It is this. A lady of education, ... living in her own house in a country town, under the eye of her neighbours, within four months of her confinement, her husband having just returned after an absence of several weeks, and having taken her children away ... for a short trip, ... submits herself *for the first time*, to the embraces of a young man whom she had known for years, and this too with the parlour door open, a light burning, the maid-servant listening..., and the criminal act, or rather acts, preceded and followed by loud and lewd conversation, laughing, crying, and kissing, that could be heard out of doors, through the curtains, the windows and the blinds!

This story was "utterly incredible," and "contrary ... to the instincts of human nature, and to the experience of every married or single man competent to give an opinion on matters of this kind."

McDougall had plenty more to say along the same lines. It was "incredible" that a woman of Eliza's religious upbringing could have used such language. It was even more remarkable that somebody who associated with the most respectable people in the town could have done so, and of course notable that, after all the attempts to blacken her name, those same respectable people still gave her their "respect, their confidence, their goodwill, and even their ardent sympathy." Add to that her "condition of life," the fact that it was claimed she had "criminal connection ... not once but twice," and the claim that the language used was "uttered in a loud tone" – all made for a story that was not credible. One could hardly expect such language even from a common prostitute "in intercourse with the other sex," unless, perhaps, she was drunk.

With that McDougall moved to dissecting the testimony of Anderson and James Campbell. Campbell had said that he had heard 16 different "expressions" overall, but, in fact, he had "forgotten" four or five of them in his examination-in-chief. They came up in cross-examination or on re-direct, including the story about California. Anderson told the committee he could hear as well from the west window as Campbell could from the front of the house, but Campbell had initially said he could hear better but then changed his mind and said equally well. Anderson had heard 12 expressions compared to Campbell's 16, yet only four of the expressions were the same. This, McDougall asserted, was not credible. They were both there to listen to what was said, they cited specific aspects of the conversations, yet their accounts did not agree on 24 of the 28 total expressions used. He did not suggest that the words used should be identical, but they ought to "agree in substance" and to come at the same time in their accounts.[13]

These discrepancies were not the only problem. Some of the expressions they did testify to were no doubt used but were perfectly innocent. They had been "distorted into vileness" by the listeners' "evil imagination." Campbell and Anderson had gone there "to hear something wrong," and as a result put the worst construction on the "fragments" they heard. McDougall expanded at some length on one example, the statement that "Robert might suspect," which Campbell heard but Anderson did not. The response, according to Campbell in his examination-in-chief, was "has Robert had anything to do with you since his return," but later in his evidence he changed this to "has Robert had any connection with you since his return." This was a crucial difference. McDougall conceded that if Gordon had asked a question about "connection," and if Eliza had answered it "in the words sworn to," one would have to conclude that "there was criminal familiarity between them." But Campbell had initially reported different words, words that might have referred to something entirely different. Realizing this, Campbell had come back the next day and given a different answer, using the word "connection." Which version was more probable? Why would Eliza, a married woman five months' pregnant, discuss with her supposed paramour whether her husband had suspicions? The contention was "too puerile for serious argument." Anderson had heard nothing of this "absurd question, and still more absurd answer," and the committee members should discount the evidence entirely.

McDougall continued in the same vein with other things Campbell claimed to have heard. He stated that Eliza had said "I have no pleasure in life," but Anderson did not hear that. Even if it had been said, there was nothing "criminal" in it. Invoking the criminal standard of proof on the heels of the word "criminal," McDougall insisted that the "presumption of innocence" must apply to any such statements "until guilt is proved by evidence that cannot be doubted." There was also a problem with the question apparently asked, "Will you come half way if I go the other?" This was supposed to be an invitation to engage in intercourse made to a young man who was apparently eager and who had already performed once, and yet he refused. "Is that the way such matters are conducted? Is this the same man who … wanted this woman three times and declared he was crazy for it," McDougall asked rhetorically, adding for good measure that apparently Anderson heard nothing of this exchange. "The floor is as good as a bed" was another expression about which committee members should be very dubious. A member of the militia might say that about camp life, but as Anderson did not hear it James Campbell was probably "romancing."

McDougall went relentlessly on. The only expression sworn to by both men was "navel." It was remarkable that Gordon could display such ignorance of human anatomy. More importantly, the word was "naval." McDougall cited other instances where Campbell testified to expressions used that Anderson did not hear, or when they both claimed to have heard the same expressions but arising in entirely different contexts. There were four of the former, including the conversation about the stereoscope, and three of the latter, in addition to those already discussed. McDougall then turned to another set of expressions – those testified to by Anderson but not by James Campbell. They included Gordon saying "you are getting stout" and "put your arms around me." Also in this category was Anderson's report of the conversation about California, and his statement that Eliza had said "kiss me." Campbell did not say this in his evidence. Surely, McDougall argued, two witnesses to the same conversation ought to have given substantially the same account.

McDougall then reverted to a note he had sounded before – the sheer improbability of much of the evidence. He specifically highlighted Campbell's claim that he heard the two kissing:

> He says he heard kissing, and that is the most remarkable thing of all – that he could hear through the curtains, windows, blinds, and other obstructions, the noise of lips meeting. You are asked to believe that two clandestine lovers, seated in a parlour, 12 feet [3.6 m] at least from the eavesdroppers, listening at the windows of a well-built brick house, … indulged in labial *smacks* that could be heard outside…. This kissing business is enough of itself to destroy the whole story of these wretched spies.

Campbell and Anderson had told two different stories, so much so that neither could be believed. The committee members should also recall Anderson's initial statement, that he had accused Gordon of attempting to seduce Eliza. That in itself negated any "presumption of guilt" that could possibly override the "presumption of innocence," which "must prevail."

McDougall was almost done for the day. He repeated his encomiums on Eliza's "irreproachable" character, and his condemnation of Robert for his efforts to find a reason to rid himself of his wife. Those efforts had "utterly failed." McDougall could find no similar case in the English divorce court records. He also condemned Blake for his suggestion that pregnant women were "apt to give free course to their passions."

The committee then adjourned, and resumed the following day at 10 a.m. McDougall began with some issues he had not mentioned the day before. The evidence of the Newsom sisters was of no value. Martha had left on 15 August, and all the statements about finding the curtains pinned together, or Eliza's boots there in the morning, were only relevant if one had "the prejudiced view of the other side." Why should a lady not, after a long day, remove her boots, a fact that Eliza had freely agreed she occasionally did? Jane Newsom was in the house on 26 August, but her evidence did not tally with that of Campbell and Anderson. She said she had gone to bed at 11:15 p.m.; they said it was 12 a.m. If they were right, she would have been awake and able to hear "the first act of criminality," which the listeners said started around midnight. Yet she heard nothing, while those outside apparently did.[14]

McDougall moved to Yeoman Gibson, who he called "the ex-mayor," presumably to stress his status and thus his reliability. He had been cross-examined and adhered strongly to the belief that he and his wife had heard singing and playing on the evening of the 26th. It was suggested that they got the wrong evening, but the fact that there was music on the 27th, which there likely was because Hettie Ham visited Eliza that evening, did not mean that there was none on the 26th. It was true that Jane Newsom had said that she also heard no music on the 26th, but McDougall simply resorted to character assassination. Jane had lost her virtue, and after that how much of her "veracity" had she retained.

McDougall then discussed what had been a major issue in the court cases, one that he had saved for the second day, the altercation in the early morning between Gordon and James Campbell. Campbell and Anderson had sworn that they left the house at 3 a.m., and McDougall had cross-examined them "at considerable length" as to how they knew that. "After much fencing" Campbell said he saw his watch by the light of the window. Before he said more on that, McDougall stressed if Campbell was shown to have been "untrue, ... substantially and knowingly false" on the time, then the senators must "distrust his truthfulness on other and more vital points." McDougall then summarized the watchers' version of what happened after they left the Campbell house, including what Gordon had allegedly said when confronted by James Campbell. But the problem with this version was that four witnesses had given different accounts of both the time and, much more important, "the tone and character of the interview." Adams, Gross, Allin, and Davidson were all independent witnesses who had "no interest in telling anything but the truth." Against them must be placed the evidence of two people who, "by their own admission," were "engaged in a conspiracy to watch, and if possible to catch, an unsuspecting woman in a position which would enable them to charge her with a crime." They may not have intended to commit perjury, but their "prejudiced minds" and "warped judgment" led them to make everything fit their previously formed opinion. Senators should ask themselves if it was "reasonable or probable" that when accused Gordon would show such indignation if he had just confessed to committing adultery? A jury had already found against Campbell and Anderson's account of the late-night meeting, and even Blake had "questioned the veracity" of the "eavesdroppers."

McDougall should perhaps have left it there, but he devoted time to an alternative argument: that even if Gordon had confessed it was dangerous to trust the admissions of co-respondents. There followed a long description of an English case in which a wealthy middle-aged husband had won a verdict in a crim. con case against a 19-year old youth who confessed in order to avoid a large damages award, only to have it proved, when the husband applied for a divorce, that his wife was a virgin and he a serial adulterer.[15] McDougall turned this into a disquisition on the iniquity of the party witness rule in crim. con. cases, and thus reinforced his earlier point about the unreliability of the verdict in *Campbell v. Gordon*. In the process he showed that he had done his research. But he also arguably showed the lack of judgment and pompous arrogance that had marred his political career. Why raise the possibility that Gordon's alleged "confession" had been uttered, even if the point of the story was that such confessions were not always true. Indeed the facts of the two cases were diametrically opposed. Robert had not won the crim. con case because of a false confession by Gordon, Gordon had not made a confession to get off lightly on damages, and nobody had ever suggested that, whatever else he may have been, Robert was a rake. Indeed, perhaps tired of listening to McDougall pontificating, Dickey brusquely told McDougall that he "over-rate[d] the effect" of *Campbell v. Gordon* on the committee.

McDougall took the hint to move on and returned to the issue of the time. Evidence in rebuttal had been called to show that James Campbell had been seen coming home at 3:30 a.m. on 27 August. But McDougall reminded committee members that if this was true, it was the second, not the first, time that Campbell had walked home from the Campbell house that night. Campbell had testified that after the confrontation with Gordon he had returned to the house, got the ladder out and tried to talk to Eliza. If he and Anderson and Gordon had in fact all initially left the house at 3, then walked down to the Campbell store, had their "discussion" with Gordon, visited the Campbell store to drink whisky, and returned to the house to put up a ladder and stood around "grumbling" because Eliza would not talk to them, it was not credible that all this could have happened in 30 minutes. Thus the rebuttal witness had rebutted Robert's case, not Eliza's. Campbell and Anderson must have left long before 3 a.m. More generally, Robert's case rested upon the Campbell/Anderson evidence, and "if they are found to have made wilful misstatements" upon three material facts – singing or no singing in the house, the admission or denial of Gordon when accused, and the time he left the house, "then I ask you, what reliance can you place upon their recollection … of the conversation that took place within the house?"

McDougall had reached the end of his forensic analysis of the evidence, but not of his speech. There remained to point out other things, including James Campbell's manner on the witness stand, "his hesitation to answer, his refusal to answer sometimes, and the way he fenced throughout…, endeavouring to evade every question which he fancied would tend to vindicate my client." This was in marked contrast to the witnesses for Eliza, who testified in "a straightforward, candid manner," and Eliza herself who was "willing to tell the *whole* truth, without reserve." The last statement was something of an exaggeration, and McDougall went back to James Campbell, criticizing him for his inaction in the face of the alleged goings on inside the house. He went for a stick with "the natural and proper purpose" of breaking in and interrupting, but then changed his mind and did nothing. This was not only improbable, but damaged Robert's case. A divorce will not be granted if the husband has connived at or agreed to the adultery. James Campbell was his brother's agent, made so for the purpose of watching the house. This made Robert effectively a "contribut[or] to his own dishonour" and disentitled him from coming to Parliament for relief.[16]

McDougall concluded by asserting that the committee should dismiss the bill, it should "find affirmatively and positively that Mrs.

Campbell is innocent." It should also find that Blake had been wrong to come to conclusions against Eliza based on her conduct prior to 26 August. That conduct was a reasonable response to Robert's neglect. A husband who is "morose or severe" to his wife, who "treats her with neglect and coldness," is not entitled to complain "if he loses her wifely solicitude or affection." Robert had paid more attention to his business interests than to his household, had neglected his wife and "compelled" her to "seek the companionship of younger people." Eliza was a very social person, musical, always wanting to entertain her friends, whom she found "more congenial than the cold, morose, negligent, absorbed husband," who thought she was only good for managing the house and the children and putting on "a happy face when he came home late at night." The senators, and likely McDougall as well, probably did think this was the proper role for a wife, but the point McDougall was making was that Robert should have played his assigned role correctly.

Overall McDougall's speech to the committee was highly persuasive, and was recognized as such – "a masterpiece of forensic eloquence" – by the *Whitby Chronicle*.[17] The *Ottawa Citizen* agreed, saying that McDougall had "conducted the case with great ability."[18] In a very well-organized, logical, and generally calm but occasionally impassioned speech, he ridiculed the evidence and the witnesses for the other side, painted Eliza in the best light he could without pretending she was faultless, and was largely responsible for a successful verdict, as discussed in the next section.

The Divorce Committee Report: Preamble Not Proved, but Then What?

McDougall's speech carried the day. By a 6–2 majority the committee decided that the preamble had not been proven. Dickey did not vote, because he felt that as chair he should not give an opinion on the merits, but also because, he later said, he found the whole proceeding "a painful experience."[19] Kaulbach and Cornwall were the dissenters.[20] According to many press reports, the result was expected, a view shared by the four official reporters for the divorce committee, who "were unanimous in believing Mrs. Campbell to be the victim of a conspiracy."[21] Most people in Whitby were delighted with the verdict, which created "considerable excitement" in the town.[22] The *Hamilton Weekly Times*' approving correspondent took pains to note that several of the senators on the committee were "able and experienced lawyers."[23] It did not say that of the four lawyers on the committee only Dickson, the non-practising lawyer, had found for Eliza. Dickey had abstained and

Kaulbach and Cornwall had voted against. The committee's verdict not only attracted comment in a number of Ontario and Montreal newspapers,[24] it was also remarked upon in the US and the UK. The *Chicago Tribune* used the story as illustrative of the difficulty of getting a divorce in Canada. The *Central Law Journal*, a St-Louis-based legal periodical, published a long paragraph about the case in its April 1876 issue, partial to Robert. The author of the article was cognizant of the three lawsuits, thought it "extraordinary" that different courts could have come to different conclusions, and was surprised that the Senate had found the preamble not proved. Testament to the "legs" that a case involving a sexual scandal could grow, the *Central Law Journal*'s article was copied verbatim in the *Irish Law Times*.[25]

A finding that the preamble had not been proved was normally the end of the matter, at least for the current session, because a petitioner could always try again with more or better evidence in a subsequent year. But on this occasion the committee report, presented to the House on 31 March, said more than that the preamble had not been proved. It also asked, in somewhat convoluted language, that Robert's bill "may not be passed without such amendments as may make it an Act providing for such a separation … as would be effected in England by a decree of judicial separation pronounced by the proper court." In other words, it asked that a bill be passed for a separation at Eliza's behest and not for a divorce at Robert's. The immediate origin of this request was a petition from Eliza that Reesor presented to the Senate on 29 March, following McDougall's closing speech.[26]

The reference to England in the committee's report was to the fact that English law had long included two forms of "divorce." Until 1857, when jurisdiction over all matrimonial disputes was given to a newly established Court for Divorce and Matrimonial Causes, spouses who wanted a legal separation could apply to the principal ecclesiastical court, the Consistory Court, for a decree of divorce *a mensa et thoro* (from bed and board) on the grounds of adultery and/or cruelty. A divorce *a mensa et thoro* did not dissolve the marriage and thus did not allow either party to remarry. In the 30-year period between 1828 and 1857 there were almost 400 such petitions in the principal Consistory Court, that of the Diocese of London, a slight preponderance of which were brought by husbands, with husbands having a much higher success rate than wives.[27] The other kind of "divorce," a divorce *a vinculo matrimonii*, which ended the marriage and allowed the parties to remarry, could not be obtained from any court before 1857, only by private Act of Parliament. English parliamentary divorces were rare, only a little over 300 Acts being passed between 1700 and 1857, because they were extremely expensive to obtain.[28] Both kinds of divorce, which I will henceforth refer to as separation (*a mensa et thoro*) or divorce (*a vinculo matrimonii*) became the purview of the Court of Divorce and Matrimonial Causes in 1857, at which time the ecclesiastical courts were largely abolished and the divorce jurisdiction of the House of Lords ended.[29]

Eliza's petition for a separation would not have been a surprise to the divorce committee members, because McDougall had already raised it with them, in the closing portion of his speech to the committee. After castigating Robert as a "morose, negligent, and absorbed" husband before the separation in August 1873, McDougall went on to discuss his conduct thereafter. Eliza was still his wife, and nothing had occurred that could justify his removing her from the house. Thus he still had a duty to support her. Yet he had tried to starve her out by telling merchants not to provide her with necessaries. Ultimately he took to the house two constables who had no legal authority to go but had been either hired or bribed by him. Eliza was dragged out against her will and against her doctor's advice. Robert's conduct "was not only cruel but entirely unwarranted in law"; it was, "in the opinion of the whole countryside, brutal." It showed that he was "a husband who had not performed and was by nature incapable of performing, those duties which he undertook … when he vowed to love, cherish, and protect his wife as long as they both should live." Given this, and given that McDougall had demolished Robert's case for a divorce, what next, he asked the committee members, "[w]hat protection does the law extend to this discarded wife?"[30]

The answer to this question required McDougall to go outside the committee's jurisdiction, to that of Parliament. He did so because, he said, Ontario law could not do anything for Eliza. It provided "no door of redress … to that unhappy woman" except the common law that gave her the right to take her husband to court in an action for necessities. That might get her "a modicum of support," but the action might fail because a court would have to deal with the argument that that the issue was *res judicata* because of Blake's judgment in the alimony case. The better remedy lay in Parliament, "the highest [court] in the land." Senators "make the law as well as administer it in divorce cases," and in the Senate Blake's judgment "will go for what it is worth, and no more." Robert had asked for a divorce and been, McDougall hoped and anticipated, rightly refused. Eliza now asked for a separation, "to be made free and independent of her husband, so that he cannot molest her, and that she may not be left without support." How much support was a matter for the Senate. But a useful example could be found in *Dundas v. Dundas*, a House of Lords divorce case where the divorce Act included a provision for an annuity for life for the wife.

McDougall proposed a separation on the grounds of desertion and cruelty. The latter was the way Robert had treated Eliza "from the beginning to the end of this conspiracy." There followed a long list of examples, including the way in which she had been ejected from the house – "an act ... unprecedented in the annals of divorce courts" – and the "attempt at starvation." They all "establish the legal offence of cruelty." If Eliza was successful in showing desertion and cruelty, she should be awarded one-third of Robert's income plus support for whatever children she was awarded custody of. It was usual in such cases, where the mother had been chaste, to award her the younger children, and he suggested she have custody of three-year-old Francis and of Edith, now nine. "Let the husband keep the boys" he said rather dismissively, suggesting that he knew, presumably from Eliza, that the older boys had sided with their father since 1873. It was not remarkable that McDougall suggested dividing custody and not awarding it to Eliza for all four children. The common law had always had a strong presumption in favour of the rights of the father to custody, a presumption that was only just beginning to be undermined and only by a minority of Canadian judges.[31]

Did Parliament have the power to pass a separation Act? McDougall had a ready answer to that question. If the Ontario courts had jurisdiction to grant a decree for separation that was the way to go. But they had no power to do so. Thus the well-known adage "no wrong without a remedy" applied, and if Parliament did not act in this case no other tribunal could do so. Section 91 (26) of the *BNA Act* gave the federal government exclusive jurisdiction over marriage and divorce. "Divorce" meant not only divorce *a vinculo matrimonii*; it also meant divorce *a mensa et thoro*, (separation) because "the greater includes the less." For Parliament – he called it "this Court" – not to pass a separation Act would be "a great wrong, a great failure of justice, a great scandal upon our laws and institutions."[32]

We can now return to Eliza's petition, which stated that Robert had "treacherously deserted" her on 25 August 1873, "without any sufficient cause, justification or provocation," taken away the children, and ejected Eliza from the marital home "with force." He had also refused to provide support for his wife and children, and repeatedly accused Eliza of adultery and tried to prove her guilty. But she was not guilty; thus, he had "outraged, ill-used and insulted her." There was no prospect of reconciliation. The petition included an extract from Eliza's evidence given to the divorce committee describing her ejection from the house on 24 September 1873, and requested "amendments" to Robert's draft bill, including that Robert should be ordered "to make adequate provision for her and the children."[33]

The Senate agreed to the proposal to refer Eliza's petition to the divorce committee, which then heard from further witnesses on each side and the respective counsel. By the narrow margin of 5–4 it decided that it could not deal with Eliza's petition without instructions from the full House as to how to handle it. The four dissenting senators did not want Eliza's petition to be considered at all and thus did not want to ask the House for guidance. The five senators also recommended that if the Senate was unable to agree on what to do in what was left of the session, scheduled to end of 12 April, proceedings should be suspended until the House met again in 1877.[34]

The Senate discussed the divorce committee's report on 5 April.[35] The debate was the first indication of what a contentious matter Eliza's petition for a separation was, raising profound legal and constitutional questions that were debated again, in the Senate and in the Commons, in 1877 and 1879. To avoid repetition I will not discuss them here, except to say that in the two weeks that remained in the session Reesor emerged as Eliza's principal advocate in the Senate, "a careful guardian of Mrs. Campbell's interests."[36] Although he had been greeted by cat calls when he started, by the end "he had aroused the sympathies of a large majority of the senators," in his story of a woman "virtually on the street" with her child, "no home, ... no income, no alimony, no credit."[37] In those same two weeks the Senate referred the petition back to the committee on 5 April by a vote of 30–16. The divorce committee met for a further two days on 7 and 8 April and produced another report on the latter day, and the full Senate discussed that report briefly on 10 April, before deciding to hold off further consideration until the 1877 session.[38] Postponement to another session was very unusual. Bills that were introduced in one session but failed to pass all three readings in both houses during that session were normally lost and had to be reintroduced the next session. Dickey was able to cite precedents of it having been done for private bills,[39] and he also made the practical argument that carrying consideration of the committee report into the 1877 session would preserve the evidence in the event of either Robert making a further application or of Eliza pressing her request for an "amended" bill.

After their deliberations on 7 and 8 April and their report on 8 April,[40] the divorce committee found Eliza's allegations in her petition to be true, and presented what they termed an "amended bill," but it was in fact an entirely different one.[41] What had been "An Act for the Relief of Robert Campbell" had become "An Act for the Relief of Eliza Marie Campbell." What had been a bill granting Robert a divorce *a vinculo matrimonii* became a bill granting Eliza a separation. What had been a preamble asserting that Eliza had committed adultery with Gordon and stating that Robert had won the crim. con. action became a preamble asserting that Robert had "treacherously deserted" Eliza, took from her the three children, violently removed her from his house, and repeatedly accused her of adultery. The operative provisions of the bill were not the usual few lines declaring the parties divorced and free to re-marry, but 10 clauses granting her a separation, which had the same "force and consequence" as one granted by the English court, giving her custody of her children Edith Holmes and Francis William Campbell, and requiring Robert to pay for the support and maintenance of Eliza and the two children, with failure to pay being a contempt of court. The amounts were left blank, to be filled in at a later stage in the parliamentary process.[42]

The committee acknowledged that it was proposing "a new precedent in legislation," and they recommended that discussion of the bill be postponed to the following session and that the evidence should be published. As we have seen, the Senate accepted the recommendation for postponement. We therefore now turn to the next Senate session, in 1877. Robert and Eliza had to wait another year, and there were clear signs that the failure to get a divorce and the turn events had taken were weighing on the former. For a week or more he had "haunted the galleries of the Senate, awaiting with feverish anxiety" to see what was decided. He looked paler and thinner than he had when the Senate started hearing his case, so much so that "[t]o those who have seen him day after day leaning over the railings of the gallery, and straining to hear ... he has become almost a spectre." He had "an almost unearthly look, as he sits hour after hour, scarcely moving a muscle, and gazing intently at those below him."[43]

12
Eliza Campbell's Separation Bill in Parliament, 1877

Introduction

The Eliza Campbell separation bill took up a good deal of the Senate's time in 1877. It was debated on six days, with the reports of the discussions totalling some 26 pages in the published debates. The session began on 8 February, but the divorce committee's reports were not discussed until 20 March, and then inconclusively. The reports were debated again on 9 April, and three days later, on the 12th, there was another long debate that ended in two tied votes, 31–31. One vote was on a motion by Alexander Campbell, the opposition Conservatives leader in the Senate and one of the upper house's leading lawyers, for the "six months" hoist.*[1] The other was on a motion by Reesor that the bill be referred to committee of the whole.[2] Campbell's motion would have killed the bill, Reesor's would have advanced it. Both lost, because a tied vote was a defeat, and thus there was a stalemate. The matter stood over for six days, and there was another long debate on 18 April, after which the same number of senators voted twice again. This time there was a slightly different group of senators present, and the same two motions were made, but Campbell's to give the bill the six-months' hoist was defeated 28–34, while Reesor's to send the bill to committee of the whole, made immediately after Campbell's, prevailed 34–28. The same day, in the evening session, the Senate went into committee of the whole on the bill and passed it, in a somewhat reduced House, 29–19. Also in committee, the draft bill from 1876 was completed by adding the amounts that Robert was to pay, which had been left blank.

* The "six-months'" hoist (sometimes three months) was a motion that a bill "not go into committee now but in six months' time." The session would be long over in six months, thus the bill would be lost.

The bill passed third reading the next day, 19 April, with only 41 senators attending. A motion to refer the bill to the very recently created Supreme Court of Canada was defeated 25–16, and one to pass it on third reading prevailed by the same number. Thus attendance went progressively down, from 62 to 48 then to 41, suggesting that senators on both sides lost interest or decided to absent themselves from a highly contentious issue. As soon as the separation bill passed third reading 19 senators entered a written protest. The bill went to the Commons on 20 April, which refused to deal with the substance before the parliamentary session ended on 28 April. Discussions of the bill nonetheless occupied six pages of *Hansard* before MPs decided that they could not proceed with it because Eliza had not given six months' notice of a divorce petition. As we saw in chapter 8, Robert had given such notice in 1875–76, but Eliza never had.

The first four sections of this chapter analyse the legal and other arguments for and against the bill, partly in chronological order and partly thematically. I first present an overview of the contending positions, and follow that with two sections on, respectively, the debates over the division of powers and over the separation of powers, drawn from the proceedings of 20 March and 9 and 12 April. As noted above, the proceedings on 12 April ended with two tied votes, which are the subject of a separate section. Thereafter I devote a section to the debates of 18 and 19 April, which involved some further discussion of legal questions but which were largely driven by senators' attitudes towards the characters and actions of the Campbells. The penultimate section of this chapter examines the changes made to the bill in committee of the whole, the third reading, and a protest by some of the senators who had voted against the bill. The final section discusses how the House of Commons dealt with the bill. The 1876 debates over the divorce committee's verdict and subsequent steps had widened the interest in the Campbell case, and the 1877 proceedings continued to be followed in the Whitby, Toronto, and Ottawa newspapers,[3] as well as by other Ontario newspapers, and the press in Quebec and Manitoba.[4]

Overview of the Arguments

The principal argument in favour of the bill was that mentioned in the previous chapter – that Eliza was the victim of a cruel injustice, and that as there was no court in Ontario with the jurisdiction to grant her a separation decree, custody of her children, and a support order, Parliament should step in and "fill the gap" in the legal system. It was true that Ontario did not have a court with jurisdiction over separation, as the courts in British Columbia, Nova Scotia, and New Brunswick did because of pre-Confederation colonial legislation and because, for British Columbia, its law was the 1857 United Kingdom Act. But the question was not whether Ontario had a court with this jurisdiction, but whether Parliament should fill the gap and pass a separation Act for an individual Ontarian. This argument necessarily involved two related legal issues. First, did Parliament have the jurisdiction to pass a separation Act given the division of powers between the federal government and the provinces delineated in sections 91 (federal powers) and 92 (provincial powers) of the *BNA Act*? The second issue was whether passing a separation Act would violate the unwritten constitutional principle, now termed the separation of powers between the legislative and the judicial branches of the constitution, although the phrase "separation of powers" was never used. Those who believed that it was constitutionally acceptable to pass a separation Act argued that "divorce" in section 91 (26) included separation; opponents said that it meant only dissolution of the marriage tie and that if Parliament passed a separation Act it would be legislating in an area of provincial jurisdiction, section 92 (13), the property and civil rights power. Second, if Parliament passed an Act giving Eliza support to be paid by Robert it would be acting as a court, making itself part of the judicial branch of the constitution, constituting itself as a court of appeal from Vice-Chancellor Blake, who had refused alimony, alimony and support being the same thing. In addition to these two principal legal arguments senators also debated two other related procedural and policy questions. Could the Senate alter the draft bill presented by Robert in 1876 so as to make it an entirely different one? Also, was it proper to pass a bill that imposed civil liabilities on a single individual?

There was another issue which dominated the debates, often intermingled with legal arguments. If Eliza was "innocent" of adultery she was, therefore, also a greatly wronged woman, the victim first of her husband's desertion and neglect and then of his cruelty. That cruelty included withholding sustenance in the weeks after 26 August 1873, and forcibly removing her from the house in September 1873. It also included a heinous conspiracy by the utterly unscrupulous Campbell brothers to use the courts and Parliament to ruin her reputation and end the marriage. Not only did Eliza merit all the "relief" Parliament could give her, but Robert needed to be held responsible, morally and financially, for a gross abnegation of his manly duty. In the circumstances it was the duty of all decent men in positions of power in Parliament to come to her aid if they could possibly do so. Those who took Robert's side argued to the contrary that Eliza had committed adultery and deserved no favourable treatment from Parliament or any other tribunal. Robert was the injured party, betrayed by his wife, and therefore was absolved from living up to his side of the marital bargain.

Supporters of both parties were also engaging in legal argument, about the common law of marital relations, the law that governed the rights, responsibilities, and duties of husband and wife.

Thirteen men spoke in the Senate debates of 20 March, and 9 and 12 April, only two of whom spoke in favour of the bill and of Eliza, with nine clearly opposed. Two senators spoke equivocally. I have included in the following brief account of the speakers not previously introduced which province each senator was from, whether they were legally trained, what branch of the Christian faith they adhered to,[5] and their party affiliation. All these factors arguably influenced their views on Eliza's separation bill. Only two senators made speeches in favour of the bill's legality: Reesor from Ontario and Dickey from Nova Scotia. The ten senators who were opposed to the bill included six lawyers: Alexander Campbell; Richard Scott from Ottawa, one of the leading anglophone Catholics in Parliament and government leader in the Senate as well as secretary of state in Alexander Mackenzie's administration;[6] François-Xavier Trudel, a Quebec Catholic and a Conservative; Henry Kaulbach; Clement Cornwall; and Nova Scotia Catholic William Miller, a Conservative. The four non-lawyers who were opposed were Amos Edwin Botsford of New Brunswick, a Conservative; Quebec Catholic and Conservative Joseph-Hyacinthe Bellerose; Edward Penny of Quebec, a Liberal and a newspaperman; and Ontario Conservative Alexander Vidal. Bellerose and Penny were legally trained, albeit not practising. Thus the collective profile of the senators who opposed the separation bill was not representative of the Senate as a whole. There were six lawyers, or eight if one counts Bellerose and Penny, four Catholics, and six Protestants, and three senators from Quebec, as opposed to no Quebec senators speaking in favour of the bill. The two senators who spoke equivocally in the debates were James Cox Aikins, a divorce committee member, and Robert Wilmot, a New Brunswick Conservative. Both voted in favour of the separation bill on 12 April.

The senators who supported the bill were joined in their advocacy by McDougall. He could not, of course, speak on the floor of the Senate, but he could try to influence public opinion. He wrote a long account of the history of the case, which was coupled with legal arguments for why the bill should be passed. It was published in late March in the *Whitby Chronicle* and, more importantly given its intended audience, the *Ottawa Citizen*.[7] Most of it comprised reasons why the Senate could and should pass the bill. His starting point was that the divorce committee had found in Eliza's favour on the central issue of adultery. As a result she had "all the privileges and benefits of her marriage contract." The divorce committee's decision had also overruled the judgments of all the Ontario courts, "inferior tribunals" he called them, which had dealt with the Campbell marriage breakdown. Parliament's jurisdiction over divorce was defined by English law, which had always recognized, and still did, a divorce *a mensa et thoro*, which was also a right very similar to separation in the civil law and thus available in Quebec.[8] Eliza could not get the benefit of the "equitable provisions" of either the *Civil Code* or the 1857 English Act because she lived in Ontario. In those circumstances only Parliament could give her relief. She had proved herself "entitled" to the relief that "the law of England and the law of every other Christian country" would provide. Since 1873 she had been living with her mother, a widow in "straitened circumstances," while her wealthy husband lived in her former home, "a comfortable mansion" and kept his relatives in "luxury," while denying to his "lawful and outraged wife" and his youngest child "the price of a loaf of bread." It was a closely and logically argued analysis, if the reader was not a lawyer, and even for lawyers his powerful if overblown rhetoric must have impressed.

The Division of Powers in the *BNA Act*

Modern constitutional scholars and practitioners and all law students are familiar with debates over the meaning of the provisions in sections 91 and 92 of the *BNA Act*. Since the 1880s the SCC and the Judicial Committee of the Privy Council (JCPC) (before 1949 when the appeal to the Privy Council was abolished) have decided myriad cases on the division of powers. Debates over sections 91 and 92 also occurred in the first decade or so after Confederation, but for the most part they did not take place in the courts, and when they did so they occurred in provincial courts of appeal, not in the SCC or the JCPC. The SCC was founded in 1875 and did not hear any cases until the following year, less than a year before the debates over the Campbell separation bill. It gave only three judgments in division of powers cases before 1880, all of them in 1879, and no judgments were given by the JCPC before 1882.[9] Thus when Canadian lawyers and politicians argued over the division of powers in the 1870s, they did so in fora other than the courts. They did so whenever the federal government considered exercising its power of disallowance of provincial legislation under sections 56 and 90 of the *BNA Act*. They did so when, in the 1870s, most provinces published statutory consolidations and revisions, an exercise that required deciding which colonial era statutes were still good law and which were not because they dealt with subjects coming under section 91, the federal powers. And they did so in the federal Parliament and provincial legislatures when somebody argued that legislation proposed was *ultra vires* as falling within the other level of government's jurisdiction.[10] The meaning of "divorce" in section 91 (26) was but one example of these parliamentary debates over the division of powers.

Dickey and Reesor were the principal speakers in favour of the bill as constitutional under section 91 (26), not a matter of property and civil rights under section 92 (13).[11] Dickey based his argument in part on the notion that the Senate was the Canadian equivalent of the House of Lords, which before 1857 could legislate the divorce or separation of individuals. Both he and Reesor made a slightly different argument to the same effect, based on the *BNA Act*. Parliament had exclusive jurisdiction over divorce, which meant both divorce and separation. Some matters of civil rights were specifically excepted from section 92 (13), including a "divorce from bed and board."[12] Moreover, if a subject was listed as a section 91 power, it necessarily meant that it had on occasion to encompass some matters that would normally be in section 92. Section 91 gave the Dominion exclusive jurisdiction in many areas, including trade and commerce, interest, the postal service, navigation, copyright, and marriage and divorce. "Every one of these subjects in some manner, directly or indirectly, affected the civil rights of the people," although they were clearly in section 91.

This argument would not be made today in such an expansive way. The SCC and the JCPC long ago scotched the claim that section 91 powers could oust provincial jurisdiction over property and civil rights in such a broad fashion, because to do so would eviscerate section 92 powers. This curtailing of federal power began very shortly after our period in *Citizens' Insurance Co. v. Parsons*,[13] a case that limited the federal trade and commerce power, and Télesphore Fournier of the SCC used s. 91 (26) as an analogy to explain why the scope of the trade and commerce power had to be limited to preserve the provincial property and civil rights power:

> The Federal Government has jurisdiction over marriage and divorce; the jurisdiction of the provinces is limited to the solemnization of marriage, which means the formalities required previous to marriage. Now the general expression, "marriage and divorce," literally interpreted, is susceptible of a very extensive meaning. Could the Federal Parliament, in such a case, on the ground that the legislation over marriage is assigned to it, extend its jurisdiction so as to regulate the civil conditions of the contract, such as dower, community of goods, and thus exclude the jurisdiction of the provinces over that portion of the civil law? On the contrary, is it not evident that the Federal Parliament should confine its legislation strictly to the conditions which have reference to the capacity or incapacity of

contracting marriage, and to reasons for prohibition, and to other conditions relating to the character of that contract, without interfering with the civil rights appertaining thereto.

Beginning with *Parsons* section 92 (13) became one of the key residual powers in the *BNA Act*.[14] But the issue was far from settled in the 1870s. A majority of the judges who ruled on the overlap between section 91 powers and the property and civil rights power in the first decade after Confederation tended to give much more leeway to the federal Parliament than the courts, especially the JCPC, did later. In *R. v. Justices of the Peace for King's County*,[15] for example, Justice William Johnstone Ritchie, then chief justice of New Brunswick and a little later one of the original six justices of the SCC, gave an extremely broad definition of the trade and commerce power in section 91 (2), saying that it included "full power over the matter to be regulated, and must necessarily exclude that interference of all other bodies that would attempt to intermeddle with the same thing." Ritchie was, like many superior court judges of the 1870s, a believer that the *BNA Act* was intended to create a constitution with a powerful central government. The point here is not whether Reesor and Dickey were right or wrong by today's doctrines; it is merely that their argument was a viable and legitimate one in 1877, even if it became much less so later.[16] Ironically, on the particular issues at stake, custody and child and spousal support, it has been accepted since the passage of the 1968 *Divorce Act* that they are included in the word "divorce" in section 91(26), although, the Campbell separation Act aside, they were never considered to be so in parliamentary divorces.[17]

Having said that, the claim that section 91(26) conferred broad powers on Parliament was very strongly resisted in 1877 because it involved the property and civil powers of one province in particular, Quebec. Quebec's laws on marital relations were an integral part of its unique private law, contained in the Civil Code. Thus when the bill first came up for debate on 20 March, Alexander Campbell, a staunch opponent, adverted to the standard explanation of why divorce was put in section 91 (26) as his reason for it not including separation. Divorce was in section 91 as a matter of "usage," out of "sheer necessity," because Ontario and Quebec did not have divorce courts in the colonial period, as Nova Scotia and New Brunswick did. If divorce had been put in section 92, a divorce court for Ontario could be created at any time, if the Protestant majority wanted it. But Catholic Quebec would never legislate judicial divorce, and thus the Protestant minority in Quebec would never have access to divorce. The only way to provide that access was for jurisdiction over divorce to be given to the federal Parliament, which could then pass individual divorce acts. But divorce meant only dissolution of the marriage. Quebec residents, Catholic and Protestant, could obtain a separation from the Quebec Superior court. Separation thus did not need to be, and was not, part of "divorce" in section 91 (26).[18]

A similar argument was made in a debate on 12 April by the ultramontane Catholic senator, lawyer and journalist François Xavier Trudel, who saw the Senate as a bulwark against liberalism. He and all other Catholic senators usually refrained from participating in debates over divorce bills, and he professed to have sympathy for Eliza, who had been found to be "innocent" of any "crime." But the Senate could not help her. Canada had two legal systems, and in neither Roman nor French law did the word "divorce" mean anything other than a dissolution of the marriage tie.[19] Trudel and another Quebec Catholic senator, Joseph-Hyacinthe Bellerose, a close friend of Trudel who had studied law but did not practise, made a similar but subtly different argument about the content of section 91 (26), one that responded to Reesor's claim that section 91 powers included all things that were incidental to them, even matters otherwise part of property and civil rights. Separation was in the Civil Code and was "an ordinary action for civil redress to enable the wife to live in a separate domicile, to put her out of the marital power," and to give her money for maintenance for herself and the children. Trudel "defied anyone to find an eminent lawyer in Quebec" who would say that this bill was within Parliament's jurisdiction.[20]

The Catholic Quebec senators were joined on this issue by Edward Goff Penny, a Quebec Protestant. A journalist and businessman who was a part owner of the *Montreal Herald* as well as its political correspondent and editor-in-chief, he had been called to the bar of Lower Canada but never practised as a lawyer. A supporter of the Lower Canadian *rouge* party and an opponent of Confederation, he had been appointed to the Senate in 1874 by Mackenzie. He was a Liberal Protestant anglophone who nonetheless recognized and supported the distinctiveness of Quebec, and argued that s. 91 (26) only gave Parliament the power to grant divorces *a vinculo,* not separations. Separation was a common action taken in the Quebec courts, whose jurisdiction would be usurped by Parliament if the bill's supporters were right. As a practical matter, moreover, if Parliament passed Eliza's separation Act it could not refuse pro forma to do so in another case, and "the whole time of the House would be occupied in the settlement of such matters." [21]

Penny was not the only Protestant to defend Catholic Quebec's jurisdiction over separation. Alexander Vidal, a banker, a Conservative from Sarnia and a former elected member of the Province of Canada legislative council, deeply sympathized with Eliza and agreed with the divorce committee's decision not to grant Robert a divorce. But he thought the division of powers argument made by Trudel and others "unanswerable." Parliament had no jurisdiction over civil rights, with the exception of marriage and divorce *a vinculo*. Alexander Campbell agreed, stating that separation "was not a divorce in the sense in which that word was ordinarily used" because the parties might come together again. The proposed bill was "distinctly an interference with civil rights and property." It interfered with property because it compelled a man to pay money to his wife on pain of contempt of court, and it interfered with civil rights because it took custody from a father and gave it to his wife.[22]

Overall, and despite what has been said above about views of the division of powers in the 1870s and about the modern post-1968 approach to the meaning of 'divorce' in section 91 (26), those opposing the separation bill on the ground that separation was a matter falling under property and civil rights had the better constitutional argument. They were right about why divorce was put into section 91 in 1867 and, whatever the merits of the analogy with section 91 powers over trade and commerce, the argument for the primacy of property and civil rights had added bite when the part of section 92 (13) at issue was the Civil Code of Lower Canada.

The Separation of Powers

To some extent the debate over the separation of powers between the judicial and other branches of government, an unwritten principle of the constitution, overlapped with that over the division of powers. If marital separation, with its incidents of alimony and custody, fell under section 92 (13) it was a matter for the courts to adjudicate, not the legislature. Eliza's supporters saw the issue as being a simple one. She had been vindicated by the divorce committee, and the same committee had recommended that Robert should "be compelled to support his wife, having found her allegations ... to be true." The question now before the Senate was whether it was Robert's duty to support his wife "or whether she should be left upon the world to sustain herself as best she could." There was no court in Ontario that could order a judicial separation, yet a guiding principle in the common law tradition was "no wrong without a remedy." Parliament was the only body that could provide justice. It had the power to redress grievances, and this was a case for doing so. The fact that in doing so Parliament would be over-ruling Vice-Chancellor Blake's judgment in the alimony case was beside the point.[23]

a027072

Figure 12.1. Senator Alexander Campbell

Source: LAC

On 12 April, in a debate on a motion to send the bill to committee of the whole, Dickey and Campbell took centre stage, both making long speeches. Campbell spoke first, insisting that it "inexpedient" to proceed further with a bill that seemed to him "so objectionable, and so fraught with what was embarrassing to the jurisdiction and future action of the House."[24] It was true that there was no action for separation available in the Ontario courts, but those courts did deal with alimony and custody, and thus those subjects were the purview of the judiciary. Parliament was not a court of appeal. The alimony question had been adjudicated, adversely to Eliza, by "one of the most eminent judges in the country." Yet the separation Act overturned a court's decision by a special Act of Parliament, something that had not happened in the United Kingdom Parliament for centuries, since the reign of Henry VIII. Equally astonishing, "strange and novel and wholly unprecedented," was that civil liability was being imposed on one man, Robert Campbell, by an Act of Parliament, which legislated that Robert owed a debt to Eliza. This was "the imposition of a parliamentary liability in an extraordinary and unjust way, distinguishing this man from his fellow subjects and placing upon him a liability which the ordinary laws of this country had not yet imposed upon him." Campbell's complaint about Acts targeting individuals was a reference to the by then anachronistic practice of passing bills imposing criminal or civil liability against named individuals. Lawyers in England would "look with wonder" at this, and like him would be "astonished."[25]

Campbell also refuted the argument that Eliza had no remedy other than Parliament. She could go back to Chancery with better evidence, evidence that included the verdict of the Senate divorce committee. This was a weak argument because the verdict of the divorce committee was not evidence, and as Dickey pointed out later any application by Eliza would be met by a claim of *res judicata*. Indeed Campbell undermined his own argument by saying that Blake was a better judge of the evidence than the senators on the committee. Campbell also stated that Eliza could support herself by running up accounts with tradesmen against her husband and every time she was sued she could go to court to make Robert pay. This argument, though legally correct, presupposed that tradesmen would give her credit and that if they did so a common law court would not accept Robert's defence that he had no duty to support an adulterous wife.

Campbell also criticized the bill as incompatible with parliamentary procedure. When Robert's preamble was not proven that should have been the end of the matter. Instead the divorce committee had proposed a different bill: "To take another step with it they must reverse each enacting clause of the original bill; they must reverse the preamble, they must reverse the title, and how it could possibly be considered that such a course of action could, by any sort of logic, be held to be an amendment of the original bill he was unable to see." This was all "perverted ingenuity," and any lawyer would find it so. If Eliza wanted a separation bill she needed to start her own parliamentary process – give notice and send in a petition.

Dickey responded to Campbell's speech, disagreeing with his fellow lawyer whose legal opinions he "greatly respected."[26] The committee had found Eliza "innocent," and she had then petitioned for relief. In the circumstances the House should provide relief if it "legally" could and relief was indeed possible. Campbell had said she could go back to court, but that was not possible because she would be told that Blake had ruled against her and that was the end of the matter. Campbell had also said that Parliament could not deal with custody or alimony as that would be usurping the courts' jurisdiction, but Dickey cited cases from the leading English text on divorce before 1857 to show that the House of Lords had ruled on both custody and alimony in the context of particular divorce *a vinculo* petitions. Indeed in some cases they had awarded alimony to a wife who had been divorced because of her own adultery. If that was the case, then "surely where the wife has been declared innocent it required no great ingenuity or argument" to insist that she could be given alimony.[27]

In response to the claim that Parliament was acting as a court of appeal, Dickey, who had called the Senate "the highest court in the land" in a debate on 9 April,[28] agreed, but said there was nothing wrong with that. The Senate was not bound by decisions of lower courts, any more than the House of Lords was. And the divorce committee had heard different evidence than that which had been presented to Chancery. Given that the powers of the English and Canadian Parliaments were coterminous, the Senate could determine whether a woman "turned out of doors and deserted" should be "entitled to relief." It could give relief to individuals, including alimony or "such other relief as their wisdom might deem meet." Here Dickey was referring to the fact that acts to benefit individuals were occasionally passed in the federal Parliament, albeit mostly in areas of section 91 jurisdiction.[29]

Other lawyer senators spoke against the bill on the issue of the separation of powers. William Miller, a Catholic from Cape Breton Island appointed to the Senate in 1867 at the age of 32, argued that the Ontario courts had dealt with the alimony question, and to overrule Blake would be a "dangerous precedent."[30] Trudel and others said that if Ontario did not have a court with a separation jurisdiction it could simply create one. Miller and other senators argued that courts were much better at finding facts than the divorce committee, which brought a rejoinder from Aikins.[31] The lawyers were joined in opposition by the legally trained Penny, who in arguing that Parliament should not be a court of appeal said the Senate was only a "quasi-judicial" body and only in divorce cases, when it acted "legislatively though on judicial grounds. Just as no court could interfere with Parliament's jurisdiction over divorces *a vinculo*, Parliament could not usurp the court's" jurisdiction over alimony. The two bodies might be said to have concurrent jurisdiction over alimony if that issue came up in a divorce *a vinculo* proceeding, but not if it arose independently. Would Parliament accede to a request by a husband to take away alimony from a wife who had been granted it by a court? Of course not, and if the Senate could not do that it could not do the opposite. Penny also pointed out, in response to the assertion that the problem was that Ontario did not have a court that could order separation, that the *BNA Act* did not give Parliament the right to interfere in some provinces but not others. If it could legislate a separation for an Ontario resident it could do so for one from Quebec, either nullifying that province's jurisdiction in the area or making itself a court of appeal for numerous cases from Quebec.[32]

At the end of the long debate, on 12 April the two tied votes mentioned in the introduction were taken.[33] The Senate was in a complete stalemate. The impasse was broken six days later after another long debate that featured the same arguments but also different ones about matrimonial powers and duties and the personalities and actions of the Campbells.

Eliza Campbell: Victim of Unjust Treatment by a Cruel Husband or a Shameless Harlot?

The legal arguments dominated the first three days of debate in the Senate, the proceedings marked by decorum with disagreements expressed respectfully and without personal invective directed against other senators or either of the Campbells. The same was not true of the next debate, on 18 April, precipitated by a motion by Reesor that the divorce committee report be referred to a committee of the whole "presently." The same numbers of senators were present, 62, albeit a slightly different 62 than had been present a week before. As he had done the week before, Campbell immediately moved an amendment to Reesor's motion, this time for a three-months' hoist.[34] Fifteen senators spoke in the debate of 18 April. Eight of them had spoken previously.[35] The seven new men included five who spoke in favour of the bill: Robert Carrall, one of the three BC senators appointed in 1871; James Dever, of New Brunswick; Billa Flint and Robert Read of Ontario; and Thomas Heath Haviland of Prince Edward Island. Of these five only Haviland was a lawyer. Two of the first-time speakers opposed the bill, and they were both lawyers: Clement Cornwall, who had been on the divorce committee, and Lawrence Power, a Liberal and the scion of one of the most powerful Nova Scotia Catholic families.[36] In the week between the tied vote and resumption of the debate there was a substantial amount of lobbying and button-holing in the corridors of the House by senators on both sides. Robert Campbell had printed and distributed a circular putting forth his views and even visited senators in their residences to press his case.[37] In the end the bill, "contested ... inch by inch," was passed, with what one newspaper called "the greatest difficulty."[38]

The same legal arguments about the division of powers and the separation between courts and legislatures were presented by the same people – Reesor and Dickey for the bill, Trudel, Vidal and Penny against it.[39] Thomas Heath Haviland Junior, a lawyer and a Conservative from Prince Edward Island and the son of his namesake who had been one of the most powerful politicians in the pre-Confederation era and who was himself sufficiently prominent to be chosen one of the first four senators from the island, also argued in favour of the bill. He cited Bouvier's law dictionary to the effect that divorce in English law included divorce *a mensa et thoro*, and the *BNA Act* was based on English law and thus gave Parliament the power to enact either kind of "divorce."[40]

The debate changed radically in tone and substance when Robert Carrall of British Columbia spoke for the first time, having not been present on the previous days when the Act was discussed. An unmarried physician who was fond of saying that that he would never marry, he did not address any of the legal questions. But he made his views abundantly clear, views based on hearing about the case from other members:[41]

> [A]lthough he had not heard or read the evidence, nor did he know the parties, yet he had heard sufficient to know the circumstances of the case, and his sympathies were with the lady, and he would vote for her in the face and teeth of the lawyers who had shut the courts in her face, the door of which she could not open. She had then come to this Senate – who were looked upon as the fathers of the country – and asked for redress for her little ones and herself. He could not argue with those lawyers, but he knew they could do what was right. After being seven years a senator of the Dominion, there was no vote he would give with more zeal and earnestness, not only in justice to the lady who had been wronged, but against the man who had taken such scandalous means of obtaining evidence to defame the character of an injured lady, and as a rebuke to the courts to which they had taken her.

This was a remarkable speech. Carrall had not read any of the more than 250 pages of evidence, had not been on the committee, and cared

e010938681

Figure 12.2. Senator Robert Carrall
Source: LAC

nothing for the legal arguments. Remarkable though the speech was, it aligned with Carrall's personality and attitudes. Born in Woodstock, Upper Canada, in 1837, he described himself as "a patriotic Canadian, descended from a race of patriotic Canadians – one of the oldest families in Canada." He was educated at Trinity College, Toronto, received his MD from McGill University in 1859, and volunteered to serve in the Union army in 1862 as a surgeon, perhaps an indication of his attachment to the anti-slavery cause. After the American Civil War he moved to British Columbia where he practised medicine, invested in mining companies, and, from 1867, actively supported the colony joining Confederation. He was one of the three British Columbia delegates to travel to Ottawa to negotiate the Terms of Union, and the only one to meet his friend John A. Macdonald, who was too ill to take part in the negotiations. Macdonald appointed him to the Senate in 1871 as one of the first three British Columbia senators, and while he was not especially interested in politics, he very much enjoyed the social scene of the capital. He complained privately that he was "worked to death *socially* – Dinners or Dances every night, and all the next day the anguish of having lost my heart which I invariably do from *one* to *four* times every night, oh! why was I created with such susceptibilities? or why on earth [are] the girls so sweet!" No surprise, perhaps, that he fell for Eliza, albeit his own idealized version of the damsel in distress, even though he had never spoken to her.

Carrall's forceful statement turned the debate over the separation bill into a personal matter as much as a legal one. Trudel and others tried to bring the discussion back to legal issues. Trudel said the validity of the bill could not be decided based on sympathy. If the constitution did not allow it, Eliza could have no redress. The next senator to speak, Henry Kaulbach, a committee member who had voted for Robert's preamble, could not let Carrall's emotional outburst go unanswered. In a previous debate in 1877 he had shown that he thought Eliza unworthy of Parliament's indulgence, and he now thoroughly denounced both her and Carrall.[42] It was "a mockery and a farce" for the separation bill to come before Parliament, the result of "sympathy for this woman" having "taken control and perverted the good judgment" of some. This was clearly aimed at Carrall, whose sympathies were "one-sided." The merits were all on the other side. He had been a member of the divorce committee and heard evidence showing that Eliza was a woman "who had been so totally reckless of the decencies of the married life, and who had asked this House to whitewash her skirts." At that point Kaulbach was interrupted by cries of "Order, Order," and by Walter Dickson, who said that his remarks were "a censure on the committee." If Dickson thought that would keep Kaulbach quiet he was wrong, because Kaulbach turned his fire onto the whole House. His colleagues had adopted the divorce committee report before the evidence had been printed, and thus the vote to adopt had been "blind."

Alexander Campbell also tried to stop him going further by saying that going into the details of the case would be "trespassing on good taste," although Kaulbach could do so if he wished.

Kaulbach was not interested in good taste. He repeated his complaint that the House had voted without having the evidence before them, "evidence that convinced him of her guilt." Robert had not, in his opinion, been treated fairly, and he singled out Reesor, accusing him of packing the committee with senators antagonistic to him and, when Robert asked for changes, something that Kaulbach claimed was usual in other cases, had refused the request.[43] This attack on the committee brought a protest from Aikins, who said that he had no sympathies one way or the other, and that Kaulbach "had no right to make such remarks." Reesor likewise objected, insisting that the committee was "fairly chosen, representing all parts of the Dominion." Kaulbach would not let go of this particular bone. He had been placed on the committee "because it was believed and avowed by ... [Reesor] that he [Kaulbach] was in favour of the woman." He then said that he had indeed initially been favourable to Eliza, and if he could have relied on her evidence he would have done so, but the evidence convinced him she was guilty of adultery. Unfortunately a majority had given her "the benefit of a doubt."

Kaulbach then moved to a combination of the divorce committee's conclusions, his view of Eliza, and the legal issues. The Supreme Court should be asked if the Senate had the right to reverse a court's judgment and had the power to change a bill from one for divorce to one for separation. The committee had done that and set aside a portion of Robert's money for Eliza "without a tittle of evidence on which to base it or to show whether he was worth a million of dollars or five cents." As for cruelty, Eliza had testified that Robert had been kind to her and the children, yet, conversely, one could not read the evidence and not be "disgusted" by her "lewd conduct." These statements about the evidence were partial, and in one case clearly wrong. Eliza had testified to Robert's kindness, but that was about an earlier period in the marriage. The kindness reference did bring a sarcastic rejoinder from James Dever, a New Brunswick businessman and Catholic who had consistently voted against divorce bills in the past.[44] Robert, he said, had been "very kind and considerate when he kicked her out of the house." In response Kaulbach justified Robert's action. Eliza had been found to have committed adultery by two courts, and given that it would have been "inconsistent with the position of a just and honourable man, a husband and father, to live in the same house with a woman ... who he believed to be an adulteress." Of course Eliza had been ejected from the house before any court had heard any of the cases, but Kaulbach was not one to let a detail like that get in his way.

Some senators told Kaulbach to stop, and Carrall proposed an adjournment, but the Speaker ruled the motion out of order when a member was speaking. After order was restored Kaulbach sailed on, intent on making the proceedings what the Toronto *Weekly Mail* called "quite a stormy debate."[45] Interruptions would not deter him, but rather would "incite him to do his duty." His duty was to continue to attack Eliza and the divorce committee:

> Adultery was a crime of which there was seldom direct proof by evidence, and the court and jury generally came to a decision from the circumstances which surrounded it. Vice-Chancellor Blake's sympathies had evidently been in favour of this woman, but even that judge was forced by the irresistible logic of facts to decide that she had been guilty of adultery. He believed there was a strong case in favour of divorce, and such was the opinion of the committee until such time as she came upon the scene, and then there seemed to be some magic about her that prejudiced the minds of honourable gentlemen in her favour. Courts always doubt the uncorroborated evidence of the accused in such cases ... A case had been made out, and ... [senators should have] ... been guided by the wisdom of Solomon, who says, "Such is the way of an adulterous woman. She eateth and wipeth her mouth, and saith, I have done no wickedness." From the evidence it would be seen that this woman was having secret correspondence with a young man in her husband's absence, of a grossly vile and sensual character, from which it could rightly be inferred that she was a fit subject for any seducer.[46]

A number of senators on both sides of the issue tried again to halt Kaulbach, including Jacques-Olivier Bureau of Quebec, a notary and a Liberal known for his efforts to have seigneurial tenure abolished, and who had voted against the separation bill on 12 April. Clement Cornwall, Kaulbach's fellow dissenter on the committee, also objected to his tone and his references to the evidence. Exactly two years later, in another debate on another attempt to pass the separation bill, discussed in chapter 14, he called the debate "a most unpleasant discussion ... on the facts of the case."[47] To Richard Scott Kaulbach's remarks were "not in good taste." Taste, said Kaulbach, had nothing to do with the issue, which was to be decided by "law and justice." He followed this with another attack on Eliza, "a woman of such licentious and depraved habits to admit of no other hypothesis than that of her guilt." These words brought cries of "Shame! Shame!", but Kaulbach stood his ground. He would not be shouted down by "sympathizers" who had not read the evidence, and if senators persisted in their denunciations of him he would go fully into the evidence. If the House was to take on the "functions of a court of law," senators could not do what Carrall had done, and simply accept what Eliza had said and award her alimony. They could not "allow their legislation to be controlled by feelings of sympathy." He "deeply felt" his obligation and his duty to go fully into the evidence, "painful and disagreeable though the character of it was." That evidence ought to lead the "guarded discretion of reasonable and just minds" to the same conclusion he had come to. But it was "useless" to go further into the issue, as some senators would not be shaken from their convictions. Nonetheless, he "trusted honourable gentlemen would hesitate before creating such a precedent as the one intended, and that law and justice, not sympathy would prevail in this matter."

Kaulbach's performance was remarkable, and suggests that there was more going on than simply a disagreement with his divorce committee colleagues about what conclusions should be drawn from the evidence and/or the rights and wrongs of the legal-constitutional arguments. At the time he was going through some professional and personal difficulties, aspects of which suggest he was obsessed with the sexual undertones of a conflict. When Beamish Murdoch, one of Nova Scotia's best-known legal and political thinkers of the nineteenth century, completed his three-volume *History of Nova Scotia* he retired to Lunenberg, the Kaulbach family's hometown, and bought a house from Kaulbach. In 1875 the Kaulbachs' house burned down, and Murdoch insisted that the Kaulbach family, including Kaulbach's wife Eunice and their five children, live with him, which they did. Murdoch died in February 1876, just before the Campbell divorce petition was heard. There followed litigation about Murdoch's will, in which his cousin Charles Beamish, who had been a beneficiary of earlier wills, was cut out in favour of Eunice Kaulbach and the Kaulbach children. Beamish alleged undue influence by Kaulbach, who had drafted the will. He claimed that in his dotage Murdoch had developed an "insane passion" for Eunice Kaulbach. The details of the extensive litigation over the will do not concern us here. What does matter is that it took place in 1875–77, overlapping with the Campbell case, and that Kaulbach's drafting of a will, which favoured his own wife and children, was highly suspicious, given that, as Murdoch's biographer notes, Kaulbach came to have a disproportionate influence over Murdoch in the last months of his life. At the very least, even without delving into the complex psychology of Murdoch's obsession with Kaulbach's wife, Kaulbach was a distracted and likely angry man when he so virulently attacked Eliza Campbell.[48]

That being said, the Campbell case was not the only one in which Kaulbach disagreed strongly and unpleasantly with his divorce committee colleagues. He behaved very similarly some 15 years later in debates over the case of James St George Dillon of Montreal. The divorce committee found that Dillon's wife had committed adultery, and Kaulbach issued a minority report stating that Dillon should not be divorced because, among other reasons, he was a Catholic, and Parliament should not exercise its jurisdiction and allow Catholics to divorce, or at least not pass an Act allowing a Catholic to remarry. Kaulbach's arguments were echoed by some Catholic senators, but in measured tones. Kaulbach made his points forcefully, with great confidence, and peppered them with castigations of those who disagreed with him. He said, for example, that the chair of the divorce committee, Sir James Gowan, "generally talks with the presumption of profound wisdom" so that "whatever he says is deserving of consideration, at least he thinks so."[49]

Kaulbach's inflammatory denunciations of Eliza and some of his colleagues brought to his feet a senator who had not previously spoken – Billa Flint of Ontario. A successful merchant and mill owner from Belleville despite having no formal education after the age of 11, Flint was a passionate Methodist and temperance advocate. He always labelled himself a Liberal, though others thought his political views changeable. Elected to the Canada West assembly and then legislative council, he was described by Mackenzie Bowell as "a man of great energy, and strong feeling, no matter which side he took, whether in politics, social life, or religious questions," and displayed those characteristics now as he took up Eliza's cause. Unlike Eliza's other champion, Carrall, he had read the evidence. As a result of doing so[50]

> he had listened with a great deal of pain to [Kaulbach's] remarks.... It was not the first time he had felt pained to hear the honourable gentleman, sheltered by his position in this House, attack an unfortunate and unprotected woman. When the honourable gentleman first discussed this question, before it went to committee he had used language ... which no gentleman would be guilty of, and twice this session he had done the same thing again. This lady was unprotected; she had been cruelly turned out of doors and deserted by her husband, and had been persecuted up to the present time by the man who sought for a divorce, and had so signally failed. The honourable gentleman had a right to his opinion, but when there were seven out of nine on the committee who had decided that the husband had no right to a bill of divorce, the honourable gentleman should in all fairness have said no more about it.

Flint not only criticized Kaulbach for rearguing the divorce committee's conclusions, he lambasted the Campbell brothers and John Anderson and came to the defence of a damsel in distress:

> It struck him as being very wrong to persecute anyone, but it was inhuman to persecute an unprotected female in the manner in which this lady had been persecuted by her husband. If he could read the evidence aright and analyse it, it seemed to him the husband, brother, and brother-in-law deserved to be prosecuted for a dastardly attempt to ruin the character of a helpless woman. He was so thoroughly satisfied on that point that if he were one of a jury of twelve men before a court, with that evidence before him, he would sit there till he died before he would render a verdict against her. He felt that the honourable gentleman had no right to attack the lady in the manner he had done.

Flint stressed that he did not know Eliza and had never seen her other than when she had been pointed out to him as she walked by to give evidence before the divorce committee. He had never spoken to her and had only spoken to Robert Campbell once "when he had been introduced to him in order to gain his [Flint's] sympathy." He had no opinion of either of them "except ... the opinion which he had formed from the evidence that she stood before the eyes of the world today – with the exception of ... her husband and a few of his friends – an innocent woman." Indeed the best evidence of Eliza's innocence "was the fact that she was considered innocent in the neighbourhood in which she resided, by all who were best acquainted with her." Kaulbach interrupted him at this point to complain that he was making statements about matters not in the evidence. Flint's response was to distinguish between law and what he considered justice:

> [Kaulbach] was a professional man, and he was not, and he felt strongly the attack that had been made on a defenceless woman. Placed as she was without a dollar to defend herself, with a wealthy husband whose unfeeling nature would not allow him to give her as much as would buy a child a dress, it was cruel to refuse her the justice which she asked at their hands. It was only justice she demanded, not sympathy.... [and] this House had the right to grant the redress which she had demanded.

Flint ended by referencing what must have been conversations he had had outside the chamber, noting that some senators had said they had some sympathy for Robert because Eliza's last letter to him had been "cold." "Was that any wonder?" he demanded. They were an ill-assorted pair, and members should consider whether "if they planted a rosebush alongside an iceberg could they expect it to bloom?"[51]

The vote on the amendment to give the bill the three-months' hoist was then taken, and lost 28–34. Reesor's original motion to send the bill to committee of the whole then passed, 34–28, with the voters reversed.[52] Nobody changed their vote from a week before. Rather, six senators who had been present on 12 April were not there to vote on the 18th, five of them members who had voted against the bill.[53] A further six senators were present on the 18th who had not been there on the 12th. Two voted for the six-month hoist and against sending the bill to committee: James Shaw of Ontario and Christian Pozer of Quebec. The other four of the newcomers voted for the bill: Matthew Cochrane of Quebec, Robert Read of Ontario, John Bourinot of Nova Scotia, and Carrall. The collective profile of the senators on each side was more or less the same as before. Carrall was an active participant in the debate, but none of the other newcomers spoke other than Read. He simply stated just before the vote that he had read the evidence and Blake's judgment carefully and concluded that there was a doubt, and he would give Eliza the benefit of it.[54]

Committee of the Whole, Third Reading, and a Protest

After a short recess the Senate moved into committee of the whole.[55] Only 48 of the 62 senators stayed for the post-recess proceedings, but we cannot say who left and who stayed because debates in committee were not reported, and on this occasion the Senate *Journals* did not list the voters in the ensuing division to accept the committee report. Eliza's supporters prevailed in that division, 29–19. In committee the operative clauses of the draft bill were amended. Robert was required to pay Eliza $600 a year in alimony, plus $200 a year for the support of the youngest child, Francis William. Eliza was only given custody of that one child, whereas the draft bill from 1876 included her 10-year-old daughter Edith as well. We do not know why Eliza, presumably, instructed Reesor to make this change. It is reasonable to think, however, that she knew that the older children had all chosen, with various degrees of psychological coercion, to say that they preferred to stay with their father. The other clauses were much the same as before, notably those giving Eliza the right to apply to a judge to vary the alimony payment, discussed in the next paragraph, and making failure by Robert to pay contempt of court.[56]

Opponents of the bill continued to express their disapproval while discussing these terms, objecting to both principle and substance.

Alexander Campbell said the custody clause was an intrusion into property and civil rights. He, Kaulbach, and Power objected to the clause that gave Eliza the right to apply to a judge to vary the sums payable if Robert's income increased; it was a "violation of the Constitution," another reference to property and civil rights or perhaps also to the separation of powers.[57] But the only substantive change effected by the opposition was to the alimony clause. Campbell, Cornwall, and Kaulbach all complained about a lack of evidence about Robert's financial position. Reesor and Dickey supplied some evidence, from what had been said before the divorce committee and from an affidavit by Eliza, but it was inconsistent. In the result $600 was agreed to. The sum was based on Robert being worth $30,000, which would produce $1,800 a year if invested at 6 per cent; it was therefore one-third of his annual income. It was also, as newly appointed Senator Adam Hope of Ontario pointed out, the same as the $50 a month interim alimony Eliza had received. Campbell proposed an amendment to have the bill state that there was insufficient evidence to fill in a precise amount for alimony, but he was defeated 29–19. The opposition's final throw of the dice was a motion by Campbell to refer the bill to the SCC, something permitted by both the Senate rules and the recently passed *Supreme Court Act*, but that was lost "on a division."[58] Campbell did, however, succeed in having the final vote deferred until after the bill had been printed, and the Senate adjourned to the next day.

The printed Campbell relief bill came up for third reading the following evening, 19 April, following afternoon debates on the Pacific railway, the customs, and the *Insolvent Act*, among other things. The proceedings lasted until midnight, with much of the time taken up with a procedural ruling by Speaker Christie and attended by seven fewer senators than the evening before, 41. The absentees were from both sides in roughly equal measure. There were further attempts to derail the bill by raising both procedural and substantive objections. Lawrence Power argued that the bill was not at the third reading stage, it was only at first reading, because it had never been before the House before. The bill introduced in 1876 had been for the relief of Robert Campbell; this one was for "another person altogether." The standard procedure was that at prorogation all bills and motions ceased, and if they were introduced in the ensuing session they had to start again.[59]

Before anybody could respond to this Clement Cornwall, who had previously only spoken briefly in defence of Kaulbach's comments, made a long speech. He disavowed any desire to comment on the substance of the divorce committee's original decision, but he "regretted … extremely" the "unseemly proceedings" of the previous day. If anything showed how unfit the Senate was to adjudicate divorce bills it was the "partial, rancorous, unseemly feelings" on display. It was a very far cry from the House of Lords, where contentious issues were left to those Lords with legal training to deal with in a "calm judicial spirit" and with knowledge of the law. Cornwall then abandoned his own calm judicial spirit to castigate his British Columbia colleague Carrall, although without naming him. He had, "with unblushing effrontery" said that he supported the bill "through sympathy with the woman charged with adultery, although he confessed that he had neither heard nor read the evidence in the case." Another member, again unnamed but obviously Flint, had done the same. Cornwall then backed off personal attacks, as he was "the last member ... anxious to stir up further feeling on the matter." He had been a member of the committee in 1876. All the members had spent many days carefully going over the evidence. He thought the preamble had been proved, and hence that Eliza "had proved herself unworthy to come to this House for the relief which she sought." Ironically given his initial comments, Cornwall then praised Kaulbach for the "earnest, lucid and eloquent speech" he had made, and insisted that justice had not been done to Robert Campbell.

Not surprisingly Cornwall's remarks brought Carrall to his feet. It was true, he said, that he had not read the evidence, "but he had obtained information on the subject from those who had heard both sides, and he considered his knowledge as full, accurate and extensive as that of any member of the committee." He was therefore able to cast his vote intelligently, "based upon knowledge co-extensive" with that heard by the committee. Reesor soon moved the third reading, and Trudel and Miller made last-ditch attempts to block the bill. Trudel moved an amendment that, as the "very essence" of the bill had been changed, it should not be read a third time. Robert Wilmot of New Brunswick said this was tantamount to a censure of the speaker, and Christie ruled it out of order. Miller made another attempt to have the bill referred to the SCC, which was defeated 25–16. The motion that the bill pass third reading then succeeded "on a division."[60]

Once the bill had passed third reading, 19 senators, 12 of them from Quebec, entered a written "dissentient," or protest. It gave seven reasons for objecting to the bill, all of which had been raised in the debates and some of which were repetitive of each other. It stated variously that section 91 (26) did not include separation, that alimony and custody were matters of exclusive provincial jurisdiction, and that in Eliza's case alimony had already been dealt with by the Court of Chancery. Three of the reasons dealt with alleged flaws in parliamentary procedure.[61] The protest convinced the *Globe* that a majority of senators had let "sympathy with the unfortunate lady" cloud their judgment. A court was the best place for her to seek justice.[62] Not surprisingly the *Whitby Chronicle* disagreed. The Senate had "done justice to Mrs. Campbell," and "removed from an unfortunate and deeply injured woman the last taint of suspicion of her chastity." Higgins singled out Flint's speech for special praise, which was marked by "sentiments credible alike to his head and heart."[63]

The House of Commons

The bill was received by the Commons on 20 April, and on a motion by Thomas Henry Gibbs, Oshawa's leading businessman and the Conservative MP for South Ontario, the riding that included Whitby, was read for the first time the same day, under the title an "Act for the Relief of Robert Campbell and Eliza Maria Campbell."[64] Gibbs proved to be the MP most in favour of the separation bill, which can likely be attributed to opinion in his hometown of Oshawa and nearby Whitby. Nothing else in his career as a very successful businessman and banker suggests that he had any interest in social causes. Indeed, quite the opposite. He was known as a harsh employer and renowned for the corrupt practices that got him elected as an MP. He served briefly in Macdonald's cabinet in 1873 but lost his post, and his seat, in 1874. He was re-elected to the Commons in a by-election in 1876 but lost his seat in the general election of 1878. In 1880 Macdonald rewarded him with a Senate seat.[65]

Following first reading the separation bill was referred, like all private bills, to the Select Standing Committee on Standing Orders, chaired by Joseph Rymal, the Liberal MP for Wentworth South.[66] McDougall lobbied MPs aggressively in support of the bill, but to no avail.[67] The committee rejected it for lack of sufficient notice. Nonetheless the next day Gibbs moved that it be placed on the orders of the day for second reading. He referred to the bill as "An Act for the Relief of Robert Campbell," and admitted that the name change was to counter the Select Committee's argument about notice. No notice had been given for an "Act for the Relief of Robert Campbell and Eliza Maria Campbell," the bill passed by the Senate, but in the 1876 session petitions giving notice of an "Act for the Relief of Robert Campbell" had been presented to both houses of Parliament which had both found the notice adequate.[68] It is likely that McDougall was the strategist. Two years later, in recounting the history of the bill in the House of Commons – by then he was an MP – he criticized the Commons' action in 1877. The Senate had postponed the bill from 1876 to 1877, which it had the power to do, and the Commons ought to have taken notice of that "as a matter of comity."[69] But less interested observers were more sanguine. "The fact is," said a commentary printed by the *Ingersoll Chronicle* and probably other newspapers, the bill was "entirely different" than Robert's original. That did not stop Eliza and McDougall from being "excessively annoyed." Robert, conversely, was "delighted beyond measure and takes no pains to conceal it."[70]

Moving that a bill rejected by the committee receive second reading was, as James Young, the Conservative MP for Waterloo South, put it, "extraordinary." Gibbs argued that the circumstances were just that, that there had been a "great injustice … done," and that if the bill was placed on the order paper the Commons could discuss the constitutional issues. His arguments held little water. Four MPs made brief speeches to the effect that the 1876 petition and bill had been for a divorce, and the bill sent up from the Senate was for a separation; thus they were two different bills, which required separate notice. Of these men only Joseph-Éduoard Cauchon, the MP for Quebec Centre, and Rymal, also alluded to the underlying substantive problem, that Parliament did not have jurisdiction. Cauchon said it was a bill that was "purely one of civil rights," and Rymal said that "[b]y some mysterious means" McDougall had "secured the passage through the Senate of a bill for alimony."[71] Rymal also read the Senate protest, and argued that if, as some members thought, a "gross injustice" had been done to "a suffering woman," Eliza's remedy was to go to court and, if that failed, to submit her own petition and bill.

Gibbs's motion did have some support, from David Blain, Liberal MP for York West, and Hector Cameron, a Toronto lawyer. Blain argued that the purpose of the notice requirement was that parties who might oppose proposed legislation would have the opportunity of appearing before the House to protect their rights. In this case that reason did not apply. Robert Campbell had been before the Senate the whole time proceedings had been going on. The Commons should accept Gibbs's motion and consider the merits. Cameron, who had seconded Gibbs's motion, argued that the substantive issue was one "of great importance" that had been "fought out with great bitterness" in the Senate and should not be dismissed on a technicality but dealt with on the merits. The discussion ended when Speaker Timothy Anglin ruled that the matter should be postponed so that he could consult parliamentary law on the subject, and Gibbs consented to that.

When the bill came up again after two days, a short debate ensued, mostly concerned with procedural questions, but everybody knew the issue was whether the Commons should be debating a separation bill. The essence of the debate was captured by Luther Holton, Liberal MP for Châteauguay who was an anglophone Quebecker devoted to protecting Quebec's distinctive law and culture. He argued that at stake was a "very important constitutional question," which MPs should not discuss so late in the session. Gibbs's motion was defeated on a division, and two days later, on 28 April, the session ended.[72] The Campbell marital breakdown had now occupied Parliament for two consecutive sessions, with no resolution. The *Whitby Chronicle* reported the news with considerable regret. While the Senate had done the right thing, in the Commons "justice has ... been balked." Gibbs had done his best to "right the lady's wrongs" in a "manly" way but had been "met by a quibble," behind which MPs and even Prime Minister Mackenzie, who had spoken against bringing the bill forward, had "shelter[ed]' ... in opposing a measure of justice which the merits of the case so urgently demanded."[73]

13
An Interlude, 1878

Introduction

Having been rebuffed by the House of Commons in 1877, Eliza tried but failed to get her separation bill through Parliament in 1878. She had not provided the required notice. This chapter deals briefly with the 1878 Senate proceedings, and then at more length with two court cases that were related, but peripheral to the Campbell matrimonial breakdown. First, in 1877, having failed to get his divorce, Robert was able to persuade one unknown member of the Ontario assembly to slip a provision amending the provincial *Dower Act* into an omnibus bill, a provision that made it possible for him to apply to court to cancel Eliza's dower interest in his land without her consent. Robert failed in this underhanded attempt to deny Eliza something that would have provided her some support in her old age if Robert had predeceased her. His attempt nonetheless testifies to his deep-rooted animosity towards her. Second, 1877 and 1878 witnessed litigation between McDougall and Robert over the legal fees that the Senate divorce committee had ordered Robert to pay for Eliza's defence in 1876. Just one aspect of the enduring battle between the Campbells, it also merits attention because it resulted in a revolutionary judgment in one area of lawyers' ethics.

During the period covered by this chapter, Eliza and Robert continued to live in Whitby, and Robert paid her nothing and also said that she should give up custody of Francis. Eliza must have found it even harder to make ends meet, because her brother James, who as we have seen was a strong emotional and financial support, died in August 1877 from a stomach ailment, a "very worthy citizen" who was "well respected by all who knew him."[1] Either because of a loss of financial support with James's death, or because she wanted the distraction as well as some money, in May 1878 she advertised her services as a music instructor. She wanted only a limited number of pupils and would give the lessons at her mother's house on Dunlop Street.[2]

McDougall remained Eliza's lawyer throughout 1878 and continued to serve as a legislator, albeit switching from provincial to federal politics. He had been a member of the Province of Canada assembly from 1859 to 1867 and won the seat of Lanark North as a Conservative in the first post-Confederation federal election, held in August-September 1867. He lost that seat in the 1872 election running as a Conservative but was elected to the Ontario legislature as an independent Liberal MPP for Simcoe South in June 1875. He was therefore a sitting MPP when he defended Eliza in the Senate in 1876, and when he helped her get her separation bill passed by the Senate in 1877. In September 1878 he resigned his seat in the Ontario assembly in order to run in the federal election held on 17 September as a Macdonald Conservative and supporter of the National policy. He won the Ontario seat of Halton. He was thus able to represent Eliza as both her lawyer in the Senate divorce committee hearing in 1879 and as an MP when the separation bill reached the Commons in 1879, a development discussed in the next chapter.

The Senate Refuses to Consider the Separation Bill, 1878

The separation bill was very quickly disposed of in 1878, rebuffed in the Senate in short order. In late February Reesor submitted a petition from Eliza, which contained two requests.[3] One was that she be allowed to prosecute her cause of divorce *in forma pauperis*. This meant simply that she would not have to pay the usual fee of $200. The request was not dealt with in 1878 because Eliza's other request to waive the notice provision for a private bill was refused. All private bills, including divorce bills, were first referred to the Senate Committee on Standing Orders and Private Bills, which determined whether the proper notice had been given. William Miller, the Nova Scotia Catholic lawyer who had been one of the principal opponents of Eliza's relief bill in 1877, was chair of that committee in 1878. In late March 1878 it ruled that Eliza's bill should not be considered for failure to give notice. Its reasons are revealing. It cited Rule 51, which required two months' notice for any private bill other than a divorce bill. Thus the committee treated Eliza's bill as an ordinary private bill, not as a divorce bill.

We can only speculate about the reasons for McDougall's decision not to give any notice of the bill he wanted to introduce in 1878. He certainly had time after the 1877 failure to provide the full six months' notice, which he had to do to maintain his position that it was a divorce bill. He may have seen not giving notice as the best tactic, given that his position in 1877 was that the separation bill was not a new bill, merely an amendment to Robert's original bill, for which notice had been given. The wording of Eliza's petition, that "a new Bill, *if necessary*, may be passed," supports this interpretation. He intended to argue that the 1877 bill was still alive. If that was the case he never got to make the argument. In specifying that Rule 51, not Rule 72, was applicable, Miller stated, albeit implicitly, that any bill contemplated by Eliza's petition was not for a divorce bill.

Whatever McDougall was trying to do, his attempt to have the separation bill introduced in the Senate in 1878 failed, albeit not without a final throw of the dice. On 26 March Reesor moved that Eliza's petition be referred to the same divorce committee that had sat in 1876 and 1877.[4] Miller immediately rose to say that the motion was out of order as his committee had reported against the petition. Speaker Christie agreed, and Reesor had to accept the ruling, but did so with bad grace. It was, he lamented, a "very great hardship" to Eliza to be "deprived of redress here, when there is no other place where she can seek for it." Eliza was said to be "in a pitiable condition" as a result of this second rebuff.[5] She did give notice in the summer of 1878 for the 1879 parliamentary session.

Legislation and Litigation over Eliza's Dower Rights, 1877 and 1878

This section deals with a minor aspect of the Campbell marriage breakdown, albeit one that may have affected the 1879 parliamentary debates over Eliza's separation bill. The issue was Eliza's dower right in all land owned by Robert during the marriage.[6] As discussed in chapter 1, although married women had very limited rights to property at common law, that law did provide some protection for widows through the law of dower. As dower could not be overridden by an *inter vivos* conveyance of the land or by a will, it made potential purchasers of land less willing to buy it because if their vendor died before his wife, her dower interest would "pop up" and deprive the purchaser of part of the value of the land during her lifetime. As land became increasingly seen as a commercial asset in the United Kingdom and North America, English judges invented a device to "bar" dower, that is, remove it from title. All that had to be done was to state in a conveyance (a deed or a will) that dower did not exist. This had to be done with the wife's consent, and all British North American colonies passed legislation specifying the procedure for a wife to be examined separately from her husband by a JP to ensure that her consent had been freely given. In 1833 the English *Dower Act* removed the need for that consent, effectively abolishing dower as a right, and leaving it up to husbands whether or not they wanted to bar dower. But the 1833 Act was not copied in the British North American colonies, so the dower right of a widow remained and was a substantive protection for wives.[7] Dower was not abolished in Canada until the matrimonial property law reforms of the 1970s.

In 1877, the year after he had been refused a divorce by the Senate, Robert tried to free his land from Eliza's dower interest, by first getting the Ontario legislature to amend the provincial *Dower Act*.[8] He did so, according to McDougall when he recounted the story in the Commons in 1879, in a "clandestine manner." It is unclear exactly how it was done, for Robert was not a member of the assembly. He must have been able to persuade a member to add a provision to an omnibus bill passed in March 1877 making 78 changes to a number of Ontario statutes, from the *Line Fences Act* to liquor licence and corporations legislation. All these changes were passed just before the province's first *Revised Statutes* were enacted, for inclusion in that revision. According to McDougall the dower provision was inserted, handwritten, in the bill at the last stage of the committee hearing, and nobody noticed, including himself, an Ontario assemblyman at the time. The provision that concerns us was section 35 of the omnibus Act and provided that if a wife had been living apart from her husband for two years, *under such circumstances as by law disentitle her to alimony*, and the husband wanted to sell his land free of dower, he could apply to a superior court judge to have dower barred. The application could be made *ex parte*, without notice to the other party, and the judge had discretion to order the dower barred without the wife's agreement.[9] McDougall called this a "villainous law" enacted "to meet this particular case," and he was certainly correct on the second point.[10] It was one of a number of small changes to the law relating to dower, which were contained in sections 34–36; that is, it was inserted between two other dower provisions, and this might well explain why nobody took any notice of it.[11] This amendment made it possible for Robert to go to court and deprive Eliza of a right she would have had on his death. While that idea no doubt pleased him, the more immediate benefit was to enhance the value of his considerable real estate holdings. Potential purchasers would pay more for land without a dower right attached than for land in which dower had not been barred.

Robert wasted little time in trying to take advantage of the new law. He engaged Alexander Grey McMillan, a Whitby lawyer,[12] to apply to

Chancery in early 1878 for the requisite order because he had "contracted to sell certain lands which he was desirous of selling." The statute allowed him to apply to any of the superior courts, and it is reasonable to assume that Robert chose Chancery in the hope that his case would be heard by Samuel Hume Blake. He did draw Blake, but was disappointed because the vice-chancellor would not exercise the discretion the statute gave him to issue an order *ex parte.* Although McMillan argued that notice to Eliza could be dispensed with, Blake refused, noting that it was well known that Robert and Eliza were both still living in Whitby, and thus there was no difficulty in serving Eliza. The English courts, in dealing with a similar provision, "in all cases" required notice to be given unless it could be shown that "unreasonable difficulties" prevented that being done.[13]

Robert could not proceed *ex parte,* but he could still try to have Eliza's dower right nullified and made a motion to do so in March 1878. Eliza was served with that notice, which was the first that she or McDougall knew about the statutory amendment of 1877. The case was heard by the senior Chancery judge, Chancellor John Godfrey Spragge. Spragge had been a successful equity lawyer, practising in partnership with common law expert John Hilyard Cameron. Both Cameron and Spragge at different times held the post of treasurer of the Law Society, the head of that organization. Spragge was the first master, a kind of junior judge dealing only with motions, in the Court of Chancery when it was established in 1837, and he was promoted first to registrar in 1844 and then to a full judge, a vice-chancellor, in 1850. He became the chancellor, the head of the court, in 1869 and was later, after the fusion of the courts of common law and equity, Chief Justice of Ontario. He died in office in 1884.[14] Robert was represented on the motion by James Bethune, Q.C., a rising star of the Toronto bar, and a bencher of the Law Society, in his mid-30s,[15] and McDougall appeared for Eliza. Argument was heard in early April 1878, and Spragge denied the application.[16]

On Robert's behalf Bethune argued that Eliza had committed adultery and had henceforth ceased to live with him. McDougall countered that she had not willingly left, but that Robert had forcibly removed her from the marital home. Spragge began by noting that if Eliza had committed adultery she would not be entitled to alimony and the fact that Robert had expelled her would be irrelevant. All that was needed to meet the statutory requirements was that they had been living apart for two years and the adultery. The question, therefore, was whether the alleged adultery was established by the evidence. In a highly technical judgment perhaps influenced by his knowledge that, as discussed below, the relevant provision in the *Dower Act* had just been amended, Spragge found nothing on the formal record of the alimony case to establish adultery. The record showed only that Eliza had sued Robert for alimony, and her suit was dismissed. Spragge was "not at liberty … to look at the evidence, or the conclusion drawn from the evidence by the learned Judge before whom the cause was heard." Spragge also dealt with Bethune's alternative argument that the crim. con. case could be used to establish adultery. It could not, Spragge held, because Eliza had not been a party to the record in that case. Thus, Spragge concluded, "there is not legal evidence of the fact of adultery by the wife, and in the absence of such proof it is not made to appear that she has been living apart from her husband under circumstances to which the statute would apply." As we will see, the chancellor's use of the phrase "not legal evidence of the fact of adultery by the wife" was important to those who argued in favour of passing the separation Act in 1879, for it was used to gainsay the argument that Parliament was overturning a Chancery decision.

In the remainder of his judgment Spragge made it clear that he knew exactly what was being argued about in Parliament concerning the constitutionality of a separation bill, because Eliza had included in her affidavit an account of her past attempts to get the bill passed and her intention to apply again. Bethune responded to this by saying that such a statute would be unconstitutional, but Spragge was not going to enter into a discussion of "so nice a question" as the meaning of marriage and divorce in the *BNA Act*, especially while proceedings were pending in Parliament. Spragge ended by noting that in the period between argument in the case and releasing his judgment the relevant clause in the *Dower Act* had been amended in another omnibus statutory amendments bill, which removed the phrase "under such circumstances as by law disentitle her to alimony" and only allowed an application to bar dower if the wife had abandoned and was living apart from her husband.[17] McDougall, as noted above a sitting MPP, took credit for that, and rightly so, for it was he who drew Premier Oliver Mowat's attention to the meaning of the 1877 amendment.[18] Spragge insisted that the repeal made no difference to his decision, but it is difficult to believe that he was not influenced by it and by his knowledge, which we can only assume, of the underhanded way that the original amendment became law. Robert had one last throw of the dice. In July 1878 he made a motion before Blake asking the vice-chancellor to amend the decree he had issued in the alimony case so that it stated the ground on which alimony had been refused. Blake declined to do so.[19]

William McDougall v. Robert Campbell for Legal Fees

As noted in chapter 8, early in the 1876 divorce proceedings, the divorce committee ordered Robert to pay Eliza $500 to enable her to defend his petition.[20] He was ordered to pay McDougall's fees from day to day, but instead promised McDougall that if he did not insist on daily payment he would pay at the end of the proceedings, after costs had been taxed.* At the conclusion of the hearing McDougall submitted his bill for legal fees to the committee, a total of $1,000, which consisted of a $100 retainer, another $100 as McDougall's fee for the first day of the divorce committee hearing, and $50 each for the subsequent 16 days of hearings. Dickey, chair of the committee, taxed his costs and ordered that Robert should pay $500. Robert simply refused to pay, and McDougall sued him in Queen's Bench for the $500 and for an additional $350, seven days' work at $50 a day, for drafting and presenting Eliza's petition for the separation and for arguing her case in 1877.[21]

The suit was heard at the Toronto Fall Assizes in 1876 by Justice Joseph Curran Morrison, without a jury. There was no need for a jury because no facts were at issue only, as explained in detail below, the legal question of whether McDougall could sue Robert for his fees. Morrison found for McDougall for the full amount, and Robert moved for a new trial in November 1876. The new trial motion was heard on 8 February 1877, before a three-judge panel of Queen's Bench judges, with judgment reserved. But the judges could not agree and ordered the case to be re-argued. A second hearing took place on 27 May, and judgment was delivered on 30 June 1877, a verdict for McDougall by a 2–1 majority. Robert appealed to the Court of Appeal, which heard the case on 18 January 1878. The court delivered its judgment dismissing Robert's appeal, on 25 June 1878.[22]

James Bethune, Q.C., Robert's counsel in the dower case, again represented him. Harrison could not do so because he had been appointed chief justice of Queen's Bench in October 1875. McDougall was represented by his oldest son Joseph Easton McDougall, who had been called to the bar in 1870 and practised with his father. He was still relatively junior but was already very well regarded on the Chancery and common law circuits. His lectures on torts given at Osgoode Hall Law School were published in 1882, the first torts book published in Canada, and he was made a Q.C. and a county court judge for York County

* Taxing costs is the procedure whereby a court will, usually on the motion of the party having to pay costs, deny items of the costs submitted on the ground that they are not a permissible cost or, more typically, reduce the costs claimed.

in 1883. He was assisted by Theodore Henry Spencer, who had been called to the bar in 1860 and practised in Toronto and other locations.[23]

The only substantial account we have of these proceedings is the reported judgment of the three Queen's Bench judges on the motion for a new trial. One of the three was Chief Justice Robert Harrison, who therefore sat on a case in which one of the parties was a former client. This would be a clear breach of judicial ethics today, but matters were viewed differently in the 1870s. Justice Morrison also sat, despite that fact that he had been the trial judge and was therefore hearing what was effectively an appeal from his own decision. Again, this is unthinkable today but standard practice in this period. Morrison immigrated to Upper Canada with his family in 1830, at the age of 14, and was called to the bar in 1839. He was active in reform politics in the 1840s and 1850s, a successful trial lawyer, and legal adviser to many businesses. He was appointed to Common Pleas in 1862 and moved to Queen's Bench in 1863. He served there for 14 years until he was appointed to the Court of Appeal at the end of 1877. Known more for his good humour than for his legal acumen, he died in Toronto in 1885.[24] He must have known McDougall, but so did most people involved in Canada West and Ontario politics in the decades before and after Confederation.

The third member of the panel was Justice Adam Wilson.[25] Wilson immigrated to Upper Canada at the age of 16 in 1830 and worked for his uncle, who owned a mill and a store in Halton County. In 1834 he moved to Toronto and apprenticed with the Robert Baldwin law firm, being called to the bar in 1839. As Baldwin became increasingly absorbed by politics Wilson did most of the firm's law work, establishing a sufficient reputation to be elected a bencher in 1850. Influenced by Baldwin he was also attracted to reform politics and was elected to the Toronto city council in 1855 and as Toronto mayor for two consecutive one-year terms in 1859 and 1860. His reform political interests extended to provincial politics, and in 1858 he unsuccessfully sued John A. Macdonald for being illegally in office after the "double shuffle" of that year.[26] In 1861 he was elected to the legislative assembly by the voters of North York, and the following year he joined the ministry of John Sandfield Macdonald and Louis Victor Sicotte along with three other reformers, including William McDougall. Thus two of the three judges who heard the motion for a new trial had close connections, one political and the other professional, with the litigants. Wilson served as solicitor general until he was dropped from cabinet in 1863. As compensation he was appointed a judge of Queen's Bench the same year. Like many judges he went back and forth between Queen's Bench and Common Pleas until he retired in 1887. His biographer dubbed him "an advocate of mild law reform."

The new trial motion panel found for McDougall by a 2–1 majority on the claim for the $500, with Wilson writing the judgment for himself and Morrison. His judgment conforms to his biographer's descriptions of his rulings as more "a gluing together of precedents" than "broad-ranging" syntheses of principles, although that was the tendency of many Ontario judges in the 1870s, who viewed their role very much as "finding" the law in the cases. He is also described as willing to rely on American law and show himself independent from English, which was more unusual. His judgment in *McDougall v. Campbell* bears out this description. His decision on the $500 claim was convoluted in its reasoning but clear enough in the result. His decision on the $300 was similar but different – unclearly reasoned and without a definite conclusion. I will deal first with the claim for the $300, which the court disallowed to some extent.

The claim for the $300 could not have been a claim by a lawyer for payment from his client because Robert was not in any sense McDougall's client when the proceedings moved from defending the divorce application to petitioning for a separation. McDougall's client at that stage was Eliza, and if Robert was to be liable for McDougall's fees it had to be on some other basis. Wilson analogized the $300 claim to a husband's common law liability to provide necessaries for his wife. He thought that a claim by another man against a husband for having expended money for a wife's "welfare and protection" might be warranted, but did not resolve that issue. Instead he said that even if the husband might be liable, it could only be for the money expended to obtain a separation and not for fees to present Eliza's claim for alimony and custody. This was because the Senate had no jurisdiction over those matters, which were for the Ontario courts to deal with. Indeed Blake had already dealt with alimony. Wilson's judgment thus displays considerable knowledge of the arguments made in the Senate in 1877, although it is hardly surprising that the arguments over the Campbell separation bill were talked about among lawyers and judges as well as among the residents of Whitby and other towns. As far as the case before Wilson was concerned, we are left with an inconclusive result. Part of the $300 might be recoverable, but only that part that had been expended on the separation aspect of the separation bill, which had yet to be ascertained.

The other claim, for $500, was dealt with at greater length by Wilson and by Harrison in his dissent. There was no doubt that the Senate had ordered Robert Campbell to pay, but, as Bethune argued on Robert's behalf, McDougall was prevented from suing for it in court by a long-standing common law rule, specifically approved of in an 1844

Canada West case,[27] that barristers could not sue either solicitors or clients for fees. Bethune's argument cannot be appreciated without a brief excursus into the structure and ideologies of the English legal profession in the eighteenth and nineteenth centuries.[28] There were, broadly speaking and ignoring differences within the two categories, two kinds of lawyers, although the word "lawyer" was not often used. A legally trained person qualified to do legal work for clients was either a solicitor, sometimes called an attorney, or a barrister. Somone seeking legal advice or assistance went first to a solicitor, and if the work required did not involve going to court – drawing up a will, conveying real estate, establishing a corporation, and the like – the solicitor did the work. If the matter required going to court, the solicitor engaged a barrister. Barristers were the elite of the legal profession. Only barristers could appear in the superior courts, and only barristers received judicial appointments. This distinction between a barrister and a solicitor went beyond what kind of work each did. Solicitors had to be approved to practise by the Law Society, a statutory body, and disciplinary control over them was exercised by judges. For barristers both entry and discipline were the preserve of the Inns of Court. Barristers could not take on work given to them directly by clients; they could only be engaged by a solicitor. Most importantly for current purposes, a solicitor was paid by the client, a barrister by a solicitor.

To this description, especially the last point about the financial relationships among barrister, solicitor, and client, must be added a social and cultural distinction between the two types of lawyers. Solicitors were invariably from the lower or middle classes; they were "men of business" who handled the legal affairs of their social equals or betters. They not infrequently went into business partnerships with their clients, were directors of companies, and the like. Barristers came from the gentry or the lower aristocratic classes, people who disdained "trade." Qualifying to be a barrister was one of the career options open to, and acceptable to, the younger sons of the landowning class. The oldest son would inherit and manage the estate, while younger sons would go into the church, the armed forces, the colonial services, or the law. They had a liberal education and "breeding." They also claimed to be independent, men of integrity and judgment, and it would detract from that independence if they were to be mere employees of the client. Their relationships *inter se* were governed by a "code of etiquette," "unwritten rules and sentiments which determined the duties of the bar" and helped maintain an "esprit de corps by which every barrister was the watchful guardian of the honour and integrity of his learned brethren." As one contemporary English legal writer put it, barristers "are recruited from the best blood of the land" and "[t]heir private lives as well as their professional conduct must be ... beyond reproach." They must "possess those qualities which united combine to form the character of the honest, fearless, independent Englishman."[29] This article was written as a long case comment to explain and approve the reasoning in *Mostyn v. Mostyn*, an 1870 case in which the English Court of Appeal had confirmed the rule that barristers could not sue for their legal fees as still good law.[30]

In line with this self-appointed status, although many barristers were able to charge high fees, the fiction was that the money they received from solicitors was "an honorarium, not a wage, as befitted the status of a gentleman."[31] An honorarium was not something the payor was required to pay, not consideration that was part of a contract, and thus, said the common law, the fees could not be sued for in court. Thus the judges in *Swinfen v. Lord Chelmsford* adverted to the crucial distinction between one who contracts and one who performs a duty: "an advocate at the English bar, accepting a brief in the usual way, undertakes a duty, but does not enter into any contract or promise, express or implied.... [A] barrister is to be considered, not as making a contract with his client, but as taking upon himself an office or duty, in the proper discharge of which not merely the client, but the Court in which the duty is to be performed, and the public at large, have an interest."[32]

As they could not sue after the fact, the practice was for the money to be paid to the barrister when he was retained, before he went to court. There was another reason justifying this arrangement as far as barristers were concerned. It shielded barristers from liability should they perform poorly or, in the rare case, not at all. Bethune adverted to this reason when making his first argument in *McDougall v. Campbell*: "If this claim is established by the plaintiff," he pointed out, "the right must bring with it the corresponding responsibility of being answerable to his client for any neglect or failure of duty which may be imputed to him." Not being liable for such made the rule "one of great consequence to the profession."[33]

The Ontario legal profession never had anything like the same rigid demarcation between barristers and solicitors. From 1797 the Law Society of Upper Canada was the regulatory body for both kinds of lawyers, and most lawyers could draw up wills and go to court to argue over their meaning.[34] The colony/province passed separate statutes for barristers and solicitors, but both were short and both delegated the power to regulate admission to practise to the Law Society.[35] In practice lawyers did specialize in either counsel or solicitorial work, just as they specialized between common law and equity or between corporate law and prosecutions, but it was a specialization derived from opportunity or personal ability or preference, not from being of a particular status. Nonetheless the English rule about counsel suing clients for fees was confirmed in 1844 by Chief Justice John Beverley Robinson of Queen's Bench. In one respect Robinson held that the common law had been changed by a local statute, which regulated court costs. If the winning party had had their costs taxed by the court, and those costs included counsel fees, counsel could recover them in a further action. But otherwise they could not. Robinson very much approved of this rule, which was one "for the advantage as well as for the honour of the profession."[36]

With this lengthy excursus I return to the decision of the Queen's Bench judges in *McDougall v. Campbell*. Wilson ruled unequivocally that the English common law rule should be abandoned in Ontario. It was a fiction. Counsel did not give their time for a "mere honorarium," and it would "not detract from their dignity or from the honour of their profession" if they, "like the rest of mankind," were entitled to sue for what was owed to them. It was not right to accept anybody's services on the promise of payment and then be able to refuse to pay, shielded by a legal rule unique to one profession. There was no reason why counsel and their clients should not be "on the footing as other men in every station and business of life."[37] The English rule was quite inapplicable in the very different circumstances of the legal professions of England and Ontario. In Ontario barristers were not a breed apart; they were one part of a united profession. Wilson concluded: "In my opinion counsel fees are recoverable by action in this Province. I do not imagine any calamity will result from a decision to that effect to the bar, to the Court, to the administration of justice, or to the country. It is in accordance with ... the actual facts and experience of business."[38] The decision was a landmark, and recognized as such by the *Canada Law Journal*.[39]

Robert Harrison dissented on this point.[40] He reviewed the history of the legal profession in England, pointing out that barristers and solicitors did very different kinds of work, and there was a good reason why solicitors could sue for their fees but barristers could not. A barrister "should be rendered as independent of the result as the Judge or jury who try a cause, and therefore his exertions should not be made to depend upon the prospect of payment of fees." Many American states had a different rule but that did not matter. He was only concerned with Ontario, and Ontario law was English law. With that he launched into a long paean to the glories of the English ways of doing things and the concomitant nobility of his chosen profession. In England it had always been "considered essential to the honour and dignity of the bar that there should be no traffic about counsel fees, no power to make contracts of hiring and service in reference to them." Maintaining a distinction between the two branches of the profession was necessary even in Ontario where they are united.'"[N]othing should be done which would have a tendency in personal conduct to lessen the honour and dignity so essential to the maintenance of a high standard of professional rectitude at the bar. I confess I never read [defences of the rule] .... without, if possible, having increased veneration and increased love for the profession to which I owe so much."

Harrison's eloquence was to no effect. It was a clarion call to arms in defence of a long tradition, but Wilson, Morrison, and the judges of the Court of Appeal were not prepared to defend tradition in a new age and a different country. It is unfortunate that we do not have available the reasons of the appeal judges, especially as a direct refutation of English law was a relatively rare event in the Ontario courts of the last quarter of the nineteenth century. As the authors of *A History of Canadian Law* have argued, this period was marked by a greater insistence than earlier on adherence to precedent and an attempt to "re-imperialize Canadian law." Countering this trend were a small number of judges who desired to "develop a distinctive domestic law suitable for Canadian circumstances." At first glance it is surprising that innovation would come in the field of legal ethics, because leaders of the profession were promulgating a "broader cultural mission" for lawyers, "aiming to make them missionaries in service of a secularized trinity: law, Britishness and civilization." But this was not aristocratic gentility; it was "modern professionalism, in which formal qualifications based on demonstrated expertise replaced gentlemanly worth as the primary claim of the professional."[41]

14
Eliza Campbell's Separation Bill in Parliament – Again – 1879

Introduction

I return in this chapter to the Campbell separation bill. Having failed so completely in getting her case before the Senate in 1878, Eliza and McDougall did things according to the book. Notice of her intention to apply to Parliament for a divorce was published in the *Canada Gazette* for the first time in July 1878, and ran for the requisite six months there, in the *Whitby Chronicle*, and in another Ontario County newspaper.[1] The notice was unique, announcing her intention to apply to the Dominion Parliament "for a bill of Divorce a *mensa et thoro* from my said husband, similar to the bill passed in my behalf by the Senate in 1877, for desertion, cruelty, and the other causes." Normally such notices simply stated that the application to Parliament was for a "Bill of Divorce," without specifying what kind of divorce, because everybody understood that divorce meant divorce *a vinculo matrimonii*. The case had become sufficiently notorious by 1878 that newspapers in Ontario and Quebec ran stories stating simply that the notice had been published.[2] Robert was served with her "Application to Parliament," dated 8 July 1878, by James Keith Gordon.[3] In the early months of 1879 Robert initiated settlement discussions with Eliza, the details of which are discussed later in this chapter. Suffice it to say here that his proposals were not ones that she, or anybody else in her position, could accept. In one instance the financial offer was derisory, and in others his terms for her living with him and the children were insulting.

This chapter analyses the parliamentary debates over Eliza's separation bill, the second time around. In many respects 1879 was a repeat of 1877: Reesor championed the bill in the Senate, and a substantial number of senators, especially ones from Quebec and those legally trained, opposed it at every turn. They used all the procedural delaying tactics

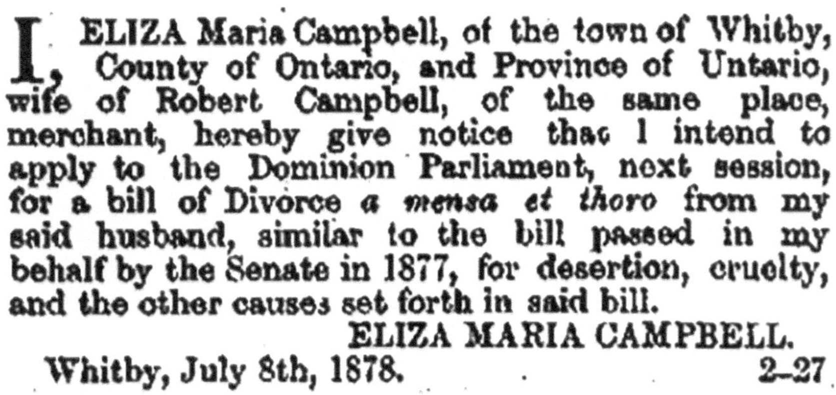

I, ELIZA Maria Campbell, of the town of Whitby, County of Ontario, and Province of Untario, wife of Robert Campbell, of the same place, merchant, hereby give notice thac I intend to apply to the Dominion Parliament, next session, for a bill of Divorce *a mensa et thoro* from my said husband, similar to the bill passed in my behalf by the Senate in 1877, for desertion, cruelty, and the other causes set forth in said bill.

ELIZA MARIA CAMPBELL.

Whitby, July 8th, 1878. 2–27

Figure 14.1. Eliza Campbell's divorce notice

Source: *Canada Gazette*, 15 July 1878 et seq

they could, including seeking to have the bill first referred to the SCC. The same legal-constitutional arguments were made as had been voiced in 1877, by both sides and in both Houses of Parliament, coupled with the same denunciations of both Robert and Eliza. Another divorce committee was struck in the Senate, heard evidence, and produced a report. Two major differences from 1877 were that the Senate passed the bill in time for it to also get through the Commons, and Eliza had a forcefully eloquent champion in the lower house – William McDougall, who had been elected the MP for Halton in the general election of September 1878 which returned John A. Macdonald to power with a majority of 137–69. Ever the maverick, McDougall had served in the Ontario assembly as a Liberal before resigning to run federally as a Conservative and a supporter of Macdonald's national policy.

The court cases between 1873 and 1875 had attracted attention in Toronto and Whitby. Robert's divorce petition in 1876 and the abortive attempt to pass a separation bill in 1877 garnered additional publicity, in Ontario and beyond, as we saw in chapters 9 through 12. In 1879 the parliamentary debates were even more widely and intensively reported and commented on. The *Whitby Chronicle*, as one would expect, carried accounts of the proceedings throughout, as did the *Globe* and the *Ottawa Citizen*.[4] Reports also appeared in other Toronto newspapers and in those in smaller Ontario towns,[5] and in Quebec.[6] In 1879 the case also attracted interest further afield, in British Columbia and in the United States.[7] Many of these newspaper reports were copied verbatim from other newspapers, and they often did no more than report the progress of the bill, and sometimes extracted what was said in debates. But occasionally they offered commentary as well.

The organization of this chapter is straightforward, dealing first with the Senate and then the Commons. Since much the same arguments were made for and against in both houses as in 1877, I will not repeat what was said in chapter 12 on the division of powers or the separate functions of the legislative and judicial branches of government. The bill passed and received royal assent on 15 May, but that was not the end of the matter. The final section of this chapter deals with Robert's unsuccessful attempt to persuade the Colonial Office in London to intervene and disallow it.

The Senate: Procedural Arguments and First and Second Readings

Reesor introduced Eliza's petition on 10 March, but it took until 4 April for a bill granting Eliza a separation to be given first reading.[8] In part the delays were Reesor's fault. He was the sponsor of the bill, as he had been in 1876–77, but was not very good at shepherding it through the Senate. Divorce bill procedure was not complicated, but it was exacting, and Reesor consistently made mistakes. Reesor's inadequacies were especially unfortunate because opponents of the bill took every opportunity to delay the process. As the *Whitby Chronicle* put it in April, invoking the oft-used distinction between law and justice, "a couple of the senators, who evidently know more about law than equity, raise technical objections and have prevented the unfortunate woman from getting simple justice."[9] Part of the problem was that Eliza also petitioned to proceed *in forma pauperis*, which meant having two Senate rules on divorce bills waived. Rule 82 specified that an applicant for a divorce had to deposit 800 copies of the draft bill with the Clerk, 600 in English and 200 in French, and Rule 82 required a $200 fee to be paid. Much time was spent discussing whether the *in forma pauperis* petition should be considered before or after the separation petition, whether the rules should be waived, and whether they applied in the first place as the bill was not a divorce bill but one for a separation and should therefore go to the Committee on Standing Orders and Private Bills. The last issue was easily turned into arguments about whether Parliament had the authority to pass a separation Act.

Other issues were raised by opponents of the bill. Kaulbach, not surprisingly, attacked Eliza, saying the separation bill was "merely a subterfuge on her part to get over this charge of adultery, for which she had been condemned in the Court of Chancery." Senator Lawrence Power demanded, and obtained, the presentation to the House of an exemplification of Blake's judgment in the alimony case. Senators insisted that James Gordon be summoned from Ottawa to testify that he had served Robert with notice of Eliza's application, despite that fact that Robert was present every day and was obviously abundantly aware of what was going on. A sense of how hard fought all these issues were can be garnered from the fact that when Gordon had done this he applied to be reimbursed for his travelling expenses for coming to the capital. Debate on a motion to do so went on for many pages in the reports of debates and ended with a tied vote, 29–29. In vain did Reesor complain at one point that "it was hardly desirable that further difficulties should be thrown in the way of the petitioner." But throwing up difficulties was the point of it all. The bill's opponents were well aware, as William Miller conceded, that they were in the minority, but they fought it to the end, exemplifying Clement Cornwall's statement that he would "object to every stage of the proceedings..., so far as it lay within his power to do so."[10]

Once the bill had received first reading on 4 April it was on its way, but Rule 76 required 14 days between first and second readings for divorce bills, and in the interim Joseph-Hyacinthe Bellerose moved successfully for a select committee to be appointed "to examine and report on the best way to properly supervise private legislation to ascertain whether private bills are within section 91 jurisdiction." The target of the proposal was obvious, although Bellerose's committee turned out not to derail or delay the bill.[11] As soon as the motion for second reading was made by Reesor, Cornwall moved an amendment to refer the bill to the SCC. A long debate principally over the division of powers ensued, at the end of which the motion to refer went down 30–22. Another long debate followed on second reading, extending until nearly midnight. In second reading the principle of a bill, not the details, was discussed, the details being hashed out in committee if the bill passed. The bill did pass second reading, "on a division."[12]

The main speakers on 18 April were the ones who had dominated the 1877 debates, with Reesor and Dickey supporting the bill and Campbell, Trudel, Miller, Penny, and Kaulbach against it. In general the debate was conducted with decorum and limited to the legal and constitutional arguments. But Kaulbach and Lawrence Power, contra the bill, and Robert Carrall and Billa Flint, in favour, departed, to a greater or lesser degree, from the strictures of polite discourse. Carrall spent some of his time on the constitutional issue, reading a summary of the English and Canadian law of divorce by Alpheus Todd, the librarian of Parliament and an internationally recognized expert on parliamentary law and the Canadian constitution. Over his long career as the librarian of the Province of Canada assembly and the federal Parliament Todd produced dozens of similar opinions for legislators. His conclusion on this occasion was that the Canadian Parliament had "ample and sufficient powers to deal with marriage and divorce, and with all legal questions growing out of the marital relation."[13] Carrall followed this with an assertion reminiscent of his earlier speeches. He would support the bill "with all the force of my character ... in the full conviction in the justice of this lady's demand, of her virtuous character, and of the complicity of her husband's friends in one of the most villainous, infernal, foul, low, and cowardly conspiracies which it has ever been my lot to have cognizance of." Carrall briefly moved to a more measured note only to very quickly again invoke his rhetoric about Robert as a cruel and unmanly man. He thought that every senator "when appealed to will not reject the petition of the unfortunate victim of a vile, low-bred conspiracy that has been entered into by a man who forcibly expelled his wife from his house without giving her anything to support her."[14]

Carrall's speech was remarkable for a man who was dying and knew it. Knowing he had only months to live, he had returned to Ottawa for the 1879 session to bring two of his beloved causes to fruition – the Campbell separation Act and another statute declaring the 1st of July Dominion Day. Shortly after the 1879 session, on 8 May, this avowed life-long bachelor married his alleged childhood sweetheart, Mrs. Elizabeth Amelia Gordon of Goderich, in order that she could inherit his property. He died on 19 September at Carrall's Grove, Ontario.[15]

On the other side of the question Kaulbach, although less intemperate than he had been in 1877, and despite having agreed not to discuss the facts of the Campbell case, could not help himself in adding invective to legal analysis. The House should not pass the bill because it would overturn a Chancery decision, a decision which rested on a finding of adultery. It was consistent with the verdict in the crim. con. case, which "stands as a record ... damnatory of the chastity of this woman." So too did Blake's judgment, which "stands for all time to come ... [as] a record of that woman's adultery – nothing now can wipe it out."[16]

For his part another opponent of the bill, Lawrence Power, chose not to attack Eliza, whose case he thought "a rather hard one." Rather he went after his older senatorial colleagues who

> do not look solely at the weight of the arguments on the two sides of the question. I believe that gentlemen of the mature years, which has fallen to the lot of most members of this House, have as warm sympathies as younger men are generally supposed to entertain; and I am very much

disposed to think that in the present case the sympathies of the House are disposed to go rather further than the law would justify them in going to assist Mrs. Campbell.[17]

One of Power's senior colleagues, Billa Flint, responded in kind, criticizing other senators for obstructionism and adopting the "man of the world" stance on the substantive question:

Legal gentlemen differ in opinion on the subject, and we, who are laymen, must use our own better judgment in the matter. My judgment leads me to do what I think is right in the case, but I cannot help thinking that it would have been far better if Mr. Campbell had settled the difficulty with his wife. He is a wealthy man, the petitioner is the mother of his children, and to save them from the stigma of having such a scandal upon his family he should have done what he could to prevent the matter going any further. What credit or honour can he derive by endeavouring to fasten upon his children for all time to come the disgrace of having a mother who was not what she ought to have been?[18]

Shortly after Flint's speech the motion to refer the bill to the SCC was put and defeated, and that to send it to a committee prevailed.

Another "Divorce" Committee

As in 1876 Reesor, the sponsor of the bill, chose the committee members. He selected six men who had served on the first committee – Dickey (chair again), Dickson, Haythorne, Leonard, Reesor, and Seymour – and three who had not – William Brouse of Ontario, James Ferrier of Quebec, and Alexander Macfarlane of Nova Scotia. Dr. William Brouse was a very recent appointment to the Senate, in 1878. He had been an adherent of the pre-Confederation Clear Grit party and sat as an independent reformer from Ontario. Ferrier was an ardent Methodist and temperance advocate and one of the richest men in Montreal. Macfarlane, Q.C., was a Conservative and a former member of the Nova Scotia assembly. He had been one of the Nova Scotia delegates to the London conference in 1866 to settle the terms of Confederation.[19] Ferrier had voted for the separation bill in 1877 and against referring it to the SCC in 1879. Macfarlane had opposed the bill in 1877 but changed his vote by 1879, and voted against the SCC reference. Brouse had not been in the Senate in 1877 but voted against the SCC reference in 1879.[20]

The most notable aspect of Reesor's choices was that the two dissenters in 1877, Cornwall and Kaulbach, were left off the committee. James

Cox Aikins was also left off, for reasons unknown. The exclusion of the two inveterate opponents of Eliza not surprisingly precipitated a debate, with Kaulbach the chief complainer. His gripes were contradictory. He decried the fact that the two were not chosen but abandoned that line when Reesor said that Kaulbach and Cornwall had declined to serve. Kaulbach shifted to saying that it would have been better if none of the 1876–77 committee members had been chosen. The committee's inquiry should be conducted in a "judicial, calm, and impartial spirit," a richly ironic statement given the tone of his own speeches. Reesor justified the retention of six members from the earlier committee by saying that they were familiar with the evidence. As for the three new men, he chose Macfarlane because "he had not expressed himself strongly on the question"; Ferrier was chosen for the same reason and because he was from Quebec and knew Quebec law, and Brouse because he was a new member and could not be accused of partiality. Kaulbach, of course, was not satisfied with these explanations, pointing out that all members of the committee "had expressed themselves in favour" of Eliza, presumably through their votes in the Senate or perhaps in private conversation.[21]

Others supported the idea that the committee should have been an entirely new one, notably Cornwall, who said that he had declined to serve because he would not be impartial. But he was sure that that was true of all the people who were on the previous committee. Miller said that it was a pity that Reesor had not chosen two or three senators who had voted differently from himself. On the other side Dickey and Ferrier supported Reesor. Dickey said that he was the only impartial person on the previous committee and as chairman had not voted on whether Robert had proved the preamble. When the question came before the Senate he had done his duty by supporting the majority of the committee. Ferrier stated that he had been surprised to find himself on the committee, for he had not been on a divorce committee since 1870. He knew nothing of the evidence in the case, and was sure he could be impartial, but he would be glad if one of the lawyers, or indeed any other senator, would take his place. The motion to appoint the committee was then carried "on a division."[22]

The committee spent the 21st and 22nd of April taking evidence and deliberating on its report. It had before it Eliza's petition and a draft bill drawn up by McDougall, which in general outline was very similar to the one passed by the Senate in 1877. Eliza was represented by McDougall, Robert by a new lawyer, George Joseph O'Doherty, who had been called to the bar in 1864 and practised in Ottawa.[23] The committee had only just sat down when Robert made the unusual announcement that he had a settlement proposal.[24] Although the senators assured him that they approved the idea of a reconciliation, his terms were unlikely to satisfy Eliza. He was willing to take Eliza back, to give her a "suite of apartments," allow her to "take charge of the children," have enough money for her support and those of the children, and even, "if she desired, to eat at the same table with him." But he would not "restore to her the conjugal rights of a wife." The committee adjourned for an hour while the Campbells met, but not surprisingly Eliza was unmoved by what was effectively another suggestion that she be an unpaid if high status servant. She was "most anxious" to get her children back, but Robert had to "receive her as his wife."

The committee immediately resumed. Eliza's testimony began with a sworn statement, which read in part:

> My husband has continued ever since the Session of 1876, and still continues to refuse to receive me into his home or contribute to my support, or to that of our child who I have with me, whose name is Francis, our youngest child. From the way my husband is living I should think he is able to contribute to my support.... By refusing to maintain me and my child, I mean he has neglected to do so. He has not offered me any support for myself or the child.

Eliza was then examined by O'Doherty, starting with questions about Robert's offer to reconcile:[25]

Q. Was there any offer from your husband to you, lately, to sink past differences and live together again?

A. His offer was that I should go and live with him, but not to forget the past. He offered to take me to Kansas. He said his idea was to go there and look for a home; but his home is in Whitby.

Q. Did you understand that his wish for you was to go with him to Kansas and live with him there as his wife, making that his home?

A. He said he wished me to travel with him and look out for a home; we were to visit different places and decide after that.

Q. Did he not say that he would condone the past?

A. No, I did not understand him to say that he would condone the past. He said that after we had lived together for a time he would think it over, and perhaps then he might. I answered that there was nothing for him to condone.

Q. Did he give you any reason for proposing to go to Kansas?

A. Yes, he said he could not take me to his home in Whitby, as he would feel disgraced by my presence there.

Q. Did you feel that you could confide in his offer or proposition to you?
A. No, I did not.
Q. Why?
A. From his conduct to me in the past.
Q. Did he not tell you that that it was on account of your position with your neighbours, and unpleasantness for the children afterwards residing in the same community?
A. No.
Q. Has he since then made an offer for you to come and live with him?
A. The same proposal made to me before, which was some time in last February, after the commencement of this session started, was renewed to me last Saturday on the same terms, except there was nothing said about Kansas. I was to go and live with him in Whitby, and make myself comfortable if I could. He said he could not withdraw his accusations, but must receive me as a guilty woman.
Q. How many meetings had you had with your husband before coming to Ottawa, that is, in the last six months?
A. Three
Q. Was the proposition to go to Kansas made to you on the17th of January?
A. I think not as early as that.
Q. At those meetings did Mr. Campbell make any other offers to you? Please tell all of them to the Committee.
A. He offered to make over a small portion of his property to trustees for me. The property was a small block of buildings in Whitby, three stores.
Q. What did Mr. Campbell pay for that block?
A. Six or seven years ago he paid four or five thousand dollars for them; but they are not so valuable now. The rent of them may be from two to three hundred dollars a year. They are not in the business part of the town. Two of them are tenanted.
Q. Was it not Mr. Campbell's proposition that the property should be vested in trustees, and that you should receive the income from it, and your children after you?
A. I was to receive the income. I do not remember that anything was said about the children.
Q. Did you not ask him to make an absolute transfer of the property?
A. Yes, I told him that if he would make over the property I would receive it.

Q. His answer?
A. He refused to do so.
Q. Did he say why?
A. He said that if I had the property in my own name I might elope with some one else.
Q. Did he say anything about your squandering it?
A. I think he did.
Q. These offers were made to you for the purposes of settlement, I suppose?
A. Yes
Q. What was that to result in?
A. If I had accepted the property, that would have ended the matter.
Q. Was that what you meant when you said you would take an absolute transfer of it?
A. Yes
Q. Did not Mr. Campbell make you, on Saturday, an unconditional offer to take you back to his house?
A. His conditions to me was that I should return to his house as a guilty woman.
Q. Did he make use of those words?
A. He said he believed his brother's accusations against me, and always would.
Q. Was not the only point of difference between you this: that you required him to state, previously to your going home to him, that he believed you to be an innocent woman?
A. That was the point of difference between us, of course. I claimed to be innocent – he said I was guilty.
Q. Did he not say he would take you back, and not refer to the past?
A. I have no recollection of his saying that.

That completed the examination by O'Doherty. The following day Eliza was back on the stand to be examined by McDougall.[26] He read out the evidence she had given to the divorce committee on 22 March 1876 about Robert's ejection of her from the house in September 1873, and asked her to reaffirm her account, which she did. There followed a few questions from McDougall and two members of the committee about Robert's settlement offers:

Q. by MacDougall: Why did you say yesterday that you could not confide in your husband when he wanted to take you back?
A. Because from his past conduct I could not risk my life with him.
Q. by MacDougall: Was that the reason, or one of the reasons, that you did not accept his proposal?
A. Yes.

Q. by MacDougall: Your husband stated, you say, that he did not wish to take you to Whitby on account of the unpleasantness of a residence there; is it not a fact that you are on friendly terms with all the respectable people of that town, male and female?
A. I enjoy the friendship and sympathy of the community and the respectable people.
Q. by MacDougall: From inquiries you made with regard to the rental of the block of buildings referred to yesterday, what was your conclusion as to the probable amount of that income?
A. About $200 or $300.
Q. by MacDougall: Was that over and above taxes and repairs?
A. No.
Q. by MacDougall: Did your husband require you, out of the rents, to pay insurance, taxes, and repairs?
A. Yes.
Q. by Robert Dickey: Did you or did you not hear your husband say yesterday, that he valued the rental of the property to be conveyed to you at $5,000?
A. Yes; so I understood him.
Q. by Alexander Macfarlane: How have you been supporting yourself?
A. I have had no means of support.
Q. by Alexander Macfarlane: How have you lived?
A. By the kindness of my relatives.

The committee deliberated on 22 April after all the evidence had been given, and the following day, 23 April, Dickey reported its findings to the whole Senate. It found the preamble proved, and presented a bill which was the draft bill authored by McDougall, with three amendments.[27] The first clause stated that Eliza "shall be and shall remain separated from the bed and board of her husband the said Robert Campbell." The second stated that Robert was required to pay Eliza $500 a year. McDougall's draft had said $600, but the committee reduced that to less than the amount the Court of Chancery had required Robert to pay in interim alimony. The third clause gave Eliza custody of Francis William, and the fourth stipulated that Robert was to pay $200 a year for his support and education during his minority.

The other clauses dealt with any future settlement and failures to abide by the terms of the bill. One clause permitted the Campbells to come to a settlement, although any such settlement had to be approved by a superior court judge. A similar clause stated that the bill's provisions would not apply should the parties reconcile. Another made the bill a document that could be registered in any registry office in Ontario, which was permitted by the *Chancery Act* for any alimony order.[28] The most unusual clause drafted by McDougall was one that the committee partially struck out. It initially stated that if there was any default by Robert in making the payments ordered, Eliza could apply to the SCC for an order compelling payment, and if Robert did not comply with that order he was to be guilty of contempt of court. The reason that the SCC was named, according to Dickey, was that a wife could not sue her husband in the Ontario courts. It is not clear why McDougall and Dickey thought Eliza could do better at the SCC, but they obviously thought she could. In the event the committee struck out the part about applying to the SCC but kept in the phrase making a default in payment by Robert contempt of court.

The Divorce Committee Report, Third Reading, and Another Protest

The debate on the committee report and the draft bill in the full Senate took place on 25 April, and began with an objection from Kaulbach.[29] He argued that Robert's offer to settle meant that there was no evidence on which the House could grant relief. Eliza should go back to her husband's house. There was also no evidence of cruelty. Robert had done nothing more than any other man would do if he thought his wife had committed adultery. He had acted in "a prudent, calm, and proper manner in ejecting that woman" from his house, and the courts had sustained his actions. Robert had "made every concession that a man possibly could to this woman" without admitting that she was innocent, and doing that would have been "contrary to his convictions." The House also had no evidence that Robert was able to pay the sum stipulated for Eliza's support. The whole thing was "pernicious in character and tyrannical in effect." He, Kaulbach, had been told that she had spent time in her "private apartments" with Robert, presumably her Ottawa lodgings, walked in the streets with him "leaning on his arm," and everybody assumed that an "amicable understanding" had been arrived at. Yet the House had subjected him to an "unheard of proceeding" without he or any other member not on the committee having seen the evidence, which had been "placed on their desks but a few hours before the meeting of the House." Dickey replied that there was no evidence that Robert would take Eliza back. He quoted extensively from Eliza's testimony to the committee. "It is no wonder under these circumstances," he said, "that they could not live together." The vote was then taken on the motion to receive the report, which prevailed 29–17.[30]

Dickey then moved that the bill be read a third time. This time Alexander Campbell took the lead in denouncing it.[31] He did not intend to make the House divide on third reading. It was pointless because "the majority of the House were evidently determined to pass the Bill, and no useful purpose could be gained by persisting in … opposition." But he had already, "with all the force he possessed," argued against the interference with the common law concerning custody and alimony, and he wanted to make a statement about other issues. The bill "invented a machinery" for the payment of alimony which was "arbitrary and exceptional," a remedy that could not be used against any other person. Payment of debts could only be normally enforced by a court process, which meant execution against a debtor's property. But the bill made non-payment by Robert contempt of court, which carried the penalty of imprisonment, and not paying a debt was not what was normally considered contempt, which meant some form of insult to the court. It was "an unusual and tyrannical provision." Another unique clause was that for registration of the bill in all registry offices. This, according to Campbell, was tantamount to giving a mortgage on all Robert's land anywhere in Ontario to Eliza. Normally a creditor could not "extort a mortgage" from a debtor, could not "take a debtor by the throat, and say you must give me a mortgage." These two clauses should certainly not be in the bill. They were a "complete departure" from the principle that the same law applied to all.

Dickey responded to both the mortgage and contempt of court arguments. While the clause might "amount to a mortgage," the fact was that the alimony payment had to be secured somehow. If the registration and contempt of court clauses were not included, a man who felt the way that Robert did about his wife would soon divest himself of his land and not pay support. On the contempt clause Dickey turned Campbell's unique remedy complaint around and asked rhetorically why Robert alone should be "above the courts of the country, and above the jurisdiction of Parliament." Reesor intervened to point out that Robert was likely to refuse to pay, giving as an example of his attitude his failure to pay McDougall's costs despite agreeing to do so in 1876. Reesor also asserted that Robert had been heard to say that "he would not pay the money … he would appeal it from court to court, until he had tired her out so that she should not be able to get the money." The debate ended when Dickey moved that the bill be given third reading the following day, which was agreed to "on a division."[32]

The third reading debate involved largely familiar arguments and familiar speakers. It also involved more rancour and personal attacks than earlier debates in 1879, and was therefore somewhat reminiscent of 1877. The first speaker was a very new senator, William Johnston Almon, appointed in 1879 and only introduced a week before. He made sure the debate started in a fractious mode by attacking Eliza. A leading Nova Scotia physician, Almon had been both an opponent of Confederation and a supporter of the southern states Confederacy, a cause to which he contributed a large sum of money. Despite his opposition to Confederation, he won one of the Halifax seats for the Conservatives in the 1872 federal election. He did not offer again in 1874 but was appointed to the Senate after MacDonald had returned to power in the 1878 election. He was very opinionated, and on this occasion forthright in his belief, having read the evidence from 1876, that "a clearer case of adultery had never been proved." It was a "crime" usually perpetrated in secret, but on this occasion there had been two witnesses. Now the Senate was being asked to pass a bill that ensured that "this man should never have a happy moment in his life again."

Carrall interrupted Almon with "I hope he will not," but Almon was not deterred. Eliza had "brought disgrace upon" Robert and his children, and now was given custody when she was not a proper person to raise a child. Not entirely logically Almon also complained that it was wrong for Robert to have to support a child that he had reason to doubt was his. Sir Frank Smith of Ontario interrupted, pointing out that Robert acknowledged paternity. This was the only comment by Smith, an extremely wealthy businessman and a leading Irish Catholic. He consistently voted for the bill, making him one of what can be termed the "silent majority," senators who did not speak but who consistently voted for Eliza's bill. Almon ignored his interruption, stating that he did not care that a good number of people believed Eliza innocent. He made a rather wild analogy to Queen Caroline, the wife of George IV, saying that Eliza, like her, was also guilty even if the mob said she was not.[33]

Eliza's most impassioned champion, Robert Carrall, who as we saw earlier was in the last months of his life, weighed in to criticize Almon and castigate Robert, keeping the temperature of debate high. He had known his fellow physician for a long time, and had respect for the new senator, but his speech on this occasion, his first, had "materially disappointed his expectations." The "old" members of the House knew more about the case than "a senator of yesterday's creation." It was presumptuous of Almon. William John Macdonald of British Columbia, a former mayor of Victoria, a Conservative, and one of the first three British Columbia senators appointed in 1871, interrupted Carrall by saying that Almon had read the evidence, to which Carrall retorted that "the evidence amounted to nothing except to show that the Senate ought, if it had the power, to have incarcerated the people who gave it." He believed that Eliza was innocent, and that her husband was a "brute." He had "treated her as only a brute would do – as no carter on the cab stand would treat his horse."[34]

Almon's colleague from Halifax, Lawrence Power, defended Almon, and not for the first time denigrated his senatorial colleagues by saying that Almon had as much ability to form an opinion as Carrall and that he did not believe that "a long experience in the high moral atmosphere of the Senate improved a man's capacity for forming a correct judgment in such matters." On the substantive issue, the bill showed that if a lady wanted to get rid of her husband, and yet be "comfortably provided for at his expense," all she had to do if she did not want to commit adultery was to act in "an exceedingly indiscreet and imprudent manner." Then, when her husband rightly cut her off, she could come to the Senate and get a bill compelling her husband to support her.[35]

There followed a heated argument among Kaulbach, Carrall, and Haviland. Kaulbach indulged in a wide-ranging denunciation of almost everybody for everything, going back to 1876. He criticized most of his senatorial colleagues for not having read the evidence, Reesor for putting people hostile to Robert on the original divorce committee, and the members of the 1879 committee for awarding Eliza $500 a year when there was evidence that she was willing to accept $300. All this brought strong rejoinders from Haviland and Carrall. The former said that it was a breach of privilege to say that any committee was packed, and Kaulbach should be censured. Carrall said that Kaulbach "had furnished an additional proof of the brutality of this thing Campbell, when he had dared to approach an hon senator and ask to be allowed to choose his jury – a jury that would be partial to his side in the case." Other senators joined the critique of Kaulbach over his attacks on the integrity of the process, but he would not back down. At one point Speaker Robert Wilmot ruled him out of order. but it made no difference. Even Alexander Campbell said that Kaulbach was out of order and should be prepared to accept that senators had done their duty and made up their minds on the evidence.[36]

For some reason, perhaps simple exhaustion, the chamber seemed to calm down, and only one further speech was made, by Alexander Vidal, giving a long summary of all the substantive issues discussed on and off since 1876. He had hoped that the "unanswerable" arguments made against the bill would have had an effect. He might not be entirely free from that "natural feeling" that every senator had for the weaker party, but he did not know either of the parties and looked only to deal with this case with the impartiality of a judge. The issue was the constitution. Divorce in the *BNA Act* means the end of the marriage tie, with the right to remarry. It did not mean separation from bed and board, or the granting of alimony, and that is what the SCC would say. It was regrettable that the House had not referred the bill there. Vidal also objected to particular provisions of the bill, especially those relating to "putting our hand ... into the pockets of an individual, by compelling him to pay a certain sum of money or be committed to prison – authorizing, in fact, imprisonment for debt."[37]

The vote was taken right after Vidal's speech and the bill passed 34–26.[38] It was not exactly the large majority that the *Whitby Chronicle* predicted, but it was not a close-run thing.[39] The result was very nearly the same as in 1877. Twenty-seven of those voting in favour had done so in 1877. Of the other seven in favour, two, Alexander Macfarlane and William Odell of New Brunswick, changed their votes from 1877, and two others, Brouse and Bull of Ontario, had not been senators in 1877. The other three in favour had not voted in 1877. Eighteen of those voting against the bill had done so in 1877. One, Almon, had not been a senator in 1877, and one changed his vote, William Henry Chaffers, an anglophone Quebec Liberal. The other six who voted against had not voted in 1877. As in 1877, there was a marked regional difference between the two sides. Sixteen Ontario senators supported the bill, only three from Quebec, all protestant anglophones. In 1877 the numbers had been 12 and seven. Conversely, voting against the bill were 11 Quebec senators and only six from Ontario. Thus the collective profile of senators for and against had not changed. As in 1877 more Catholics and lawyers voted against the bill than for it. Thus we can conclude that the legal arguments were persuasive to the legally trained and to Quebec senators, who were most concerned about property and civil rights in this case because the 92 (13) rights at stake were integral parts of that province's distinctive Civil Code.

Immediately after the bill passed 24 of the 26 senators who had voted against it entered another "dissentient."[40] Eleven of the 24 Quebec senators signed it, as did six from Ontario, four from Nova Scotia, and one each from New Brunswick, Manitoba, and British Columbia. The separation bill was halfway home. The hurdle on which it had fallen in 1877, the House of Commons, was still before it.

The House of Commons

The MPs who dealt with the Campbell separation bill in 1879 did so for effectively the first time, the Commons having quickly dispatched the 1877 bill. Perhaps for this reason it passed the Commons with much less trouble and rancour than there had been in the Senate. The Campbell case was of course known about in Ottawa, and both sides worked to prepare the ground. McDougall was now an MP, and between the separation bill passing the Senate and its being debated in the Commons he rushed into print the pamphlet reproducing his 1876 speech to the divorce committee and distributed it to all MPs and the newspapers.[41] The speech had been published in the *Whitby Chronicle* in 1876, but now he wanted a much wider audience. McDougall added a short introduction, an emotional appeal for Eliza coupled with a manifesto on behalf of all women ill-treated by unmanly husbands:

> The resistance of an intelligent, brave, and virtuous woman – as all those best qualified to judge believe her to be – against the persecution and ill-treatment of a coarse, ill-natured, penurious, and unprincipled husband, has made the CAMPBELL DIVORCE CASE not only a *cause célèbre*, but has conclusively established the fact that in Ontario, as the law now stands, a married woman has few rights which a husband is bound to respect. If a husband wishes to put away his wife, he need only provide himself with two witnesses to watch at her window when some neighbour is paying her a visit, to report a conversation implying criminal intercourse, … and he may then kick her into the street and leave her there to starve.

Such a husband could then take his fabricated case to Parliament and secure a divorce. Robert had only been thwarted in his evil designs by "a woman of spirit" who was supported by reputable neighbours and who "resolved that in defence of her honour and the reputation of her children she would follow him to Parliament." It had been a "prolonged … desperate struggle," but she had been finally vindicated by the Senate. She could only now be deprived of her rights if Canadian justice was "reserved for men and denied to women." Surely the MPs would not want that to be said of them?[42]

Although a Brantford, Ontario, newspaper reported that Robert had tried again to settle with Eliza after the Senate passed the bill, without success, that was likely not true.[43] If it had been true it would surely have been more widely reported. In fact Robert had done his own lobbying throughout the 1879 session. As soon as Eliza's petition had been presented to the Commons, he wrote to John A. Macdonald to demand that he oppose the bill in both Houses and also sent the judgments in the crim. con. and alimony cases to the clerk of the Commons. He told Macdonald that Eliza's petition was "vexatious" and lamented that it was "too bad that a man situated as I am has to spend the savings of years of toil to get redress."[44] There is no reply from Macdonald on record. Robert also circulated a paper to senators and MPs stating the familiar argument that the proceedings were an attack on the Ontario courts by making Parliament a Court of Appeal from Chancery. He either included in his circular, or distributed in another one, copies of the "jottings" found in Eliza's secretaire in 1873, which were described by McDougall as "ingeniously patched together and made to appear as if they were the actual letters written to her paramour."[45] It is more than possible that McDougall decided to produce and distribute the pamphlet containing his 1876 speech to the divorce committee in response – or vice versa. Robert's machinations did not endear him to the *Ottawa Citizen*, which expressed the hope that "this matter which has now occupied too much attention, will be set at rest and a very ordinary and tardy act of justice done."[46]

The separation bill was formally recorded as having been received by the Commons in the evening session on Monday 28 April, in the limited time set aside for private bills, one hour twice a week. It was immediately read for the first time; as in the Senate first reading was purely formal with no debate.[47] The bill came up again four days later, on Friday 2 May, again in the part of the evening session reserved for private bills.[48] McDougall made a long speech on this occasion. He was the only speaker, and he took up all the time allotted to private bills with what the *Ottawa Citizen* described as a "clear, able speech."[49] His arguments, and those of other MPs who spoke on subsequent days, were very much a repeat of what had been said in the Senate in 1877 and 1879, and thus they are not dealt with in detail here. They were listened to attentively by both parties. Robert sat in the public gallery, "for the purpose of watching [over] his interests," and Eliza was also present, sitting in the ladies' gallery.[50]

McDougall began with a recitation of proceedings since the marriage breakdown, like many politicians gilding the lily and exercising his best rhetorical flourishes. The divorce committee's decision on Robert's petition was "almost ... unanimous" that Robert had "utterly failed to make out his charge against his wife." In September 1873 he had tried to "starve" Eliza out of the family home, and when that failed, he "violently" took her from her bed and "threw her out on the veranda in a cruel, heartless, brutal manner." The relief she requested from Parliament was "the ordinary relief given in all civilized countries under such circumstances." The Senate had passed the 1877 bill by "a decisive vote," but it failed in the Commons because of a "technical objection." He hoped that the "new and ... juster Parliament" elected in the 1878 general election would treat her better this time. The Senate had passed the bill, by a narrower margin than it merited, because several senators who were on Eliza's side "on the merits of her case" were persuaded by the constitutional arguments to vote against her. He needed to make it clear that the bill was not for a divorce *a vinculo*, which he knew many people objected to; thus it was "not objectionable on the religious or moral grounds so often urged against divorce bills." It was simply separation, the kind of divorce that was available under the Civil Code of Lower Canada. Thus he wanted Eliza to get what she would have been entitled to in Quebec and in England, a separation. Such a separation was available to women in "the circumstances proved in evidence" in "all civilized countries."[51] A reporter for the *Montreal Daily Witness* astutely noted that McDougall had laid particular stress on the fact that Eliza was "merely" asking for a separation, so as to 'quiet the apprehension of members opposed to divorce bills [on] principle".[52]

With that McDougall moved to those who said that it was a parliamentary overruling of the Court of Chancery. He asserted that " [t]here has been no decision in any Court which legally convicted Mrs. Campbell of the crime of adultery." His justification for saying this was Spragge's statement in the dower case, which he read out, that "there is not legal evidence of the fact of adultery by the wife." McDougall was playing games with the word "legal." Spragge had used those words but meant only that adultery was not mentioned in Blake's formal judgment. McDougall was careful to quote Spragge's exact words, and hoped that as a result "he would not again hear the statement in Parliament that, by doing justice to Mrs. Campbell, we were reversing the decision of a Court." McDougall also cited Spragge to support the idea that "marriage and divorce" included both types of "divorce," by repeating his statement in the dower case that it would be "unseemly" for him to comment on that issue and rhetorically asked "[w]hy "unseemly" if Parliament had, in the opinion of the learned judge, no jurisdiction in the case." This was a misleading argument. Spragge had simply meant that as a judge it was "unseemly" for him to comment on a matter that was political and controversial; his use of that word did not suggest that Spragge himself had any opinion on the question. From this red herring, McDougall asserted that it was "perfectly clear" that "the whole subject of marriage and divorce" was within Dominion jurisdiction. To refuse Eliza would be to "to ignore right and deny justice."[53]

McDougall then turned to Robert, who had come to Ottawa and offered to be reconciled to Eliza on conditions she could not accept. He wanted her to be "a sort of upper servant, to look after his table and his children." She naturally declined. McDougall also castigated Robert for not caring about the effect of the case on his children. If he had cared about them it would be "greatly to [their] advantage" to have Parliament's verdict in their mother's favour, to have it "recorded on the Statute book of their country" that the adultery accusation was false. It would be better for the children to be able to say, "Our father was mistaken; he was under a delusion; he was the victim of a conspiracy." Eliza, said MacDougall, "spoke as a wise and prudent and loving mother" would "instinctively" do in such a case. But what did Robert do? Eliza's "unreasoning and vindictive" husband refused, and "gave the lie to his proposal" by distributing to MPs the circular containing copies of what he claimed were the letters found in her secretaire. In fact the jottings were extracts, "harmless and unmeaning as such," copied from books. She was "addicted to literature," which "proved an unfortunate pastime in her case." McDougall had found the books in the library. He was sorry to say that "even a learned Judge drew the illogical inference that, because a letter, expressed in familiar and affectionate terms, was found in her desk addressed to one party, therefore she ought to be found guilty of adultery with another party."[54] McDougall's "scathing description of the husband's conduct" brought a "a loud cheer" from MPs. Eliza, also present, watched what one reporter described as "the most painful inflictions on Robert."[55]

At that McDougall moved second reading, and the bill was referred to the Select Standing Committee on Miscellaneous Private Bills, of which McDougall was a member.[56] The Commons *Journals* did not report committee meetings, but journalists could attend and a number did so. Robert appeared without counsel and tried to head off the proceedings by offering to take Eliza back and support her. This was too little too late, and was probably seen as insincere by MPs who had read or heard about his reconciliation offer when the bill was before the Senate divorce committee. He received a "very indifferent hearing," including from the Quebec MPs who were partial to Eliza and generally in favour of giving her what she would have received from the Quebec Superior Court. The committee "reported" the bill, advanced it in the parliamentary process, by a margin of 25 votes to 9.[57] Five days later McDougall moved third reading of the bill.[58]

McDougall's motion for third reading precipitated an inconclusive debate of one hour, curtailed by the time limitation for private bills. There were only three speakers in addition to MacDougall in the time available, and they all opposed the bill: Prime Minister Macdonald; David Mills, a leading lawyer, constitutional theorist and former minister of the interior under Alexander Mackenzie; and James McDonald of Pictou, Nova Scotia, a Halifax lawyer and minister of justice in Macdonald's cabinet who later became a judge of the Nova Scotia Supreme Court.[59] Mills was the first speaker, and opposed the Bill on jurisdictional grounds. Parliament had jurisdiction over divorce, and divorce clearly meant only divorce *a vinculo*. English law recognized both kinds of "divorce," but instructions to colonial governors, which said that divorce bills had to be reserved for London's approval, never referred to bills of separation. Separation therefore meant something quite different to divorce. The drafters of the *BNA Act* knew the rule of statutory construction that when a general power was conferred, and express exceptions made to it, those exceptions had to be strictly construed. Thus when the provinces were given a general power over property and civil rights that would have included marital relations, and marriage and divorce were "expressly carved out" of the general power, divorce meant only the end of the marriage, not separation. Even without strict construction it was "perfectly obvious" that the word "divorce" in section 91 "had not the slightest reference to the subject of divorce from bed and board." In addition, McDougall's argument about a lack of a court to decree separation made no sense. There was no need for a court to decree separation. Separation "was a simple matter of fact." When it happened all the courts had to do was decide if it was a case for alimony. Eliza had already gone to court for alimony, the court had said no, and McDougall was now appealing from Chancery to Parliament. Parliament had no jurisdiction over alimony. If it did it could deal with dower and married women's property, with a wife's right to contract separate from her husband, and with custody and guardianship. In short, "the whole subject of property and civil rights within the limits of the domestic relations would be usurped." Mills ended his speech by moving the six-months' hoist.[60]

James McDonald spoke next, giving a long and repetitive speech, which added little of substance to the debate. The essential issue was the constitution, and it would be "something to be deplored if, from any sentiment of sympathy," Parliament "should be led beyond its domain." He agreed with Mills that divorce meant ending the marriage tie, and the matters dealt with in the separation bill were therefore *ultra vires* Parliament's jurisdiction. McDougall gave a much shorter speech than McDonald, one that lightly brushed over the legal questions by asserting that the Senate had found in favour of the bill and the Commons should respect that. He was principally intent on arguing that Eliza had a compelling case. The evidence in her favour was "abundant," and she was the victim of a conspiracy by witnesses who had lied. The debate ended with the Prime Minister, a very short speech of only three sentences, in which he said that the hour allotted to private bills having expired, the matter should stand over as public business could not be he held up over one case. His "very strong" opinion was that his minister of justice was right, and he would take another opportunity to express his views at "some length."[61] The Commons then took up the latest report from the Committee of Supply.

Four days later, on the evening of Tuesday 13 May, the debate was resumed. Twelve people spoke, including the four who had spoken previously. Of the eight others five were in favour of the bill: lawyer Hector Cameron of British Columbia; Désiré Girouard, also a lawyer, of Quebec; and James McCuaig, Duncan McMillan, and Samuel Lane of Ontario. Three spoke against the bill, all Quebeckers: Joseph Mousseau, Michel Coursol, and Felix Geoffrion. John A. Macdonald began the debate, his speech being a relatively rare opportunity for us to read the approach to the division of powers of the man long associated with a centralist vision of the *BNA Act* when the issue he was dealing with was one that he firmly believed belonged in section 92.[62] The bill was *ultra vires*. The line between federal and provincial powers was easily marked, and there could be "little or no hesitation" in deciding where it was to be drawn here. Section 91 gave the Dominion jurisdiction over the "formation and dissolution of the marriage tie," and over no other related issues. A separation did not involve breaking the marriage tie. The *BNA Act* assigned issues relating to people who were husband and wife to the provinces, pursuant to the property and civil rights power. Macdonald also insisted that it was "exceedingly inexpedient to mingle ... the judicial and legislative power."

McDougall responded with a familiar argument: There were two different kinds of divorce.[63] But rather than detail the constitutional arguments, as he had done earlier, he asked for "justice" over law. The Senate should be deferred to and Eliza, the victim of a conspiracy, deserved justice. "[A] large committee of able and experienced men in the Senate, some of whom were lawyers, and one or two of them very distinguished lawyers," had heard the evidence and decided in Eliza's favour. In the circumstances "it was not too much to expect that Parliament should exercise its power and do justice." McDougall was supported by Hector Cameron, a Conservative lawyer who represented North Victoria, B.C., and briefly stated that "after much consideration" he thought that Parliament had jurisdiction. Chancery could award alimony, but "it could not grant those separate rights, such as were obtained by a woman who had been granted judicial separation, and the Local Legislature could not do so without interference with the subject of marriage and divorce."[64]

Constitutional theorist and provincial rights advocate David Mills rose to move the six-months hoist in a long speech against the bill.[65] For constitutional historians there is an irony in seeing the intellectual guru in Ontario Premier Oliver Mowat's long campaign for provincial rights and Macdonald, the arch advocate of a strong central government, on the same side of an issue.[66] Mills's biographer has dubbed him "one of the ablest constitutional theorists of his generation." On this occasion he repeated at greater length his arguments on the meaning of divorce in English law and British colonial policy on divorce in the empire. He also took the provincialist position that property and civil rights had a broad scope, and that while "marriage and divorce" had been "carved out" of civil rights, the phrase must be interpreted narrowly to allow section 92 (13) to "operate to its full extent." Mills attacked McDougall as someone who was sincere but whose legal opinions had been "largely" influenced by having been Eliza's counsel; we "all know to what an extent ... relation to the party interested biased one's judgment."

Mills was followed by Quebec lawyer Désiré Girouard, a Conservative who, perhaps surprisingly, supported the bill.[67] His views were surprising because he was from Quebec, and one of only five Quebec MPs who supported the bill while 17 did not. Girouard was a lawyer, and his party leader, Macdonald, was firmly against the bill. His stance on this occasion did his career no harm; in 1895 he became a judge of the Supreme Court of Canada. He had a reputation as a leading lawyer and for independence of thought on legal and political questions, which he certainly displayed on this occasion. For Girouard the question of jurisdiction was "a nice point," not entirely clear. But he was persuaded that Eliza had a deserving case, and as there was no court in Ontario that could grant relief, it was the duty of Parliament to come to her aid. If this was a divorce bill he would vote against it as a Catholic. But it was not a divorce bill, just one for separation, and "[h]e considered they were here performing the duties of a Judge of the Superior Court of Quebec in a case of *separation de corps et des biens*, and this Parliament was the only tribunal that could grant such relief to parties living in Ontario." Echoing the views of some senators, he expressed strong sympathy for Eliza, who had been subjected to "the grossest insult that could be addressed to any woman, and especially to a lady of fine feelings," and castigated Robert for that and for not providing for his wife.

No such chivalric sentiments were exhibited by another Quebec MP, Joseph-Alfred Mousseau, a Conservative and a lawyer who had practised both civil and criminal law for 20 years with the firm of Mousseau, Chapleau, et Archambault. He was only 40 years old and saw himself as part of the next generation of Quebec leaders and perhaps as a result began his speech by deprecating "those old and venerable gentlemen" in the Senate.[68] Eliza had failed to get alimony in court, and she wanted to persuade Parliament to reverse Blake's judgment. He had listened with "much pleasure" to what Macdonald, one of the fathers of Confederation and "one of the masters of constitutional law," had said. McDougall had not "dare[d] enter into the merits of the question" in his response. The word "divorce" in the *BNA Act* clearly referred only to the marriage tie, and to take a different view would leave to the "absurd" result that property and civil rights would be greatly reduced in scope.

Five more short speeches were made, none contributing new arguments.[69] At this point, with the time for private bills expired and it being 12:15 a.m. on 14 May, an amendment was moved that the amounts Robert had to pay be reduced from $500 a year to $300 for Eliza, and from $200 a year to $100 for six-year-old Francis. The motion was defeated, although the record does not say by what margin. The vote was then taken on Mills's amendment to give the bill the three- or six-month's hoist, which was defeated 56–38.[70] The bill then passed third reading, "on the same division reversed," the announcement of the vote being loudly applauded by many MPs. It was then returned to the Senate, with amendments, for its concurrence. The Senate concurred without making any further amendments. The bill received royal assent a day later. It was the first "divorce" bill not to be reserved by the governor-general for London's approval, that requirement having been ended with the appointment of a new governor-general, the Marquis of Lorne, in 1878.[71]

The 94 MPs voting on the bill was less than half of the total of 206 MPs, a comparatively smaller proportion of the members who attended the various debates in the Senate. The vote was essentially a contest between Ontario and Quebec MPs. Three-quarters of the Ontario MPs voted in favour (44 of 59), while 86 per cent of the Quebec MPs voted against (17 of 21). Only 14 of the MPs from the other five provinces voted, and they split 8–6 in favour of the bill. The bill succeeded because fully a half of the Ontario MPs turned out to vote in favour (44 of 88), while only a quarter of the Quebec MPs (17 of 65) turned out to vote against.

The Separation Act of 1879

In many respects the 1879 Act, appendix 3, was very similar to the bills that passed the Senate in 1877 and 1879. All the Acts decreed that the parties were separated from bed and board, provided for the payment of alimony and child support, gave Eliza custody to some of the children, albeit two in 1877 and just one in 1879, and prescribed penalties for any shortfall by Robert. But two aspects of the bills were very different between 1877 and the final 1879 version. The earlier versions, including the 1879 Senate bill, were titled "An Act for the Relief of Robert Campbell and Eliza Maria Campbell." That title was initially used because retaining Robert's name was necessary given the fiction that Eliza had only petitioned for amendments to Robert's bill of 1876. I have no explanation for its continued use in 1879, when the bill was one requested by Eliza alone. Perhaps the parliamentary clerks thought that a separation Act was truly for the "relief" of both parties in the way that an Act ending the marriage tie was not. But if that is true one is left asking why the Commons changed the name to "An Act for the Relief of Eliza Maria Campbell." The name change is never mentioned in the records.

A more important change, and one somewhat contradictory to the name change, was made in the Commons to the preamble. The final version of the preamble was much longer than any previous versions, all of which told only one side of the story. The 1879 Act told both versions before finally getting to the operative provisions. As a result it was very nearly three full pages in the statute book. It began with the marriage, then moved to the adultery accusation and the crim. con. and alimony cases, and then stated that as a result Robert "was desirous of having the ... marriage dissolved." All other divorce Acts continued by shortly stating that the preamble had been proved and the marriage dissolved. In contrast the Campbell Act preamble shifted to another version of the story, beginning with the marriage and moving through Robert's desertion, his ejection of Eliza from the house, his failure to support her, his attempts to prove the adultery, and his other acts of cruelty. Two crucial sentences then followed:

> And whereas the evidence produced by the said Robert Campbell did not prove that his wife, the said Eliza Maria Campbell, had ever committed adultery with the said George Gordon, or with any other person; and whereas the evidence produced ... proved that the said Robert Campbell had treated his wife, the said Eliza Maria Campbell, with cruelty; that he deserted her on [25 August 1873] ... ; that he had not since lived or cohabited with her; that he had not made any provision for her support and maintenance and for the support and maintenance of their youngest child.

The next part detailed the legislative history of the bill, including the failure for lack of notice in the Commons in 1877, before finally moving to the operative provisions. There is no record of why the Act included all this detail, but it was in fact an accurate account of a long, drawn-out parliamentary battle.

The Campbell separation Act was unique, the only separation Act passed by Parliament in the century between 1867 and the ending of the last vestiges of Parliament's jurisdiction over divorce in 1968. Contemporary commentators quickly came to the same conclusion as the Act's opponents, that Parliament had exceeded its jurisdiction in passing the Act. The leading scholar of Parliament's jurisdiction and procedure, John George Bourinot, stated in 1892 that the Act, which his father had voted for as a Nova Scotia senator, was *ultra vires*, "a precedent doubtful in its character and not likely to be cited as authoritative in the future." Bourinot knew why it had been passed – the case evoked "much sympathy" for Eliza.[72] Bourinot was correct that the Act would not be a precedent, but it was not forgotten while Canada still had parliamentary divorce for some provinces. It was referred to as an *ultra vires* statute in two early twentieth-century textbooks on divorce, and came up in the parliamentary debates of the 1920s over whether divorce jurisdiction should be given to the Ontario courts. One of the arguments deployed by those in favour of doing so was that a divorce court could deal with alimony and child custody, matters corollary to divorce, while Parliament could not. When the question of Parliament's jurisdiction came up, some members were well aware that it had only ever passed one separation Act, in the Campbell case. Minister of Justice Ernest Lapointe had had his staff research the case, and he quoted the views of John A Macdonald and David Mills noted here.[73]

Robert Campbell's Last Stand: Disallowance

Robert did not give up even when the bill passed the Commons. His final move was to try to have the Act disallowed by the London government even though it had not been routinely reserved.[74] He petitioned the crown sometime in early June 1879, sending along all the evidence. In response the secretary of state for the colonies, Sir Michael Hicks-Beach, asked Ottawa for information to justify his decision to advise against interfering. He assumed that Parliament was "satisfied that there are good reasons, either in the conduct of Robert Campbell, or otherwise," for granting Eliza alimony, even though she had been "convicted" of adultery. Obviously at that stage London only had Robert's one-sided account to go on. Cabinet referred the matter to Alexander Campbell, the government leader in the Senate.

Campbell's report briefly reviewed the history of the Act. He then said that had the royal instructions been the same as they were before the appointment of the current Governor-General the Marquis of Lorne in 1878, the bill would have been reserved for London's opinion, and the law officers of the crown would have had the opportunity to give an opinion on the evidence and the constitutionality of the legislation. Under the new royal instructions that did not happen. Campbell had opposed the bill, but he was not going to recommend that London should disallow a piece of Canadian legislation. Yet he left the door open to London to do that. He simply noted, without comment, the constitutional argument, the fact that the Act overturned a decision of Chancery, and the senators' dissent in which the arguments against the bill were "fully stated." He even indicated his agreement with those reasons; there was no doubt that alimony and custody were subjects of provincial jurisdiction, and that the alimony issue had been decided by Chancery. But he made no recommendation: "It must rest with Her Majesty's government to determine the course to be pursued under the powers expressly reserved to the Crown by the Canadian constitution." The cabinet approved Campbell's report and forwarded it to Hicks-Beach. The colonial secretary tersely ducked the issue, noting that "I have not seen any sufficient reason for advising Her Majesty to exercise the power of disallowance with regard to this Act."

15
The Principals after 1880 – Winners and Losers

William McDougall, George Gordon, and James Campbell

This chapter is principally about the lives of Robert and Eliza after their epic parliamentary battle. But I begin with the other leading characters in the story. William McDougall's successful advocacy of Eliza's cause gave impetus to his legal career, which had been only a footnote to his life before 1876.[1] In 1880 he moved to Ottawa and acted in a number of high-profile cases, including the well-known Andrew Mercer estate litigation, in which he represented Andrew F. Mercer, very likely the illegitimate son of the wealthy Andrew Mercer who died intestate.[2] As one contemporary put it, "No one can read his argument before the Supreme Court in [*Mercer*] … without regretting that he did not earlier apply himself to the legal profession."[3] To this encomium we might add his speech to the divorce committee in the Campbell case. McDougall was created a Queen's Counsel in 1881, the year he declined a judgeship and the lieutenant-governorship of British Columbia. He should have taken one of those posts when he had the chance, because his political career and personal life did not go so well thereafter. He switched his support from the Conservatives to the Liberals because he was disappointed at not being taken into the cabinet when Macdonald returned to power after the 1878 general election but was not re-elected to the Commons in the 1882 election or when he tried again in 1887. In 1890 he seriously injured his spine when he stepped from a moving train at Cobourg. He disappeared from public life thereafter but lived another 15 years. He died in 1905 at the age of 83, after a "long and trying illness" and left virtually no estate for his family.

We saw earlier that by the time that the Senate divorce committee hearing was underway George Gordon had left for Manitoba. He had still been in Whitby in late 1875 when he was charged with assaulting a servant girl who worked for his father. The case was dropped when the complainant failed to appear, and soon afterwards Gordon joined many other Ontarians in moving west, probably, given his farming background, to take up land under the *Dominion Lands Act*'s homesteading provisions. The 1881 federal census lists him as a farmer living in Marquette in the inter-lake region, some 40 kilometres west and a little north of Winnipeg. In 1881 he married his cousin Jane Brand, daughter of James Bell Brand, the brother of his mother Christine Gordon, née Brand. Jane Brand was five years George's junior and had lived and worked as a governess in the United Kingdom in the 1870s before emigrating, which she did around 1879. George and Jane Gordon had two daughters, Alice and Vera. At some point before 1901 the Gordon family moved to Lisgar, Manitoba, and at some time after that to British Columbia. George Gordon died in Nanaimo in 1919, aged 78. He suffered no long-term adverse effects from being part of the Campbell family scandal of the 1870s.[4]

James Campbell seems similarly to have overcome being branded by some as a perjurer. He stayed in Whitby until 1895. One might have expected him to have been something of a pariah in a community that did not believe that Eliza had committed adultery, for people would therefore have concluded that he and John Anderson had fabricated their stories, and perjured themselves in three court hearings and before the Senate divorce committee. Initially James Campbell may indeed have been not well regarded. He ran for election as reeve of Whitby in 1880, but was challenged by one Charles King, whose candidacy the *Whitby Chronicle* championed, stating that James Campbell had left "no stone unturned and no means unresorted to to secure his" election. The ratepayers "would grievously wrong themselves and perhaps do Whitby lasting harm" were they to choose "such a man as Mr. Campbell," who was supported only by people who were actually laughing at him and/or were "discontented malcontents"; his "begging and praying and entreating of votes" would cause him to lose. He did lose quite handily, which the *Chronicle* saw as the triumph of "merit and intelligence" over "brag and bluster." Perhaps not coincidentally the vacant position of deputy reeve was filled by Yeoman Gibson.[5]

Yet something changed in the community's attitude in the following year, and in 1881 he was elected reeve. He stayed in Whitby until 1895, prospered, and became a much-respected member of the community. After a hiatus in the early 1880s, advertisements for "R & J Campbell" appeared again in the *Whitby Chronicle* in mid-1883, and continued to run in the mid- to late 1880s, even though, as discussed below, Robert left Whitby in 1885 leaving James to run the business alone.[6] He stayed in Whitby until 1895, a prominent and active member of the community. He made summer visits to the United Kingdom to buy stock, served two terms as mayor of Whitby, and was sufficiently well known to have his out-of-town trips to attend the funerals of relatives noticed in the press. His term as mayor elicited fulsome praise from the *Chronicle*, by then run by Higgins's successsor; he was "the best man in what we believe to have been the best council for years."[7] He retired in 1895 and moved with his family to Chicago. Like Robert, therefore, the great Campbell divorce saga did nothing to damage his social or economic standing in the long term. He died in Chicago on 15 June 1921, aged 82, and his body was returned to Ontario county for burial in the Union Cemetery, Oshawa. His wife, Rebecca née Tweedie, also died in Chicago, on 4 November 1925, and was also buried in Union Cemetery, Oshawa.[8]

Robert Campbell and the Campbell Children

Although there was a rumour in 1880 that Robert intended to renew his application to Parliament for a divorce, he never did so. He was apparently advised by "influential senators" not to try again because he would fail.[9] More importantly, he had already decided, very soon after Eliza's separation Act had become law, to seek another way to rid himself of her – the American legal system. He was divorced by an order of the Lancaster County Court, Lincoln, Nebraska, on 19 March 1880.[10] Nebraska had only entered the Union a decade before, in 1869, and Robert settled in the state capital, Lincoln, a city of just 13,000. Robert spent the second half of 1879 there, satisfying the six-months' residency required to file for divorce, and on 5 January 1880, his local lawyer, Lionel C. Burr, filed a petition with the Lancaster County district court to dissolve his marriage with Eliza. He alleged adultery by Eliza, one of a number of grounds for divorce under Nebraska law, as well as "extreme cruelty," a ground for either divorce or separation from bed and board.[11] His petition recounted the familiar story of Eliza's alleged adultery with Gordon and was followed in early March by a reply from Eliza in response to her being served in Whitby. She told the story of Robert's desertion of her in August 1873, her ejection from the family home, his failure to get a divorce from Parliament, and her own separation Act. Thus she was able to bring to the attention of the court a formal finding that she had not committed adultery, and that Robert was guilty of cruelty and desertion. She also swore that Robert had paid her nothing under the Act yet was worth over $100,000, and demanded that the Nebraska court not grant the divorce without also requiring Robert to pay her support.

There is no way of knowing if Robert expected Eliza to contest the divorce, but when she did he had to gather his own evidence, in the form of affidavits from James Campbell and John Anderson taken in Whitby in March. A week after the evidence was taken Robert filed his response to Eliza's reply. It reiterated his accusation of adultery with Gordon and also stated that her letters to Parks showed that she had also been intimate with him. Thus, he insisted, he had the right to remove her from his house, which he had done with minimal force. He detailed the crim. con. and alimony cases and their verdicts but did not mention the defamation action. He had gone to the Senate "fortified" by Blake's judgment, but that body had denied his petition and passed the separation Act after a long process, one that cost him over $10,000. At that point, "exhausted in mind and means [he] became thoroughly disgusted with the laws of such a country"; he renounced his allegiance, a purely symbolic gesture given that it was impossible to do so without having first acquired citizenship in another state, for one would otherwise be stateless.[12] He insisted that the parliamentary proceedings were not a bar to another petition to Parliament for divorce or to his application to the Nebraska court.

The court appointed a referee, one R.D. Steares, who held a hearing in his office on 17 March, the same day that Robert filed his reply. Robert attended with Burr; Eliza did not attend but was represented by two local lawyers. Steares was charged with "find[ing] issues of law and fact," but could not have done anything more than review Eliza's and Robert's statements and the affidavit evidence from James Campbell and John Anderson, for he submitted his report to the court the next day, 18 March. In three short paragraphs he stated that Eliza had committed adultery, that she was "not a proper or fit custodian of the children," and that Robert should get his divorce. It was an easy way to earn his $25 fee. The next day, 19 March, the court granted Robert a decree of divorce. Robert was one of hundreds, perhaps thousands of Canadians who obtained American divorces in this period, because for so many a parliamentary divorce was the only kind available in Canada, an expensive, time-consuming process, and a divorce was much easier to obtain through an American state court. Robert did not choose the United States because of the expense, but because he had failed in Ottawa. It was common for Ontario residents to get divorced in Michigan or New York rather than in the Midwest, and Robert may have chosen Nebraska because he had his eye on moving to that region. Recall that he talked about relocating to Kansas in 1879, when he asked Eliza to go there with him on such unfavourable terms. To my knowledge Robert was the only unsuccessful petitioner to Parliament who turned to the United States for a divorce, but others may have done so.[13]

His divorce secured, Robert soon came to a settlement with Eliza. We know very little about the terms of the settlement. We know only that McDougall was Eliza's counsel, that the two sides negotiated in 1880, and that some time in 1881 the Court of Chancery approved a settlement under section 7 of the separation Act. The principal terms were that Eliza released her dower interest in Robert's land and received a lump sum, paid to trustees, which relieved Robert of any further support obligations. All the sparse entry in Spragge J.'s benchbook tells us is that he approved the settlement after interviewing Eliza privately in his chambers to ensure that her consent was freely given, as required by provincial dower legislation.[14] We can only speculate about why Robert decided to do this, but the most likely reason was to get rid of Eliza's dower interest. As discussed below, he did sell up and move to the United States in 1885 and was likely contemplating doing so earlier. His land would be worth more on the market without the purchaser having to worry that Eliza might later claim her dower.

Robert likely moved between Whitby and Lincoln Nebraska in 1881 and 1882, going into business as a dealer in real estate in Lincoln.[15] On 18 March 1882, almost two years to the day after he obtained his divorce, he married Janet (Jeannie) Laird, in Lincoln, local Baptist minister C.T. Chaffee officiating.[16] She was 40 years old, 8 years younger than Robert, and a spinster.[17] She was not from Nebraska, but Ontario. Like Robert she was from a Scots Presbyterian background. She had been born in Airdrie, Scotland, in 1842 or 1843, and sometime between 1851 and 1861 moved as a child with her parents and five younger siblings, four boys and a girl, to Kent County in southwestern Ontario. The patriarch Joseph Laird took up farming near Blenheim in the district of Harwich. According to the 1861 census Janet worked as a teacher at one point, when she was a young woman barely out of her teens, but later censuses, those of 1871 and 1881, do not give any occupation for her, simply listing her as a member of Joseph Laird's household.

Robert had therefore transformed his life in the three years after Eliza's separation Act was passed by Parliament. He settled his financial obligations to Eliza, got divorced, and remarried. This account leaves many questions unanswered, and probably unanswerable. Most notably, when did he meet Janet Laird and decide to marry her? Was it while the parliamentary battles of 1877 to 1879 were going on, or sometime thereafter? Given that Robert got divorced in Nebraska and married her there two years later it is reasonable to think that he knew her in 1879 or 1880. But there is no evidence of that. Whenever they first met, how did a woman living on a farm near Harwich encounter a Whitby businessman and see enough of him to decide to marry him? Blenheim is approximately 260 kilometres southwest of Toronto, Whitby some 45 kilometres farther east, and there is no evidence either that Robert visited Kent County or that Janet Laird spent time in Toronto or Whitby. Robert kept the marriage a secret from people in Whitby. It is never mentioned in the *Whitby Chronicle*, even though he continued to maintain a residence in Whitby in the early 1880s and the *Chronicle* reported his returns from one of his trips to Nebraska.[18] That Janet Laird did not leave Kent County permanently before 1881 is evidenced by her presence in the 1881 census for that county.

We also do not know why Robert chose Nebraska, well to the west of Ontario, to get a divorce. Given that, as discussed below, he ultimately chose Missouri as his new home, and that during the Senate divorce committee hearings in 1879 he suggested that Eliza could go with him to Kansas, he likely had a general interest in moving to the prairie Midwest. What we probably can say is that the reconciliation proposal during the Senate divorce committee proceedings was an entirely insincere attempt to persuade Eliza to abandon her attempts to have the separation Act passed. At the same time that he made the proposal he was contemplating an American divorce from her and may have developed a relationship with Janet Laird. His machinations in this regard speak volumes about his character. Had Eliza agreed to his proposal he would have been freed of any legal obligation to pay support and could have taken her to the United States and very quickly divorced her.

Although everything was in place for Robert to move to the US and start a new life with a new wife in 1882, he did not leave Canada for good until 1885. He and all four of his children, including the youngest, Francis William, and his unmarried sister Elizabeth, are listed on the 1881 census as living in Whitby, as is James Campbell. Thus at some point between the passage of the separation Act in 1879 and the census of 1881 Francis went to live in his father's household, perhaps an aspect of the settlement between Robert and Eliza. Eliza may have been persuaded to agree to this because the wealthy Robert could give their son a better material life than she could. But it must nevertheless have been a bitter pill to swallow. Robert had ignored Francis's birth and done nothing to support him and Eliza for more than six years. Through her long struggle Eliza had only Francis of her four children to nurture. And now she lost him as well.

Advertisements for the R. & J. Campbell firm do not appear in the *Whitby Chronicle* in 1880, 1881, or 1882, the years when Robert spend a fair bit of his time in Lincoln, but the firm was not dissolved. It was presumably run by James. Three years after his re-marriage, in 1885, Robert left Whitby and Canada for good and settled in Marshall, Missouri. His intention to do so was reported in the *Pickering News* in May 1885,[19] but there was nothing about it in Whitby newspapers until July. He announced his departure for "the west" directly in the *Whitby Chronicle*, and indirectly through advertisements – SELLING OUT! SELLING OUT! – in the same newspaper, as well as others putting his real estate up for sale. His land included a 50-acre farm near Greenwood, which was "under good cultivation" and came with a "comfortable House, barn, stables, sheds, orchard, firewood, etc.," as well as 154 acres of good bush land near Southampton. He also offered for sale his Whitby real estate – the family home, a two-storey brick house that was "one of the most desirable residences in Whitby," and three stores in the Ontario block on Brock Street with an adjoining vacant lot. The farm was sold privately to a George Wilson in September 1885 for $2,900, but Robert had no luck with his house or the town lots. They were put up for auction that month but the sale fell through, and he rented them out instead.[20]

We can only speculate about why he left Whitby and moved to Missouri. Perhaps he did not want to continue living in a place where he was unpopular, and equally his new wife also did not want to set up her marital home in the same town as his former wife. More probably, he left Canada because he would have been open to a prosecution for bigamy. Whether an American divorce would be recognized in Canada was uncertain in the 1870s and early 1880s. Anybody researching the question would have found a series of English precedents that collectively stood for the principle that so long as the applicant for a divorce was domiciled in the jurisdiction which granted the divorce, and the divorce was valid by the law of the foreign jurisdiction, then the divorce would be recognized by an English court, and therefore also by a Canadian one.[21] Had the validity of Robert's divorce ever been litigated, however, doubts could have been raised about whether Robert had ever been domiciled in Nebraska. The common law test for domicile required an intention to stay in the new jurisdiction permanently, which Robert clearly did not have. He had gone there for the six months required to establish residency and get a divorce, and had stayed a little longer, but he never settled in that state, returning from time to time to Canada. When Canadian courts did address the validity in Canada of foreign divorces, they produced inconsistent judgments.[22] For current purposes the point is that we do not know, and in the years immediately after his marriage to Janet Laird Robert did not know, whether his Nebraska divorce would be recognized in Canada were he to return, and therefore whether he could possibly be prosecuted for bigamy. All Robert knew was that there was one person who might have reported him to the police – Eliza. As it turned out this was never an issue.

Robert selected Marshall, Missouri, for his new life with Janet Campbell (née Laird), the county seat of Saline County, which is located roughly in the middle of the land-locked state. Saline County was named after the area's salt springs and established in 1820, the year that Missouri entered the Union as a slave state in the famous Missouri Compromise of that year.[23] The Missouri that Robert went to was a segregated state, as was so much of the South in the era of Jim Crow. Marshall was founded in 1839, named after John Marshall, Chief Justice of the United States. Before the Civil War the county's economy was primarily plantation agriculture (tobacco and hemp), and it remained agricultural thereafter, although plantations disappeared as the now free black population moved elsewhere. Marshall's population was no more than around 2,700 in 1880, though it did grow to almost twice that by 1900. Its current population is only 13,806.

Robert lived in Marshall for 30 years, until his death in 1915. The broad outlines of his life there can be reconstructed from the obituaries for him and Janet Laird Campbell, a biographical sketch published in a history of Saline County,[24] his and Janet Campbell's and his children's appearances in Marshall newspapers, and his will. The author of the biographical sketch knew about his marriage to Eliza in Canada in 1864, about her father being Rev. Byrne, and about the four children. One assumes that Robert himself provided this information. The author either did not know, or kept quiet about, the marriage breakdown; the reader is left to assume that his first wife had died. Robert himself clearly made some effort to conceal his past, reporting on his 1900 US federal census form that he had been married to Janet Laird for 33 years. Robert made a very good new life for himself, albeit one marked by one family tragedy, the premature death of his oldest son, Robert Junior. Here I will first discuss his family, and then his business dealings, and a few other matters.

All four of Robert's children eventually moved to Missouri with him. That included Frank (Francis), who was in a school in Canada in 1887, presumably a private boarding school, and moved to Marshall in 1893 after he finished school. He became a dealer in real estate, in partnership with his father, married and had children, and in 1901 Robert bought a house for him in Marshall for $1,000. He lived a very long life in the Marshall area, dying in 1966 at the age of 93.[25] The Campbells' oldest son, Robert Campbell Junior, was 21 when he moved with his father to Marshall. Only a few months later, in December 1885, he married a local woman, Minnie Eakin, the daughter of James Eakin, "one of Saline County's most prominent and highly respected citizens." They had two children, Helen and Robert. Robert Junior went into the dry goods business in partnership with his father for three years and from 1888 ran it on his own after his father sold his interest to him and concentrated on buying and selling real estate. His Marshall store, "The Fair," was described in 1890 as "one of our large dry goods establishments," and Robert Junior was said to be "young, full of enterprise and popular." In 1890 he moved his business to Boonville, 43 kilometres from Marshall, and shortly afterwards bought the local newspaper as well, the *Boonville Bee*. He died on October 10th, 1899, of typhoid fever, at the age of 36. He was a "good husband and father," well known and liked in "social and business circles." His widow and children moved in with Robert, sharing the large house on East North Street, Marshall.[26]

The Campbells' second son, James Bremner Campbell, became a farmer in Saline County, some 15 kilometres from Marshall. He seems to have been successful. In 1905 he offered for sale "3 fresh cows with calves, 14 well-bred cows in calf to fine Hereford bulls, 4 yearling Hereford heifers, 1 2-year-old shorthorn bull." He died in Saline County in 1957 at the age of 91. The Campbells' daughter Edith, 19 when she accompanied her father and brothers to Missouri, enjoyed her life as a "bright young thing" in Marshall, entertaining other young people in the family home and, in 1891, taking a three-month trip with her father to the United Kingdom, Europe, and Canada. On 4 October 1892, she married Marshall physician Baylor M. Spotts. They had at least three children: Jean Laird Spotts born in 1894, Margaret Spotts, and Catherine Ann Spotts.[27] Regarding his children, as in many other respects Robert therefore emerged as a "winner" from his long and bitter battle with Eliza.

Robert's family connections were not limited to his children. He also maintained good relations with his extended family, including the one he acquired by marrying Janet Laird. His spinster sister Elizabeth lived with Robert and his children in Whitby until they all went to Missouri, and then moved to Toronto sometime before 1891 and set up house with her widowed sister, Ann Ross. Around the turn of the century she moved to Marshall, perhaps to be taken care of by her brother's money and the extensive care it could provide for an elderly single lady of about 73. She died there at Robert's house in November 1907, around 80 years old.[28] Robert's nieces, Kate and Annie Anderson, daughters of John Anderson and Robert's sister Jane, visited on different occasions, Kate staying for some months and helping with Robert's bookkeeping. "Miss Ross" of Canada, daughter of one of Robert's sisters,

Catherine or Ann, also visited. Janet Laird Campbell's niece, also called Janet, spent time with her aunt and uncle by marriage. She stayed long enough in Missouri to meet and then marry Charles Dugas Steel, a local farmer from the nearby community of Slater. Janet Laird Campbell also had her sister Mary to stay in 1907 while Robert was on a business trip to the United Kingdom. And there were likely others whose presence in Marshall was not captured in the pages of the local newspapers. Janet Laird Campbell became a pillar of the community, hosting parties in the family home on East North Street, taking a leading role in a woman's literary society, and the Presbyterian Church's foreign missionary work. Obituaries do not provide a balanced assessment of a life, but hers are notable for their fulsome praise of a woman "universally esteemed for her Christian life," someone who "was always the same undemonstrative, calm, and upright and loving and gentle and true woman."[29]

When Robert first moved to Marshall he took up the trade that had served him so well in Whitby. The first mention of him in a local newspaper is from August 1886, and shows that by then he was already reasonably well known in the town as a retail merchant. It was not an announcement of his arrival but of the news that he was about to go to New York and Chicago "and other points in quest of his fall stock goods." He did well in the business, presumably because he had the two principal attributes needed to make good: He was an experienced businessman and he brought a lot of money with him. As noted above he created a partnership with his son Robert Campbell Junior, and he retired from that position in 1888. He then concentrated on real estate acquisitions, which kept time from being "a burden on his hands." In 1907, for example, he bought two stores in nearby Slater, 16 kilometres away, bringing his total to eight and making him the largest owner of real estate in that town. As this example demonstrates, he owned property not only in Marshall but in other communities in Saline county. His last will, drafted by himself and executed in Canada, divided his estate of some US$350,000, some $11 million in current money, between his widow, Clara née Shier (about whom more below), his surviving children Frank, James, and Edith, and Robert Campbell Junior's children. Clara Shier Campbell's interest was left in trust, and litigation ensued over the duration of the trusteeship and other issues, which was not resolved for seven years.[30]

When he was not looking after his business interests Robert travelled a good deal, to visit his children who lived in other Missouri counties, or to Canada, including Toronto and Whitby, or to Colorado, Kansas City, the United Kingdom, and Europe. He was a supporter of prohibition and in 1911 he became an American citizen. His life in Marshall was not without personal losses. As noted above, his oldest son Robert Junior died relatively young, at 36, in 1899. Nearly two decades later his wife of 26 years, Janet, died of epilepsy, on 20 May 1908. She was principally taken care of in her last years by Minnie Campbell, the widow of Robert Campbell Junior.[31]

Five years later, on 17 July 1913, Robert married for a third time, at the age of 80. His new wife, Clara Emma Shier, aged 69, was a spinster and a long-time resident of Whitby, where her father, John Shier, was one of the leading citizens. John Shier had been born in Scotland in 1808, emigrated to the United States in 1829, moved to Oshawa in 1845 and in 1850 relocated to Whitby. He was the Ontario County Engineer from 1854 to 1867, the provincial land surveyor, and the county's clerk from 1877 until his death in 1882. He also served as chairman of the Whitby Board of School Trustees and secretary-treasurer of the Ontario County Agricultural Society. As another of Whitby's prominent citizens, Robert Campbell would surely have known John Shier and probably also Clara, who would have been 29, about Eliza's age, when the Campbells' marital problems were the talk of Whitby. When and how Robert and Clara Shier reconnected is unknown. They were married in the Presbyterian Church on Bathurst Street, Toronto. Robert was listed on the affidavit required by the provincial *Marriage Act* as retired and a widower. Clara likely lived in Toronto, at 26 Ellerbeck Avenue, the house also of her sister Mary, who was one of the two witnesses. Today there is no street of that name. The other witness was Annie Anderson, the daughter of John Anderson and Robert's niece.[32]

Robert lived only eighteen months more after his marriage to Clara Shier, dying at his home in Marshall on 23 February 1915. One obituary called him "a splendid citizen" who "had the respect and esteem of all who knew him," but obituaries are like that. Another was more prosaic; he was "one of the county's wealthiest and more substantial citizens." He was buried in Ridge Park Cemetery, Marshall, where his son Robert Junior had been buried, and his other son, Frank, would be interred 50 years later. His death was reported in the *Globe* and later reprinted in the *Canadian Statesman* of Bowmanville, perhaps more because of who his third wife was, the daughter of a prominent Ontario county resident, than because of him. The very brief report states simply that he was "late of Whitby" and the "beloved husband of Clara Shier." Clara Shier returned home to Toronto and to her house on Ellerbeck Avenue, where she died 7 years later.[33]

Eliza Campbell and Her Family

Eliza Campbell's life of 30 more years after her parliamentary triumph of 1879 was in marked contrast to Robert's, George Gordon's, and James Campbell's. The 1879 Act was the ultimate pyrrhic victory. She had an Act of Parliament ordering Robert to pay her $500 a year, but she had not been able to obtain custody of her three older children, and as noted above she did not keep Francis either, who went with his father. She did get some money by way of the settlement with Robert in 1881, but likely only enough for a modest existence in Whitby and later in Toronto.

As we saw in previous chapters, Eliza continued to live in Whitby with her mother and younger sister Annie throughout the 1870s. Her widowed sister, Bethiah, had moved to Toronto when she remarried in 1874, and her father and her brother James had died in the 1870s. In 1882 Henrietta Byrne moved to Toronto with Annie and took up residence in a rented house at 168 Teraulay Street, now Bay Street, just to the east of the University of Toronto. She therefore lived in "The Ward," St John's Ward, a densely populated area of mostly working-class people of British and Irish origin, or of African Canadians who were refugees from the pre-Civil War southern United States and their descendants. In the twentieth century this area acquired the reputation of a slum, even more crowded with residents who came with the successive waves of immigrants from eastern and southern Europe. But in the 1880s and 1890s it was a "predominantly working-class area with pockets of poverty."[34] The Byrnes were not working class, but they likely experienced poverty, albeit "genteel poverty." In 1885 Henrietta and Annie moved to another rented house a short distance away, at 197 McCaul Street, south of College Street, and also part of the Ward, where Henrietta died on 16 August 1886, at the age of 88. Her death and her marriage to Rev. Byrne were duly noted in the *Whitby Chronicle*.[35] Annie Byrne remained in the McCaul Street house until 1889, when she moved again, this time to 158 Robert Street. She continued to move frequently, as renters tend to do, but not far. In 1896 she was on Dundas Street near Sheridan Street, and a year later she was on Major Street at No. 256.

Eliza joined Annie sometime before 1891. It is possible, even likely, that she had moved to Toronto with her mother and sister in 1883, but she is not listed as a resident before 1901. The first concrete evidence of her living in Toronto is the 1901 census. The enumerator recorded the sisters as the only occupants of the house on Major Street, with Annie designated as head of the household and Eliza as the "No 2 resident of the house." Both still professed to belong to the Congregationalist faith, and neither claimed an occupation. They were living on their own means. According to the city directories Annie continued to reside at 256 Major Street at least for the next decade.

Eliza died on the 20th of January 1910, at the age of 66, at the house she shared with Annie on Major Street. The *Globe* gave the cause of death as heart failure, which of course everyone dies of. The death record gives the cause as influenza and pneumonia.[36] She was buried in Mount Pleasant Cemetery, with no tombstone, just a plan stone slab marking the place where she was interred.[37] Her next of kin is given in the cemetery register as George Ham, the oldest son of her sister, Bethiah Johnston, who lived at 392 Shaw Street with his 75-year-old mother, his wife Minnie, and their four children. Bethiah lived another 10 years, dying in May 1920.[38] Annie Byrne, the youngest of Rev. Byrne's children, never married and outlived all her siblings, dying in 1935 at the age of 87. Remarkably, she lived her final years, and died, in Marshall, Missouri, although I have no idea when she moved there and how such a reconciliation between the family of Robert Campbell and his estranged wife's sister took place. She was buried in Ridge Park Cemetery, Saline County, the final resting place of her erstwhile brother-in-law and his second wife.[39]

This is a frustratingly brief account of 30 years or so of a person's life after her triumph in the Senate in 1879. It is brief largely because Eliza lived an uneventful life after 1880, certainly compared to the dramatic and painful events of the previous seven years. She had some money from the settlement with Robert, and Henrietta might have had a small pension from the London Missionary Society, but if she did it could not have been much. There is nothing to indicate that Eliza or Annie had any way of earning income. They probably lived on her settlement, which was enough that when she died, she had an estate to be administered by her nephew George Ham.[40] The one concrete thing that we do know about Eliza is that her matrimonial breakdown in 1873 ruined her life. She lost all her children, never saw her grandchildren, and surely never forgot the adultery accusation. Nor did others forget that she was still married to Robert, he having failed in his attempt to divorce her in Canada. The *Globe's* brief death notice was headed "Death of Mrs. Robert Campbell" and had "Eliza Maria Byrne" as the sub-heading.[41] She probably considered herself still to be Robert's lawful wife.

16
Conclusion

As I researched, wrote, and talked about this book I was often asked an obvious question: What did happen between 9 p.m. and the early hours of the morning in the Campbell family home on 26 August 1873? I always gave three answers, and still do: I do not know, I will never know, and it does not matter to me, although of course it mattered very much to Eliza and Robert Campbell. It mattered especially to Eliza, which is why I chose the main title of this book. Her whole life after 26 August 1873 was a defiant denial of what she had been accused of.

What matters for current purposes is that the Campbell case provides a detailed insight into large themes in the socio-legal history of marriage and divorce in later nineteenth-century Ontario. Central to the law governing gender relations was the marriage bond, its importance highlighted by the fact that the one thing this unhappy couple could not do, for legal and social reasons, was to separate amicably, sort out the finances, do what is best for the young children, and perhaps find happiness in another relationship. Today the law facilitates all these outcomes, even if a marital breakdown does not always work out well.

But in the 1870s in Ontario there was no legal route to an amicable separation. Eliza Campbell was unhappy in her marriage, but trapped in it. She had no independent means, and no way to take the drastic step of leaving her husband and maintaining a relationship with her children. Had she left the marriage her husband, her family, and her community would have shunned and condemned her. She would have been reminded that marriage was about wifely obedience, maternal rectitude, and, most of all, duty. If happiness was also part of the mix, that was fortunate, but it was not required. Eliza would have had no claim to support and could not have sued for custody. The large mistake she made, which everybody involved with the legal proceedings that followed the crisis of August 1873 could agree, was to be flirtatious with young men of her own age. That way of easing the burden of the dull everyday was always going to end in trouble.

Not so for Robert Campbell. He was no more happy in the marriage than she was. But he cared less about that than she did. For him the marriage was an orderly household and a reliable and respectable "guardian" for his children – not their children. He was advancing in the world of commerce, accumulating wealth, travelling annually to the "old country." He was in the world, and wanted and needed a wife who was not, a wife who remained confined to a woman's world. When he saw that he could no longer have those things in Eliza he also did not have an easy route out. To get rid of her he seized upon what might seem to some to be very slight reasons to separate. It cannot be stressed enough that his decision to separate from Eliza was taken within an hour or two of finding a letter she had received from Godfrey Parks, and it was final and absolute. He did not discuss that letter with her, did not even tell her that he had obtained it. He prepared the ground for ending the marriage by taking the children well away, and arranged for her to be watched while he was gone so that he could confirm his suspicions. Had he simply ended their relationship the community would have condemned him, and the law would have required him to support her financially. Only by proving adultery could he escape social disapprobation and financial responsibility. Whether or not James Campbell and John Anderson did fabricate a story, Robert certainly had reason to want them to.

This book is about the various ways in which the law and the legal system were used by both parties to the marriage to deal with their conflict. The three court cases fought between 1873 and 1875 involved three different causes of action, but they all turned on one factual question – the one I said at the beginning of this conclusion that I did not know the answer to, and never would. People at the time also struggled with that question, and there were stark differences of opinion. One jury of middling men believed Eliza, one similarly constituted did not, although the latter could hardly have come to a different verdict on such one-sided evidence. Conversely every judge that dealt with this case, men of a different class than the jurors, did not believe Eliza. In the Senate, comprised of men of approximately the same class as the judges, she was not viewed so uniformly. Indeed opinions of her were for some senators diametrically opposed to their colleagues. She was either a much-wronged woman or one who had done much wrong herself. Different senators read the evidence very differently, while some did not need to read the evidence to know what they thought. Senators on both sides considered the evidence in light of their attitudes to marriage and men's and women's responsibilities within that institution, and against their assessments of the character of Robert and Eliza, and came to very different conclusions about who had failed to live by the prevailing codes of marital relations, codes both legal and social.

Gender is the principal lens through which I have told this story, and the conclusion is inescapable that the law and the patriarchal society that made that law were heavily stacked against Eliza. She won in the Senate, but it took a long time and, more importantly, her victory availed her little or nothing in the long run. That the law in the 1870s did not favour women's equality is hardly a surprising conclusion, and this book did not need to be written to make that point. But the book does show the particular ways in which inequality played out in one woman's life. Even the senators who supported Eliza grounded that support in the idea that their manly task was to come to the aid of a damsel in distress, a woman who could not act for herself. It is probably more apt to say that Robert lost in Parliament, not that Eliza won. She was able to secure a support order and custody of her youngest child. But in the end she did not even attempt to get custody of the other three, and Robert evaded the support order until he used it as a bargaining chip to rid his land of her dower right.

Gender relations is not the only theme explored here. For constitutional historians there is a rare glimpse of a debate about the division of powers in the 1870s and in Parliament. Histories of the evolution of the Canadian federal constitution after 1867 are overwhelmingly focused on the courts, especially the Judicial Committee of the Privy Council, and on the period from the early 1880s. Yet arguments over the scope of federal powers versus that of the provincial property and civil rights power were at the centre of the debate over the constitutionality of Eliza Campbell's separation Act. It was raised in other political controversies, but historians have not studied the parliamentary aspect of division of powers disputes to anything like the extent they have examined judicial decisions. More attention should be paid to Parliament in this context to provide a fully rounded understanding of our constitutional history, not one limited to a world dominated by the courts.

The other major constitutional question raised by the Campbell case was whether an Act of Parliament could effectively overturn a finding of fact made by a court in a dispute between individuals. This is not an issue that has contemporary resonance, belonging to an earlier phase of our constitutional history when people could still make the argument that Parliament was the highest court in the land, an argument derived from viewing the Senate as the equivalent to the House of Lords. It was not an unreasonable claim, even if it was incorrect. In this period the Senate did operate as a quasi-judicial body.

This legal historical account of the Campbell matrimonial dispute has also provided glimpses into the elite of the legal profession in Ontario, into practising lawyers and judges. Both Robert Harrison and Malcolm Crooks Cameron were at the top of their professional careers when they faced off against each other in the criminal conversation and defamation cases, and it was perhaps fitting that each secured one jury verdict and one defeat. They did not confront each other when the dispute moved to Chancery, a different forum than the common law courts in which the judge, not the jury, decided the key factual findings. If the talents of individual lawyers mattered at common law but much less so in Chancery, they came to the fore in a very unusual "court," the divorce committee of the Senate of Canada. In that forum an indifferent politician and a man who had not honed his legal talents for the first 50 plus years of his life, William McDougall, commanded the stage. His defence of Eliza Campbell combined an adroit handling of hostile witnesses with a masterful exercise in forensic reasoning before an unusual "jury" – nine senators, four of whom were lawyers.

Family and community support also played a significant role in the outcome of the legal and parliamentary struggles Eliza Campbell endured. She was emotionally and financially supported by her parents, siblings, and neighbours through the six-year long struggle to vindicate her reputation, and also doggedly championed by David Reesor in the Senate. Finally, given that a parliamentary divorce was a legislative process as much as a judicial one, the vagaries of parliamentary procedure also played a role. In this respect, while the Senate could devote many hours to the case, ultimately the separation Act passed the Commons in part because the government wanted to see the issue go away as quickly as possible without wasting valuable parliamentary time on it. Yet one solution to the problems that parliamentary divorce posed for the working of Parliament – the abolition of parliamentary divorce and the vesting of jurisdiction in the courts – was never seriously contemplated in this period, even though the United Kingdom had taken that step in 1857, a decade before Confederation. It did not happen for Ontario until 1930. It would take two world wars and greatly changed social mores to alter Canadians' conviction that easier access to divorce would result in the fatal weakening of the institution of marriage, and hence of society itself.

Appendix 1
Eliza Campbell's Petition to the Senate, 29 March 1876

Senate Journals, 23 April 1879, 166–167

To the Honourable the Senate of the Dominion of Canada in Parliament Assembled.

The Petition of Eliza Maria Campbell, wife of Robert Campbell, of the Town of Whitby, in the County of Ontario, in the Province of Ontario, in the Dominion of Canada, merchant,

Respectfully sheweth:
That your Petitioner was lawfully married to the said Robert Campbell by her father, the Reverend J.T. Byrne, and in her said father's house at Whitby, aforesaid, on the 6th day of April, 1863.

That on the 25th August 1873, about four months before the birth of the fourth and last child, issue of the said marriage, the said Robert Campbell, without any sufficient cause, justification or provocation, treacherously deserted her, the Petitioner, his wife, and took away from her the three children they then had, and that he has ever since lived, and kept the said children apart from her.

That he refused to return and did not return to his house while she remained in it; that on the 24th September, 1873, he did, with force and violence, and with the assistance of two constables, but without warrant, remove her from the said house, and that he has ever since refused and does still refuse to receive her or their youngest child therein.

That he has neglected and refused, and does still neglect and refuse, to support or maintain her, his wife, or their said child, or furnish them or either of them with the necessaries of life, according to his rank, means and condition.

That he has repeatedly, openly and publicly, accused her of having committed adultery, and has vainly endeavoured to prove her to have been guilty of that crime.

That she has not been guilty of adultery.

That he has petitioned Parliament for the dissolution of his marriage with her on the ground of adultery, alleged by him to have been committed by her, and a Bill founded on his said Petition is now before Parliament.

That the said Robert Campbell has treated her, your Petitioner, with cruelty, and has outraged, ill used and insulted her.

That there is no prospect of the said Robert Campbell ever being reconciled to your Petitioner.

That your Petitioner is desirous of being divorced *a mensa et thoro*, or separated as to bed and board from the said Robert Campbell.

That she is advised that there is no court or tribunal in the Province of Ontario by whose decree such a separation can be effected.

That your Petitioner is without means of her own for her support and that of her child or children.

That by a decree of the Court of Chancery of Ontario alimony has been refused to her, and she is advised that there is no means of obtaining and judicial revision or reconsideration of the question of her rights to alimony open to her or within her reach.

That your Petitioner is desirous of being allowed to retain the care and custody of her youngest child, and to have, in addition, the care and custody of her only daughter, at least, if not of her other children.

Wherefore your Petitioner humbly prays that the said Bill may not be passed without such amendments as may make it an Act providing for such a separation between her and the said Robert Campbell as would be effected in England by a decree of judicial separation pronounced by the proper court, and providing also for the said Robert Campbell being compelled to make due and adequate provision for her support and that of her children, and proving also for her having the care and custody of at least the two youngest of her children; and that your Petitioner may have such further and other relief in the premises as to your Honourable House may seem meet; and your Petitioner, as in duty bound, will ever pray.

Eliza M. Campbell
Ottawa, 29th March, 1876

Appendix 2
Eliza Campbell's Separation Bill, 1877

Senate Journals, 18 April 1877, 248–253

This bill was the one drafted in 1876 and then amended in Committee of the Whole in 1877. The version that came out of Committee of the Whole was the one that passed the Senate but was not considered by the Commons.

An Act for the Relief of Robert Campbell and Eliza Maria Campbell

And whereas the said Eliza Maria Campbell hath by her petition humbly set forth that she was lawfully married to the said Robert Campbell in her father's house at Whitby on the sixth day of April, A.D. 1863, that on the 25th August A.D. 1873 about four months before the birth of the fourth and last child, issue of the said marriage, the said Robert Campbell, without sufficient cause, treacherously deserted her, took her away from her their three children, and has since lived and kept the said children apart from her; that on the 24th September A.D. 1873, the said Robert Campbell, with force and violence and with two constables, but without warrant, removed her from his house, and has ever since refused to receive her or their youngest child therein; that he has since refused to maintain her or their child or to furnish them with necessaries according to his means and condition; that he has repeatedly accused her of adultery and endeavoured to prove her guilty; that she has not been guilty of adultery; that he has petitioned Parliament for the dissolution of his marriage with her; that the said Robert Campbell has treated her with cruelty, and ill-used and insulted her; that there is no prospect of reconciliation; that she, the petitioner, desires to be divorced a *mensa et thoro*;

that there is no court in Ontario by whose decree such divorce can be effected; that she is without means for her own or for her child or children's support; that the Court of Chancery for Ontario having refused her petition for alimony, she is without means to secure a revision of that judgment, and that she desires to have the care and custody of her youngest child and of her only daughter; and the said Eliza Maria Campbell prayed that the said bill might not be passed without amendments, which would make it an Act providing for such a separation between her and the said Robert as would be effected in England by a decree for "judicial separation," and compelling the said Robert Campbell to make adequate provision for her support, and the support of her children, and giving her the care and custody of at least the two youngest of her children.

And whereas, the evidence produced by the said Robert Campbell did not prove that his wife, the said Eliza Maria Campbell, had ever committed adultery with the said George Gordon or with any other person;

And whereas, the evidence produced as well by the petitioner as by the Respondent, proved that the said Robert Campbell treated his wife, the said Eliza Maria Campbell with cruelty; that he deserted her on the 25th day of August A.D. 1873; that he has not since lived or cohabited with her; that he has not made any provision for her support and maintenance or for the support and maintenance of their youngest child;

And whereas, it is expedient to grant the prayer of the petition of the said Eliza Maria Campbell for a Divorce from bed and board.

1. From and after the commencement of this Act the said Eliza Maria Campbell shall be and shall remain separated from the bed and board of her husband the said Robert Campbell.
2. The separation hereby authorized and provided shall, except as hereinafter provided, have the same force and the same consequences as a judicial separation in England, under a decree for a judicial separation pronounced by the proper Court there at the commencement of this Act.
3. The said Robert Campbell shall pay annually to his said wife for her support and maintenance the sum of 600 dollars during her separation as aforesaid, in two equal half-yearly instalments payable on the first days of May and November in every year.
4. The said Eliza Maria Campbell may, after the commencement of this Act, have the custody and care of one of the children of the said marriage, viz: John Francis Campbell during her separation as aforesaid.

5. The said Robert Campbell shall pay annually to his wife the said Eliza Maria Campbell the sum of $200 for the support and education of the said child while he remains in her custody during her separation as aforesaid. The said sum of $200 shall be payable half-yearly in equal instalments of $100 on the first days of May and November each month.
6. It shall be lawful for the said Eliza Maria Campbell at any time or times hereafter to apply to a Judge of one of the Superior Courts of Ontario, and the said Judge is hereby authorized and empowered to grant her application, for a rule or summons to the said Robert Campbell to shew cause why he should not pay to the said Eliza Maria Campbell an additional sum for her support or maintenance, and if the said Judge shall find that the sum of $600 is not equal to one third of the annual income of the said Robert Campbell, he may order and direct the said Robert Campbell to pay to his wife, the said Eliza Maria Campbell, in half-yearly instalments as aforesaid, such additional sum as shall, together with the said sum of $600, be equal to one-third of the annual income from every source of the said Robert Campbell.
7. If the said Robert Campbell shall neglect or refuse for the space of ten days after the same is due, to pay or cause to be paid into the hands of the said Eliza Maria Campbell or her attorney, lawfully appointed, any one of the said instalments, or any instalment as increased by the Order of a Judge as aforesaid, he shall be deemed guilty of a contempt of Court.
8. The said Robert Campbell and the said Eliza Maria Campbell may agree that upon the payment of a certain sum of money in hand, or upon the conveyance of a certain amount of property to her for her sole and separate use, the said Robert Campbell shall no longer be liable to pay the half-yearly instalments aforesaid or any of them, but no such agreement shall have any force or effect until it has been approved by a Judge of one of the Superior Courts of Ontario, whose approval, after hearing the parties, shall be endorsed on the instrument containing the agreement.
9. Before and until the making and approval of an agreement as aforesaid, this Act may be registered in any Registry Office in Ontario, and such registration shall have the same force and effect as the registration of an Order or Decree of the Court of Chancery under section four of the Act of the late Province of Canada, entitled "An Act to amend the Consolidated Statutes respecting

the Court of Chancery," passed in the seventeenth year of Her Majesty's reign. [1854].

10. If, and whenever the said Eliza Maria Campbell and Robert Campbell shall become reconciled and cohabit as man and wife, this Act shall thereafter have no farther or other operation or effect than a decree for judicial separation would have in England under like circumstances.

Appendix 3

Eliza Campbell's Separation Act, 1879

Whereas Robert Campbell, of the Town of Whitby, in the County of Ontario, in the Province of Ontario and Dominion of Canada, merchant, by his petition to Parliament in the Session of 1876 set forth, that on the sixth day of April, … [1863] he was lawfully married to Eliza Maria Byrne, at Whitby, in the County of Ontario, in accordance with the rites and ceremonies of the Congregational Church of Canada; that the said marriage was duly authorized by licence duly issued; that the said Robert Campbell and Eliza Marie Byrne lived and cohabited together as husband and wife from the date of such marriage up to … [25 August 1873]; that the said Eliza Maria Byrne, although the lawful wife of the said Robert Campbell, did commit adultery with one George Gordon, at various times in the town of Whitby, in the said County of Ontario, in the said Province of Ontario, previous to and during the month of August…. [1873], in particular on …[26 August 1873] in the said town of Whitby; that the said Robert Campbell made discovery of the said adultery …; that the said Robert Campbell, since the discovery of the said adultery…, refused to cohabit, and had not cohabited with his said wife, and had since lived apart from her; that the said Eliza Maria Byrne had, since the discovery of the said adultery, lived at the town of Whitby aforesaid separate and apart from the said Robert Campbell; that the said Robert Campbell, subsequent to the discovery of the said criminality, brought an action for criminal conversation in Her Majesty's Court of Queen's Bench for Ontario, against the said George Gordon, and recovered a verdict in the said action against the said George Gordon for one thousand five hundred dollars and entered judgment thereon; that the said Robert Campbell and the said Eliza Maria Byrne so living apart as aforesaid, the said Eliza Maria Byrne brought a suit against the said Robert Campbell in Her Majesty's Court of Chancery for Ontario, seeking to recover and obtain an allowance for alimony from the said

Robert Campbell, which said suit was defended by the said Robert Campbell on the ground of said adultery hereinbefore mentioned ..., the said Court did order and declare that the said Bill of Complaint of the said Eliza Maria Byrne be, and the same was thereby, dismissed out of the said Court; that the said Robert Campbel was desirous of having the said marriage dissolved, annulled, and put an end to, so that he might be free from the same, and could contract matrimony with any other person or persons with whom it would have been lawful for him to contract matrimony, if the said Robert Campbell and Eliza Maria Byrne had not intermarried; and that there were four children issue of the said marriage; and the said Robert Campbell prayed that the said marriage might be dissolved, and out an end to, and that the issue of his marriage with the said Eliza Maria Byrne, and also the issue of any such future marriage, might be declared legitimate;

And whereas the said Eliza Maria Campbell, by her petition presented during the same session, humbly set forth that she was lawfully married to the said Robert Campbell, in her father's house at Whitby, ... [in 1863]; that on ... [25 August 1873], about four months before the birth of the fourth and last child, issue of the said marriage, the said Robert Campbell, without sufficient cause, treacherously deserted her, took away from her their three children, and had since lived and kept the said children apart from her; that on ... [24 September 1873] the said Robert Campbell, with force and violence, and with two constables, but without warrant, removed her from his house, and had ever since refused to receive her or their youngest child therein; that he has since refused to maintain her or their child, or to furnish them with necessaries according to his means and condition; that he had repeatedly accused her of adultery, and endeavoured to prove her guilty; that she had not been guilty of adultery; that he had petitioned Parliament for the dissolution of his marriage with her; that the said Robert Campbell had treated her with cruelty, and ill-used and insulted her; that there was no prospect of reconciliation; that she, the petitioner, desired to be divorced *a mensa et thoro*; that there is no court in Ontario by whose decree such divorce can be effected; that she was without means for her own or her children's support; that the Court of Chancery of Ontario having refused her petition for alimony, she was without means to secure a revision of that judgment, and that she desired to have the care and custody of her youngest child and of her only daughter; and the said Eliza Marie Campbell prayed that the Bill might not be passed without amendments which would make it an Act providing for such a separation between her and the said Robert Campbell as would be effected in England by a decree for "judicial separation," and compelling the said Robert Campbell to make adequate provision for her support and the support of her children, and giving her the care and custody of at least the two youngest of her children;

And whereas the evidence produced by the said Robert Campbell did not prove that his wife, the said Eliza Maria Campbell, had ever committed adultery with the said George Gordon, or with any other person;

And whereas the evidence produced as well by the petitioner as by the respondent, proved that the said Robert Campbell had treated his wife, the said Eliza Maria Campbell, with cruelty; that he deserted her on [25 August 1873] ... ; that he had not since lived or cohabited with her; that he had not made any provision for her support and maintenance and for the support and maintenance of their youngest child;

And whereas the Senate, in the Session of 1877, granted the prayer of the said Eliza Maria Campbell for a divorce from bed and board, and passed a bill for that purpose, with provisions for her support and maintenance and for the support and education of her child;

And whereas the said Bill was not passed by the House of Commons, on the ground that sufficient notice had not been given of the said Bill according to the rules of that House;

And whereas the said Robert Campbell still refuses to receive his said wife into his domicile or to maintain and support her while living apart from him;

And whereas the said Eliza Maria Campbell has by her petition prayed that a new Bill may be passed identical in terms as nearly may be with the said Bill of 1877;

And whereas it is expedient to grant the prayer of the said Eliza Maria Campbell: Therefore Her Majesty, by and with the advice and consent of the Senate and Huse of Commons of Canada, enacts as follows:-

1. From and after the commencement of this Act, the said Eliza Maria Campbell shall be and shall remain separated from the bed and board of her husband the said Robert Campbell.
2. The separation hereby authorized and provided shall, except as hereinafter provided, have the same force and the same consequences as a judicial separation in England, under a decree for judicial separation pronounced by the proper court there, at the commencement of this Act.
3. The said Robert Campbell shall pay annually to his said wife for her support and maintenance the sum of five hundred dollars during her separation as aforesaid, in two equal instalments, payable half-yearly, on the last days of May and November in each year.

4. The said Eliza Maria Campbell may, after the commencement of this Act, have the custody and care of one of the children of the said marriage, namely, Francis William Campbell, during her separation as aforesaid.
5. The said Robert Campbell shall pay annually to his said wife, the said Eliza Maria Campbell, the sum of two hundred dollars for the support and education of the said child, while he remains in her custody during the separation as aforesaid. The said sum of two hundred dollars shall be payable in equal half-yearly instalments, on the last days of May and November in every year during the minority of the said child.
6. If the said Robert Campbell shall neglect or refuse for the space of ten days after the same is due, to pay or cause to be paid into the hands of the said Eliza Maria Campbell or her attorney … any one of the said instalments, it shall be lawful for the said Eliza Maria Campbell to apply to a judge of one of the superior courts of Ontario, or to one of the county judges of Ontario, and the said judge is hereby authorized and empowered to grant her application for an order to the said Robert Campbell to pay the instalment or instalments then over due, together with the costs of the said application and order, and if he shall disobey the said order, he shall be deemed guilty of a contempt of court.
7. The said Robert Campbell and the said Eliza Maria Campbell may agree that upon the payment of a certain sum of money in hand, or upon the conveyance of a certain amount of property to her for her sole and separate use, the said Robert Campbell shall no longer be liable to pay the half-yearly instalments aforesaid, or any of them; but no such agreement shall have any force or effect until it has been approved by a judge of one of the superior courts of Ontario, whose approval, after hearing the parties, shall be endorsed on the instrument containing the agreement.
8. Before and until the making and approval of an agreement as aforesaid, this Act may be registered in any registry office in Ontario; and such registration shall have the same force and effect as the registration of an order or decree of the Court of Chancery, under section 44 of chapter 40 of the Revised Statutes of Ontario.
9. If, and whenever, the said Eliza Maria Campbell and Robert Campbell shall become reconciled and cohabit as man and wife, this Act shall thereafter have no further or other operation or effect than a decree for judicial separation would have in England under like circumstances.

Notes

1. Introduction

1 *An Act for the Relief of Eliza Maria Campbell*, SC 1879, c 79. Reproduced as appendix 3 in this book. Private Acts to benefit individual persons or corporations were invariably entitled "*An Act for the Relief of*" the person or entity who had petitioned for the Act.
2 John Alexander Gemmill, *The Practice of the Parliament of Canada upon Bills of Divorce* (Toronto: Carswell & Co, 1889), 49.
3 For the number of parliamentary divorce Acts passed between 1867 and 1914 see Jim Phillips, Philip Girard, and R. Blake Brown, *A History of Law in Canada Volume II: Law for the New Dominion, 1867–1914* (Toronto: Osgoode Society for Canadian Legal History and University of Toronto Press, 2022), 547. The total of 263 given there has been slightly augmented by further research since the book was published.
4 Parliamentary divorce is discussed in the excellent leading study of Canadian divorce history, James G. Snell, *In the Shadow of the Law: Divorce in Canada, 1900–1939* (Toronto: University of Toronto Press, 1991), but in tandem with judicial divorce and with more emphasis on the social than the legal aspects.
5 Suzanne Zeller, "William McDougall," *DCB online*. It is, however, very briefly mentioned in the entry for McDougall in a contemporary biographical dictionary, *The Scot in British North America*, ed. William J. Rattray (Toronto: Maclear, 1880), 584–90, and in a fictionalized biography of him, Daniel Livermore, *Wandering Willie: The Memoirs of William McDougall 1822–1905: Canada's Forgotten Father of Confederation* (Burnstown, Ont.: Burnstown Publishing, 2020).
6 Catherine Evans, "The Case as Episode: Murder and Migration in Colonial Australia," in *In Between and Across: Legal History without Boundaries*, eds.

Jacob Cogan and Kenneth Mack (Oxford: Oxford University Press, 2024), 143.

7 On the genre see Jeffrey L McNairn, "Intersecting Legal and Intellectual Histories," *Journal of the Canadian Historical Association* 32, no. 1 (2022): 97. See also, inter alia, Steven Bednarski, "On Microhistory and Pedagogy," in *A Poisoned Past: The Life and Times of Margarida de Portu, a Fourteenth-Century Accused Prisoner* (Toronto: University of Toronto Press, 2014), chap. 1.

8 Natalie Zemon Davis, *The Return of Martin Guerre* (Cambridge, Mass.: Harvard University Press 1983); A.W. Brian Simpson, *Leading Cases in the Common Law* (Oxford: University Press, 1996), and *Cannibalism and the Common Law: The Sory of the Tragic Last Voyage of the Mignonette and the Strange Legal Proceedings to Which It Gave Rise* (Chicago: University of Chicago Press, 1986).

9 Jim Phillips, "The Trials and Travails of Eliza Maria Campbell: Law and Gender in Ontario in the 1870s," in *Essays in the History of Canadian Law, Volume XII: New Essays in Women's History*, eds. Lori Chambers and Joan Sangster (Toronto: Osgoode Society for Canadian Legal History and University of Toronto Press, 2023); Jim Phillips and Rosemary Gartner, *Murdering Holiness: The Trials of Franz Creffield and George Mitchell* (Vancouver: University of British Columbia Press, 2003); and Jim Phillips and Jeremy Martin, "*Manitoba Fisheries v. The Queen*: The Origins of Canada's *De Facto* Expropriation Doctrine," in *Property on Trial: Canadian Cases in Context*, eds. Bruce Ziff, Eric Tucker, and James Muir (Toronto: Osgoode Society for Canadian Legal History and Irwin Law, 2012).

10 For Canadian examples of work on leading cases see, inter alia, books published by the Osgoode Society for Canadian Legal History: Constance Backhouse, *Reckoning with Racism: Police, Judges and the RDS Case* (Toronto: University of Toronto Press, 2022); Robert Sharpe and Patricia McMahon, *The Persons Case: The Origins and Legacy of the Fight for Legal Personhood* (Toronto: University of Toronto Press, 2022); James W. St. G. Walker, *"Race," Rights and the Law in the Supreme Court of Canada: Historical Case Studies* (Waterloo: Wilfrid Laurier University Press, 1997).

11 For notable Canadian examples see Ian Radforth, *Jeannie's Demise: Abortion on Trial in Victorian Ontario* (Toronto: Between the Lines, 2020), and *Deadly Swindle: An 1890 Murder in Backwoods Ontario That Gripped the World* (Toronto: Osgoode Society for Canadian Legal History and University of Toronto Press, 2024); Robert J. Sharpe, *The Lazier Murder: Prince Edward County, 1884* (Toronto: Osgoode Society for Canadian Legal History and University of Toronto Press, 2011). For the Quebec civil law doctrines dealing with the emotions see Eric Reiter, *Wounded Feelings: Litigating Emotions in Quebec, 1870–1950* (Toronto: Osgoode Society for Canadian Legal History and University of Toronto Press, 2019). For

a multi-jurisdictional account of family, religion and law see Bettina Bradbury, *Caroline's Dilemma: A Colonial Inheritance Saga* (Vancouver and Sydney: University of British Columbia Press and University of New South Wales Press, 2019). For an American example see Michael Grossberg, *A Judgment for Solomon: The d'Hauteville Case and Legal Experience in Antebellum America* (Cambridge: University Press, 1996). For labour law see Judy Fudge and Eric Tucker, eds., *Work on Trial: Canadian Labour Law Struggles* (Toronto: Osgoode Society for Canadian Legal History and Irwin Law, 2010), and R.W. Kostal, "Conservative Insurrection: Great Strikes and Deep Law in Cleveland, Ohio and London, Ontario, 1898–1899," in *Essays in the History of Canadian Law Volume VIII: In Honour of R.C.B. Risk*, eds. G. Blaine Baker and Jim Phillips (Toronto: Osgoode Society for Canadian Legal History and University of Toronto Press, 1999). For property law see Bruce Ziff, *Unforeseen Legacies: Reuben Wells Leonard and the Leonard Foundation Trust* (Toronto: Osgoode Society for Canadian Legal History and University of Toronto Press, 2000).

12 Carolyn Strange, "Wounded Womanhood and Dead Men: Chivalry and the Trials of Clara Ford and Carrie Davies," in *Gender Conflicts: New Essays in Women's History*, eds. Franca Iacovetta and Mariana Valverde (Toronto: University of Toronto Press, 1992). One of the two cases examined by Strange is also the subject of Charlotte Gray, *The Massey Murder: A Maid, Her Master, and the Trial That Shocked a Nation* (Toronto: Osgoode Society for Canadian Legal History and Harper Collins, 2013). See also Karen Dubinsky and Franca Iacovetta, "Murder, Womanly Virtue and Motherhood: The Case of Angelina Napolitano, 1911–1922," *Canadian Historical Review* 74 (1991): 505.

13 Phillips and Gartner, *Murdering Holiness.*

14 See Constance Backhouse, "'Bitterly Disappointed' at the Spread of 'Colour Bar Tactics': Viola Desmond's Challenge to Racial Segregation, Nova Scotia 1946," in *The African-Canadian Legal Odyssey: Historical Essays*, ed. Barrington Walker (Toronto: Osgoode Society for Canadian Legal History and University of Toronto Press, 2012), and *Colour Coded: A Legal History of Racism in Canada* (Toronto: Osgoode Society for Canadian Legal History and University of Toronto Press, 1999).

15 For the critiques in this paragraph and the next see McNairn, "Intersecting Legal and Intellectual Histories." For another review of the genre noting some of these critiques, see Sarah Hamill, "Review of Legal History," *Social and Legal Studies*, 28 (2019): 538.

16 Richard Danzig, "Hadley v. Baxendale: A Study in the Industrialization of the Law," *Journal of Legal Studies* 4 (1975): 249; quotation below at 250.

17 It would be otiose to provide extensive references for this by now self-evident proposition. For an overview of women's history in

nineteenth-century Canada, see Alison Prentice et al., *Canadian Women: A History* (Toronto: Harcourt, Brace Jovanovich, 1999). For a case study of one of the professions that women had access to, see Alison Prentice, *From Private Servant to Public Servant: Status, Sex and Hierarchy in the Mid-Nineteenth Century Ontario Teaching Profession* (Toronto: Ontario Institute for Studies in Education, 1979). For suffrage see Joan Sangster, *One Hundred Years of Struggle: The History of Women and the Vote in Canada* (Vancouver: University of British Columbia Press, 2018). For the law and the legal system generally, see Constance Backhouse, *Petticoats and Prejudice: Women and Law in Nineteenth-Century Canada* (Toronto: Osgoode Society and Women's Press, 1991).

18 See, inter alia, Constance Backhouse, "Nineteenth Century Canadian Rape Law, 1880–1902," in *Essays in the History of Canadian Law, Volume II*, ed. David Flaherty (Toronto: Osgoode Society and University of Toronto Press, 1981); Karen Dubinsky, *Rape and Heterosexual Conflict in Ontario, 1880–1929* (Chicago: University of Chicago Press, 1993); Carolyn Strange, "Patriarchy Modified: The Criminal Prosecution of Rape in York County, Ontario, 1880–1930," in *Essays in the History of Canadian Law, Volume V: Crime and Criminal Justice*, eds. Jim Phillips, Tina Loo, and Susan Lewthwaite (Toronto: Osgoode Society and University of Toronto Press, 1994).

19 Constance Backhouse, "Pure Patriarchy: Nineteenth-Century Canadian Marriage," *McGill Law Journal* 31 (1986), 264 at 265. Quotations from Gemmill, *The Practice of the Parliament of Canada*, 262. Backhouse also cites, among many other contemporaries, the views of Goldwyn Smith, a leading intellectual of the 1870s, who wrote that "the husband's headship" was as inseparable an incident of Christian marriage "… as its indissolubility" (at 299).

20 William Blackstone, *Commentaries on the Laws of England* (London and Chicago: Facsimile edition of the first 1765 edition, University of Chicago Press, 1979), Book 1, 430.

21 James Schouler, *A Treatise on the Law of Domestic Relations Embracing Husband and Wife, Parent and Child, Guardian and Ward, Infancy, and Master and Servant* (Boston: Little Brown, 1870), 10. There were no Canadian treatises on the law of domestic relations published in this period and, as a result, Canadian judges often referred to English and American texts in their judgments. Such texts laid out the basic principles of the common law doctrines shared by both and by Canadian common law jurisdictions. See, inter alia, in addition to Schouler, *Law of Domestic Relations*, William Pinder Eversley, *Law of the Domestic Relations, Including Husband and Wife, Parent and Child, Guardian and Ward, Infants, and Master and Servant* (Edinburgh

and London: Ballantyne Press, 1885), and Charles Crawley, *The Law of Husband and Wife* (London: William Clowes, 1892).

22 Note that in the title of Schouler, *Law of the Domestic Relations*, above, "domestic relations" includes master and servant law. For an explanation see Luke Taylor, *Constructing the Family: Marriage and Work in Nineteenth-Century English Law* (Toronto: University of Toronto Press, 2023), and Philip Girard, 'Why Canada Has No Family Policy: Lessons from France and Italy," *Osgoode Hall Law Journal* 32 (1994): 579, esp. at 584–6.

23 Lori Chambers, *Married Women and Property Law in Victorian Ontario* (Toronto: Osgoode Society for Canadian Legal History and University of Toronto Press, 1997), and "Married Women and Businesses," *Ontario History* 104 (2012): 45; Philip Girard and Rebecca Veinott, "Married Women's Property Law in Nova Scotia, 1850–1910," in *Separate Spheres: Women's Worlds in the 19th-Century Maritimes*, eds. Janet Guildford and Suzanne Morton (Fredericton: Acadiensis Press, 1994); Constance Backhouse, "Married Women's Property Law in Nineteenth-Century Canada," *Law and History Review* 6 (1988): 211; Chris Clarkson, *Domestic Reforms: Political Visions and Family Regulation in British Columbia, 1862–1940* (Vancouver: University of British Columbia Press, 2007); Sheri Allen, "One Hundred Years of Solicitude: Judicial Resistance to the Reform of Married Women's Property Law in the West," *Dalhousie Journal of Legal Studies* 4 (1995): 175.

24 Constance Backhouse, "Shifting Patterns in Nineteenth-Century Canadian Custody Law," in *Essays in the History of Canadian Law Volume I*, ed. David Flaherty (Toronto: Osgoode Society and University of Toronto Press, 1981); Rebecca Veinott, 'Child Custody and Divorce: A Nova Scotia Study, 1866–1910," in *Essays in the History of Canadian Law Volume III: Nova Scotia*, eds. Philip Girard and Jim Phillips (Toronto: Osgoode Society and University of Toronto Press, 1990); Philip Girard, "Children, Church, Migration and Money: Three Tales of Child Custody in Nova Scotia," in *Children's Vices in Atlantic Literature and Culture*, ed. Hilary Thompson (Guelph, On.: Children's Press, 1995); Susan Boyd, *Child Custody, Law and Women's Work* (Don Mills, Ont.: Oxford University Press, 2003), chap. 2.

25 Constance Backhouse, "Involuntary Motherhood: Abortion, Birth Control and the Law in Nineteenth-Century Canada," *Windsor Yearbook of Access to Justice* 3 (1983): 61; Radforth, *Jeannie's Demise.*

26 Constance Backhouse, "The Tort of Seduction: Fathers and Daughters in Nineteenth-Century Canada," *Dalhousie Law Journal* 10 (1986): 45; Martha Bailey, 'Servant Girls and Masters: The Tort of Seduction and the Support of Bastards," *Canadian Journal of Family Law* 10 (1991): 137.

27 Phillips, Girard, and Brown, *A History of Law in Canada Volume II*, 519.

28 Philip Girard, Jim Phillips, and R. Blake Brown, *A History of Law in Canada Volume I: Beginnings to 1866* (Toronto: Osgoode Society for Canadian Legal History and University of Toronto Press, 2018), 349.
29 Tim Streeton and Krista Kesselring, "Introduction: Coverture and Continuity" in *Married Women and the Law: Coverture in England and the Common Law World*, eds. Stretton and Kesselring (Kingston and Montreal: McGill-Queen's University Press, 2013), 4.
30 The significance of marriage as the perceived bedrock social institution of this period has been the subject of many studies, too numerous to list here. Surveys may be found in Snell, *In the Shadow of the Law*, and the same author's "The White Life for Two: The Defence of Marriage and Sexual Morality in Canada, 1890–1914," *Social History-Histoire Sociale* 26 (1983): 311; Backhouse, "Pure Patriarchy," 265–6 and *passim*.
31 See, for two examples a century apart, *Cartwright v. Cartwright* (1853), 3 De G M & G 1982, 43 ER 385 (Chancery), and *Re Hurshman* (1956), 6 DLR (2d) 615 (B.C. Supreme Court).
32 Schouler, *Law of Domestic Relations*, 53. See also Chambers, *Married Women and Property Law*, 15–16.
33 For nineteenth-century Canadian attitudes to love and marriage see W. Peter Ward, *Courtship, Love and Marriage in Nineteenth-Century English Canada* (Kingston and Montreal: McGill-Queen's University Press, 1990).
34 Schouler, *Law of Domestic Relations*, 23.
35 For the use of this phrase see Strange, "Wounded Womanhood and Dead Men."
36 Alimony Case Report.

2. The Town of Whitby, the Campbell and Byrne Families, and the Campbell Marriage to August 1873

1 For the history of Whitby see Leo Johnson, *History of the County of Ontario, 1615–1875* (Whitby: Corporation of the County of Ontario, 1973), and "Abram Farewell," *DCB online*; Brian Winter, *Chronicles of a County Town: Whitby Past and Present* (Whitby: Published by the author, 1999), and *A Town Called Whitby* (Whitby: R. Huff Production, 1967); *Centennial Handbook: The County Town Ontario County* (Whitby: Town of Whitby, 1955; and J.E. Farewell, *Ontario County: Short Notes as to the Early Settlement and Progress of the County* (Whitby: Gazette-Chronicle Press, 1907; reprinted by Mika Publishers, Belleville, 1972, as *County of Ontario*). The last is the first full-length study of the town's history, written by a descendant of a prominent early settler and Whitby lawyer in the later nineteenth and early twentieth centuries. *Chronicles of A County Town* is a collection of 133 newspaper articles written over many years by Winter, the long-serving town archivist.

2 Robert J. Surtees, *Indian Land Surrenders in Ontario, 1763–1867* (Ottawa: Indian and Northern Affairs Canada, 1984), 4. The region and many other parts of Ontario were also included in the 1923 Williams Treaties: see Robert J. Surtees, *Treaty Research Report: The Williams Treaties (1923)* (Ottawa: Indian and Northern Affairs Canada, 1986).

3 *Whitby Chronicle*, 28 Feb. 1861.

4 See *An Act to Make Certain Alterations in the Territorial Divisions of Upper Canada*, SPC 1851, c 5; *An Act to Incorporate the Town of Whitby, and to Define the Limits Thereof*, SPC 1854, c 28; Winter, *Chronicles of a County Town*, 70–82. The new county of Ontario had 11 townships, including Whitby, Pickering, and Uxbridge. In 1857 Whitby township was split into Whitby and East Whitby, and East Whitby was annexed by Oshawa in 1922.

5 For Higgins and the *Chronicle* see Winter, "The First Chronicle," in *Chronicles of a County Town*, 1–4.

6 *Illustrated Historical Atlas of Ontario County* (Toronto: J.H. Beers and Co, 1872; reprinted by Mika Books, Belleville, 1972); William H. Higgins, *The Life and Times of Joseph Gould: Reminiscences of Sixty Years of Active Political and Municipal Life* (Toronto: C. Blackett Robinson, 1887).

7 Winter, *Chronicles of a County Town*, 106–7.

8 Much of what follows on Eliza Byrne's family is based on census and vital statistics records located through ancestry.com and familysearch.org. For the Byrnes's transatlantic crossing see the online US Immigration Records, Mfilm M237, Line 14, List Number 665. For the Rev. Byrne see generally his obituary in *Whitby Chronicle*, 26 Nov. 1874, and Farewell, *County of Ontario*, 68.

9 For Congregationalism see the current church's website www.cccc.ca, and for the LMS, best known for its work in Africa and Polynesia, see Cecil Northcott, *Glorious Company: 150 Years Life and Work of the London Missionary Society 1795–1945* (London: Livingstone Press, 1945). Most Canadian congregationalist churches joined with the Methodists and many Presbyterians to form the United Church in 1925. In 1965 a few Congregationalists left that body and affiliated with the American Conservative Congregational Christian Conference because they did not care for the theological liberalism of the United Church. In 1988 that church's decision to ordain non-celibate gay ministers caused more churches, many in southern Ontario, to leave and form the Congregational Christian Churches of Canada.

10 Allen P. Stouffer, *The Light of Nature and the Law of God: Antislavery in Ontario, 1833–1877* (Kingston and Montreal: McGill-Queen's University Press, 1992), 165.

11 Henrietta does not appear at all in this story. She married (see Rev. Byrne's obituary in *Whitby Chronicle*, 26 Nov. 1874) and likely moved away

from her parents soon after the family got to the new world. Samuel is mentioned a few times, as living in California.

12 Chana Kroll, "The Story of Batyah (Bithiah): A Transformed Identity," at *chabad.org/the Jewish Woman/article_cdo.*

13 *Whitby Chronicle*, 13 Oct. 1864; "Norman George Ham," LSO/PMD.

14 *Hamilton Spectator*, 4 June 1861 and 8 June 1864.

15 *Whitby Chronicle*, 15 Dec. 1864. This is the first issue in which I could find an advertisement. He bought the business from a George Bannister. In 1871 Byrne took on a 17-year old apprentice, Thomas Whitfield, who opened his own business when Byrne died in 1877: Whitby Archives.

16 Ontario County Marriage Registers, 1858–1869, on ancestry.com; Minnesota State Census, 1895, on family search.org.

17 *Whitby Chronicle*, 9 Apr. 1863.

18 In addition to the specific references given in the footnotes below, as with the Byrne family and many other individuals in this book, what follows on the Campbell family is based in part on seven Canadian censuses taken between 1851 and 1911: the Canada West censuses for 1851 and 1861, and the federal censuses of 1871, 1881, 1891, 1901, and 1911. Census information was first located through the online source ancestry.com, as was vital statistics (births, marriages and deaths) information. I have also used familysearch.org and findagrave.com. See also the entries for Robert Campbell, James Campbell, and Rebecca Tweedie in Whitby Archives. The only published account of Robert Campbell's family background and life is William Barcley Norton, *Past and Present of Saline County, Missouri* (Indianapolis and Chicago: Bowen & Co, 1910), 605–7. This was the source for Robert's obituaries published in the newspapers for Marshall, Missouri, and its environs. Marshall was where Robert moved to in 1885 and where he lived the last 30 years of his life. See *Weekly Democrat-News*, 25 Feb. 1915; *Saline County Weekly Progress*, 26 Feb. 1915; *Saline County Citizen*, 27 Feb. 1915; *Slater News-Rustler*, 25 Feb. 1915; *Slater News*, 25 Feb. 1915.

19 *Dictionary of Scottish Church History and Theology*, eds. N. Cameron et al. (Edinburgh: T & T Clark, 1993).

20 To give just one example, in her testimony in her suit for alimony, discussed in chapter 6, Eliza said "she could not mind" when a certain thing happened: *Whitby Chronicle*, 30 Apr. 1874. Since Eliza was born in Canada and her parents in England, she surely picked the phrase up from Robert. "Mind" is a word still commonly used by Scots for "remember."

21 An 1873 advertisement said that Robert had "been before the public for the last 22 years in Whitby": *Whitby Chronicle*, 30 Oct. 1873.

22 For the marriage see *Whitby Chronicle*, 1 Nov. 1860.

23 *Saline County Weekly Progress* (Marshall, Missouri), 29 Nov. 1907; *Pickering News*, 6 Dec. 1907.
24 *Whitby Chronicle*, 3 Apr. 1862.
25 *Whitby Chronicle*, 30 Oct. 1873.
26 Advertisement for John Saunders, boots and shoes, and business card for James Keith Gordon, barrister and attorney: *Whitby Chronicle*, 11 May 1871 and 25 Jan. 1872. See generally the many advertisements in the *Whitby Chronicle*, *passim*, 1860s and early 1870s, and in the *Whitby Gazette*'s occasional extant issues, 6 and 27 Oct. 1870. See also "Brian Winter's Historical Whitby," *Whitby Free Press*, 21 July 1978.
27 See, inter alia, *Whitby Chronicle*, 14 Nov. 1867 and 6 Feb. 1873.
28 *Whitby Chronicle*, 2 Apr. 1874; *Hamilton Weekly Times*, 13 Apr. 1876; Alimony Case Report, para. 22.
29 For the marriage see *Whitby Chronicle*, 27 Oct. 1864. For other information on James Campbell's family see Obituary of Rebecca Campbell in *Evening Telegram* (Toronto), 11 Nov. 1925, and *Gazette and Chronicle* (Whitby), 12 Nov. 1925; *Whitby Chronicle*, 11 Oct. 1895; and Winter, *Chronicles of a County Town*, 34–6.
30 *Whitby Chronicle*, 30 Apr. 1874; Minutes of Evidence, 197. For more on Adams see chapter 6 and for Gibson see chapter 7.
31 *Whitby Chronicle*, 12 May 1864, 25 Dec. 1865, 21 Nov. 1867, and 18 Dec. 1873.
32 Floor Plan, Exhibits 16 and 17 in Minutes of Evidence, 32.
33 Gross is discussed in more detail in chapters 3 and 5; the quotations are from Minutes of Evidence, 225. There is no explanation for why Martha left on 15 August 1873, to be replaced by Jane.
34 *Globe*, 16 Oct. 1873.
35 Alimony Case Report, para 22; Minutes of Evidence, 197.
36 Minutes of Evidence, 9; *Globe*, 27 Mar. 1874; *Whitby Chronicle*, 2 Apr. 1874.
37 *Whitby Chronicle*, 23 Oct. 1873.
38 Ibid., 2 and 30 Apr. 1874.
39 Ibid., 2 Apr. 1874.
40 Minutes of Evidence, 9.
41 *Whitby Chronicle*, 30 Apr.1874
42 Minutes of Evidence, 27, Exhibit 3.
43 Ibid., 13.
44 Ibid., 27–8, Exhibit 5. Emphasis in original.
45 For the Gordon family see 1871 Census; *Globe*, 16 Oct. 1873 and 27 Mar.1874; "James Keith Gordon," LSO/ PMD; James K. Gordon's obituaries in *Toronto Daily Star*, 24 Nov. 1909, and *Globe*, 25 Nov. 1909. For lawyers in Whitby see any issue of the *Whitby Chronicle*. In October 1873

Gordon's office was over Addison's store on Brock Street: *Whitby Chronicle*, 9 Oct. 1873.

46 *Globe*, 27 Mar. 1874, and *Whitby Chronicle*, 2 Apr. 1874.

47 *Whitby Gazette*, 23 Oct. 1873.

48 *Globe*, 27 Mar. 1874.

49 Alimony Case Report, para. 31.

50 Although she may well have talked about the bed being "mussed up" in the lawsuits, the only place she is recorded as having said it was before the Senate divorce committee in 1876: see Minutes of Evidence, 35.

51 For these three men see Whitby Archives. Quotations in this paragraph from *Globe*, 16 Oct. 1873; *Whitby Chronicle*, 2 Apr. 1874.

52 See Whitby Archives, and, inter alia, an advertisement for R.H. Jameson advertising a variety of clarets, champagne, highland whisky and rye whisky: *Whitby Chronicle*, 11 Sept. 1879.

53 *Globe*, 28 Mar. 1874.

54 See *Whitby Chronicle*, 30 Oct. 1873, and subsequent issues.

3. Robert Campbell's Separation from Eliza, August 1873

1 *Whitby Chronicle*, 2 April 1874; *Globe*, 23 October 1873.

2 Reproduced in Minutes of Evidence, 27, Exhibit 4.

3 Reproduced in Alimony Case Report, para 26; emphasis added. For some reason only a small part of this, the first sentence only, was reproduced in Minutes of Evidence,28, Exhibit 5.

4 *Monsieur Sylvestre*, 212 and 217. These page references are to an 1883 edition published by Roberts Brothers of Boston and entitled *The Hermit*.

5 James Hare, *A Treatise on the Conduct of God to the Human Species, and on the Divine Mission of Jesus Christ* (1809). The full sentence from the original reads: "The two greatest duties of man are worshipping God in spirit and truth, and in making happy the human heart: certainly there is no pleasure on earth so exquisite, so sublime, or so pure."

6 Franklin Square Song Collection: *Songs and Hymns for Schools and Homes, Nursery and Fireside, Volume 7* (New York: Harper, 1891), 83. The song was written by W. Landson.

7 See, inter alia, Elizabeth Harlan, *George Sand* (New Haven: Yale University Press, 2004), and Ruth Jordan, *George Sand: A Biography* (London: Constable, 1976).

8 *Globe*, 27 Mar. 1874; *Whitby Chronicle*, 4 Apr. 1874.

9 Minutes of Evidence, 21; NWMP Personnel Records, LAC, RG 18, Vol 10037; John Althouse, "The North-West Mounted Police Cemeteries at Fort MacLeod," online at www.abgenealogy.ca. For the reasons John A. Macdonald created the force and the first deployment to the west see

Roderick C. Macleod, *The North-West Mounted Police and Law Enforcement, 1873–1905* (Toronto: University of Toronto Press, 1976), chaps. 1 and 2.

10 For Coulthard's evidence to this effect see *Whitby Chronicle*, 30 Apr. 1874; and for Coulthard's business and the fact that he served on the town council see the issues of 14 April 1864 and 1 January 1874. Coulthard was later reeve of Oshawa, an Ontario county councillor, and warden of the county: Whitby Archives.

11 Quotations in this paragraph from *Whitby Chronicle*, 2 Apr. 1874, and *Globe*, 27 and 28 Mar. 1874.

12 Quotations in this paragraph from *Globe*, 27 Mar. 1874 and Minutes of Evidence, 87.

13 *Globe*, 27 Mar. 1874.

14 Alimony Case Report, para. 27.

15 *Globe*, 16 Oct. 1873.

16 Minutes of Evidence, 42.

17 The deposition was entitled "Overheard conversation between G. Gordon and Mrs. R. Campbell, that took place on the evening of 26th August and morning of 27th, 1873." It is in Alimony Case Report, para. 27.

18 Ibid., para. 30.

19 Quotations from Minutes of Evidence, 43. I have not cited the other occasions on which nearly identical testimony was given.

20 Minutes of Evidence, 64.

21 Quotations in this paragraph from *Globe*, 16 Oct. 1873 and 27 Mar. 1874; *Whitby Gazette*, 23 Oct. 1873; *Whitby Chronicle*, 23 Oct. 1873 and 2 Apr. 1874.

22 *Whitby Gazette*, 23 Oct. 1873.

23 A stereoscope was a device for viewing a pair of separate images, left eye and right eye views of the same scene, as a single three-dimensional image. It was invented in the 1830s and became a popular form of home entertainment from the mid-nineteenth century. Sets of stereo-cards could be bought by those who owned one. See Ray Zone, *Stereoscopic Cinema and the Origins of 3-D Film, 1838–1952* (Lexington: Kentucky University Press, 2007).

24 For the words and music of "Kathleen Aroon" see *Music for a Nation: American Sheet Music 1870–1885*, music by J.C. Alden Jr. For "I'll Take You Home Again Kathleen," see *American Old Time Song Lyrics* – Traditional Music Library, at *yumpu.com/en/document/view/11555728*. For "A Pirate's Serenade," written by John Thomson, first published in 1838 and republished in the US, see *Historic Sheet Music Collection*, 322, at *digitalcommons.conncoll.edu/sheetmusic/322.*

25 For the floriography movement see Geraldine Laufer, *Tussie-Mussies: The Victorian Art of Expressing Yourself in the Language of Flowers* (New York: Workman Publishing, 1993). A tussie -mussy was a nosegay, worn

or carried as a fashion accessory to convey a message. *The Language of Flowers* was a six-page poem, the second verse of which begins with some lines stating the general message: "There is a language in each flower, / That opens to the eye, A voiceless – but a magic power, / Doth in earth's blossoms lie." It was published in Catherine Waterman, *Flora's Lexicon: An Interpretation of the Language and Sentiment of Flowers with an Outline of Botany and a Poetical Introduction* (Philadelphia: Herman Hooker, 1840). (Waterman became Waterman Esling when she married in 1840 but she continued to publish as Waterman thereafter.)

26 Quotation from John Wilders, "Book Review," in *Modern Language Review* 74 (1979), 655–6. For the leading modern edition see *Hudibras*, ed. John Wilders (Oxford: Clarendon Press, 1967), and for useful commentaries see A.S. Hargreaves, "Hudibras," in *Oxford Companion to British History*, ed. John Cannon (Oxford: University Press, 2009) and William C. Horne, "'Between th' Petticoat and Breeches': Sexual Warfare and the Marriage Debate in *Hudibras*," *Studies in Eighteenth-Century Culture* 11 (1982): 133.

27 *Whitby Chronicle*, 27 Mar. and 2 and 30 Apr. 1874.

28 See, inter alia, ibid., 27 Mar. 1874.

29 Lawler ran one of the principal grocery stores in the mid- to late nineteenth century. Winter, *Chronicles of a County Town*, 108–10.

30 See variously Alimony Case Report, para. 27; *Globe*, 16 Oct. 1873; *Whitby Chronicle*, 23 Oct. 1873.

31 See variously Alimony Case Report, para. 27; *Whitby Gazette*, 23 Oct. 1873; *Globe*, 16 Oct. 1873.

32 *Whitby Chronicle*, 27 Mar. 1874

33 Alimony Case Report, para. 27; *Whitby Gazette*, 23 Oct. 1873.

34 *Globe*, 27 Mar. 1874.

35 *Globe*, 16 Oct. 1873.

36 *Whitby Chronicle*, 30 Apr. 1874; Minutes of Evidence, 215, 225, 230, 251 and 252 (quotation).

37 Quotations in this paragraph from Gross's testimony before the Senate, in Minutes of Evidence, 214; *Globe*, 28 Mar. 1874; and *Whitby Chronicle*, 2 Apr. 1874. Gross was born in Germany in 1807, educated in Holland, and was for some years resident in the UK, running the family business after his father's death. In 1850 he emigrated to the US, and after a couple of years moved to Canada West, living in Cobourg and then Goderich. In 1859 he moved to Whitby and opened his hardware business, which later became Gross & Granger. He owned "considerable property" in the town, and his hardware store was on the opposite side of Brock Street from the Campbell stores, and a little to the south. See Minutes of Evidence, 211; and numerous advertisements in the *Whitby Chronicle*. For his role as Eliza's "chaperone" in Ottawa see below, chapter 10.

38 *Whitby Chronicle*, 30 Apr. 1874.
39 The letter is reproduced in Minutes of Evidence, 182–183, Exhibit 20. There is no copy of the letter dated August 29th, but the evidence makes it clear that it was to the same effect.
40 Alimony Case Report, para. 32; *Globe*, 27 Mar. 1874.
41 *Whitby Chronicle*, 2 Oct. 1873.
42 Minutes of Evidence, 219. It is uncertain whether a fund was actually established for Eliza, but Gross thought plenty of people were willing to contribute to one: Minutes of Evidence, 215.

4. Eliza Campbell's Ejection from the Family Home, September 1873

1 This account of Eliza's forcible removal from the family home is based on Minutes of Evidence, esp. at 131–3, and on proceedings taken against Robert by Eliza before the Whitby magistrates and reported in *Whitby Chronicle*, 2 and 9 Oct. 1873, and *Whitby Gazette*, 9 Oct. 1873. As in previous chapters only quotations are footnoted.
2 Minutes of Evidence, 26.
3 Robert Harrison Diaries, AO, F 1328, entry for 22 Sept. 1873 [hereafter Harrison Diaries]. For Harrison and the lawsuit see chapter 5. Harrison was told about Eliza's ejection the evening it happened: Harrison Diaries, entry for 25 Sept. 1873.
4 Dr. Robert John Gunn was born on 14 February 1815 at Caithness, Scotland. He took a medical degree at Edinburgh University, practised in Thurso in his native Caithness for two years, and came to Canada West in 1842, settling in Whitby where he was a physician and surgeon for 58 years. He was also mayor of Whitby in 1862 and 1867–68, as well as a councillor for many other years, a JP, surgeon to the county jail, and an elder of the Presbyterian Church: see Whitby Archives.
5 *Whitby Chronicle*, 2 Oct. 1873. See the same source for the certificate.
6 For Bryan's appointment see ibid., 9 Oct. 1873.
7 Town government, including policing, was done under the authority of the *Municipal Act*, SPC 1849, c 81. For the importance of the Act see J.H. Aitchison, "The Municipal Corporations Act of 1849," *Canadian Historical Review*, 30 (1949): 107, and David Siegel, "Robert Baldwin and Responsible Local Government in Ontario," *Journal of Canadian Studies*, 53 (2019): 296. Under the *Municipal Act* town councils were authorized to appoint a chief constable and as many constables as was deemed necessary. For constables see Adam Wilson, *The Constables' Guide: A Sketch of the Office of Constable* (Toronto: Maclear & Co., 1859). For the organization of Whitby's police force see John E. Prichard, "Town Administration," in *Centennial Handbook*, 23

8 Quotations in this paragraph from *Whitby Chronicle*, 2 Oct. 1873.
9 Quotations in this paragraph from ibid., 2 and 9 Oct. 1873.
10 Ibid., 2 Oct. 1873.
11 Ibid.
12 Ibid., 2 Oct. 1873 and 2 Apr. 1874.
13 What follows on the assault prosecution is from ibid., 2 and 9 Oct. 1873. The former covered the proceedings on 30 September and gave a very brief summary of 1 October, presumably because the reporter did not have time to write up more between the court adjourning at 8 p.m. on 1 October, and the paper needing to be set up to come out on 2 October. A much longer account of Wednesday, 1 October appeared in the *Chronicle* of 9 October. Greenwood also at various times owned a clock factory and a sewing machine company in the town. Although he lived in a large house on Henry Street he was not very successful in his various enterprises and in 1875 had to resign as mayor because of his financial difficulties: see Whitby Archives, and *Whitby Free Press*, 3 Dec. 1975.
14 For Draper see Winter, *Chronicles of a County Town*, 51–5 and 143.
15 *Whitby Chronicle*, 2 Oct. 1873.
16 *An Act Respecting the Duties of Justices of the Peace, out of Sessions, in Relation to Persons Charged with Indictable Offences*, SC 1869, c 30.
17 Canada West was the only British North American colony to have a system of salaried, full-time county attorneys to oversee and conduct criminal prosecutions. Elsewhere criminal prosecution was either private, or carried out by ad hoc appointees. See Girard, Phillips, and Brown, *History of Law in Canada Volume I*, 572–7; Paul Romney, *Mr. Attorney: The Attorney-General for Ontario in Court, Cabinet and Legislature, 1791–1899* (Toronto: Osgoode Society and University of Toronto Press, 1986), 218–31; Marvin Bloos, "The Public Prosecutions Model for Upper Canada," *Criminal Law Quarterly*, 32 (1989–1990): 69; and Desmond Brown, "James Robert Gowan," *DCB online.* Farewell was the son of Ontario county grandee Abram Farewell and the author of *County of Ontario.* See Leo Johnson, "Abram Farewell," *DCB online.*
18 Smith was born in Nova Scotia in 1833 and moved to Whitby in 1849. In 1876–77 he was mayor of Whitby, and in 1889 was made a county court judge for Ontario county: see Whitby Archives, and LSO/PMD.
19 This was implicitly the view propounded by then vice-chancellor of the Court of Chancery Oliver Mowat in 1872, in *Cronk v. Cronk* [1872] OJ No. 206.
20 This account of the proceedings on 30 September, including all quotations, is from *Whitby Chronicle*, 2 Oct. 1873.
21 For what follows on 1 Oct., see ibid., 9 Oct. 1873, and *Whitby Gazette*, 9 Oct. 1873, quotations from *Whitby Chronicle*. This issue of the *Whitby Gazette* is

one of the few that is extant and is shorter than the report in the *Chronicle*. It also refers to its report of the first day in the previous week's issue, but that has not survived.

22 Quotations from *Whitby Chronicle*, 9 Oct. 1873, and *Whitby Gazette*, 9 Oct. 1873.

23 *Whitby Gazette*, 9 Oct. 1873.

24 *Whitby Chronicle*, 11 and 18 Dec. 1873. The Quarter Sessions records for Ontario County for 1873 or 1874 have not survived.

25 Testimony of James A. Campbell, no relation to the Campbell family featured in this book, reported in *Globe*, 27 Mar. 1874.

26 *Whitby Chronicle*, 11 Sept. 1873 and 2 Oct. 1873. Quotations in the next two paragraphs are from the latter source.

27 James's statement has not survived but is referred to in Harrison Diaries, entry for 25 Sept. 1873.

28 This is a very much simplified description of the phenomenon of vigilante action taken against those who offended a community's sense of right and wrong. For a more detailed discussion see Bryan Palmer, "Discordant Music: Charivaris and Whitecapping in Nineteenth-Century North America," *Labour/Le Travail* 3 (1978): 5–62. For the charivari in Ontario see Susanna Moodie, *Roughing It in the Bush, or Forest Life in Canada* (Toronto: Hunter Rose, revised edition, 1871), chap. 11, "The Charivari." For a detailed north American example see Phillips and Gartner, *Murdering Holiness*, 45–54.

29 *Whitby Chronicle*, 2 Oct. 1873.

30 Ibid., 30 Oct. 1873, 5 Nov., and 4, 11 and 18 Dec. 1873.

31 Ibid., 18 Dec. 1873.

32 Elizabeth Campbell was listed as a member of Robert Campbell's household on the 1881 census. She had not been there in 1871.

33 *Whitby Chronicle*, 23 Mar. 1877 and *Ottawa Citizen*, 26 Mar. 1877.

34 *Whitby Chronicle*, 2 Oct. 1873.

5. The Campbells Go to Court I: Robert Campbell v. George Gordon for Criminal Conversation, 1873

1 What follows on the Ontario court system is drawn from Christopher Moore, *The Court of Appeal for Ontario: Defining the Right of Appeal, 1792–2013* (Osgoode Society for Canadian Legal History and University of Toronto Press, 2014), chap. 1; John D. Blackwell, "William Hume Blake and the Judicature Acts of 1849: The Process of Legal Reform at Mid-Century in Upper Canada," in *Essays in the History of Canadian Law Volume 1*; Margaret Banks, "The Evolution of the Ontario Courts, 1788–1981," in *Essays in the History of Canadian Law Volume II*. Here I deal only with the three superior civil courts because those were the ones in which the

lawsuits involving the Campbells were conducted. There were also lower, inferior, courts of civil jurisdiction, county and division courts, which dealt with cases involving smaller amounts of money.

2 For more on the Ontario Court of Chancery see chapter 7 dealing with the alimony case.

3 SPC 1853, c 175, s 2.

4 *Administration of Justice Act*, SPC 1849, c 63.

5 See *Administration of Justice Act*, SO 1873, c 8, s 1 and *Administration of Justice Act*, SO 1874, c 7, s 23. For more detail see Phillips, Girard and Brown, *History of Law in Canada Volume II*, 90–2, quotation at 91.

6 For the history of the crim. con. action in eighteenth- and nineteenth-century Britain see, inter alia, Susan Staves, "Money for Honour: Damages for Criminal Conversation," *Studies in Eighteenth-Century Culture* 11 (1982): 279, and Lawrence Stone, "Honor, Morals, Religion and the Law: The Action for Criminal Conversation in England, 1670–1857," in *The Transmission of Culture in Early Modern Europe*, eds. Anthony Grafton and Ann Blair (Philadelphia: University of Pennsylvania Press, 1990). For consortium, which in its origins included servants as well as wives, see Jeremy Weinstein, "Adultery, Law and the State: A History," *Hastings Law Journal*, 38 (1986): 195, at 216–18, and Jacob Lippman, "The Breakdown of Consortium," *Columbia Law Review*, 30 (1930): 651.

7 Stella Tillyard, *A Royal Affair: George III and His Scandalous Siblings* (London: Random House, 2020); Diane Atkinson, *The Criminal Conversation of Mrs. Norton: Victorian England's "Scandal of the Century" and the Fallen Socialite Who Changed Women's Lives Forever* (London: Preface Publishing, 2012).

8 For this case see the short account in Laura Hanft Korobkin, *Criminal Conversations: Sentimentality and Nineteenth-Century Legal Stories of Adultery* (New York: Columbia University Press, 1998), 57–60, quotation at 59.

9 *An Act to Introduce the English Law as the Rule of Decision in All Matters of Controversy Relative to Property and Civil Rights*, SUC 1792, c 1.

10 Crim. con is discussed in Backhouse, "Pure Patriarchy," 291–5, but only through two reported cases from the 1890s that considered whether the action should also be available to wives against women who committed adultery with their husbands. For other cases see *Frank v. Carson*, [1864] OJ No. 147. See also other cases in which the crim. con. action was mentioned even though the case was about something else. In *Hogle v. Ham*, [1825] OJ No. 8 (K.B.), a seduction case, the defendant applied for a new trial after the jury had given its verdict, arguing that the girl's father had given his consent to her sleeping with the defendant, and that this was a bar to the action, as it was in crim. con. In *Phipps v. Moore*, [1848] OJ No. 43 (Q.B.), a dower case, the issue was whether there had been a lawful marriage,

and Robinson C.J. said in passing that the only circumstances in which reputation could not serve as proof of marriage were indictments for bigamy and actions for crim. con. (para. 16).

11 See *Crim. Con.: A Trial. William Henry Hall, Plaintiff against Major George Barrow, Defendant, for Criminal Conversation with the Plaintiff's Wife, Supreme Court, at Halifax, Nova-Scotia, 20th July, 1820* (Halifax, 1820). Hall sued Barrow for £5,000, but the jury awarded him just £400.

12 For cases in the law reports see *McMillan v. Jelly*, [1867] OJ No. 150 (CP), and *Patterson v. McGregor*, [1869] OJ No. 73 (QB). For parliamentary divorce and crim. con., and the Martin case, see Gemmill, *The Practice of the Parliament of Canada*,153 and 155–159.

13 *Lellis v. Lambert*, (1897) 24 OAR 653 at 662.

14 *Quick v. Church*, [1893] OJ No. 76 (Q.B.); *Lellis v. Lambert*, cited above.

15 *Skinner v. Allen*, (1977) 18 OR (2nd) 3 at 9 (C.A.).

16 For Harrison see Carole Stelmack, "Robert Alexander Harrison," *DCB online*, and *The Conventional Man: The Diaries of Ontario Chief Justice Robert A. Harrison, 1856–1878*, ed. Peter Oliver (Toronto: Osgoode Society for Canadian Legal History and University of Toronto Press, 2003).

17 Harrison Diaries, entry for 1 Sept. 1873. I have relied on the original rather than the published diaries because the latter are far from complete. That Harrison told Robert that he thought that Robert had a good chance of success is from Minutes of Evidence, 252.

18 *Whitby Chronicle*, 11 Sept. 1873; AO, RG 22–5806–0–6, York County Assize Minutes 1872–1875, 171.

19 Harrison Diaries, entries for 22, 25, 26, and 27 Sept. 1873. The two had a further meeting on 14 October, and on that same day Harrison met with his witnesses.

20 For the Whitby fall assizes see *Whitby Chronicle*, 28 Aug. 1873, and for the lack of time see Robert Harrison's address to the jury in the 23 Oct. issue of the same newspaper, discussed later in this chapter.

21 There are no Canadian studies of the systematic use of juries in civil trials, although accounts of individual cases heard by juries are plentiful. For a refutation of the shibboleth that the civil jury was in decline in England in this period see Micheal Lobban, "The Strange Life of the English Civil Jury, 1837–1914," in *"The Dearest Birth Right of the People of England": The Jury in the History of the Common Law*, eds. John W. Cairns and Grant McLeod (Portland, Ore: Hart, 2002). For criticisms of the jury generally see R. Blake Brown, *A Trying Question: The Jury in Nineteenth-Century Canada* (Toronto: Osgoode Society for Canadian Legal History and University of Toronto Press, 2009). For the "speedy trials" legislation and the criminal trial in the 1870s see Phillips, Girard, and Brown, *A History of Law in Canada Volume II*, 437–9.

22 *Whitby Chronicle*, 23 Oct. 1873. This paragraph summarizes the relevant legislation in 1873, which was the *Jurors and Juries Act*, CSUC 1859, c 31. This became, with very little amendment, *An Act Respecting Jurors and Juries*, RSO 1877, c 48. Quotations and other specific references are from sections 3, 7, 15, and 105–7 of the 1859 Act.
23 For what follows on Cameron see "Matthew Crooks Cameron," LSO/PMD and A. Margaret Evans, "Sir Matthew Crooks Cameron," *DCB online*, from which the quotations are taken.
24 See Harrison Diaries, passim.
25 Whelan was defended by the aforementioned John Hilyard Cameron, grand master of the Orange Lodge.
26 *Whitby Chronicle*, 26 Nov. 1874.
27 Harrison Diaries, entry for 15 Oct. 1873.
28 *Whitby Chronicle*, 1879, passim.
29 For John Wilson Bengough see principally Ramsay Cook, "John Wilson Bengough," *DCB online;* Terry "Aislin" Mosher and Peter Desbarats, *The Hecklers: A History of Canadian Political Cartooning and a Cartoonists' History of Canada* (1979); and Stanley Kutcher, "John Wilson Bengough: Artist of Righteousness," (MA Thesis, History, McMaster University, 1975). For the Bengough family see also Whitby Archives. Unfortunately for me Bengough did not draw a cartoon referencing the crim. con. case. His overriding interest was politics, not other kinds of scandal.
30 *Whitby Gazette*, 23 Oct. 1873.
31 *Globe*, 16 Oct. 1873; *Whitby Gazette*, 23 Oct. 1873.
32 *Globe*, 16 and 17 Oct. 1873; *Mail*, 16 Oct. 1873; *Whitby Chronicle*, 23 Oct. 1873; *Whitby Gazette*, 23 Oct. 1873. Somewhat ironically the *Whitby Chronicle* issue of 23 October is one of the very few missing, but fortunately Robert Harrison cut the report out and pasted it into his diary, entry for 25 October 1873.
33 *Weekly Mail* (Toronto), 28 Nov. 1873; *Montreal Herald*, 18 Oct. 1873.
34 For the *Chronicle*'s publication schedule, see the notice "To Correspondents," in *Whitby Chronicle*, 11 May 1876.
35 Simon Greenleaf, *A Treatise on the Law of Evidence* (Boston: Little Brown, 9th edition, 1858), 254.
36 *An Act to Amend the Law of Evidence in Civil Cases*, SO 1869, c 13, s 5 (c). For an approving editorial see "Law of Evidence in Ontario," *Canada Law Journal*, 7 (1871) 173–4. For the English reforms see UK Statutes, 1826, c 16 (party witness) and 1853, c 83 (spousal immunity).
37 *An Act to Amend the Law of Evidence*, SO 1873, c 10, s 3.
38 *Globe*, 16 Oct. 1873.
39 Ibid.
40 Ibid. Neither of the Whitby newspapers reported the re-examination.

41 Italics in original in *Whitby Chronicle*, 23 Oct. 1873.
42 *Whitby Gazette*, 23 Oct. 1873.
43 This account of the evening recess is from *Globe*, 16 Oct. 1873.
44 Harrison Diaries, entry for 16 Oct. 1873.
45 This is my estimate of the date from the evidence of one of the rebuttal witnesses, James Campbell, who gave the date as "a week ago last Wednesday." He said this on Tuesday, 16 October, so last Wednesday was 10 October, and a week before that was 3 October.
46 For these individuals see Whitby Archives.
47 For Gross having been subpoenaed see Minutes of Evidence, 217 and 219. For his evidence in the other trials see chapters 6 and 7. Potential witnesses were kept in an anteroom while other testimony was taken.
48 The Rev. Byrne was not, of course, a Presbyterian but a Congregationalist. Perhaps Cameron did not know this, but more likely he thought the jury would see Presbyterians as more mainstream and automatically respectable.
49 Harrison Diaries, entry for 16 Oct. 1873. Quotation from Harrison in the next paragraph from the same source.
50 Ibid.
51 The executions are in Minutes of Evidence, 28–30, Exhibits 7 and 8.
52 The quotation is from Gibson's testimony before the Senate divorce committee more than two years later: Minutes of Evidence, 192.
53 *North Ontario Observer*, 2 Apr. 1874. The Tichborne case involved Richard Tichborne, the heir to the family fortune and baronetcy of that name. He was presumed to have died in a shipwreck in 1854 at the age of 25. His mother would not believe he had died, and was convinced he was in Australia. She advertised widely there, a campaign which brought forward a claimant in 1866. Lady Tichborne accepted him, but other family members did not. His claim went to the Court of Chancery in 1871, which found him to be an imposter. He was then successfully prosecuted for perjury in a subsequent case and given 14 years imprisonment. See, inter alia, Rohan McWilliam, *The Tichborne Claimant: A Victorian Sensation* (London: Hambledon, 2007), and Zadie Smith, *The Fraud* (London: Penguin Books, 2022).
54 *Daily Advertiser* (London), 23 Mar. 1874; *Ottawa Free Press*, 30 Nov. 1874. See also *Ontario Reformer* (Oshawa), 3 and 17 Oct. 1873; *Newmarket Courier*, 23 Oct. 1873; *Waterloo Advertiser*, 26 Mar. 1874.
55 This was the word used by George Gross before the Senate divorce committee: Minutes of Evidence, 216.
56 Harrison Diaries, 25 Oct. 1873.
57 *Whitby Chronicle*, 30 Oct. 1873.
58 Winter, *Chronicles of a County Town*, 134.
59 Minutes of Evidence, 216.

60 *Canada Law Journal*, 10 (February 1874), 31–32.
61 *Whitby Chronicle*, 6 Nov. 1873.
62 These proceeding were reported in the *Globe*, 22 Nov. 1873, 30 Nov. 1874, and 18 Sept. 1875, in the *Whitby Chronicle*, 27 Nov. 1873 and 2 Apr. 1874, and in the *Whitby Gazette*, 20 Sept. 1875. The *Globe* report of 30 Nov. 1874 was also published in the *Ottawa Free Press* of the same date. The following account is an amalgam of all reports.
63 "New Trials for Felony," *Canada Law Journal*, 13 (December 1877) 352, emphasis in original. See to similar effect the *Eighth Report of His Majesty's Commissioners on Criminal Law* (London: HMSO, 1845), 20: "A new trial in civil proceedings is allowed on the plain and simple ground that the practice is essential to justice for the purpose of correcting errors in its administration ... which require remedy."
64 The affidavit was sworn before John Homer Greenwood on November 19th, 1873, and is reproduced in Minutes of Evidence, 226.
65 Minutes of Evidence, 236–7.
66 *Globe*, 3 Mar. 1875.
67 *Globe*, 18 Sept. 1875.

6. The Campbells Go to Court II: Eliza Campbell (Robert Campbell *et ux*) v. James Campbell for Defamation, 1874

1 *Whitby Chronicle*, 11 Sept. 1873; AO, RG 22–5806–0–6, York County Assize Minutes 1872–1875, 239.
2 See Chambers, *Married Women and Property Law*, 21.
3 See Justice John Wellington Gwynne's judgment on James Campbell's motion for a new trial: Defamation Case Report, para. 3.
4 *Whitby Chronicle*, 2 Oct. 1873.
5 *Married Women's Property Act*, SO 1871–1872, c 16, s 9, and *Married Women's Property Act*, SO 1884, c 19, s 2 (2).
6 George Wingrove Cooke, *A Treatise on the Law of Defamation* (Philadelphia. US Edition, T. and J.W. Johnson, 1846), 76. For the use of this text in Ontario at this time see *Regina v. Patteson*, [1875] OJ No. 6 (QB). The Ontario statute on defamation was very short and largely procedural, the common law remained the governing source of defamation law: *An Act Respecting Actions of Libel and Slander*, CSUC 1859, c 103.
7 *North Ontario Observer* (Port Perry), 2 Apr. 1874.
8 For this motion see *Globe*, 2 and 3 Oct. 1873. For Dalton see "Robert Gladstone Dalton," LSO/ PMD. He became master in chambers of the Supreme Court after the passage of the *Judicature Act* of 1881: George Smith Holmested, *A Manual of Practice for the High Court of Ontario* (Toronto: Rowsell and Hutchison, 1881), 18.

9 For Osler and his famous family see, inter alia, Henry James Morgan, *The Canadian Men and Women of the Time: A Handbook of Canadian Biography* (Toronto: William Briggs, 1898), 788 and 874; Moore, *The Court of Appeal for Ontario*, 265; Patrick Brode, "Britton Bath Osler," *DCB online*.

10 For these men see *Canadian Biographical Dictionary*, 350–4, and *Globe*, 20 Dec. 1884 (Bethune); Moore, *The Court of Appeal for Ontario*, 260–1 (Moss); Christopher Moore, "Newman Wright Hoyles," and Jamie Benidickson, "Sir William Glenholme Falconbridge," both in *DCB online*.

11 *Globe*, 2 and 3 Oct. 1873, and Defamation Case Report, paras. 16 and 17. The cases cited were all about lawsuits started in someone's name where the alleged plaintiff argued that it had been done without authority. In every instance the motion was successful because no authority to bring the suit had been given, but these cases were not directly on point because Eliza had instructed Cameron to institute the litigation. One of the cases was Canadian{ *Shaw v. Ormiston*, [1855] OJ No. 197. The others were English: *Chambers v. Donaldson*, (1808), 9 East 472; *Hammek and Corporation of Plymouth v. Fillis*, (1818) 2 Chitty 170; and *Hubbart v. Phillips*, (1845) 13 M & W 703.

12 *Globe*, 25 and 27 Feb. 1874.

13 Graham Parker, "Sir John Hawkins Hagarty," *DCB online*.

14 *Globe*, 27 and 28 Mar. 1874; *Mail*, 27 and 28 Mar. 1874; *Whitby Chronicle*, 2 Apr. 1874; AO, RG 222–390–13, Box 106, Envelope 3, Benchbook of John Hagarty.

15 For the Ontario newspapers see below, this chapter, and *The Union*, 2 Apr. 1874; and for Montreal see *Montreal Daily Witness*, 27 Mar. 1874.

16 *Globe*, 27 Mar. 1874. See also Harrison Diaries, 26 and 27 Mar. 1873. The court house was "crowded to excess" on the first day and "densely packed" on the second.

17 *Globe*, 27 Mar. 1874.

18 The *Globe*, ibid., said that Harrison did cross-examine, and got Campbell to say that "he paid no particular attention to what the present defendant said about Gordon." The *Whitby Chronicle*, 2 Apr. 1874, said there was no cross-examination.

19 *Globe*, 27 March 1874.

20 Ibid.

21 Ibid.

22 Minutes of Evidence, 216.

23 *Globe*, 28 Mar. 1874.

24 For the Allins see Winter, *Chronicles of a County Town*, 134, and the advertisements in *Whitby Chronicle*, 1870s, passim.

25 *Globe*, 28 Mar. 1874.

26 *Globe*, 28 Mar. 1874.

27 Minutes of Evidence, 199.
28 Quotations in this paragraph and the next three from *Globe*, 28 Mar.1874.
29 Ibid.
30 Ibid.
31 Ibid.
32 This paragraph is largely from the Toronto *Leader*, evening edition, 27 Mar. 1874. See also Harrison Diaries, 28 Mar. 1874.
33 The Toronto *Leader*, 27 Mar. 1874, had a slightly different version of the deadlock, with 10, not 12, jurors for Eliza and two against.
34 Issue of 28 March 1874.
35 *Whitby Chronicle*, 2 and 9 Apr. 1874.
36 Ibid, 21 May 1874, and 1881 Census.
37 *Whitby Chronicle*, 9 Apr. 1874.
38 Port Perry *North Ontario Observer*, 2 Apr. 1874. See also a brief report in the London *Daily Advertiser*, 28 Mar. 1874.
39 *Whitby Chronicle*, 15 July 1875; *Whitby Gazette*, 9, 16, 23, and 30 Sept. 1875.
40 See Paul Romney, "Sir John Wellington Gwynne," *DCB online.*
41 Harrison Diaries, 20 and 21 May 1874.
42 *Globe*, 22 May 1874, 27 May 1875, and 23 Dec. 1875; *Daily Leader* (Toronto), 22 May 1874 and 28 May 1875. These reports simply state that the motion for a rule *nisi* was successful in May 1874 and that Cameron "shewed cause" why it should not be made absolute in May 1875.
43 What follows on the arguments made is from Defamation Case Report. Harrison's arguments are at paras. 15 and 17 and Cameron's at para. 16.
44 (1871) 7 L.R. (Q.B.) 112.
45 Defamation Case Report, paras. 30–1.

7. The Campbells Go to Court III: Eliza Campbell v. Robert Campbell for Alimony, 1874–1875

1 See *Whitby Chronicle*, 2 Oct. 1873; OA, RG 22–3809–0–5, Court of Chancery Master/Deputy Registrar's Docket Books 1872–1879, 84.
2 *Soules v. Soules*, [1851] O J No. 250, para. 5 The *Chancery Court Act*, SUC 1837, c 2, stated that the court had the jurisdiction of the English Court of Chancery.
3 For the operation of the Court of Chancery in alimony cases in nineteenth-century Ontario see Chambers, *Married Women and Property Law*, chap 2; and Chambers and John Weaver, "Alimony and Orders of Protection: Escaping Abuse in Hamilton-Wentworth, 1837–1900," *Ontario History* 95 (2003): 113.
4 Holmested's father Arthur was also a Chancery official, having been appointed the first clerk of records and writs of that court in 1862. George Smith Holmested held various posts as a court official before and after the

fusion of the courts by the 1881 *Judicature Act*, rising to be senior registrar and accountant of the Supreme Court, a post he held until he retired in 1923. He was also a widely published author in legal journals on many subjects. See "George Smith Holmested: An Appreciation," *Canadian Bar Review* 6 (1928): 452.

5 See "Arthur Godfrey Molson Spragge," and "John Hoskin," both in LSO/PMD; Brian Morison, "John Godfrey Spragge," *DCB online*; Curtis Cole, *Osler, Hoskin & Harcourt: Portrait of a Partnership* (Toronto: McGraw-Hill Ryerson, 1995); and "McCarthy, Osler, Hoskin, and Creelman, 1882–1902: Establishing a Reputation, Building a Practice," in *Beyond the Law: Lawyers and Business in Canada, 1830–1930*, ed. Carol Wilton (Toronto: The Osgoode Society and University of Toronto Press, 1990)

6 "William Alexander Foster," LSO/PMD, and *Canada First: A Memorial of the late William A. Foster, Q.C.* (Toronto: Hunter Rose, 1890).

7 SO 1871–1872, c 16, s 1.

8 For the proceeding before Holmested see Interim Alimony Case Report, quotations in this paragraph at para. 3 and in the next at para. 4. See also *Globe*, 26 Nov, 1873, and a brief report in the *Ontario Reformer* of Oshawa, 28 Nov.1873.

9 *Globe*, 1 Apr. 1876.

10 *Administration of Justice in the Court of Chancery Act*, SPC 1850, c 50, s 1 and *Court of Chancery Act*, SPC 1857, c 56, s 6. For the distinction between common law and equity, the best short description, which discusses both the English origins and the operation of Chancery courts in what is now Canada, is Philip Girard, "History and Development of Equity," in *The Law of Trusts: A Contextual Approach*, eds. Mark Gillen and Faye Woodman (Toronto: Emond, 4th ed., 2021). For Chancery reform in England and Ontario see Michael Lobban, "Preparing for Reform: Reforming the Nineteenth-Century Court of Chancery, Parts I and II," *Law and History Review*, 22 (2004): 389 and 565; Elizabeth Brown, "Equitable Jurisdiction and the Court of Chancery in Upper Canada," *Osgoode Hall Law Journal* 21 (1983): 275.

11 Transcripts of the Evidence in *Campbell v. Campbell*, AO, Court of Chancery Civil Suits Case Files, RG 22–409, Container B109512, File 269.

12 See John D. Blackwell, "Samuel Hume Blake," *DCB online*.

13 See James G. Snell, "Thomas Moss," *DCB online*, and "The West Toronto by-election of 1873 and Thomas Moss," *Ontario History*, 58 (1966): 236.

14 "Daniel McMichael," LSO/PMD; Evans, "Matthew Crooks Cameron," *Senate Journals*, 22 May 1872, 103–4.

15 *Globe*, 16 Sept. 1875.

16 As noted in chapter 2, the *Whitby Chronicle* was a weekly that appeared on Thursdays. There was a brief paragraph on the case in the *Whitby*

Chronicle, Thursday 23 Apr. 1874, which simply listed the first four witnesses, the fourth being John Anderson, who gave testimony on the 22nd, and stated that nothing more could be said because the paper had to be sent to the presses.

17 Blake's judgment was reported in Alimony Case Report. For Robert's deposition see para. 25.

18 *Whitby Chronicle*, 23 Apr. 1874.

19 *Oshawa Reformer*, no date, cited in *Whitby Chronicle*, 7 May 1874.

20 The *Chronicle* did not specify that this happened on the first day, but it seems most likely given that it was on the first day that Robert's witnesses testified in chief and that at the start of the second say Cameron's witnesses were heard from.

21 Alimony Case Report, paras. 31 and 32.

22 Ibid., paras. 28–9.

23 Ibid., para. 30.

24 *Whitby Chronicle*, 8 July 1875.

25 See Whitby Archives and *Whitby Chronicle*, 4 Jan. 1895.

26 Stanton had emigrated from Ireland to Whitby in 1856 at the age of 19. He worked for the *Chronicle* for almost 50 years, and died in 1908: Whitby Archives.

27 Laing was born in Scotland and emigrated to Canada West in 1841. He had been the mayor of Whitby in 1863–64, and in 1874 was the city treasurer: Whitby Archives.

28 Only Calvery said this, but given that Stanton corroborated what Calvery said he had heard Campbell say at the defamation trial he must have been there also.

29 What follows on Blake's remarks in urging reconciliation is derived from the report in the *Whitby Chronicle*, 30 April 1874, and on the closing speech given by William McDougall, counsel for Eliza in the Senate, in 1876, and later published in *The Campbell Divorce Bill: Women's Rights in Ontario. Parliament as a Court of Justice* (Ottawa: Privately Published, 1879).

30 There is no mention of Cameron having read out the letter in the press report, but later in his speech Blake referred to the letter as having been read on the first day of the trial.

31 For Robert's account see Minutes of Evidence, 12–13, and for Eliza's, 133–4.

32 See Blake's Decree, 15 Sept. 1875, in Minutes of Evidence, 31. The issuing of the judgment was reported in *Whitby Gazette*, 23 Sept. 1875, and *Globe*, 16 Sept. 1875.

33 *Whitby Chronicle*, 26 Nov. 1874; Probate Record, 9 April 1875, England & Wales, Index of Wills and Probates, 1853–1943.

34 *Whitby Chronicle*, 25 Feb. 1875.

35 Ibid., 15 July 1875.

36 Ibid., 10 and 17 June, and 28 Sept. 1875.
37 James Bremner 1875, Elgin Sheriff Court, National Records of Scotland, Wills and Testaments Reference SC26/39/12, 218–42, quotation at 241. I am grateful to Philip Augustine of Ottawa, a lawyer who has a long-standing interest in the Campbell case and who has done voluminous research on it, for sharing this reference with me.
38 For all of this see variously *Whitby Chronicle*, 30 Mar., 1 July, and 4 and 18 Nov. 1875.
39 Minutes of Evidence, 181–2.
40 The arguments are reproduced in the official report of Blake's decision released some months later: Alimony Case Report, paras. 1–10. Quotations from Moss's arguments in this paragraph and the next are at para. 3. The account in the case report is short and cannot reflect all that was said. I have augmented the case report from Blake's assessment of the evidence, discussed below, which refers in a number of places to counsels' arguments.
41 Quotations from Cameron's arguments are from Alimony Case Report, paras. 4 and 12.
42 Quotations from Moss's reply are from ibid., paras. 6–8.
43 Blake's judgment lists 24 cases cited by Cameron and Moss, but does not say who cited which ones: ibid., para. 10.
44 [1865] OJ No. 147; quotation below at para. 57.
45 As we will see in chapter 11, in England before 1857 divorces could only be obtained in the House of Lords, and applying to Parliament required a prior decision from the Court of Chancery or an ecclesiastical court.
46 John Aylife, *Forms of Ecclesiastical Law; or, the Mode of Conducting Suits in the Consistory Courts* (London: W. Bening, 1844).
47 Quotations in this paragraph from Alimony Case Report, paras. 13 and 14.
48 (1810), 2 Hag Con 1, 161 ER 648.
49 *Lord Cadogan v. Lady Codogan*, 1796, cited in *Loveden v. Loveden*, above; *Burgess v. Burgess*, (1804), 2 Hag Con 229, 161 ER 590; and *Chambers v. Chambers*, (1810) 1 Hag. Con. 445, 161 ER 610.
50 Thomas Poynter, *A Concise View of the Doctrine and Practice of the Ecclesiastical Courts in Doctors Commons on Various Points Relative to the Subject of Marriage and Divorce* (Philadelphia: John Little, 2nd ed., 1836); quotations in this paragraph from Alimony Case Report, para. 20.
51 Quotations in this paragraph from Alimony Case Report, para. 20.
52 Quotations in this paragraph from ibid., para. 23.
53 Quotations in this paragraph and the next two from ibid., paras. 27, 33, and 34.
54 Ibid., para. 36.
55 *Proverbs*, chapter 30, verse 20.

56 Quotations in this paragraph from Alimony Case Report, para. 37.
57 Ibid., paras. 3, 41, 44, 46 and 47.
58 McDougall, *The Campbell Divorce Bill,* 3. For more on this pamphlet see chapter 11.
59 *Whitby Chronicle,* 7 Jan. 1875.
60 "Interesting Review of the Whitby Scandal," *Ingersoll Chronicle,* 6 Apr. 1876, letter from Whitby.
61 *Hamilton Weekly Times,* 13 Apr.1877.
62 *Whitby Gazette,* 23 Sept. 1875.

8. Robert Campbell Petitions Parliament for a Divorce, 1876

1 Kim Smith-Maynard, "Divorce in Nova Scotia, 1750–1900," in Philip Girard and Jim Phillips, eds., *Essays in the History of Canadian Law Volume III: Nova Scotia* (Toronto: Osgoode Society and University of Toronto Press, 1990); J.M. Bumsted and Wendy Owen, "Divorce in a Small Province: A History of Divorce in Prince Edward Island from 1833," *Acadiensis,* 20 (1991): 86; Girard, Phillips, and Brown, *A History of Law in Canada Volume I,* 351–3. The Nova Scotia assembly also passed one divorce Act despite divorce being available through a court: *An Act to Dissolve the Marriage of Anne Kidston with Richard Kidston,* SNS 1834, c 44.
2 Section 129 did not refer to Prince Edward Island which was not a province in 1867, but section 146 of the *BNA Act* was to the same effect for future provinces and territories.
3 A colony's reception date is the date on which all English law, common law and statute, was received into a colony. After the reception date the common law continued to be received, but English statutes were not unless they were made specifically applicable to a colony or colonies. The British Columbia Supreme Court held that the UK Act of 1857 was received in the colony in 1872, although that was in a case about protection orders for deserted wives: Christopher Clarkson, *Domestic Reforms: Political Visions and Family Regulation in British Columbia, 1862–1940* (Vancouver: University of British Columbia Press, 2007), 47–8. The court did not find it had jurisdiction to grant divorces until the 1877 case of *M. Falsely Called S. v. S.* (1877) 1 BCR 25. For reception see Girard, Phillips, and Brown, *A History of Law in Canada Volume I, passim,* esp 278–80 for the criminal law, and Phillips, Girard, and Brown, *A History of Law in Canada Volume II,* 118–19 and 538. The 1857 UK Act is discussed in greater detail in chapter 11, below.
4 For divorce in Ontario before 1867 see Gemmill, *The Practice of the Parliament of Canada,* 17–19, and Backhouse, "Pure Patriarchy," 270–1. A divorce court bill was introduced in the Upper Canada assembly in

1833–34, but it did not even reach second reading: *Journals of the Legislative Assembly of Upper Canada*, 19 and 28 November 1833, 9 and 17. In 1858, 1859, and 1860 there were brief discussions of introducing a statute equivalent to the 1857 UK Act, but no Act was passed.

5 *Walker v. Walker* [1919] AC 947 (PC); *Board v. Board* [1919] AC 956 (PC).

6 The 1857 UK Act did not apply to Ireland. Thus residents of the island had to apply to Parliament for a divorce. For people in Northern Ireland after the partition (1922), the situation remained the same until 1939, when judicial divorce was inaugurated. There was no mechanism to get a divorce in the Republic of Ireland after partition, and its unavailability was reinforced in 1937 when a new constitution prohibited divorce. Judicial divorce did not become available until 1996. See Diane Urquhart, *Irish Divorce: A History* (Cambridge: University Press, 2020), and "Ireland and the *Divorce and Matrimonial Causes Act*, 1857," *Journal of Family History*, 38 (2013): 301.

7 It was not accepted, however, by some Quebec legal commentators. Thomas-Jean-Jacques Loranger, author of *Commentaire sur le Code civil dus Bas-Canada* (2 vols., Montreal, 1873 and 1879) and a judge of the Quebec Superior Court, railed against s. 91(26) in his *Commentaire* as a violation of natural law because only the church could rule on the validity of a marriage tie. Joseph Frémont agreed with him in *Le divorce et la separation de corps* (Quebec City: Imp. A Côté et cie, 1886). For Loranger see Jean-Charles Bonenfant, "Thomas-Jean-Jacques Loranger," *DCB online*. I am indebted to Nicholas Kasirer for these references.

8 *An Act for the Relief of Joseph Frederick Whiteaves*, SC 1869, c 95; *An Act for the Relief of John Horace Stevenson*, SC 1870, c 75; *An Act for the Relief of John Robert Martin*, SC 1873, c 126; *An Act for the Relief of William Henry Peterson*, SC 1875, c 98.

9 This was the case of George Jones of Port Perry, whose 1869 petition for a divorce from his wife Ann Martin was rejected by the Senate divorce committee because it had not provided sufficiently precise allegations of when, where, and with whom the alleged adultery had taken place. Ann Martin was therefore unable to effectively defend the action: see *Senate Journals*, 9 June 1869, 165.

10 *An Act for the Relief of Mary Bates*, SC 1878, c 87. The substantial preponderance of male petitioners in the early years after Confederation was not reproduced in subsequent years. Between 1868 and 1914 45 per cent of divorce Acts were passed for women. Among Ontario residents women were a slight majority of petitioners: see Phillips, Girard, and Brown, *A History of Law in Canada Volume II*, 546–7.

11 *The Union* (Toronto), 2 Apr. 1874. For Martin's two failed attempts see *Senate Journals* and *Senate Debates*, Mar. and Apr. 1870, passim; and Apr.

and May 1872, passim; *Commons Journals* and *Commons Debates*, 31 May and June 1872, passim.

12 *Senate Rules*, Section 16, Bills of Divorce, Rule 72. For parliamentary divorce procedure see Gemmill, *The Practice of the Parliament of Canada*, chap. 4, and "Parliamentary Divorce in Canada," *Canadian Law Times* 8 (1888): 52; John George Bourinot, *Parliamentary Procedure and Practice* (Montreal: Dawson, 1884), 668–80.

13 *Canada Gazette*, 27 June 1874–30 Jan. 1875.

14 *Whitby Chronicle*, 26 Nov. 1874.

15 *Canada Gazette*, 3 July to 31 Dec. 1875. Very few issues of the *Whitby Gazette* have survived for 1874, but f from September have, and they all carried the notice: *Whitby Gazette*, 9, 16, 23, and 30 Sept. 1875.

16 *Ottawa Citizen*, 10 July 1875, and *Ottawa Free Press*, 10 July 1875.

17 *BNA Act*, s 22. For the history of the Senate see Robert MacKay, *The Unreformed Senate of Canada* (Toronto: McClelland and Stewart, 2nd ed., 1963); Janet Ajzenstat, "Bicameralism and Canada's Founders: The Origins of the Canadian Senate," in *Protecting Canadian Democracy: The Senate You Never Knew*, ed. Serge Joyal (Montreal and Kingston: McGill-Queen's University Press, 2003), and James Bowden, "The Founders' Senate – and Ours," *Dorchester Review,* (2019): 55. See also Eugene Forsey, "Alexander Mackenzie's Memorandum on the Appointment of Extra Senators, 1873–1874," *Canadian Historical Review*, 27 (1946): 189.

18 *BNA Act*, s 23. Quotation from Macdonald in A.G. Doughty, "Notes on the Quebec Conference, 1864," *Canadian Historical Review* 1 (1920): 31.

19 Section 127 begins: "If any Person being at the passing of this Act a Member of the Legislative Council of Canada, Nova Scotia, or New Brunswick, to whom a Place in the Senate is offered," and goes on to say that those people must accept or decline the offer within thirty days. But it does not actually say senators must be appointed from the Legislative Councils. Bowden, "The Founders" Senate,' at 57–58, wrongly states that it does.

20 The original Senate was comprised of 36 Conservatives, 8 Liberal-Conservatives, 27 Liberals, and 1 Reformer. In 1876 there were five more senators than in 1867, with Conservatives and Liberal-Conservatives having a larger majority (48) over Liberals (26) than was the case in 1867. These calculations are mine. These labels are confusing to modern readers because, as with all terms describing a political ideology, they have meant different things at different times in different polities. The origins of the term "Liberal-Conservative" go back to the 1850s when moderate Reformers and Conservatives from Canada West joined with the *Bleus*, Conservatives from Canada East, to form a government. Liberal-Conservative was the official name of the Conservative Party until

1873, although most MPs and senators of that party called themselves Conservatives. In 1864 the political deadlock in the Province of Canada was broken by the "Great Coalition" of Liberal-Conservatives, Liberals, and the *Parti Bleu*, which came together to effect the Confederation of the original four provinces, an arrangement which crucially involved ending the deadlock in the Province of Canada by dividing it into two provinces.

21 Only Quebec senators were actually appointed to represent an electoral district (*BNA Act*, s 22), a requirement designed to assure that there would be appropriate representation for the anglophone protestant minority. Although senators from other provinces were not required to be appointed for electoral districts, they were nonetheless drawn from each region of a province.

22 For Reesor see *The Canadian Biographical Dictionary and Portrait Gallery of Eminent and Self-Made Men, Ontario Volume* (Toronto: American Biographical Publishing Company, 1880), 697–8.

23 *Senate Debates*, 12 Apr. 1877, 352.

24 *Senate Journals*, 21 Feb. 1876, 34.

25 *Senate Debates*, 25 Mar. 1875, 292–3. For Smith see Mark McGowan, "Sir Frank Smith," *DCB online*.

26 *Senate Debates*, 21 Feb. 1876, 41.

27 *Daily Citizen* (Ottawa), 19 Feb. 1876.

28 *Senate Debates* and *Senate Journals*, 22 Feb. 1876, 42 and 38. On the same day Robert also completed the formality of presenting the same petition for a divorce to the Commons. It was referred to the Commons standing committee on standing orders, which found it in order: *Commons Journals*, 22, 24, and 25, 73, 79, and 82–3.

29 *Senate Journals*, 8 Mar. 1876, 61–63.

30 Gerald Tulchinsky, "James Ferrier," *DCB online*.

31 For the selection of the committee see *Senate Journals*, 8 Mar. 1876, 63.

32 *An Act for the Relief of James Albert Manning Aikins*, SC 1892, c 78.

33 Information on the Ontario senators from David G. Burley, "James Aikins," and Christopher Andreae, "Elijah Leonard," both in *DCB online*; *The Canadian Biographical Dictionary*, 161–2 (Dickson); and Parliament of Canada biography website (Seymour).

34 Information on Kaulbach from Shirley Elliott, *The Legislative Assembly of Nova Scotia, 1758–1983: A Biographical Directory* (Halifax: Province of Nova Scotia, 1984), 175, and Philip V. Girard, *Lawyers and Legal Culture in British North America: Beamish Murdoch of Halifax* (Toronto: Osgoode Society for Canadian Legal History and University of Toronto Press, 2011), 186. For Dickey see Robert Barry Dickey, *Canadian Encyclopedia online*.

35 Information on Haythorne and Cornwall from Andrew Robb, "Robert Poor Haythorne," *DCB online*, and J.B. Kerr, *Biographical Dictionary of*

Well-Known British Columbians, with a Historical Sketch (Vancouver: Kerr & Begg, 1890), 130–3.

36 Of the seven prior committees, three had sat on the case of John Robert Martin, whose bill was twice rejected by the Commons, in 1870 and 1872, before passing in 1873. For prior service on divorce committees see *Senate Debates*, 30 Apr. 1868, 234; *Senate Journals*, 14 and 31 May 1869, 87–8 and 127–8; 28 Mar. 1872, 81; 17 Apr. 1873, 101; 5 Mar. 1875, 86.

37 *Senate Journals*, 10 Mar. 1876, 68–9. The select committee report states only that her petition for support "was complied with … to her satisfaction," but the amount is given in ibid., 31 Mar. 1876, 138.

38 "William Walker," LSO/PMD; *Ottawa Journal*, 19 Jan. 1897.

39 For McIntyre see William Cochrane and John Castell Hopkins, eds., *The Canadian Album. Men of Canada; Or Success by Example in Religion, Patriotism, Business, Law, Medicine, Education and Agriculture, Containing Portraits of Some of Canada's Chief Businessmen, Statesmen, Farmers, Men of the Learned Professions and Athers; also, an Authentic Sketch of Their Lives, Object Lessons for the Present Generation, and Examples to Posterity* (4 vol., Brantford, On: Bradley, Garretson & Co., 1891–1896), Vol 4, 509, and LSO/PMD.

40 For McDougall see Zeller, "William MacDougall"; Foster J.K. Griezic, "William McDougall and the North and North Lanark By-election, 1864," *Ontario History* 59 (1967): 1; R.S. Longley, "Cartier and McDougall: Canadian Emissaries to London, 1868–1869," 26 *Canadian Historical Review* 26 (1945) 25; Henry James Morgan, *The Canadian Men and Women of the Time: A Handbook of Canadian Biography* (Toronto: W. Briggs, 1898), 689–91; John Charles Dent, comp, *The Canadian Portrait Gallery* (4 Vols. Toronto: Magurn, 1880–1881), Vol 4, 148; Rattray, ed., *The Scot in British North America*, 584–90; and Livermore, *Wandering Willie*. For his role in the Red River crisis of 1869, see Phillips, Girard, and Brown, *A History of Law in Canada Volume II*, chap. 7.

41 The partnership is not mentioned in LSO/PMD, for either Gordon or McDougall, which makes it likely that if there was ever a partnership it was a "one-off."

9. The Senate Divorce Committee I: The Case for Robert Campbell

1 *The Times* (Ottawa), 13 Mar. 1876.

2 *The Union* (Toronto), 2 Apr. 1874.

3 Senate Rules, 6 – Rules 3 and 4.

4 For the number of staff reporters see George Clark-Holland, "The Red Chamber – An Appreciation of the Canadian Senate," *The Canadian Magazine of Politics, Science, Art and Literature*, May-October 1911, 158–9.

5 *Le journal du cultivateur et de L'ouvrier*, 25 Nov. 1876 (my translation).

6 This assessment is, admittedly, an impressionistic one, derived from reading over two hundred parliamentary divorce cases for a wider study of the period prior to 1914.

7 *Globe*, 22 and 23 Feb.; and 9, 14, 15, 16, 21, 23, 24, 25, 29, 30, and 31 Mar. 1876.

8 *Ottawa Citizen*, 19 Feb. and 2 Mar. 1876.

9 *Guelph Mercury*, 24 Feb. 1876; *Ingersoll Chronicle,* 30 Mar. 1876; *Hamilton Weekly Times*, 13 Apr. 1876; *Kingston Daily News*, 24 Feb. 1876; *British Whig* (Kingston), 13 Mar. 1876; *Acton Free Press,* 9 and 30 Mar. 1876; *Ottawa Times*, 22 Feb. and 13, 15, and 16, 23, and 29 Mar. 1876; *Ottawa Citizen*, 23 Feb., and 20, 22, 23, and 30 Mar. 1876. This is not a comprehensive list. It includes only those newspapers for which issues are still extant and have been digitized and made available on newspapers.com. The same is true for the Quebec and American newspapers cited immediately below.

10 *Montreal Herald and Daily Commercial Gazette*, 22 and 23 Feb., and 9 and 30 Mar. 1876; *Montreal Daily Witness*, 30 Mar. 1876; (Montreal) *Morning Chronicle and Commercial and Shipping Gazette*, 31 Mar. 1876; *La Minerve*, 22 and 29 Mar. 1876; *Quebec Daily Mercury*, 20 Mar. 1876; *Manitoba Free Press*, 3 and 11 Mar. 1876; *Chicago Tribune*, 31 Mar. 1876; *Daily Herald and Empire*, (Dayton), 15 July1876; *Springfield Daily Republican*, 15 July 1876; *Daily State Journal* (Jefferson City), 7 Apr. 1876.

11 Radforth, *Deadly Swindle*. See also generally Paul Rutherford, *A Victorian Authority: The Daily Press in Late Nineteenth-Century Canada* (Toronto: University of Toronto Press, 1982).

12 Exhibit 1, Minutes of Evidence, 4. For the first day see Minutes of Evidence, 2–19. References are only provided for quotations.

13 The newspaper that reported this exchange, the *Hamilton Weekly Times*, 13 Apr.1876, report dated 3 April, said that the committee had deemed the evidence "inadmissible." That could not have been true because inadmissible evidence by definition cannot be admitted. Dickey probably meant "not directly relevant."

14 Minutes of Evidence, 27–8, Exhibits 3–6.

15 Ibid., 28–32, Exhibits 7 and 8 (Execution Warrants), 9 (Chancery Decree), and 16–17 (Floor Plans). The portrait of Eliza and the views of the house were not reproduced in the Senate report. The lack of the portrait is especially unfortunate, because I have not been able to find any picture of her.

16 Ibid., 9.

17 McDougall's cross-examination of Robert is at ibid., 10–21 and 23–7.

18 Quotations in this paragraph at ibid., 10–11.

19 Ibid., 13–15.

20 Minutes of Evidence, 17–18.

21 Quotations in this paragraph and the next at ibid, 18–19.
22 This is a rough calculation from reading the minutes aloud slowly (one hour) and allowing extra time (another hour or two) for pauses, changes of questioner, and the presentation and confirmation of exhibits.
23 This paragraph on the final part of McDougall's cross-examination is from Minutes of Evidence, 20–1.
24 There was a *Ladies Journal* published in Toronto, a magazine "devoted to Literature, Fashion, Domestic Matters, etc." according to its masthead. It started publishing in the mid-1870s. Early Canadiana's (www.canadiana.org) run starts with Volume 5, 1881. Alternatively, Walker could have been referring to the *Young Ladies Journal*, an illustrated periodical marketed to a young, female, middle-class audience. It was published from 1864 to 1920. See www.virtual-exhibits.library.queensu.ca/young-ladies-journal.
25 Quotations in this paragraph and the next two at Minutes of Evidence, 21–3.
26 Quotations in this paragraph and the next at ibid., 23–6.
27 Martha Newsom's direct examination and re-examination are at ibid., 33–5 and 38, and Jane Newsom's at 39. McDougall's cross-examination of Martha Newsom is at 35–7, and of Jane Newsom is at 40–1.
28 Quotations in this paragraph and the next from McDougall's cross-examination at ibid., 36.
29 Quotations in this paragraph and the next two from McDougall's cross-examination at ibid., 37, 39, and 41.
30 Ibid., 44.
31 Quotation in this paragraph from Minutes of Evidence, 45.
32 Quotations in this paragraph and the next two from ibid, 48–51.
33 Quotation in this paragraph from ibid., 54.
34 Quotations in this paragraph from ibid., 54–5.
35 This paragraph is from ibid, 56–60; the quotations are from 57 and 60.
36 This paragraph is from ibid., 60–2, quotations at 62, except for Robert's direct examination the day before, which is at 42.
37 This paragraph is from ibid., 62–5, quotations at 62, 64 and 65.
38 This paragraph is from ibid., 65–6.
39 This paragraph is from ibid., 66–70; quotations at 69 and 70.
40 This paragraph and the next are from ibid., 70–7.
41 This paragraph is from ibid., 73–4.
42 This paragraph is from ibid., 77–9; quotations at 78 and 79.
43 This paragraph is from ibid, 80–2; quotations at 81 and 82.
44 Anderson's examination in chief is at ibid, 82–6, quotation at 85.
45 Quotations from ibid, 88 and 95.
46 This paragraph is from ibid, 95–9; quotation at 98–9.
47 This paragraph and the next are from ibid., 99–101; quotations at 100 and 101.
48 This paragraph is from ibid., 102–5.

49 Ibid., 105–21, Exhibit 18. The exhibit was not exactly the same as the judgment reported in *Grant's Chancery Reports* because the Senate journal version does not have the headnote or the summaries of arguments by counsel. It was submitted to the committee before it was reported. It ends with a declaration by A. Grant, reporter, dated 7 February 1876, that the 49 pages of manuscript he put in were a correct copy of Blake's judgment.
50 *Hamilton Weekly Times*, 13 Apr. 1876, report date 4 April.

10. The Senate Divorce Committee II: The Case for Eliza Campbell and Rebuttal Witnesses

1 The motion was not mentioned in the committee's report, but it was reported in the *Ottawa Citizen*, 20 Mar. 1876.
2 *Hamilton Weekly Times*, 13 Apr. 1876, report dated 4 April. See also for Eliza's arrival, *Ottawa Citizen* and *Ottawa Times*, 22 Mar. 1876.
3 "Interesting Review of the Whitby Scandal," *Ingersoll Chronicle*, 6 Apr. 1876, by-line "Whitby March 31." The same story was reprinted in *Whitby Chronicle*, 6 Apr. 1876.
4 Minutes of Evidence, 122–82.
5 *Hamilton Weekly Times*, 13 Apr. 1876, report dated 3 April.
6 This paragraph is from Minutes of Evidence, 125; quotations at 122 and 124.
7 This paragraph and the next two are from ibid., 125–34; quotations at 130, 131, and 134–5.
8 *Ottawa Times*, 23 Mar. 1876; *Hamilton Weekly Times*, 13 Apr. 1876, report dated 3 April.
9 This paragraph is from Minutes of Evidence, 135–41.
10 This paragraph is from ibid., 142–8; quotations at 142 and 147.
11 This paragraph is from ibid., 144 and 148–51.
12 This paragraph is from ibid., 151–3; quotations at 151 and 153.
13 This paragraph from Minutes of Evidence, 153–4.
14 This paragraph from Minutes of Evidence, 154–63; quotations at 156, 158, and 160.
15 This paragraph from Minutes of Evidence, 163–8; quotations at 167.
16 This paragraph, including quotations, from Minutes of Evidence, 168–70.
17 This paragraph from Minutes of Evidence, 171–2.
18 This paragraph from Minutes of Evidence, 172–6; quotation at 175.
19 Minutes of Evidence, Exhibit 20, 182–3.
20 This paragraph from Minutes of Evidence, 177–80; quotations at 179–80.
21 This paragraph from Minutes of Evidence, 179. The letter from Eliza to Robert about Bremner is Exhibit 19, 182. Death certificate and newspaper report of Bremner's death courtesy of Philip Augustine of Ottawa.
22 This paragraph from Minutes of Evidence, 180–2; quotation at 180.
23 *Hamilton Weekly Times*, 13 April 1876, report dated 3 April.

24 *Whitby Chronicle*, 30 March 1876.
25 This paragraph from Minutes of Evidence, 183–6; quotation at 186.
26 This paragraph from Minutes of Evidence, 186–90; quotations at 186 and 187.
27 This paragraph from Minutes of Evidence, 190–3; quotations at 193
28 This paragraph from Minutes of Evidence, 195–8; quotations at 195, 197, and 198.
29 This paragraph from Minutes of Evidence, 198–203. The short deposition was entered as Exhibit 22, in Minutes of Evidence, 226.
30 This paragraph from Minutes of Evidence, 204–8. Mitchell could not have appeared as a witness because he had left the province by 1876: ibid., 229.
31 *Hamilton Weekly Times*, 17 Apr. 1876, report dated April 4. This paragraph on Adams's testimony from Minutes of Evidence, 208–9; quotation at 209.
32 *Whitby Chronicle*, 30 Mar. 1876.
33 Ibid., 27 Apr. 1876, letter dated 7 April.
34 This paragraph is from ibid., 211–4; quotations at 212 and 214.
35 This paragraph and the next, including quotations, are from ibid, 214–5. It is not clear what word or words the printers left out, or why they did so.
36 This paragraph is from ibid., 216–8.
37 This paragraph is from ibid., 219–24; quotations at 219 and 222.
38 This paragraph is from ibid., 225.
39 This paragraph and the next are from ibid., 227–32; quotations at 229
40 For Bandell, spelled Braudell or Baudel in some sources, who had briefly testified in the Chancery case, although what he said was not reported, see *Whitby Chronicle*, 2 Jan. 1868, and Winter, *Chronicles of a County Town*, 150–1. He did very well in the hotel business. He ran the Western House until 1875, when he acquired the Whitby House, a new building on Dundas Street West. It burned down in 1879, but was rebuilt, and he operated it until his death in 1896.
41 This paragraph is from Minutes of Evidence, 232–6.
42 This paragraph is from ibid, 236–43.
43 This paragraph is from ibid, 244–7; quotations at 245–7.
44 This paragraph is from Minutes of Evidence, 247–50.
45 *Whitby Chronicle*, 6 Apr. 1876.
46 This paragraph is from Minutes of Evidence, 250–4; quotations at 252.
47 *Ottawa Citizen*, 30 Mar. 1876; *Whitby Chronicle*, 30 Mar. 1876.

11. The Senate Divorce Committee III: Counsels' Speeches and the Committee's Report

1 "Philemon Pennock," LSO/PMD.
2 William McDougall, *The Campbell Divorce Bill: Women's Rights in Ontario. Parliament as a Court of Justice* [hereafter *McDougall's Speech*]; *Whitby Chronicle*, 18 and 25 May and 1 June 1876.

3 *McDougall's Speech*, 6.
4 Ibid., 3.
5 Ibid., 6, and *Senate Journals*, 10 Mar. 1875, 110.
6 *McDougall's Speech*, 6.
7 Quotations in this paragraph are from *McDougall's Speech*, 6–8.
8 Quotations in this paragraph are from *McDougall's Speech*, 8. Emphasis in original.
9 Quotations in this paragraph are from *McDougall's 1876 Speech*, 8–9. "He who comes into equity must come with clean hands" is one of the maxims of equity promulgated by text writers in the early to mid-eighteenth century and distilled from previous cases. Maxims are statements of general principles, not specific legal rules. This one means that if a litigant asks the court for a remedy he or she must not have acted wrongly themselves. However, the clean hands doctrine does not mean that someone who has acted wrongfully cannot obtain an equitable remedy. It applies only if there is a nexus between the applicant's wrongful act and the rights he or she wishes to enforce. Hence it might be seen as a good illustration of Jeffrey Hackney's observation that "most maxims do not today greatly figure in judicial language, and their principal harm is, by their banality, to reduce manifestations of justice to the level of simple chatter, and thereby to devalue the underlying conscience": Jeffrey Hackney, *Understanding Equity and Trusts* (London: Fontana Press, 1987), 29.
10 See G.M. Craig, "Marshall Spring Bidwell," *DCB online*.
11 Quotations in this paragraph are from *McDougall's Speech*, 9–10.
12 Quotations in this paragraph and the next three are from ibid., 10–11.
13 Quotations in this paragraph and the next three are from ibid., 12–14.
14 Quotations in this paragraph and the next two are from *McDougall's Speech*, 15–17.
15 This was a case reported in the *Westminster Review* in 1856, in which the husband and wife were Mr. and Mrs. Hunt, and the young man a Mr. Portman, son of Lord Portnam. Quotations in this paragraph and the next are from ibid., 18–19.
16 Quotations in this paragraph and the next two are from ibid., 20. Emphasis in original.
17 Issue of 18 May 1876, announcing the newspaper's intention to publish it in three parts.
18 *Ottawa Citizen*, 7 Apr. 1876.
19 *Senate Debates*, 20 Mar. and 12 Apr. 1877, 227 and 350.
20 The committee report is at *Minutes of Evidence*, 1–2 and *Senate Journals*, 29 Mar. 1876, 166.

The report did not say the decision was a majority one, but this came out later in the debate over the report: *Senate Debates*, 5 Apr. 1876, 295, 20 Mar. and 12 and 19 Apr. 1877, 228, 424, and 438, and 18 Apr. 1879, 307.

21 Holland, "The Red Chamber," 158. For correct predictions of the verdict see, inter alia, *Ingersoll Chronicle*, 30 Mar. and 6 Apr. 1876; *Whitby Chronicle*, 30 Mar.1876; *Hamilton Times*, 13 Apr. 1876; *Montreal Daily Witness*, 30 Mar. 1876.
22 "Interesting Review of the Whitby Scandal," *Ingersoll Chronicle*, 6 Apr. 1876, by-line "Whitby, March 31."
23 *Hamilton Times*, 13 Apr. 1876, report dated 3 April.
24 See, in addition to the newspapers already mentioned, *Guelph Mercury*, 24 Feb. and 7 Apr. 1876; *North Ontario Observer* (Port Perry), 20 Apr. 1876; *Montreal Daily Witness*, 30 Mar. 1876; *Montreal Herald*, 9 Mar. 1876; *Morning Chronicle* (Montreal), 7 Apr. 1876; *Evening Star* (Montreal), 19 Apr. 1876).
25 "Divorce in Canada. The Great Difficulty Attending that Legal Formality," *Chicago Tribune*, 31 Mar. 1876; *Central Law Journal*, 21 Apr. 1876, 1; *Irish Law Times and Solicitors' Journal*, 10 (1876), 361. In contrast there was nothing about the case in the Toronto-based *Canada Law Journal*.
26 The petition, not reproduced in the Senate Journal in 1876, is at *Senate Journals* 23 Apr. 1879, 166–7, and is reproduced below as appendix 1. Its presentation was reported in *Ottawa Citizen*, 30 Mar. 1876.
27 The best account of the operation of the Consistory Court in the nineteenth century is a biography of its principal judge, Stephen Waddams, *Law, Politics and the Church of England: The Career of Stephen Lushington, 1782–1873* (Cambridge: Cambridge University Press, 1992), ch. 5.
28 On English parliamentary divorce see Sybil Wolfram, "Divorce in England, 1700–1857," (1985) 5 *Oxford Journal of Legal Studies* 155 and Stuart Anderson, "Legislative Divorce – Law for the Aristocracy," in *Law, Economy and Society, 1750–1914: Essays in the History of English Law,* eds. Gerry Rubin and David Sugarman (Abingdon: Professional Books, 1984).
29 *Divorce and Matrimonial Causes Act*, UK Statutes 1857, c 85.
30 Quotations in this paragraph and the next are from *McDougall's Speech*, 21.
31 Quotations in this paragraph are from *McDougall's Speech*, 22. On custody law in this period see Phillips, Girard, and Brown, *History of Law in Canada II*, 552–60.
32 Quotations in this paragraph are from *McDougall's Speech*, 22–3.
33 The petition is at *Senate Journals*, 29 Mar. 1876, 131 and was also reproduced later in *Senate Journals*, 23 Apr. 1879, 166–7.
34 For all this see *Senate Journals*, 29 and 31 Mar. 1876, 131 and 137. From later statements in the Senate *Debates* we know that those opposed were Dickey, Dickson, Kaulbach, and Cornwall, and that the five in favour were Aikins, Haythorne, Leonard, Reesor, and Seymour. *Senate Journals*, 5 Apr. 1877, 161, and *Senate Debates*, 9 Apr. 1877, 316.
35 For the debate see *Senate Debates*, 5 Apr. 1876, 293–5, quotations below at 294 and 295.
36 *Whitby Chronicle*, 13 Apr. 1876.

37 Ibid., reproducing a report in the *Hamilton Times*.
38 *Senate Journals*, 5, 8, and 10 Apr. 1876, 161, 178–81, and 200; *Senate Debates*, 5 and 10 April 1876, 295 and 323–4.
39 Principal among his sources was the "bible" of parliamentary procedure, Erskine May's *Treatise on the Law, Privileges, Proceedings, and Usages of Parliament*. May was a barrister and variously librarian and clerk to the UK House of Commons, and the first edition of his work was published in 1844. It was regularly brought out in updated editions, the first nine editions being edited by May himself before his death in 1886. The Senate probably using the seventh edition, published in 1873. The work is still considered the standard work on parliamentary practice; the 25th edition was published in 2019.
40 *Senate Journals*, 8 Apr. 1876, 178–81.
41 See appendix 2.
42 For the final amounts see the 1879 Act in appendix 3.
43 *Whitby Chronicle*, 13 Apr. 1876, reproducing a report from the correspondent of the *Hamilton Times*.

12. Eliza Campbell's Separation Bill in Parliament, 1877

1 For Campbell see Donald Swainson, "Sir Alexander Campbell," *DCB online*. A father of Confederation, Campbell held a variety of cabinet posts under Macdonald although not that of Minister of Justice until 1881.
2 A committee of the whole is a meeting of a legislative body at which the rules are those of committee meetings but all members of the legislative body are present, with somebody other than the Speaker in the chair. In Parliament it meets after the bill has been given second reading and then goes into committee on the details. When the committee of the whole discussions are complete the Speaker resumes the chair, and the chair of the committee reports to the full membership, that is, to the same members who took part in the committee of the whole discussions.
3 *Whitby Chronicle*, 12, 19, and 26 Apr. and 3 May 1877; *Globe*, 23 Feb., 21 Mar., and 11, 13, 19, 21, 23, 25, 27, and 30 Apr. 1877; *Weekly Mail* (Toronto), 23 and 30 Mar., and 6, 13, 20, and 27 Apr. 1877; *Ottawa Citizen*, 21 Mar. and 13 Apr. 1877.
4 *Hamilton Times*, 19 Apr. 1877; *Ingersoll Chronicle*, 17 May 1877; *Daily Telegraph* (Quebec), 24 Mar. 1877; *Quebec Saturday Budget*, 28 Apr. 1877; *Montreal Star*, 21 Mar. 1877; *Montreal Daily Witness*, 13 and 24 Apr. 1877; *Sherbrooke News*, 19 Apr. 1877; *Manitoba Free Press*, 28 Apr. 1877.
5 I have only stated this for Catholics. If no religious affiliation is given if the senator was a Protestant.
6 For Scott see Brian Clarke, "Richard Scott," *DCB online*. Scott held a number of other ministerial posts in Mackenzie's government. He is best

known for his support of prohibition (the *Canada Temperance Act* of 1875 was always referred to as the *Scott Act*) and for having been a prominent advocate throughout his career of separate schools, having championed them when involved in Upper Canadian politics in the 1860s. He steered the *Northwest Territories Act* through the Senate in 1875, legislation that established separate schools in the territories, and later was a principal defender of them during the Manitoba Schools question.

7 *Whitby Chronicle*, 23 Mar. 1877; *Ottawa Citizen*, 26 Mar. 1877.

8 For separation in the *Civil Code of Lower Canada* see, inter alia, Phillips, Girard and Brown, *A History of Law in Canada Volume II*, 159–62; Marie Aimée Cliche, "Les Séparations de corps dans le district judiciaire de Montréal de 1900 à 1930," *Canadian Journal of Law and Society* 12 (1997): 71, and "Les procès en séparation de corps dans la région de Montréal, 1795–1879, *Revue d'histoire de l'Amérique française* 49 (1995): 3. Separations were available under articles 187 and 188 of the *Civil Code*, which provided that a husband could demand one on the grounds of his wife's adultery, but a wife could only do so if, in addition to the adultery, the husband kept his "concubine" in the conjugal domicile.

9 For the constitution and the courts in this period see principally John T. Saywell, *The Lawmakers: Judicial Power and the Shaping of Canadian Federalism* (Toronto: Osgoode Society for Canadian Legal History and University of Toronto Press, 2002), ch. 2; and R.C.B. Risk, "Canadian Courts Under the Influence," *University of Toronto Law Journal* 40 (1990): 687, at 690–700.

10 For the disallowance power see Phillips, Girard, and Brown, *A History of Law in Canada Volume II*, 71–3, and Robert Vipond, "Alternative Pasts: Liberal Legalism and the Demise of the Disallowance Power," *University of New Brunswick Law Journal* (1990) 39: 126. For the very extensive correspondence between the federal and all provincial governments over disallowance, see W.E. Hodgins, comp., *Correspondence, Reports of the Minister of Justice, and Orders in Council Upon the Subject of Dominion and Provincial Legislation, 1867–1895* (Ottawa: Government Printer, 1896). For statutory consolidations in the 1870s, see Phillips, Girard, and Brown, *A History of Law in Canada Volume II*, 120–33.

11 This section is an amalgam of the debates in March and on 9 and 12 April 1877. I have only provided footnote citations for quotations.

12 *Senate Debates*, 9 Apr. 1877, 315.

13 [1880] SCJ No. 4, quotation below at para. 92. The JCPC upheld the SCC: (1881) 7 AC 96 (PC).

14 Peter Hogg, *Constitutional Law of Canada* (Toronto: Carswell, 5th edition, 2007).

15 (1875) 15 NBR 535; quotation below in this paragraph at 539.

16 For Ritchie, whose views on the scope of the trade and commerce power had changed by 1879, and for changing judicial views of the paramountcy

of the trade and commerce power in the 1880s, see Gordon Bale and E. Bruce Mellett, "Sir Willam Johnstone Ritchie," *DCB online*, and Risk, "Canadian Courts under the Influence," 700 et seq.

17 See in particular the 1920s debates on whether Ontario should move from parliamentary divorce to judicial divorce. All participants were adamant that Parliament did not have jurisdiction over "corollary relief," custody and support: See Nina Patti and Jim Phillips, "The Demise of Parliamentary Divorce in Ontario: The 1930 Divorce Act," forthcoming in University of Toronto Law Journal, 2025.

18 *Senate Debates*, 20 Mar. 1877, 227. The same argument had been made shortly after Confederation by George-Étienne Cartier. He claimed that the placing of divorce in section 91 had the support at the time of the Catholic bishops, because "it would be wrong on the part of the Catholics to refuse to Protestants a right which [they] … believed they should possess": *Commons Debates*, 23 Mar. 1870, 678. See also the analysis of why certain subjects were put in section 91 and others in section 92 in Jim Phillips and Tom Collins, "The Colonial Origins of the Division of Powers in the *British North America Act*," in *Law, Life and the Teaching of Legal History: Essays in Honour of G. Blaine Baker*, eds. Ian Pilarczyk, Angela Fernandez, and Brian Young (Montreal and Kingston: McGil Queen's University Press, 2022).

19 *Senate Debates*, 12 Apr. 1877, 355. Trudel had represented the parish council of Notre-Dame, which refused to give Liberal and anti-clerical printer Joseph Guibord a burial in a Catholic cemetery. See Nadia Eid, "Francois Xavier Trudel," and Jean-Rock Rioux, "Joseph Guibord," both in *DCB online*.

20 *Senate Debates*, 9 and 12 Apr. 1877, 315 and 355. For Bellerose, who had previously been a federal MP and was the man responsible for insisting that the Senate debates were translated into French in 1877, see Marcel Caya, "Joseph-Hyacinthe Bellerose," *DCB online*.

21 Senate Debates, 18 Apr. 1877, 421. For Penny see Lorne Ste. Croix, "Edward Goff Penny," *DCB online*.

22 *Senate Debates*, 12 and 18 Apr. 1877, 348 and 421. For Vidal see Morgan, *Canadian Men and Women of the Time*, 1040–1.

23 *Senate Debates*, 9 Apr. 1877, 315–6.

24 For Campbell's speech see ibid., 12 Apr. 1877, 347–50; quotations in this and the next two paragraphs from the same pages.

25 Bills imposing criminal liability and the death sentence on individuals were known as Bills of Attainder, and were not infrequently employed during the Wars of the Roses and the Tudor period to get rid of political opponents or of persons considered untrustworthy. The last Act of Attainder passed in the UK Parliament was in the case of Lord Edward Fitzgerald, leader of the 1798 Irish rebellion. The bill sentenced Fitzgerald to death for treason,

but he died from wounds inflicted when he was captured. Bills imposing lesser criminal sentences and or civil liability were called Bills of Pains and Penalties. For Fitzgerald see Stella Tillyard, *Citizen Lord: Edward Fitzgerald* (London: Chatto & Windus, 1977); for a Bill of Pains and Penalties brought against East India Company employees for their defalcations in the late eighteenth century see Jim Phillips, "Parliament and Southern India, 1781–83: The Secret Committee of Inquiry and the Prosecution of Sir Thomas Rumbold," (1988) 7 *Parliamentary History*: 81.

26 For Dickey's speech see *Senate Debates*, 12 Apr. 1877, 350–2; quotations in this and the next two paragraphs from the same pages.

27 On House of Lords practice Dickey cited John MacQueen, *A Practical Treatise on the Appellate Jurisdiction of the House of Lords & Privy Council, Together with the Practice on Parliamentary Divorce* (London: Maxwell, 1842).

28 *Senate Debates*, 9 Apr. 1877, 277.

29 Ibid., 12 Apr. 1877, 351–2. Between 1867 and 1878 Parliament passed six such acts, although only one was called a "relief act." One was to provide support for a widow and children: *An Act to enable Her Majesty to provide for the widow and children of the late Honorable Thomas D'Arcy McGee*, SC 1868, c 77. Two were to issue patents to individuals despite the fact that the *Patent Act*, SC 1869, c 11, provided an administrative mechanism for approving patents: see *An Act to enable James Blanchfield Smith to obtain an extension of the patent of a certain invention*, SC 1869 c 72, and *An Act to enable Ozro Morrill to obtain a patent for certain inventions and improvements in sewing machine shuttles*, SC 1876 c 75. Two were naturalization Acts: *An Act to Naturalize Eli Clinton Clark*, SC 1869, c 118 and *An Act to Naturalize Anson Greene Phelps Dodge*, SC 1872, c 118. The only "relief act" so named was for a corporation: *An Act to Grant Relief to the Canada Agricultural Insurance Company*, SC 1878, c 38.

30 *Senate Debates*, 20 Mar. 1877, 228. For Miller, who was the youngest person ever summoned to the Senate, see Alan Marble, *Nova Scotians at Home and Broad: Biographical Sketches of Over Six Hundred Native Born Nova Scotians* (Windsor, N.S. Lancelot Press, 1977), 300.

31 *Senate Debates*, 12 Apr. 1877, 353–4.

32 Ibid., 354.

33 *Senate Journals*, 12 Apr. 1877, 219–20. The result would have been different had not David Christie of Ontario, the Speaker, voted against the six-months' hoist and for advancing the bill to Committee of the Whole. At this time there was no rule limiting the Speaker's ability to vote on any motion. The Commons rules stipulated that the Speaker could only vote to break a tie, but the Senate rules were silent on the question: *Commons Rules*, Rule 9. Christie, a successful farmer and agricultural promoter, was a one-time radical reformer, a "clear grit," who had by Confederation lost

some of his fire and was allied with Liberal mainstay George Brown. He had been briefly secretary of state in the Alexander Mackenzie minority administration of 1873–74, but when Mackenzie won a majority in the 1874 election, he was moved to being Speaker of the Senate. See J.M.S. Careless, "David Christie," *DCB online*.

34 *Senate Debates*, 18 Apr. 1877, 356, and *Senate Journals*, 18 Apr. 1877, 245.

35 Aikins, Campbell, Dickey, Kaulbach, Penny, Reesor, Trudel, and Vidal.

36 Power had been educated at the Catholic University of Ireland and Harvard, and was admitted to the Nova Scotia bar in 1866. His father, Patrick Power, was a federal MP for Halifax from 1867–72 and 1874–78, and his influence with Mackenzie secured his son the Senate appointment earlier in 1877 at the age of 36. He later authored *The Manitoba School Question from the Point of View of a Catholic Member* (1896): see Marble, *Nova Scotians at Home and Abroad*, 331, and David Flemming, "Patrick Power," *DCB online*.

37 *Senate Debates*, 12 and 18 Apr. 1877, 349 and 425.

38 *Hamilton Weekly Times*, 19 Apr. 1877.

39 *Senate Debates*, 18 Apr. 1877, 420–2.

40 Ibid., 422. Haviland was citing John Bouvier, *A Law Dictionary Adapted to the Constitution and Laws of the United States of America and of Several States of the American Union* (2 vols. Philadelphia: Childs and Peterson, 1856). First published in 1839 it was frequently revised, before and after Bouvier's death in 1851, with the sixth edition coming out in 1856 and the eighth in 1859. The 1856 edition is the one most commonly found in law libraries, which is why I have cited it here. For the Havilands see Ian Ross Robertson, "Sir Thomas Heath Haviland," *DCB online*. Thomas Heath Haviland Junior served in the Senate until he was appointed by Macdonald as lieutenant-governor of Prince Edward Island in 1879.

41 For Carrall's speech see *Senate Debates*, 18 Apr. 1877, 421–2. For Carrall see Dorothy Blakey Smith, "Robert Carrall," *DCB online*.

42 Kaulbach's speech is at *Senate Debates*, 18 Apr. 1877, 422–5. His earlier remark was about his disagreement with the majority of the divorce committee, insisting that there was "evidence of a criminal nature that would not justify this House in giving that woman what she claimed": ibid., 20 Mar. 1877, 228.

43 Kaulbach provided no examples of the committee being changed, and in fact none of the seven previous committees, three for one case in successive sessions, had been altered after they were named. But committees might have been changed while membership of them was canvassed before they were officially named.

44 For Dever see John Alexander Gemmill, *The Canadian Parliamentary Companion 1891* (Ottawa: Durie & Son, 1891), 47–8. Dever was the only New Brunswick senator to vote against the first divorce Act passed by

Parliament, that for Joseph Whiteaves, and voted similarly in the case of John Stevenson in 1869. He also opposed the bills for John Robert Martin in 1870 and 1872 and absented himself from the 1873 vote in the same case: *Senate Journals*, 30 Apr. 1868, 14 May 1869, 28 Mar. 1870, and 29 May 1872, 248, 79, 84–5, and 133–4.

45 Issue of 27 April 1877.

46 *Senate Debates*, 18 Apr. 1877, 423. The quotation is from the King James version of the Bible, Book of Proverbs, Chapter 30, Verse 20, and as noted in chapter 7 was used by Vice-Chancellor Blake in his judgment in the alimony case.

47 *Senate Debates*, 18 Apr. 1879, 285.

48 For all of this see Girard, *Beamish Murdoch of Halifax*, 186–91. For Murdoch's *History* see *A History of Nova Scotia, or Acadie* (3 vols. Halifax: James Barnes, 1856–1867); for the litigation over the will see *In re Beamish Murdoch's Will* (1878) 12 NSR 428 (Supreme Court).

49 *Senate Debates*, 15 May 1894, 68.

50 *Senate Debates*, 18 Apr. 1877, 424. For Flint see Larry Turner, "Billa Flint," *DCB online.*

51 *Senate Debates*, 18 Apr. 1877, 425. The reporter for Ottawa *Daily Citizen* was struck by this statement, calling it "a beautiful contrast": *Daily Citizen* (Ottawa), 20 Apr. 1876.

52 *Senate Journals* and *Senate Debates*, 18 Apr. 1877, 245 and 425.

53 The missing five who had previously voted against the bill were George Alexander and James Skead of Ontario, Jacques Olivier Bureau of Quebec, Archibald Woodbury McLellan of Nova Scotia, and Abner McLellan of New Brunswick. The senator who had supported the bill on the 12th but was absent on the 18th was George Howlan of Prince Edward Island.

54 *Senate Debates*, 18 Apr. 1877, 425.

55 For what follows in this paragraph on the Committee of the Whole proceedings see *Senate Journals* and *Senate Debates*, 18 Apr. 1877, 246–53 and 425–6.

56 For the bill see appendix 2.

57 *Senate Debates*, 18 Apr. 1877, 426.

58 Senate Rule 55 provided that the Senate could, at any time before the final passage of a private bill, refer the bill to the SCC "as to any point or matter in connection with such bill." Section 53 of the *Supreme and Exchequer Courts Act* is much less well known than the Court's reference power, in section 52 of the original Act (section 54 of the current Act), which has often been, and still is, used by governments to obtain the court's opinion on the constitutionality of controversial public law questions. It provided that the Court, "or any two of the Judges thereof, shall examine and report upon any private bill presented to the Senate or House of Commons and referred to the Court under any rules or orders made by the Senate

or House of Commons." "Private bills" did not mean private members bills, but any bill that confers "special powers or benefits (in excess of or in conflict with the general law) upon one or more persons or group of persons (including corporate entities) or to exempt them from the application of a statute." The origins of this private bill reference power are in traditional House of Lords practice. The section has only been invoked by the Senate, not the Commons, and has been very little used, only three times and not since 1882. See Carissima Mathen, *Courts without Cases: The Law and Politics of Advisory Opinions* (New York: Hart, 2019), 71–2, quotation at 72. The governor-general could have referred the Bill pursuant to the *Supreme Court Act* even if the Senate did not.

59 *Senate Debates*, 19 Apr. 1877, 437.
60 Ibid., 440.
61 *Senate Journals,* 19 Apr. 1877, 261.
62 *Globe,* 25 Apr. 1877.
63 *Whitby Chronicle*, 3 May 1877.
64 *Commons Journals,* 20 Apr. 1877, 301. For the other 1877 Commons proceedings on the bill see ibid., 23 and 26 Apr. 1877, 313 and 335; and *Commons Debates*, 24 and 26 Apr. 1877, 1757–60 and 1837–40.
65 For Gibbs see Leo Johnson, "Thomas Nicholson Gibbs," *DCB online.*
66 See Elwood Jones, –Joseph Rymal," *DCB online.*
67 *Ingersoll Chronicle,* 17 May 1877.
68 It was standard practice for any petitioner for a private bill to present his or her petition to both Houses, even though divorce bills were always first taken up in the Senate.
69 *Commons Debates,* 2 May 1879, 1707.
70 *Ingersoll Chronicle,* 17 May 1877.
71 Cauchon had been a senator from 1867 to 1872, when he was elected to the Commons: Andrée Désillets, "Joseph Eduoard Cauchon," *DCB online.* The other MPs who spoke against Gibbs's motion were Colin MacDougall, a lawyer and the MP for Elgin East, Ontario; James Fraser Forbes, MP for Queen's County, Nova Scotia; Timothy Warren Anglin, the Speaker and the Liberal MP for Gloucester, New Brunswick; and Prime Minister Alexander Mackenzie.
72 For Holton and Anglin see H.C. Klassen, "Luther Hamilton Holton" and William Baker, "Timothy Warren Anglin," both in *DCB online.*
73 *Whitby Chronicle*, 3 May 1877.

13. An Interlude, 1878

1 *Whitby Chronicle*, 2 Aug. 1877.
2 *Whitby Chronicle*, 2 May 1878.

3 For what follows on Eliza's petition see *Senate Journals,* 27 Feb. and 4, 8, and 22 Mar. 1878, 63, 66, 69, and 100. See also *Montreal Gazette,* 19, 22, and 25 Mar. 1878
4 *Senate Debates,* 26 Mar. 1878, 292. There was no mention of this motion in the *Senate Journals* for 26 March, presumably because it was ruled out of order, as discussed below.
5 *Huron Expositor,* 29 Mar. 1878.
6 For dower in this period see Philip Girard, "Land Law, Liberalism, and the Agrarian Ideal: British North America, 1750–1920," in *Despotic Dominion: Property Rights in British Settler Societies,* eds. John McLaren, Nancy E. Wright, and A.R. Buck (Vancouver: University of British Columbia Press, 2005; Girard, Phillips, and Brown, *A History of Law in Canada Volume I,* 357–8 and 616–7; Phillips, Girard, and Brown, *A History of Law in Canada Volume II,* 510–3.
7 See for example the Ontario *Dower Act,* RSO 1877, c 126, s 5, which provided: "A married woman may bar her dower in any lands … by joining with her husband in a deed or conveyance thereof in which a release of dower is contained."
8 The events recounted here were told by McDougall in his speech to the Commons introducing Eliza's divorce bill in May 1879: *Commons Debates,* 2 May 1879, 1709. They were also described by Reesor in *Senate Debates,* 21 Mar. 1879, 118–9.
9 *An Act to Provide for Certain Amendments to the Law,* SO 1877, c 8, s 35. Section 35 became section 10 of the *Dower Act,* RSO 1877, c 126. My emphasis.
10 *Commons Debates,* 2 May 1879, 1709.
11 Neither the *Journals* of the Ontario assembly nor the reports of legislative debates in the newspapers make any mention of this provision. The progress of the bill can be followed in *Journal of the Legislative Assembly of Ontario,* 8, 14, and 26 Feb. and 1 and 2 Mar. 1877, 117, 139, 165, 184–5, and 191. There was no official reporting of Ontario legislative debates in this period. For very brief mentions of the omnibus bill, which do not discuss section 35 but do discuss various amendments to the liquor license laws, see *Globe,* 9 and 27 Feb., and 2 and 3 Mar. 1877.
12 McMillan was called to the bar in 1864 and practised in Elora, Galt, and Guelph before settling in Whitby: see "Alexander Grey McMillan," LSO/PMD. Since this was a motion to proceed *ex parte,* nobody appeared for Eliza.
13 See Dower Case Report No 1, quotations at paras. 2 and 3 of OJ. See also the reports of the motion in *Globe,* 20 and 21 Feb. 1878.
14 Brian Morrison, "John Godfrey Spragge," *DCB* online.
15 See "James Bethune," LSO/PMD.
16 Dower Case Report No 2, quotations below at paras. 8, 9, 11, and 13. See also the very brief report in the *Globe,* 5 Mar. 1878.

17 *An Act to Make Certain Amendments in the Revised Statutes*, SO 1878, c 8, s 13. The progress of the bill can be followed in *Journal of the Legislative Assembly of Ontario*, 4, 6, 7, 8 and 11 Mar. 1878, 154, 174, 188, and 213.
18 See *Globe*, 6 March 1878, reporting an assembly debate in which McDougall spoke briefly about the *Dower Act*. See also to the same effect *Commons Debates*, 2 May 1879, 1879. John Charles Dent called the dower amendment "one of the most important measures" of 1878 in his entry for Mowat in *The Canadian Portrait Gallery* (Toronto: Magurn, 1881), 4, 91.
19 *Globe*, 4 July 1878, and *Guelph Mercury*, 4 Apr. 1879; *Senate Journals*, 21 Mar. 1879, 115.
20 This section is largely based on the Legal Fees Case Report. See also "McDougall v. Campbell," *Canada Law Journal*, Dec. 1877, 362.
21 Legal Fees Case Report, paras. 9 and 10.
22 For all this see Legal Fees Case Report, paras. 5, 16, and 17; OA, RG 22–561, Pleadings Book, Court of Appeal, MS 6242 and 6243. For brief press reports of McDougall's success see *Globe*, 23 Sept. 1876, 12 Mar., 28 May, and 29 June 1877, 18 and 19 Jan., and 25 and 26 June 1878; *Ottawa Times*, 31 Oct. 1876; *Daily British Whig* (Kingston), 28 May 1877; *Montreal Daily Witness*, 1 Nov. 1876, and 12 Mar. 1877; and, somewhat remarkably, *Saint John Daily News*, 6 Nov. 1876. See also Harrison Diaries, 8 Mar. 1877.
23 For both see LSO/PMD. For McDougall see Livermore, *Wandering Willie*, 191, and Joseph Easton McDougall, *Law Lectures: Subjects Torts and Negligence Delivered before the Law Students at Toronto, at Osgoode Hall* (Toronto: Rowsell & Hutchison, 1882).
24 See the collaborative entry for him in *DCB online*.
25 See Graham Parker, "Sir Adam Wilson," *DCB online*, from which the quotations in this paragraph and the next are taken.
26 Under the Act of Union of 1840 assembly members who joined the cabinet were required to resign their seats and seek re-election, but this rule did not apply to a minister who resigned from one position and took another within a month. In late July 1858 the Cartier-Macdonald ministry was forced to resign when their proposal to locate the capital permanently in Ottawa was defeated in the assembly, and a short-lived government led by George Brown and Antoine-Aimé Dorion replaced it. The new ministry lasted only a week, resigned, and the governor asked Cartier and Macdonald to come back. On 6 August all the ministers took a different portfolio than they had occupied before resigning in July, and then they all reverted to their original posts on 7 August. Thus no by-elections were required. See generally Donald Creighton, *John A. Macdonald: The Young Politician* (Toronto: MacMillan, 1952), 261–8. For the case see *Macdonnell v. Macdonald* [1858] OJ No. 314 (Common Pleas).
27 *Baldwin et al. v. Montgomery*, [1844] OJ No. 142 (Queen's Bench).

28 What follows is a short summary of the structure of the English legal profession, drawn from Daniel Duman, "Pathway to Professionalism: The English Bar in the Eighteenth and Nineteenth Centuries," *Journal of Social History* 13 (1980): 615, and Philip Girard, "The Making of the Canadian Legal Profession: A Hybrid Heritage," *International Journal of the Legal Profession* 21 (2014): 145.
29 "On the Right of Counsel to Recover His Fees," *Law Magazine and Law Quarterly* 29 (1874): 295–323 at 323.
30 (1870) LR 5 (Ch.)
31 Duman, "Pathway to Professionalism," 616 and 619.
32 (1860) 5 H. & N. 890, 157 E.R. 1436 at 1448, Pollock C. B. For a contemporary approving discussion of this issue see "On the Right of Counsel to Recover His Fees."
33 Legal Fees Case Report, para. 24. For the history of lawyers' liability for negligence see John Covell, "Liability for Negligence for Members of Professions," Ll.M. Thesis, Durham University, 1989.
34 See Girard, Phillips, and Brown, *A History of Law in Canada Volume I*, 272–3 and 467–9.
35 *Barristers Act*, RSO 1877, c 139; *Solicitors Act*, RSO 1877, c 140.
36 *Baldwin v. Montgomery*, [1844] O. J. No. 143, at para. 4.
37 Legal Fees Case Report, para. 54.
38 Ibid., para. 66.
39 *Canada Law Journal*, 13 (1877), 362.
40 Harrison's dissenting judgment is at Legal Fees Case Report, paras. 72–126; quotations below at paras. 85 and 124–125.
41 Phillips, Girard, and Brown, *A History of Law in Canada Volume II*, 135, 186 and 187.

14. Eliza Campbell's Separation Bill in Parliament – Again – 1879

1 *Canada Gazette*, 15 July 1878 et seq; *Whitby Chronicle*, 11 July 1878, et seq. I have not been able to find the notice in another Ontario county newspaper.
2 *Globe*, 15 July 1878; *Ottawa Citizen*, 13 July 1878; *Hamilton Daily Times*, 13 July 1878; *Acton Free Press*, 18 July 1878; *Montreal Gazette*, 15 July 1878; *Quebec Saturday Budget*, 20 July 1878.
3 *Senate Journals*, 28 Mar. 1879, 109.
4 *Whitby Chronicle*, 13 Mar., 3, 10, and 24 Apr., and 1, 8, and 15 May 1879; *Globe*, 8, 12–14, 19, 20, 24, 29, and 31 Mar. and 4, 7, 8, 21, 22, 23, 25, 26, 28, and 29 Apr. and 2, 3, 5, 10, 14, and 15 May 1879; *Ottawa Citizen*, 14 and 31 Mar. and 3, 4, 13, 17, 22, 23, 25, 26, and 28–30 Apr., and 1, 3, 6, 10, and 14 May 1879.
5 *Weekly Mail* (Toronto), 28 Mar., and 4 and 11 Apr., and 16 May 1879; *Hamilton Spectator*, 28 Feb. 1879; *Daily British Whig* (Kingston), 29 Mar.

1879; *Daily Expositor* (Brantford), 4 and 21 Apr. 1879; *Canadian Post* (Lindsay), 2 May 1879; *Waterloo Advertiser*, 2 May 1879; (Belleville) *Intelligencer*, 15 May 1879; *York Herald*, 22 May 1879; *Glencoe Transcript*, 22 May 1879; *Grey Review*, (Durham) 22 May 1879. This is likely only a partial list, compiled from newspapers available on-line.

6 *Montreal Gazette* 28 Feb. and 19 Mar. and 3, 4, 7, 8, 17, 19, and 26 Apr. 1879; *Montreal Herald*, 11 and 13 Mar. and 24 Apr. and 3, 12, 14, and 15 May 1879; *Montreal Daily Witness*, 13, 22, and 29 Mar., and 3, 4, 19, 21, 23, and 24 Apr., and 2, 3, 5, 12, and 14 May 1879; *Montreal Daily Star*, 23 Apr. and 10 May 1879; *Evening Post* (Montreal), 28 Mar. and 17 Apr., and 10 and 14 May 1879; *True Witness and Catholic Chronicle* (Montreal), 2 Apr. 1879; *Morning Chronicle* (Montreal), 29 Apr. and 3 May 1879; *Evening Mercury* (Quebec City) 1 Apr. and 12 May 1879; *Daily Telegraph* (Quebec City), 17 and 25 Apr. 1879; *Le Courrier du Canada*, 30 Apr. and 5 and 12 May 1879; *Le Journal de Québec*, 30 Apr. 1879; *Le courier de St-Hyacinthe*, 27 Mar., and 13 and 16 May 1879; *La Gazette de Sorel*, 7 May 1879. This is likely only a partial list, compiled from newspapers available on-line.

7 *Daily Colonist* (Victoria), 14 and 30 May 1879; *Chicago Tribune*, 24 and 27 Apr., and 5 and 7 May 1879; *Daily Inter-Ocean* (Chicago), 23, 26, and 30 Apr. 1879.

8 *Senate Journals*, 10 Mar. 1879, 66. For the arguments over the bill between then and first reading see ibid., 12, 13, 17, 21, and 27 Mar., 1, 2, 3, 4, and 18 Apr. 1879, 78, 80, 86, 99, 105, 109–10, 119, 123–4, 127–9, 131, and 151–2; *Senate Debates*, 12, 17, 21, 27, and 28 Mar., 1, 2, 3, 4 7, 18 Apr. 1879, 82–86, 89, 114–20, 145–7, 161–6, 195–6, 199–200, 220, 230, 251, 278–82.

9 *Whitby Chronicle*, 3 Apr. 1879. See also *Guelph Mercury*, 4 Apr. 1879: "much feeling is being created in the Senate by two or three lawyers … who resort to every possible technical expedient to prevent [Eliza] … getting simple justice."

10 *Senate Debates*, 21 Mar. and 18 Apr. 1879, 120 and 279.

11 *Senate Journals*, 7 Apr. 1879, 135. The committee did not report until after the separation bill had passed second reading and been sent to committee, and when it did it recommended that rather than have a separate committee on constitutionality the private bills committee be tasked with looking into that question for every bill: ibid., 21 Apr. 1879, 156.

12 *Senate Journals*, 18 Apr. 1879, 153; *Senate Debates*, 18 Apr. 1879, 282–308

13 *Senate Debates*, 18 Apr. 1879, 287. Having emigrated to Upper Canada with his parents in his teens, Todd first worked as an assistant librarian for the Upper Canada assembly in 1836 and served as the assistant and then chief librarian for that body and its successors until his death in 1884. Self-educated, his two-volume *On Parliamentary Government in England: Its Origin, Development, and Practical Operation* (London: Longmans

Green, 1867–69) made him an authority throughout the empire and was translated into French, German, Spanish, and Italian. He published many other works, notably *Parliamentary Government in the British Colonies* (London: Longmans Green, 1880). See Bruce Hodgins, "Alpheus Todd," *DCB online*.

14 Quotations in this paragraph from *Senate Debates*, 18 Apr. 1879, 286.

15 Smith, "Robert Carrall"; *An Act to Make the First Day of July a Public Holiday, by the Name of Dominion Day*, SC 1879, c 47.

16 *Senate Debates*, 18 Apr. 1879, 296–8.

17 Ibid., 299–300.

18 Ibid., 301.

19 For these men see Donald Swainson, "William Henry Brouse" and Gerald Tulchinsky, "James Ferrier," both in *DCB online*, and J.A. Gemmill, ed., *The Canadian Parliamentary Companion* (Ottawa: Durie, 1891), 57.

20 For the appointment of the committee see *Senate Journals* and *Senate Debates*, 18 Apr. 1877, 154 and 305.

21 *Senate Debates*, 18 Apr. 1877, 305–6.

22 Ibid., 306–8.

23 See "George Joseph O'Doherty," LSO/PMD.

24 Robert's intervention was not reported in the *Senate Journals*, which did not report committee proceedings. This information was provided by a reporter and published in the *Whitby Chronicle*, 24 Apr. 1879, the *Daily Expositor* (Brantford), 21 Apr. 1878, the *Hamilton Spectator*, 21 Apr. 1879, and the *Globe*, 21 Apr. 1879; the quotations in this paragraph are from the last-named.

25 *Senate Journals*, 23 Apr. 1879, 163–5.

26 For what follows on 22 Apr. 1879, see *Senate Journals*, 23 Apr. 1879, 165–6.

27 There is no extant copy of the text of the bill presented to the House by the committee. The account given here is reconstructed from the 1877 bill, the 1879 Act, the *Senate Journals* of 23 April 1879 reproducing the amendments, and the *Senate Debate* of April 24th on the adoption of the committee report.

28 RSO 1877, c 40, s 44.

29 For what follows on Kaulbach's objection, see *Senate Debates*, 24 Apr. 1879, 367–9.

30 *Senate Journals* and *Senate Debates*, 24 Apr. 1879, 174 and 369.

31 For what follows see *Senate Debates*, 24 Apr. 1879, 369–1.

32 *Senate Journals*, 24 Apr. 1879, 174.

33 Almon's speech is at *Senate Debates*, 25 Apr. 1879, 373–4. For Almon see Allan E. Marble, "William Johnston Almon," *DCB online*, and *Senate Journals*, 18 Apr. 1879, 150, and for Smith see Mark McGowan, "Sir Frank Smith," *DCB online*. Queen Caroline was disliked by George IV and

supported by the masses, but then opinion turned against her when it was shown that she had taken lovers: see Thomas W. Laqueur, "The Queen Caroline Affair: Politics as Art in the Reign of George IV," *Journal of Modern History* 54 (1982): 17 and Nicholas Rogers, "Royal Soap? Class and Gender in the Queen Caroline Affair," *Left History* 12 (1994): 12.

34 *Senate Debates,* 25 Apr. 1879, 374. For Macdonald see Parliament of Canada biography.

35 *Senate Debates,* 25 Apr. 1879, 374–5.

36 Ibid., 375–8; quotation at 375.

37 Ibid., 378–9.

38 *Senate Journals* and *Senate Debates,* 25 Apr. 1879, 185–8 and 379–80.

39 *Whitby Chronicle,* 24 Apr. 1879.

40 *Senate Journals,* 25 Apr. 1879, 187–8.

41 McDougall, *Woman's Rights in Ontario.* For its distribution to MPs see *Ottawa Citizen,* 3 May 1879.

42 McDougall, *Woman's Rights in Ontario,* 2. McDougall here threw in a remarkable gratuitous insult of the senators who had vigorously opposed the bill. Their stance on the bill showed a disregard for women's rights, which could in turn "be inferred from their own marital relations."

43 *Daily Expositor* (Brantford), 26 Apr. 1879. The newspaper said that Robert offered to restore Eliza "to all rights and privileges," that is, to take her back as his wife. Eliza, however, doubtless distrustful, insisted on Robert stating in writing that the adultery allegation was untrue, and that Robert would not do.

44 Robert Campbell to Sir John A. Macdonald, 10 Mar. 1879, LAC, Macdonald Papers, Vol. 356.

45 No copy of Robert's circular(s) has survived. What is said here is from what McDougall said about it in *Commons Debates,* 2 May 1879, 1710. For the existence of Robert's circular, though not its contents, see also *Chicago Daily Tribune,* 7 May 1879.

46 *Ottawa Citizen,* 3 May 1879.

47 *Commons Journals,* 28 Apr. 1879, 321.

48 Ibid., 2 May 1879, 350. The Commons allowed much less time for private bills than the Senate because the need to deal with government business was paramount. Private bills were given only an hour in the Wednesday and Friday evening sessions, starting at 7.30, although a bill could be debated on more than one day. Private bills were also dealt with on Mondays, after the routine business (the presentation of petitions, committee reports, and motions) was taken care of, but could only be introduced on that day, with no further discussion. For the Commons procedure see *Commons Rules,* Rule 19, and John George Bourinot, *Parliamentary Procedure and Practice* (Montreal: Dawson, 1884). Bourinot

was clerk of the House of Commons. His father, John Bourinot, was a senator for Nova Scotia from 1867 to 1884 and voted for the Campbell bill in 1879.

49 *Ottawa Citizen*, 3 May 1879.

50 *Globe*, 2 May 1879; (Belleville) *Intelligencer*, 15 May 1879.

51 *Commons Debates*, 2 May 1879, 1707–8.

52 *Montreal Daily Witness*, 3 May 1879.

53 *Commons Debates*, 2 May 1879, 1708–10.

54 Ibid., 1710.

55 (Belleville) *Intelligencer*, 15 May 1879.

56 *Commons Journals*, 2 May 1879, 350; *Globe*, 3 May 1879.

57 *Ottawa Citizen*, 6 May 1879; *Montreal Daily Witness*, 5 May 1879; *Montreal Gazette*, 6 May 1879. Thirty four MPs voting in committee was a large number, but in fact the committee had 64 members, although the quorum was only 7: *Commons Journals*, 20 Feb. 1879, 22.

58 *Commons Journals*, 5 and 9 May 1879, 357 and 410.

59 For Mills and James McDonald see Robert Vipond, "David Mills," and P.B. Waite, "James McDonald," both in *DCB online*. Mills was an MP from 1867 to 1882 and again from 1884 to 1896. He served as minister of the interior in the Mackenzie government in the 1870s. For Mills, the compact theory of federalism, and provincial rights see Vipond, "David Mills," the same author's *Liberty and Community: Canadian Federalism and the Failure of the Constitution* (Albany, N.Y.: State University of New York Press, 1991), and F. Murray Greenwood, "David Mills and Co-ordinate Federalism, 1867–1903," *University of Western Ontario Law Review* 16 (1977): 93.

60 Mills's speech is at *Commons Debates*, 9 May 1879, 1878–9. See also *Commons Journals*, 9 May 1879, 410.

61 For the speeches of James MacDonald, McDougall, and John A. Macdonald see *Commons Debates*, 9 May 1879, 1879–83.

62 *Commons Debates*, 13 May 1879, 2004–5.

63 Ibid., 2005.

64 Ibid.

65 Ibid., 2005–7. The *Commons Debates* said three months, the *Journals* six months: *Commons Journals*, 13 May 1879, 431.

66 Vipond, –David Mills."

67 *Commons Debates*, 13 May 1879, 2007–8. For Girouard see Michael Lawrence Smith, "Désiré Girouard," *DCB online*.

68 For Mousseau see Andrée Désilet, 'Joseph-Alfred Mousseau', *DCB online*. For his speech see *Commons Debates*, 13 May 1879, 2008–9.

69 *Commons Debates*, 13 May 1879, 2009–10. Three Ontario MPs, James McCuaig, the Conservative member for Prince Edward County, Duncan Macmillan, a lawyer representing Middlesex East, and Samuel Lane, a

Conservative and a lawyer from Grey North, all supported the bill. Two Quebec senators, Felix Geoffrion, a man with little formal education but a notary, a successful businessman, and long-time Liberal with Quebec nationalist leanings, and Charles-Joseph Coursol, a talented lawyer and a Conservative representing Montreal East, opposed the bill for by now familiar reasons. For these men see Marcel Caya, "Felix Geoffrion," and Lorne Ste-Croix, "Charles-Joseph Coursol," both in *DCB online*.

70 *Senate Debates* and *Senate Journals*, 13 May 1879, 2010–1 and 431–2. The *Journals* got the number of those opposing wrong, at 37, but listed the same 38 MPs as the *Debates*.

71 *Commons Journals* and *Senate Journals*, 14 and 15 May 1879, 433 and 439 and 289–90; *Montreal Daily Witness*, 12 May 1879. Until Lorne's appointment in 1878 the royal instructions to governors-general specified that all divorce Acts were to be reserved. This instruction was omitted from those given to Lorne in 1878, and thereafter no divorce bills were reserved: see William E. Hodgins, comp., *Correspondence, Reports of the Minister of Justice, and Orders in Council upon the Subject of Dominion and Provincial Legislation, 1867–1895* (Ottawa: Government Printing Bureau, 1896), 59–60.

72 Bourinot, *Parliamentary Procedure and Practice*, 2nd edition 1892, 752 and 753.

73 *Commons Debates*, 3 May 1929, 2222–3. See also a reference to the Act to the same effect by J.S. Woodsworth, *ibid.*, 22 Feb. 1929, 380. The text books referred to are Robert Victor Sinclair, *The Rules and Practice Before the Parliament of Canada Upon Bills of Divorce* (Toronto: Carswell, 1915), 58–60, and Robert Ramsey Evans, *The Law and Practice Relating to Divorce and other Matrimonial Causes* (Calgary: Burroughs, 1923), 405. The Ontario courts were given divorce jurisdiction in 1930: see Patti and Phillips, 'Demise of Parliamentary Divorce.'

74 For what follows see Secretary of State for Colonies Sir Michael Hicks-Beach to governor-general, 27 Sept. and 30 Dec. 1879; Report of Alexander Campbell, 5 Nov. 1879; Minute of Cabinet, 15 Dec. 1879 and 27 Jan. 1880, all in LAC, RG 2, Privy Council Office, Series A – 1 – a, PC No. 1880.

15. The Principals after 1880 – Winners and Losers

1 For McDougall's career after 1879 see, in addition to the sources cited below, Zeller, "William McDougall."

2 See Frederick H. Armstrong, "Andrew Mercer," *DCB online*, and *Ontario (Attorney-General) v. Mercer*, (1883) 8 AC 767 (PC). The principal legal issue in the Mercer case was whether the federal or provincial government was entitled to the estate of a person who died intestate without heirs and whose property therefore escheated to the crown. The case went through

the Ontario courts and the Supreme Court of Canada before a final decision by the JCPC ruled in favour of the province. The money was used to establish the Andrew Mercer Reformatory for women.

3 Rattray, *The Scot in British North America*, 589.

4 For this paragraph see *Whitby Chronicle*, 4 and 18 Nov.; Canadian census 1881 and 1901; 1871 England and Wales Census; *Nanaimo Daily News*, 4 Feb. 1919; *Montreal Star*, 1 Sept. 1879, list of UK passengers arriving on S.S. *Circassian*.

5 Quotations from *Whitby Chronicle*, 25 Dec. 1879 and 8 Jan. 1880. For the county council elections of 1880 and 1881 see also Farewell, *Ontario County*, 146.

6 See *Whitby Chronicle*, 8–29 June 1883 1883–5, 1887, 1889–91, and 1893, passim. Not all issues of the *Chronicle* have survived for this period; these references are simply a sampling of those that have.

7 *Whitby Chronicle*, 1 Jan. 1892. For the other details in this paragraph see ibid., 17 Oct. 1887, 3 Sept. 1889, 2 Jan. and 18 Dec. 1891, 1 and 8 Jan. 1892, 21 Dec. 1894 and 4 Oct. 1895.

8 *Whitby Chronicle*, 11 Oct. 1895; *Gazette and Chronicle* (Whitby), 30 July 1914; *Evening Telegram* (Toronto), 7 June 1921.

9 The rumour was published in the *Daily Advertiser* of London, Ontario, 23 Jan. and 11 Feb. 1880; *Quebec Daily Telegraph*, 24 Jan. 1880; *Morning Chronicle and Commercial and Shipping Gazette* (Montreal), 24 Jan. 1880; *Montreal Evening Post*, 23 Jan. 1880; *Quebec Saturday Budget*, 31 Jan. 1880; *Daily Colonist* (Victoria), 10 Feb. 1880; and *Manitoba Free Press*, 23 Jan. 1880.

10 For Robert's Nebraska divorce see, in addition to the other sources cited here, Nebraska State Archives (History Nebraska), RG207 Lancaster County, District Court, Series 3 and Sub-Series 1, Civil Appearance Dockets, 1868–1957, Vol. I, 147–8, and Civil Case Files, Box 28 1879–1880, Case #2611.

11 All references to Nebraska divorce law and procedure are from *The Compiled Statutes of the State of Nebraska* (Omaha: Gibson, Miller and Richardson, 1881), chap. 25. The grounds for divorce are listed at sections 6 and 7.

12 British subject status was considered at common law to be indelible. The *Naturalization Act*, UK Statutes 1870, c 14, allowed it but only when becoming a citizen of another country.

13 For Canadians getting divorced in the US in a slightly later period see James G. Snell, "The International Border as a Factor in Marital Behaviour: An Historical Case Study," *Ontario History* 81 (1989): 289 at 297–9; and Snell, *In the Shadow of the Law, passim.* American divorces being sought by Canadians occasionally came up in parliamentary debates on Canadian divorce law or on individual cases in this period.

14 For the settlement see AO, RG 22–390, Benchbook of John Spragge, Box 71, No. 27, 31, Re Campbell, and *Daily Advertiser* (London) 11 Feb. 1880. For barring dower see *Married Women's Real Estate Act*, RSO 1877, c 127. The settlement was made pursuant to section 7 of the separation Act.

15 *Lincoln Nebraska State Journal*, 28 Feb. and 3 Mar. 1882.

16 For the marriage see Marriage Licence and Certificate, Nebraska State Archives, accessed via *ancestry.com; Lincoln Journal Star* and *Lincoln Daily News*, 20 Mar. 1882.

17 For Janet Laird see her obituaries, all largely identical, in four Marshall, Missouri newspapers: *Saline County Citizen*, 23 May 1908; *Saline County Weekly Progress*, 22 May 1908; *Weekly Democrat-News*, 23 May 1908; and *Marshall Republican*, 22 May 1908. For her family background see Canadian censuses, 1861, 1871, and 1881. Specific census references were first located through the online sources ancestry.com and familysearch.com.

18 *Whitby Chronicle*, 18 July 1884.

19 *Pickering News*, 1 May 1885.

20 *Whitby Chronicle*, 18 and 25 July; 22 and 29 Aug.; 12, 19, and 26 Sept.; and 3 Oct. to 12 Dec. 1884.

21 These cases are all reviewed in a leading English case, *Harvey v. Farnie*, (1882) 8 AC 43, decided by the House of Lords in 1882.

22 Compare *Magurn v. Magurn*, [1885] OJ No. 185 (C.A.), with *Stevens v. Fisk*, a Supreme Court of Canada decision given in the same year and reported in [1885] *The Legal News*, No 6, 42–8, and No. 7, 53–6. The issue of the validity of foreign divorces did come up in two parliamentary divorce cases proceedings in 1887, involving Susan Ash and William Lavell. The problem in each case was that one of the parties had obtained an American divorce, which, if valid, would have prevented the other party from getting a Canadian one because one cannot get divorced from the same person twice. Both cases are summarized in Gemmill, *The Practice of the Parliament of Canada*, 186–9.

23 The Missouri Compromise was an agreement between the southern slave states and the northern free states, brokered when both Maine and Missouri fulfilled the requirements for statehood. Northern states opposed the admission into the Union of more slave states, while southern states wanted some to be admitted so that the balance of power remained largely the same. Maine was admitted as a free state, Missouri as a slave state, and Congress passed legislation prohibiting slavery in the remaining Louisiana Purchase lands north of the 36 degrees 30 minutes parallel. See Richard H. Brown, "Missouri Crisis, Slavery and the Politics of Jacksonianism," in *Essays on Jacksonian America*, ed. Frank Gatell (New York: Holt, Rineheart & Winston, 1970), and John Craig Hammond, "President, Planter, Politician: James Monroe, the Missouri Crisis, and the Politics of Slavery,"

Journal of American History 105 (2019): 843. For the history of Missouri see William Parrish, Charles Jones, and Lawrence O. Christensen, *Missouri: The Heart of a Nation* (Columbia: University of Missouri Press, 3rd edition, 2004). For Marshall, Missouri see wikipedia.

24 William Barclay Norton, *Past and Present of Saline County Missouri* (Indianapolis and Chicago: Bowen & Co, 1910), 605–7. Robert's obituaries in Marshall newspapers (see note above) were all largely taken from this sketch.

25 For Frank Campbell see Norton, *Past and Present of Saline County,* 606, *Saline County Weekly Progress*, 2 Apr. 1887; *Weekly Democrat News,* 1 Feb. 1901; US Federal Census, 1920 and 1930; Frank Campbell, Ridge Park Cemetery, Marshall, Missouri, on findagrave.com.

26 For Robert Campbell Jr., see Norton, *Past and Present of Saline County,* 606; Obituary in *Weekly Democrat News*, 14 Oct. 1899; Robert Campbell and Minnie S. Eakin, 2 Dec. 1885, in Missouri, County Marriage, Naturalization, and Court Records, 1800–1991; *Saline County Weekly Progress*, 18 June 1887, 3 and 10 Mar. 1888, 21 Feb. 1890; *Slater News Rustler*, (Slater, Missouri), 9 Apr. 1892; *Pickering News*, 25 Dec. 1885.

27 This paragraph on James Bremner Campbell and Edith Campbell is from Norton, *Past and Present of Saline County,* 606; *Saline County Weekly Progress*, 12 Dec. 1890, 8 May and 26 June 1891; *Marshall Republican*, 15 Feb. 1901; *Saline County Citizen*, 16 May 1908; *Weekly Democrat News*, 4 Nov. 1905, 8 Aug. 1908, 13 Mar. 1913, and 25 Feb. 1915; Marriage Records and Missouri Death Certificates, 1910–1969, Missouri State Archives, accessed via *ancestry.com*.

28 *Pickering News*, 6 Dec. 1907; 1881 and 1891 Census.

29 This paragraph is from *Saline County Weekly Progress,* 31 Oct., 28 Feb. and 7 Nov. 1890, 30 Mar. 1894, 15 Mar. 1895, 15 Dec. 1897, 9 Sept. 1899, and 22 May 1908; *Saline County Citizen,* 18 Nov. 1896 and 1 June 1907; *Weekly Democrat-News*, 28 Oct. and 4 Nov. 1905.

30 This paragraph is from Norton, *Past and Present of Saline County,* 606–7; *Saline County Citizen,* 2 Nov. 1907 and 6 Mar. 1915; *Saline County Weekly Progress,* 4 Oct. 1907, 2 Dec. 1910 and 30 June 1911; Ledger Book of Missouri Wills, 547–53, accessed via ancestry.com; *Weekly Democrat-News,* 27 Dec. 1917, 13 July, and 23 Nov. 1922. The estate litigation went to the Missouri Supreme Court: see *Campbell v. Spotts,* 331 Mo. 974, 55 S.W.2d 986 (1932) Supreme Court of Missouri.

31 See her four obituaries in Marshall newspapers, cited above in note 18. For this paragraph see also *Saline County Weekly Progress*, 14 Aug. 1886, 26 June 1891, 25 Dec. 1895, 31 Aug. 1898, 7 Oct. 1910, 29 Dec. 1911, and 18 Oct. 1912; *Saline County Citizen*, 18 May 1907, 23 July 1910, and 30 Mar. 1912; *Weekly Democrat-News*, 8 Aug. 1908; *Marshall Republican,* 7 Oct. 1910.

32 This paragraph is from Robert Campbell, "Ontario Marriages, 1926–1938," Affidavit pursuant to the Ontario Marriage Act, accessed via ancestry.com; Winter, *Chronicles of a County Town*, 41.

33 This paragraph is from *Globe*, 26 Feb. 1915; *Canadian Statesman* (Bowmanville), 4 Mar. 1915; *Mail and Empire* (Toronto), 17 Apr. 1922; Robert's will, reference above note 29, and his obituaries in *Weekly Democrat News*, 25 Feb. 1915; *Saline County Citizen*, 27 Feb. 1915; *Saline County Weekly Progress*, 26 Feb. 1915; *Slater News-Rustler*, 25 Feb. 1915; and *Slater News*, 27 Feb. 1915. All of the obituaries were cribbed with minor changes from Norton, *Past and Present of Saline County*, 605–7. See also his death certificate, Missouri State Archives, 796/6992, attending physician his son-in-law Baylor Spotts, and Robert Campbell, Ridge Park Cemetery, Marshall, on findagrave.com.

34 See John Lorinc et al., *The Ward: The Life and Loss of Toronto's First Immigrant Neighbourhood* (Toronto: Coach House Books, 2015), quotation at 13.

35 For what follows on Henrietta and Annie Byrne, and Eliza Campbell, see *Toronto City Directories* (Toronto: R.L. Polk & Co, various years), for 1882, 219; 1884, 393; 1885, 291; 1886, 132; 1887, 350; 1888, 400; 1889, 475; 1890, 522; *Toronto City Directories* (Toronto: Might Directories Ltd, 1897), 525; *Whitby Chronicle*, 20 Aug. 1886; Death Record of Henrietta Byrne, Ontario Deaths, 1869–1937, No. 2293, accessed via ancestry.com; Ontario Tax Assessment Rolls, 1834–1899, and City Tax Roll, Toronto, 168 Teraulay Street, 197 McCaul Street, and 158 Robert Street; for Henrietta Byrne, 1884–1886; for Annie Byrne, 1886, 1888–1890, 1896 and 1897; Census of 1901 – all accessed via familysearch.com.

36 *Globe*, 25 Jan. 1910; Ontario Deaths 1869–1950, accessed via ancestry.com.

37 Mount Pleasant Cemetery, Plot 3327. Today her final resting place is indicated by a different grave marker, a stone slab with the words "ELIZA MARIA CAMPBELL, 1844–1910" and underneath the words "I DID NOT COMMIT ADULTERY." It was placed there in 2017 by Philip Augustine, a retired Ottawa lawyer, and his daughter Alexandra, a Toronto filmmaker. The Augustines hope to make a multi-episode TV series of the Campbell case, and five other Ontario cases from the period. See https://victorian-justice.com.

38 Death Record for Bethiah Johnston, Archives of Ontario, MS935, accessed via ancestry.com.

39 Ridge Park Cemetery Index, 1875–1963, accessed via ancestry.com.

40 See Notice to Creditors, *Toronto World*, 19 Mar. 1910.

41 *Globe*, 25 Jan. 1910.

Index

2025 Robert Sharpe, *My Life in the Law: Lawyer, Scholar, Judge*
Eric Adams and Jordan Stanger-Ross, *Challenging Exile: Japanese Canadians and the Wartime Constitution*
Carolyn Strange, *Fatal Confession: A Girl's Murder, a Man's Execution, and the Fitton Case*
Jim Phillips, *I Did Not Commit Adultery: Marital Conflict and the Law in Ontario in the 1870s*

2024 Adam Dodek, *Heenan Blaikie: The Making and Unmaking of a Great Canadian Law Firm*
Colin Campbell and Robert Raizenne, *A History of Canadian Income Tax Volume II, 1948–71*
Wayne Sumner, *Prairie Justice: The Hanging of Mike Hack*
Ian Radforth, *Deadly Swindle: An 1890 Murder in Backwoods Ontario That Gripped the World*

2023 Lori Chambers and Joan Sangster, eds., *Essays in the History of Canadian Law Volume XII: New Perspectives on Gender and the Law*
C. Ian Kyer, *The Ontario Bond Scandal of 1924 Re-examined*
Jonathan Swainger, *The Notorious Georges: Crime and Community in British Columbia's Northern Interior, 1909–25*

2022 Jim Phillips, Philip Girard, and R. Blake Brown, *A History of Law in Canada Volume II: Law for the New Dominion, 1867–1914*
J. Barry Wright, Susan Binnie, and Eric Tucker, eds., *Canadian State Trials Volume V: World War, Cold War and Challenges to Sovereignty, 1939–1990*
Constance Backhouse, *Reckoning with Racism: Police, Judges and the RDS Case*

2021 Daniel Rûck *The Laws and the Land: The Settler Colonial Invasion of Kahnawà:ke in Nineteenth-Century Canada*
Lyndsay Campbell, *Truth and Privilege: Libel Law in Massachusetts and Nova Scotia, 1820–1840*
Martine Valois, Ian Greene, Craig Forcese, and Peter McCormick, eds. *The Federal Court of Appeal and the Federal Court: Fifty Years of History*
Colin Campbell and Robert Raizenne, *A History of Canadian Income Tax Volume I: The Income War Tax Act 1917–1948*

2020 Heidi Bohaker, *Doodem and Council Fire: Anishinaabe Governance through Alliance*
Carolyn Strange, *The Death Penalty and Sex Murder in Canadian History*

2019 Harry Arthurs, *Connecting the Dots: The Life of an Academic Lawyer*
Eric Reiter, *Wounded Feelings: Litigating Emotions in Quebec, 1870–1950*
2018 Philip Girard, Jim Phillips, and Blake Brown, *A History of Law in Canada Volume 1: Beginnings to 1866*
Suzanne Chiodo, *The Class Actions Controversy: The Origins and Development of the Ontario Class Proceedings Act*
2017 Constance Backhouse, *Claire L'Heureux-Dube: A Life*
Dennis G. Molinaro, *An Exceptional Law: Section 98 and the Emergency State, 1919–1936*
2016 Lori Chambers, *A Legal History of Adoption in Ontario, 1921–2015*
Bradley Miller, *Boarderline Crime: Fugitive Criminals and the Challenge of the Boarder, 1819–1914*
James Muir, *Law, Debt, and Merchant Power: The Civil Courts of Eighteenth-Century Halifax*
2015 Barry Wright, Eric Tucker, and Susan Binnie, eds., *Canadian State Trails Volume IV: Security, Dissent and the Limits of Toleration in War and Peace, 1914–1939*
David Fraser, *"Honorary Protestants": The Jewish School Question in Montreal, 1867–1997*
C. Ian Kyer, *A Thirty Years' War: The Failed Public /Private Partnership that Spurred the Creation of The Toronto Transit Commission, 1891–1921*
2014 Christopher Moore, *The Court of Appeal for Ontario: Defining the Right of Appeal, 1792–2013*
Dominique Clément, *Equality Deferred: Sex Discrimination and British Columbia's Human Rights State, 1953–84*
Paul Craven, *Petty Justice: Low Law and the Sessions System in Charlotte County, New Brunswick, 1785–1867*
Thomas Telfer, *Ruin and Redemption: The Struggle for a Canadian Bankruptcy Law, 1867–1919*
2013 Roy McMurtry, *Memoirs and Reflections*
Charlotte Gray, *The Massey Murder: A Maid, Her Master and the Trial That Shocked a Nation*
C. Ian Kyer, *Lawyers, Families, and Businesses: The Shaping of a Bay Street Law Firm, Faskens 1863–1963*
G. Blaine Baker and Donald Fyson, eds., *Essays in the History of Canadian Law Volume 11: Quebec and the Canadas*
2012 R. Blake Brown, *Arming and Disarming: A History of Gun Control in Canada*

Eric Tucker, James Muir, and Bruce Ziff, eds., *Property on Trial: Canadian Cases in Context*
Shelley A.M. Gavigan, *Hunger, Horses, and Government Men: Criminal Law on the Aboriginal Plains, 1870–1905*
Barrington Walker, ed., *The African Canadian Legal Odyssey: Historical Essays*

2011 Robert J. Sharpe, *The Lazier Murder: Prince Edward County, 1884*
Philip Girard, *Lawyers and Legal Culture in British North America: Beamish Murdoch of Halifax*
John McLaren, *Dewigged, Bothered, and Bewildered: British Colonial Judges on Trial*
Lesley Erickson, *Westward Bound: Sex, Violence, the Law, and the Making of a Settler Society*

2010 Judy Fudge and Eric Tucker, eds., *Work on Trial: Canadian Labour Law Struggles*
Christopher Moore, *The British Columbia Court of Appeal: The First Hundred Years*
Frederick Vaughan, *Viscount Haldane: The Wicked Step-father of the Canadian Constitution*
Barrington Walker, *Race on Trial: Black Defendants in Ontario's Criminal Courts, 1850–1950*

2009 William Kaplan, *Canadian Maverick: The Life and Times of Ivan C. Rand*
R. Blake Brown, *A Trying Question: The Jury in Nineteenth-Century Canada*
Barry Wright and Susan Binnie, eds., *Canadian State Trials Volume 3: Political Trials and Security Measures, 1840–1914*
Robert J. Sharpe, *The Last Day, the Last Hour: The Currie Libel Trial*

2008 Constance Backhouse, *Carnal Crimes: Sexual Assault Law in Canada, 1900–1975*
Jim Phillips, R. Roy McMurtry, and John Saywell, eds., *Essays in the History of Canadian Law. Volume 10: A Tribute to Peter N. Oliver*
Gregory Taylor, *The Law of the Land: Canada's Receptions of the Torrens System*
Hamar Foster, Benjamin Berger, and A.R. Buck, eds., *The Grand Experiment: Law and Legal Culture in British Settler Societies*

2007 Robert Sharpe and Patricia McMahon, *The Persons Case: The Origins and Legacy of the Fight for Legal Personhood*
Lori Chambers, *Misconceptions: Unmarried Motherhood and the Ontario Children of Unmarried Parents Act, 1921–1969*

Jonathan Swainger, ed., *The Alberta Supreme Court at 100: History and Authority*

Martin Friedland, *My Life in Crime and Other Academic Adventures*

2006 Donald Fyson, *Magistrates, Police and People: Everyday Criminal Justice in Quebec and Lower Canada, 1764–1837*

Dale Brawn, *The Court of Queen's Bench of Manitoba 1870–1950: A Biographical History*

R.C.B. Risk, *A History of Canadian Legal Thought: Collected Essays*, edited and introduced by G. Blaine Baker and Jim Phillips

2005 Philip Girard, *Bora Laskin: Bringing Law to Life*

Christopher English, ed., *Essays in the History of Canadian Law Volume 9: Two Islands, Newfoundland and Prince Edward Island*

Fred Kaufman, *Searching for Justice: An Autobiography*

2004 John D. Honsberger, *Osgoode Hall: An Illustrated History*

Frederick Vaughan, *Aggressive in Pursuit: The Life of Justice Emmett Hall*

Constance Backhouse and Nancy Backhouse, *The Heiress versus the Establishment: Mrs. Campbell's Campaign for Legal Justice*

Philip Girard, Jim Phillips, and Barry Cahill, eds., *The Supreme Court of Nova Scotia, 1754–2004: From Imperial Bastion to Provincial Oracle*

2003 Robert Sharpe and Kent Roach, *Brian Dickson: A Judge's Journey*

George Finlayson, *John J. Robinette: Peerless Mentor*

Peter Oliver, *The Conventional Man: The Diaries of Ontario Chief Justice Robert A. Harrison, 1856–1878*

Jerry Bannister, *The Rule of the Admirals: Law, Custom and Naval Government in Newfoundland, 1699–1832*

2002 John T. Saywell, *The Law Makers: Judicial Power and the Shaping of Canadian Federalism*

David Murray, *Colonial Justice: Justice, Morality and Crime in the Niagara District, 1791–1849*

F. Murray Greenwood and Barry Wright, eds., *Canadian State Trials Volume 2: Rebellion and Invasion in the Canadas, 1837–1839*

Patrick Brode, *Courted and Abandoned: Seduction in Canadian Law*

2001 Ellen Anderson, *Judging Bertha Wilson: Law as Large as Life*

Judy Fudge and Eric Tucker, *Labour before the Law: Collective Action in Canada, 1900–1948*

Laurel Sefton MacDowell, *Renegade Lawyer: The Life of J.L. Cohen*

2000 Barry Cahill, *"The Thousandth Man": A Biography of James McGregor Stewart*

A.B. McKillop, *The Spinster and the Prophet: Florence Deeks, H.G. Wells, and the Mystery of the Purloined Past*
Beverley Boissery and F. Murray Greenwood, *Uncertain Justice: Canadian Women and Capital Punishment*
Bruce Ziff, *Unforeseen Legacies: Reuben Wells Leonard and the Leonard Foundation Trust*

1999 Constance Backhouse, *Colour-Coded: A Legal History of Racism in Canada, 1900–1950*
G. Blaine Baker and Jim Phillips, eds., *Essays in the History of Canadian Law Volume 8: In Honour of R.C.B. Risk*
Richard W. Pound, *Chief Justice W.R. Jackett: By the Law of the Land*
David Vanek, *Fulfilment: Memoirs of a Criminal Court Judge*

1998 Sidney Harring, *White Man's Law: Native People in Nineteenth-Century Canadian Jurisprudence*
Peter Oliver, *"Terror to Evil-Doers": Prisons and Punishments in Nineteenth-Century Ontario*

1997 James W. St. G. Walker, *"Race," Rights and the Law in the Supreme Court of Canada: Historical Case Studies*
Lori Chambers, *Married Women and Property Law in Victorian Ontario*
Patrick Brode, *Casual Slaughters and Accidental Judgments: Canadian War Crimes and Prosecutions, 1944–1948*
Ian Bushnell, *The Federal Court of Canada: A History, 1875–1992*

1996 Carol Wilton, ed., *Essays in the History of Canadian Law Volume 7: Inside the Law – Canadian Law Firms in Historical Perspective*
William Kaplan, *Bad Judgment: The Case of Mr. Justice Leo A. Landreville*
Murray Greenwood and Barry Wright, eds., *Canadian State Trials Volume 1: Law, Politics and Security Measures, 1608–1837*

1995 David Williams, *Just Lawyers: Seven Portraits*
Hamar Foster and John McLaren, eds., *Essays in the History of Canadian Law Volume 6: British Columbia and the Yukon*
W.H. Morrow, ed., *Northern Justice: The Memoirs of Mr. Justice William G. Morrow*
Beverley Boissery, *A Deep Sense of Wrong: The Treason, Trials and Transportation to New South Wales of Lower Canadian Rebels after the 1838 Rebellion*

1994 Patrick Boyer, *A Passion for Justice: The Legacy of James Chalmers McRuer*

Charles Pullen, *The Life and Times of Arthur Maloney: The Last of the Tribunes*
Jim Phillips, Tina Loo, and Susan Lewthwaite, eds., *Essays in the History of Canadian Law Volume 5: Crime and Criminal Justice*
Brian Young, *The Politics of Codification: The Lower Canadian Civil Code of 1866*

1993 Greg Marquis, *Policing Canada's Century: A History of the Canadian Association of Chiefs of Police*
Murray Greenwood, *Legacies of Fear: Law and Politics in Quebec in the Era of the French Revolution*

1992 Brendan O'Brien, *Speedy Justice: The Tragic Last Voyage of His Majesty's Vessel* Speedy
Robert Fraser, ed., *Provincial Justice: Upper Canadian Legal Portraits from the Dictionary of Canadian Biography*

1991 Constance Backhouse, *Petticoats and Prejudice: Women and Law in Nineteenth-Century Canada*

1990 Philip Girard and Jim Phillips, eds., *Essays in the History of Canadian Law Volume 3: Nova Scotia*
Carol Wilton, ed., *Essays in the History of Canadian Law Volume 4: Beyond the Law – Lawyers and Business in Canada 1830–1930*

1989 Desmond Brown, *The Genesis of the Canadian Criminal Code of 1892*
Patrick Brode, *The Odyssey of John Anderson*

1988 Robert Sharpe, *The Last Day, the Last Hour: The Currie Libel Trial*
John D. Arnup, *Middleton: The Beloved Judge*

1987 C. Ian Kyer and Jerome Bickenbach, *The Fiercest Debate: Cecil A. Wright, the Benchers and Legal Education in Ontario, 1923–1957*

1986 Paul Romney, *Mr. Attorney: The Attorney General for Ontario in Court, Cabinet and Legislature, 1791–1899*
Martin Friedland, *The Case of Valentine Shortis: A True Story of Crime and Politics in Canada*

1985 James Snell and Frederick Vaughan, *The Supreme Court of Canada: History of the Institution*

1984 Patrick Brode, *Sir John Beverley Robinson: Bone and Sinew of the Compact*
David Williams, *Duff: A Life in the Law*

1983 David H. Flaherty, ed., *Essays in the History of Canadian Law Volume 2*

1982 Marion MacRae and Anthony Adamson, *Cornerstones of Order: Courthouses and Town Halls of Ontario, 1784–1914*

1981 David H. Flaherty, ed., *Essays in the History of Canadian Law Volume 1*

Kolibri 360 GmbH
Ferdinand-Jühlke-Straße 7
99095 Erfurt, Deutschland
produktsicherheit@kolibri360.de